FINANCIAL AND MONETARY POLICY STUDIES

volume 15

For a list of the volumes in this series see final page of the volume.

THE FLOW OF FUNDS IN THEORY AND PRACTICE

THE FLOW OF FUNDS IN THEORY AND PRACTICE

A Flow-Constrained Approach to Monetary Theory and Policy

by

Jacob Cohen
University of Pittsburgh

1987 **KLUWER ACADEMIC PUBLISHERS**
DORDRECHT / BOSTON / LANCASTER

Distributors

for the United States and Canada: Kluwer Academic Publishers, P.O. Box 358, Accord Station, Hingham, MA 02018-0358
for the UK and Ireland: Kluwer Academic Publishers, MTP Press Limited, Falcon House, Queen Square, Lancaster LA1 1RN, UK
for all other countries: Kluwer Academic Publishers Group, Distribution Center, P.O. Box 322, 3300 AH Dordrecht, The Netherlands

Library of Congress Cataloging in Publication Data

Cohen, Jacob, 1918-
The flow of funds in theory and practice : a flow-constrained approach to monetary theory and policy / Jacob Cohen.
p. cm. -- (Financial and monetary policy studies ; 15)
Bibliography: p.
Includes indexes.

ISBN-13: 978-94-010-8145-0 e-ISBN-13: 978-94-009-3675-1
DOI: 10.1007/978-94-009-3675-1

1. Money. 2. Monetary policy. 3. Flow of funds. I. Title.
II. Series.
HG221.C678 1987
332.4--dc19 87-21316
CIP

ISBN-13: 978-94-010-8145-0

Copyright

CONTENTS

Introduction 1

Chapter I
The Transaction: The Basic Building Block . . . 3

Chapter II
Equilibrium. 30

Chapter III
Disequilibrium 58

Chapter IV
Money and Banking in the Flow of Funds 79

Chapter V
The Degree of Netness: Stocks vs. Flows 93

Chapter VI
Policy Implications. 103

Chapter VII
An Idealized Set of Accounts 121

Chapter VIII
Simple Model Building: The Sector and
Transaction Identities 163

Chapter IX
Flow-Flow Models 181

Chapter X
A Stock Market Model 196

Chapter XI
Portfolio Balance Models 210

Chapter XII
Disequilibrium Models. 251

Chapter XIII
"Direct Linkage" Policy Models 276

Chapter XIV
The Strength and Limitations of
Flow-of-Funds Analysis 302

References 310

Name Index 330

Subject Index. 335

". . . every exit [is] an entrance somewhere else."
--Tom Stoppard, Rosencrantz and Guildenstern Are Dead

ACKNOWLEDGMENTS

The following acknowledgments are made for permission to publish:

Allen Sinai for material from the 1977 preliminary draft of The Financial System of the DRI Model. (Chapter XII)

The Journal of Money, Credit, and Banking for table 6 from David Backus et al., "A Model of U.S. Financial and Nonfinancial Economic Behavior," vol. 12, no. 2., Special Issue (May 1980). Copyright © 1980 by the Ohio State University Press. (Chapter XI); and for fig. 1 and table 2 from David Backus and Douglas Purvis, "An Integrated Model of Household Flow-of-Funds Allocations," The Journal of Money, Credit, and Banking, vol. 12, no. 2, Special Issue (May 1980). Copyright © 1980 by the Ohio State University Press. (Chapter XI)

Ray C. Fair for figures on pages 95 and 96 of Fair, A Model of Macroeconomic Activity, vol. 2, The Empirical Model. Ballinger Publishing Company, Cambridge, Mass., 1976. (Chapter XII)

Journal of Post Keynesian Economics, pp. 263-66 of Cohen and Kenkel, "A Credit Model Featuring External Finance and Scale Economies," vol. 2, no. 2 (Winter 1979-80), by permission of M. Sharpe, Inc., Armonk, New York 10504. (Chapter XII)

Brookings Institution for figure on p. 102 of Gurley and Shaw, Money in a Theory of Finance (Washington, D.C., 1960). (Chapter II)

American Economic Association for table on p. 108 of Brainard-Tobin, "Pitfalls in Financial Model-Building," American Economic Review Proceedings (May 1968). (Chapter XI)

Journal of Economics and Business for table 2, pp. 74-75 and Data Directory, pp. 80-82 in Cohen and Miller, "A Flow-of-Funds Model of the Stock Market," (Winter 1973). (Chapter X)

U.N. Statistical Office for table 2.17 opposite p. 32 of UN, A System of National Accounts (New York, 1968). (Chapter VII)

Quarterly Review of Economics and Business for tables on pp. 29, 30, 31, 32 of Cohen, "Direct vs. Indirect Controls as Instruments of Monetary Policy," (Fall 1970). (Chapter XIII).

Lexington Books, D. C. Heath & Co., for three tables on pp. 82, 108, 124 in P. H. Hendershott, Understanding Capital Markets, vol. 1, A Flow-of-Funds Financial Model, (Lexington, Mass., 1977). (Chapter XI)

Prentice-Hall Inc., for figure 18.5 on p. 294 of Smith, Money and Financial Intermediation: The Theory and Structure of Financial Systems (Englewood Cliffs, N.J., 1978). (Chapter I)

Economica and Miles Fleming for tables on pp. 134 and 141 in "The Timing of Payments and the Demand for Money," _Economica_ 31 (May 1964). (Chapter I); _Economica_ and Sten Thore for figure on p. 44 in "Credit Networks," _Economica_ 36 (February 1969). (Chapter I)

Rivista Internazionale di Scienze Ecnomiche e Commerciali for table on pp. 262-63, in "Tying Loose Ends in Monetary Theory in a Moneyflows Framework," vol. 21, no. 3 (1974). (Chapter III)

Martin H. Wolfson for material on p. 131 of Martin H. Wolfson, _Financial Crises_ (M. E. Sharpe, Inc., 1986).

Iowa State University Press for material on pp. 11-13, 279-281 of Cohen, _Money and Finance_ (1986).

My thanks to Kathy McLaughlin for first-rate typing. Also I am indebted to Jennifer Mayo and Edward Hilker for their assistance.

INTRODUCTION

The central emphasis in the book is on the transaction and the constraints that its architecture imposes on a discussion of monetary theory and policy. Because of their comprehensiveness and discipline the flow-of-funds accounts are the ideal vehicle for theorizing about real and financial interaction. Such interaction can best be understood when real and financial transactions are expressed in a common flow dimension. Each decision by economic agents is seen as two-ended in terms of markets: one market supplies the source of funds and the second market absorbs these funds. A matrix of interdependent markets is featured throughout the theoretical discussion. Credit markets, and the bank credit market in particular, become the source of disturbance in the theoretical model, but the necessary involvement of the money market is also stressed. Theories of financial instability and crisis now receiving considerable attention are part of the more general theory of the flow of funds. The rationale for the monetary authority to target credit rather than the monetary aggregates emerges from the analytical discussion.

A flow-constrained analysis clarifies interest-rate determination, provides a helpful format for discussing equilibrium and disequilibrium, integrates credit markets with the familiar IS-LM framework, and identifies a class of missing equations in macro-monetary theory. The prototype of the missing equations is an equation explaining monetary dissaving in terms of a series of arguments only one of which will be the stock of real balances or real wealth. Since it is monetary dissaving that influences spending behavior, a distinction is thereby drawn between the wealth effect (dissaving) and the wealth variable (the stock of real balances). The well-known convention is to identify (mistakenly) the wealth variable with the wealth effect.

After describing the leading national flow-of-funds accounts, the study focuses on the empirical work based on the accounts. Beginning with simple model-building, organized around the identities of the accounts, successive chapters deal with circular flow, financial market, portfolio balance, disequilibrium, and policy models. A final chapter evaluates the strength and limitations of flow-of-funds analysis.

Empirical studies offer considerable support to the central importance of credit markets. Flow-flow relations do well in explaining sector expenditures and flows in and out of financial markets. As is the case with choice-theoretical relations they do less well in explaining financial asset behavior. On the macro-level, a flow of funds cycle, with the key market being the bank credit market, seems well established. For forecasting purposes advantage should be taken of the a priori information offered by the accounting identities.

The flow-of-funds accounts are unique in the scope they offer for macro-monetary analysis. Both the theory and the practice of the flow of funds deserve more attention.

CHAPTER I
THE TRANSACTION: THE BASIC BUILDING BLOCK

It was the obvious importance of finance that led to the development of transactions (flow-of-funds) accounts. The accounting framework was designed to show that uses of funds of decision-making sectors were constrained by financial sources of funds in addition to real sources (income), and secondly that financial uses of funds of one sector were linked to the financial sources of funds of a second sector.

Failure to theorize within such a framework of constraints explains various loose ends in monetary theory. More than this, the flow of funds suggest a unique paradigm, supplementing the well-known monetarist and Keynesian approaches. We can speak interchangeably of flow-of-funds theory independent of any set of economic accounts and a theory of the flow of funds which theorizes about such accounts. A study of real-financial interaction in a "complete systems" setting leads to a focus on credit markets and a "creditist" hypothesis. This does not mean that money goes unnoticed. Our creditist paradigm considers changes in cash flow as a necessary condition for disturbances and leakages in the economy.

We begin with an analysis of the transaction as the basic building block.

THE TRANSACTIONS MATRIX

Analyzing the Transaction.

The basic building block of the flow of funds is the transaction. The transaction has both substantive and payment sides and involves at least two parties ("transactors"). These characteristics provide the ingredients of a "quadruple entry" accounting structure.

A's Account		B's Account	
Dr (Uses)	Cr (Sources)	Dr (Uses)	Cr (Sources)
A's Purchase____	Decrease in money holdings____	Increase in money holdings____	B's Sale____

Thus, A's purchase from B is debited and the resultant reduction in money holdings credited, with a reversal of these entries on B's statement.

We can jump from a quadruple entry system to an "octuple entry" system if we assume that A's purchase will ordinarily be offset by a sale. Player A now sells a bond to player B.

A's Account		B's Account	
Dr (Uses)	Cr (Sources)	Dr (Uses)	Cr (Sources)
Increase in money holdings____	A sells a bond____	B buys a bond____	Decrease in money holdings____

At this stage, A experiences no change in money holdings and in effect bond sales finance its purchases. The same effect of an octuple entry system will be achieved sans money flows in the case of sales on credit.

An octuple entry system typifies Robert Clower's "dual decision" process (Clower, 1956). Every transactor has his feet implanted in two markets: his decision to purchase in one market is constrained by the sources of funds provided by a second market, or, alternatively, his sources of funds decision is conditioned (if not constrained) by the uses planned for a second market. His analysis, however, is confined to two markets only--the labor and product markets. The constraining effect of the bond and money markets is not considered.

The Market Matrix.

The flow constraints on each market can be generalized in a market matrix. I assume "i" sectors active in four markets--output (P), bonds (B), inputs (L), and money (M). Thus, for the ith sector, assuming activity in all markets, the sectoral identity can be stated as:

I.1 $P_i + B_i + L_i + M_i = {}_iP + {}_iB + {}_iL + {}_iM$

where the subscripts to the right of the symbol indicate uses of funds in the designated markets and to the left indicate markets providing sources of funds.

The individual categories of uses are constrained by sources of funds in the same way that total uses are constrained. The four uses of funds of a sector can then be expressed in the following four identities:[1]

I.2
$$P_i = {}_iPP_i + {}_iBP_i + {}_iLP_i + {}_iMP_i$$
$$B_i = {}_iPB_i + {}_iBB_i + {}_iLB_i + {}_iMB_i$$
$$L_i = {}_iPL_i + {}_iBL_i + {}_iLL_i + {}_iML_i$$
$$M_i = {}_iPM_i + {}_iBM_i + {}_iLM_i + {}_iMM_i$$

Each equation links the various sources of funds (${}_iP$, ${}_iB$, etc.) to individual uses of funds.[2] When the independent variables are viewed column-wise, they indicate the allocation of a given source of funds among alternative uses. Viewed row-wise they describe the allocation of various sources to a given use. Since sources of funds indicate the supply of commodities or financial claims, and uses of funds indicate the demand for commodities or claims, the right-hand side of the four flow-of-funds identities can be expressed as a matrix of interlocking market flows. Such a matrix is given below after transposing columns and rows in order to show demand down the columns and supply across the rows.

Table I.1
The Market Matrix

Supply \ Demand	$P_i(p)$	$B_i(\frac{1}{r})$	$L_i(W)$	$M_i(r_m)$
${}_iP(p)$	PP	PB	PL	PM
${}_iB(\frac{1}{r})$	BP	BB	BL	BM
${}_iL(W)$	LP	LB	LL	LM
${}_iM(r_m)$	MP	MB	ML	MM

The first letter in the elements of the matrix indicate the market in which sales are taking place in order to finance demand in the market indicated by the second letter. Since the second letter is the same down each column, the column vectors of the matrix represent the demand side of each of the four markets. In the same way, the initial letter is the same across the rows so that the rows indicate the supply side of each of the four markets. The first column and row define demand and supply in the product market and so on for the remaining three markets. Going across the rows the sum of the marginal propensities to use funds out of each source of funds is unity. Going down the columns of the matrix, the partial derivatives of the various sources of funds with respect to a use of funds similarly add up to unity.

Demand and supply flows which have reference to the same second market constitute a "submarket" of the market in question. For example, the bond submarket of the product market is defined by BP (the money demand for commodities financed by the sale of bonds) and PB (the money demand for bonds financed by the sale of commodities). Similarly, the elements of the matrix involving "M" and "L" flows can be paired into the money and input submarkets of the product markets.[3] Money intermediates these two-market transactions. But increases in sector money holdings over the period (uses side) or decreases in money holdings (sources side) are the only money market (M) transactions.

Within each market, transactions are carried on by the various transactor-sectors. As shown, the elements of the matrix are aggregations of sector demand and supply. Leading sectors include households, business, government, and finance. In an "open economy" the "rest of the world" would be an additional sector. In some markets only one sector may appear on one side of the market. For example, we shall assume that households are the unique seller of inputs (labor services) and business will be the unique seller of output.

<u>The Market Equations.</u>

The dual decision process is necessarily valid in an ex post sense since each use of funds involves a corresponding amount of sources of funds. In an ex ante "notional" sense the dual decision process implies that plans to buy in one market are associated with plans to sell in a second and that these joint plans constitute a single dependent variable on the demand side of one market and the supply side of a second. As such they are a function of a series of explanatory variable including prices, interest rates, income, assets, and expectational variables.

A generalized equation for the ith sector would look as follows:

I.3 $\ _{i}XY^{i} = {}_{i}XY_{i}\ (p, EXP, r, \bar{M}_{i}, \bar{A}_{i}, \bar{S}_{i}, I)$

where

$X, Y,$ = two markets

p = commodity price variables, including rates of change

EXP = expectational variables

r = interest rate variables

$\bar{M}_i$ = holdings of money balances by the ith sector

$\bar{A}_i$ = other financial asset holdings by the ith sector

$\bar{S}_i$ = stocks of physical assets (fixed assets, inventories) of the ith sector

I = institutional constraints, such as reserve requirements for banks, or taxes

The "own prices" for a sector operating in a given market are shown on the fringes of the matrix in Table I.1 where "p" indicates the commodity price level, "1/r" the reciprocal of the market rate of interest, "W" the money price of inputs, "r" the market rate of interest, and "r_m" the own rate of interest on money balances. The notation $B_i(\frac{1}{r})$, for example, states that the demand for bonds is a function of the reciprocal of the market interest rate. Both demand and supply functions when plotted against "own" prices can be positively sloping since the quantity axis is measured in dollars rather than physical quantities. Thus the demand curves in the first three markets in the case of inelastic demand could be rising curves. In the case of the money market, the supply of money curve would be negatively sloping. As the cost of money creation goes up (measured by the implicit or explicit return on checkable deposits), given the prices in other markets, less money will be supplied to finance other-market purchases. This negative slope would also apply to holders of money balances who will supply more money balances as the return from holding such balances declines. The demand curve for additional money holdings will be positively sloped. Amounts demanded increase with higher interest returns. The stability conditions are assumed to be satisfied in all markets with excess demand driving up the price in the first three markets and driving down the return on money in the money market.

In analyzing a single market in this way, the focus is on its "own price" variable. This means that we ignore the "shift variables" for this market (e.g., the influence of reserves and reserve requirements on the supply side of the money market) and that we ignore the variables influencing second market decisions. In effect, the second market decisions are influenced solely by the change in own price in the first market.

The cells along the diagonal of the matrix represent each market's "own" submarket. The first value, PP, embraces the business sector, signifying the use of retained business earnings to buy output (investment goods).[4] The PP submarket can reflect unplanned depletions or increases in inventories, with the size of PP being decreased in the former case and increased in the latter. These diagonal elements are common to both the demand and supply sides of a given market and as a result they do not determine prices.[5]

The equilibrium condition in each market requires that the excess demands in the submarkets other than the "own" submarket sum up to zero. In the product market, for example, the equilibrium condition is that (BP - PB) + (LP - PL) + (MP - PM) equal zero. Assuming that the first three markets clear, since the fourth market is made up of a subset of the submarkets of the first three markets, the solution for the fourth market is given once the solution is known for the first three markets.

The market matrix is on a high level of abstraction. For example, the demand and supply functions in the bond market describe the purchase and sale of both "old" and "new" financial claims per period of time. The sale of old financial claims (nonmonetary financial dissaving) may be influenced by variables other than those affecting the sale of new financial claims. The diagonal term in this market, BB, variously describes sectors' shifting among financial assets or refunding outstanding issues. It also includes the borrowing-lending activities of financial institutions--the sale of their own liabilities for the sake of financial investment.

I shall identify the "input" market (L) with the market for labor services (again measured in dollar terms). The "LP" and "PL" cells will be the important elements in the input market. The diagonal term LL indicates the household sector's supplying of labor for the purpose of hiring direct labor-service, e.g., domestic help.

The money market is on the same flow-of-funds basis as the first three markets. The supply side refers to the supply of <u>additional</u> money balances per period of time by the banking sector with MB being the leading element on the supply side. The demand side refers to the demand for additional money balances by the nonbank sectors financed by the sale of output, bonds, or labor. The supply of additional money balances is supplemented by planned dishoarding of existing money balances by nonbank sectors which will be spent in the three remaining markets. Unlike the other markets in equilibrium, each submarket of the money market will "disappear" in the stationary state.[6] Money of course continues to pass from hand to hand in payment for transactions but in equilibrium <u>average</u> money holdings over the period equal desired <u>average</u> holdings. It is in this average sense that we define equilibrium in the stationary state. Under equilibrium growth conditions, an excess supply of money balances in the bond submarket will match an excess demand in the product and labor submarkets. The MM diagonal term denotes switches between components of the money supply by the nonbank sector; that is, between currency and demand deposits.

Given i sectors and n markets, and assuming that each sector is involved in every market, the precise number of independent relations in the flow-constrained model will be defined by the following formula:

I.4 $$i[n(n-1)] + in + (n-1) = in^2 + n-1$$

For example, given six sectors and four markets, each sector will have a demand and supply relation in each of twelve submarkets--the initial 16 submarkets minus 4 "own" submarkets. Each of these submarket relations will appear twice--once as a demand function in one market and once as a supply function in a second market. The total number of demand and supply relations will therefore be 6 (x) 12 = 72. To these 72 relations must be added 24 "own" submarket relations (e.g., $_iP_{P_i}$--one for each sector in each market). The six budget constraints will each solve for one supply or demand variable, thus reducing the number of independent supply and demand relations to 66. Three independent market clearing equations solve for three price variables. The total number of independent equations in this hypothetical model will be 99--(72) + (24) + (3).

Theoretical advantage. The submarket formulation of the bond market resolves long-standing difficulties with the "loanable funds" approach to the bond market. When flows in the money market (increases in the money stock, and hoarding demand for money) and in the product market (saving and investment flows) are aggregated to give the supply and demand for bonds, three possible equilibrium interest rates have to be reconciled (Harris, 1981, chapter 15). Either the component market curves have to be manipulated in some arbitrary way so that the money and product markets clear at the same interest rate or one has inconsistent rates established in each market.[7]

This dilemma is avoided in a submarket analysis of the bond market. Now flows in the money and product markets become the second market associated with the supply and demand for bonds. In the money submarket of the bond market the relevant flows are MB and BM, in the product submarket, PB and BP. Including the input market that encompasses household saving, the two-ended flows are LB and BL. Now disequilibrum in the individual submarkets of the bond market does not matter since in all cases demand and supply refers to bonds. Summing up demand and supply in the individual submarkets yields one unique interest rate for the bond market.

A similar criticism can be offered of equation-dropping in a Walrasian system of equations. Assume excess demand equations for the product, bond and money markets with the arguments being relative prices, the interest rate on bonds, endowments of commodities and money with the system closed by a definition of the price level. With n equations in the goods market, the addition of the bond and money markets make for n + 2 equations. Adding the definition of the absolute price level, there are now n + 3 equations to determine n relative prices of goods, the absolute price level, and the rate of interest. According to Walras's law, there are only n + 2 independent equations to determine the n + 2 prices, including the rate of interest. It has been traditionally argued that it is a matter of indifference whether the bond market or money equation is dropped, thus suggesting the equivalence of loanable funds and liquidity preference theories (Harris, p. 313). From the standpoint of the flow-constrained model, the bond market cannot be treated as independent of the product and money markets in the determination of the bond interest rate. Goods may be sold to buy bonds or bonds may be sold to buy products, money is created to buy bonds, bonds are sold to add to average money holdings. The Walrasian system is incapable of handling such intermarket flows.[8] This interdependence, of course, applies to every market and requires a systematic "dual-decision" approach.[9]

THE SECTOR CONSTRAINTS

The unit-sum identities apply to individual sectors as they do to markets. Thus for the ith sector, expenditures in the product market are wholly explained by sources of funds in this and the other three markets:

$$\text{I.5} \qquad \frac{\partial P_i}{\partial_i P} + \frac{\partial P_i}{\partial_i B} + \frac{\partial P_i}{\partial_i L} + \frac{\partial P_i}{\partial_i M} = 1$$

and similarly for the other uses of funds columns of the market matrix (Table I.1). The row-sum identities specify that a given source of funds is fully exhausted by uses of funds in this and the other three markets. Thus for sources in the product market:

$$\text{I.6} \qquad \frac{\partial P_i}{\partial_i P} + \frac{\partial B_i}{\partial_i P} + \frac{\partial L_i}{\partial_i P} + \frac{\partial M_i}{\partial_i P} = 1$$

and similarly for the other supply of funds rows.[10]

A series of zero-sum constraints apply to sector sources and uses in response to interest-rate changes. Since the identity of sources and uses must be retained, any effect on one side must be balanced by effects on the other side. Thus we write:

$$\text{I.7} \qquad \frac{\partial P_i}{\partial r} + \frac{\partial B_i}{\partial r} + \frac{\partial L_i}{\partial r} + \frac{\partial M_i}{\partial r} - \left(\frac{\partial_i P}{\partial r} + \frac{\partial_i B}{\partial r} + \frac{\partial_i L}{\partial r} + \frac{\partial_i M}{\partial r}\right) = 0$$

An increase in the market interest rate on a particular bond which leads by substitution to an increase in demand for that asset must be offset by decreases in other uses of funds or by increases in sources of funds. Given more than one interest rate, symmetry constraints can be imposed on the individual financial equations.[11] The response of a given financial variable to a second interest rate should be the same as the response of the second financial variable to the first interest rate. For example, if purchases of Treasury bonds decrease in response to an increase in yields on corporate bonds (holding the yield on Treasury bonds constant), purchases of corporate bonds should increase to the same extent, given a relative increase in the yield on Treasury bonds. We will denote the interest rate on the first financial asset acquired on the ith sector by rl, the second by r2. The liability issued by the ith sector carries a third interest rate, r3. These numbers also identify financial assets and liabilities. Now the three symmetry conditions are:

I.8 $\frac{\partial B_{i1}}{\partial r_2} = \frac{\partial B_{i2}}{\partial r_1}$

I.9 $\frac{\partial B_{i1}}{\partial r_3} = -\frac{\partial {}_iB_3}{\partial r_1}$

I.10 $\frac{\partial B_{i2}}{\partial r_3} = -\frac{\partial {}_iB_3}{\partial r_2}$

With the introduction of financial liabilities, the negative response of asset purchases to an increase in the cost of borrowing must match the positive response of borrowing to an increase in the yield on assets.

The a priori information provided by these constraints must be considered in any estimation procedure. For example, suppose we were estimating the above equations--two financial asset and one financial liability equation (Hendershott, 1977, chapter 4; Wachtel, 1981a, p. 585). Using our previous notation:

I.11 $B_{i1} = a_1 r_1 + a_2 r_2 + a_3 r_3 \quad a_4 ({}_iP)$

I.12 $B_{i2} = a_5 r_1 + a_6 r_2 + a_7 r_3 + a_8 ({}_iP)$

I.13 ${}_iB_3 = a_9 r_1 + a_{10} r_2 + a_{11} r_3 + a_{12} ({}_iP)$

The a priori knowledge is that:

I.14 $a_1 + a_5 - a_9 = 0$

I.15 $a_2 + a_6 - a_{10} = 0$

I.16 $a_3 + a_7 - a_{11} = 0$

I.17 $a_4 + a_8 - a_{12} = 1$

I.18 $a_2 = a_5$

I.19 $a_3 = -a_9$

I.20 $a_7 = -a_{10}$

By substitution, the equations can be rewritten as:

I.21 $B_{i1} = a_1 r_1 + a_2 r_2 + a_3 r_3 + a_{4i} P$

I.22 $B_{i2} = a_2 r_1 \, (a_7 + a_2) r_2 + a_2 r_3 + a_{8i} P$

I.23 $_iB_3 = (a_1 + a_2) r_1 - a_7 r_2 +$
$(a_3 + a_7) r_3 + (a_4 + a_8 - 1)_i P$

These parameters can now be estimated simultaneously by "stacking" the equations, as if they were a single equation (Hendershott, Wachtel). The flow-of-funds restrictions could also be enforced by estimating each equation by itself but with a common set of regressors. This is preferable to residual estimation of one of the equations but runs the danger of having inconsistent signs for the coefficients (Hendershott, p. 52; Cohen, 1972, p. 13). Hendershott's stacking method enforces consistency although not necessarily guaranteeing that the variables or the signs of the coefficients are the correct ones. If the coefficients are incorrect because the individual equations ought to be specified differently, or because symmetry conditions do not hold, stacking (pooling) the data "averages out" the errors in the individual equations rather than providing "correct" estimates.[12]

THE PAYMENTS SIDE

The market matrix compresses out the payments (money flow) side of the transaction. Thus, for example, the sale of bonds to buy products--BP--nets out the intermediating money payment--BM→MP. In the market matrix, "M" transactions are reserved for changes in average money holdings over the payment period. Assuming that money balances are only held for medium of exchange (transactions) purposes, day-to-day balances will vary as payments are made. Concentrating on the payments side means literally a concentration on the flow of funds.[13]

The Payments Matrix. The payments matrix shown below (based on Fleming, 1964), estimates cash balances for sectors with different patterns of receipts and payments. The figures in the columns of Table I.2 represent payments, those in the rows, receipts. Expenditure patterns follow a five-day cycle. Households are represented by H and firms by A, B, C, D, and E. Households pay daily for their purchases. Firms make payments at weekly intervals. Each transactor is represented by five columns and five rows. For example, firm A makes intermediate payments of 60 on day 2 and 25 on day 4 to firms D and E, respectively, and income payments of 5 on day 5 to households H. Firm A receives receipts on day 1 of 60 and 20 on day 3 from firms C and B and daily receipts of 2 from H. (Presently the underlined figures of 60 and 120 in the A and B columns are to be ignored.) Total payments and receipts are shown at the bottom of the columns and at the side of the rows, respectively.

The table records the weekly settlements for trade credit extended between business firms. The household sector in contrast pays daily for its purchases (there is no consumer credit) and is paid weekly by the business sector for the services it has rendered during the week.

Below the total payments row is a row showing minimum daily balances. Given the payments structure these are the least amount of balances that a transactor can hold during the week. On one day minimum balances will be zero. Beyond this

TABLE I.2 THE PAYMENTS MATRIX

Payments

Receipts		A					B					C					D					E					H					TR
		1	2	3	4	5	1	2	3	4	5	1	2	3	4	5	1	2	3	4	5	1	2	3	4	5	1	2	3	4	5	
A	1											60															2					
	2																											2				
	3								20																				2			90
	4																													2		
	5																														2	
B	1																					35					3					
	2												100															3				
	3																												3			150
	4																													3		
	5																														3	
C	1																										5					
	2																											5				
	3																		100										5			180
	4																								55					5		
	5																														5	
D	1	60																									6					
	2		60																									6				
	3								120																				6			210
	4									120																				6		
	5																														6	
E	1																70										4					
	2																											4				
	3																												4			115
	4				25																									4		
	5																														4	
H	1																															
	2																															
	3																															100
	4																															
	5					5					10					20					40					25						
TP				90					150					180					210					115					100			845
NB	1	62	4	26	3	0	38	141	124	7	0	95	0	105	165	150	28	94	0	126	92	39	43	47	21	0	60	40	20	0	80	322
NB	2	62	4	26	3	0	62	165	28	31	24	95	0	105	165	150	4	70	96	102	68	39	43	47	21	0	60	40	20	0	80	322
NB	3	62	4	26	3	0	38	141	4	7	0	95	0	105	165	150	0	66	92	98	64	39	43	47	21	0	60	40	20	0	80	294
NB	4	14	16	38	15	12	38	141	4	7	0	95	0	105	165	150	48	54	80	86	52	39	43	47	21	0	60	40	20	0	80	294
NB	5	2	6	26	3	0	38	141	4	7	0	95	0	105	165	150	0	6	32	38	4	39	43	47	21	0	60	40	20	0	80	234

<u>Source</u>: Fleming, 1964, p. 34.

day the sum of payments and receipts (for the five-day cycle) will be equal. For example, firm A can end day 5 with zero balances because over the next 5 days total receipts match total expenditures. In the case of firm C, this equality applies to total receipts and expenditures beginning on day 3. But on other days, each transactor is seen to have positive money balances. Such balances are inevitable in view of the timing pattern of receipts and expenditures. Adding up all minimum balances yields the economy's demand for money. Initially, it is 322.

To economize further on cash balances, the timing of payments has to be altered. If creditors could receive payment on low cash days, and debtors make payment on high cash days, minimum balances could be reduced. This can be illustrated in terms of the matrix. Now B agrees to pay 120 to D on day 3 (as shown by the underlined 120) instead of day 4. The week's trade credit from D to B starts and matures on day 3 rather than day 4. In the week the change is made, B pays 120 x (4/5) = 96 to D on day 3 because only four days' credit has to be settled at this point. This leads to an increase of 120 - 96 = 13 in B's daily cash balance as shown by row MB2. The MB2 row shows that B now has a positive money balance of 24 on day 5, and D has 4 on day 1. They can now reduce their money balances on all days by these amounts. Required average money balances decline. This is shown by the MB3 row. In the same way if D changes its credit to A so that it gets paid on day 1 instead of day 2, the change in minimum balances is given by MB4. The last MB5 row shows how the demand for money (average balances) can be reduced in this case. Rearranging the timing of payments is not cost free. Searches have to be made for the necessary "double coincidence" of preferences. These involve the cost of time in addition to the money costs of acquiring information. Interest is saved by paying off bank debts, thus reducing the money supply.

Money balances are used not only to make payments on current account but also on capital account. We can take the behavior of firm C in relation to households as an illustration of this function of money balances. We now assume that firm C issues long-term securities every day 3 which are purchased by households on that day. This financial investment by households replaces previous consumption expenditures. The demand for money balances stays the same in row MB_1 despite the financing of investment in the place of consumption.

Rearranging the payments structure could be accomplished by a lending transaction. In terms of Table I.2, it is as if A and B made one-day loans to D. This gives us a more general approach to optimizing cash balances. Knowing his/her payments structure, the transactor can temporarily dispose of excess cash by financial transactions. It will pay him to do this so long as the marginal cost of making such transactions (acquiring an asset and then disposing it) is less than the interest gained.

The more frequent payments will similarly reduce the minimum amount of average balances in relation to total payments. In a second matrix (Table 1.3), households have their income and expenditures increased by 50 percent and firm payments for intermediate purchases are made twice as often. The result is an increase in total payments at the same time that minimum balances are reduced (as compared with MB_1 in the first matrix, Table I.2).

A Payments Network. The payments matrix has its limitations in describing money flows. It is not set up to handle additions to money balances via depository institutions. Algebraic manipulation to produce "money" and "credit multipliers" is not feasible. An alternative description of the payments mechanism is provided by so-called credit networks (Thore, 1969; Thore, 1970; Thore and Kydland, 1972).

A credit network is illustrated in Figure I.1. It is seen to consist of nodes and interconnecting directed links. The nodes represent the nonfinancial sector (households and firms), P; commercial banks, B; and non-bank financial institutions, I. The directed links stand for cash flows: x_{PB} and x_{PI}--

TABLE I.3 PAYMENTS MATRIX WITH MORE FREQUENT PAYMENTS

PAYMENTS

RECEIPTS		A					B					C					D̄					E					H					
		1	2	3	4	5	1	2	3	4	5	1	2	3	4	5	1	2	3	4	5	1	2	3	4	5	1	2	3	4	5	TR
A	1											60															3					
	2												30															3				
	3								20																				3			135
	4									10																				3		
	5																														3	
B	1																					35					4					
	2												100															4				
	3																												4			225
	4														50										20					4		
	5																														4	
C	1																										8					
	2																	50					25					8				
	3																		100										8			270
	4																								55					8		
	5																														8	
D	1	30																									9					
	2		60					60																				9				
	3																												9			315
	4									120																				9		
	5																														9	
E	1																70										6					
	2																											6				
	3																												6			172
	4				25															35										6		
	5					12																									6	
H	1																															
	2																															
	3																															150
	4																															
	5					8					15					30					60					37						
TP				135					225					270					315					172					150			1,267
MB_1		33	6	29	17	0	39	83	67	11	0	47	0	108	121	99	12	91	0	94	43	41	22	28	19	0	90	60	30	0	120	262

Source: Fleming, p. 141.

FIGURE I.1 A CREDIT NETWORK

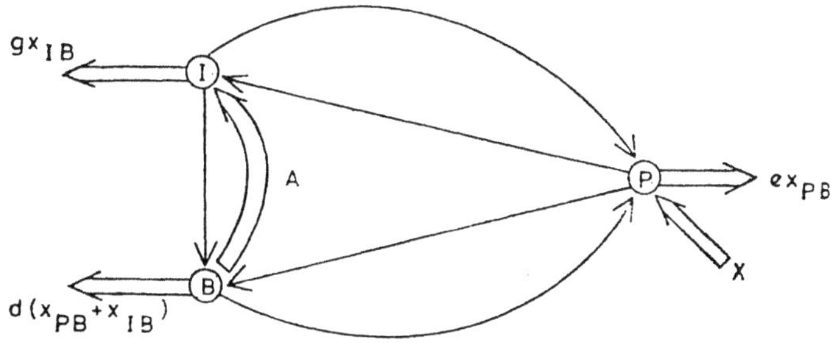

Source: Thore, 1964, p. 44.

changes in public deposits in banks and institutions respectively; x_{IB}--changes in deposits of institutions in banks; and x_{BP} and x_{IP}--changes in bank and institutional lending to the public. The flow "A" from B to I represents an exogenous shift of public deposits.

Cash enters the network by an exogenous influx of high-powered money. High-powered money leaves the network through the efflux channels of the system. The efflux at P indicates the public cash leakage--the desired change in public cash holdings. The effluxes at B and I represent changes in required or desired cash reserves of banks and financial institutions. Static equilibrium is reached in the network when desired holdings equal actual holdings of high-powered money. Determinacy depends on the following parameters which define the outflows of cash:

r = X_{PI}: X_{IP}, i.e., the marginal redeposit ratio on institutional lending

c = the marginal cash/own commercial bank deposits ratio P desires to hold

d = the marginal cash/deposits ratio B is required or desires to hold

f = the marginal reserves, cash and bank deposits/ liabilities ratio I is required or desires to hold

g = the marginal cash/own commercial bank deposits ratio I is required or desires to hold

Cash flows are summarized in the "incidence matrix." It has one row for each node and one column for each link in the network. An outflow from a given node is indicated by a minus, the inflow by a plus. Thus, for example, the flow from the public to the commercial banks in the second column is recorded by a -1 in the P row and a +1 in the B row.

I.24

	X_{BP}	X_{PB}	X_{IB}	X_{IP}	X_{PI}
P	+1	-1	0	+1	-1
B	-1	+1	+1	0	0
I	0	0	-1	-1	+1

Using this matrix and the "Kirchoff conservation conditions" which stipulate that the total outflow from any node must equal total inflow into the same node a system of linear equations emerges.

I.25

	X_{BP}	X_{PB}	X_{IB}	X_{IP}	X_{PI}	
P	+1	-1		+1	-1	$= -X+eX_{PB}$
B	-1	+1	+1			$= +A+d(X_{PB}+X_{IB})$
I			-1	-1	+1	$= -A+gX_{IB}$

The unknown variables are the column variables. The right-hand side of each equation shows the influx and efflux from the node, with the former being denoted by a minus, and efflux by a plus sign.

The equation system is completed with the definitions for r and f. This makes it possible to solve for the five flows: xBP, xPB, xIB, xIP, and xPI. The resultant credit multipliers are similar to those derived in more conventional ways (see, e.g., Shepperd and Barrett, 1965).

By means of a linear programming approach, this "direct" solution of the network is contrasted with the dual. The direct solution is in keeping with the quantity theory, the dual is consistent with the "general equilibrium" approach of Tobin and Brainard (p. 53). The right-hand sides of the dual program (Thore, 1969, p. 48) show demand prices of the capital flowing over each link (maximum interest rate borrowers would pay), the left-hand sides show the supply price of the capital flow. Thus from a general mathematical point of view the quantity and Keynesian approaches are shown to be two sides of the same coin (p. 54).

A serious limitation of network theory is the literal meaning that has to be given to cash flows. Banks and non-banks lend cash (high-powered money) which is redeposited by the public and reloaned until high-powered money leaks into desired holdings. Since deposits are always considered an advance of funds to financial "intermediaries," their unique leakage effect (as compared with other moneyflows) is obscured.[14] A Markov matrix (introduced in the following section) makes clear this distinction.

Payments as a Markov Chain. That demand deposits are not transmitted and (depending on reserve requirements) time deposits are only partly transmitted can be illustrated by means of a transition matrix for the moneyflows process (Smith, 1971, chapter 12; 1978, chapter 18).

In the following matrix the heading on the rows indicate the "state" the funds are in, and the heading on the columns the next state. The values in each row add to 1 and record the expected distribution of funds as they move from state to the next. These values are called transition probabilities. The first row of the matrix is the "absorbing state." The timing of all flows is coordinated by having a planning vector for direct consumption and investment expenditures (C_p and I_p). This takes care of the two-stage decisions involved in financial intermediation (1978, p. 294). The process begins with income (Y) and moves through various types of expenditures back to income at a later stage or into the absorbing state. Given the

TABLE I.4 A TRANSITION MATRIX

	H	C_p	I_p	C	I	R	F	B	Y
H	1.0	0	0	0	0	0	0	0	0
C_p	0	0	0	1.0	0	0	0	0	0
I_p	0	0	0	0	1.0	0	0	0	0
C	0	0	0	0	0	0	0	0	1.0
I	0	0	0	0	0	0	0	0	1.0
R	0	0	0	0.2	0.8	0	0	0	0
F	0.1	0	0	0.2	0.7	0	0	0	0
B	0.25	0	0	0.1	0.65	0	0	0	0
Y	0.2	0.4	0.1	0	0	0.2	0.1	0	0

Source: P. F. Smith, 1978, p. 294.

transition probabilities, the flow of funds through successive states of the process can be traced by computing successive powers of the transition matrix (1971, p. 203).

The distribution vector H indicates that any funds moving into this state are completely absorbed. Leakages occur when values in the absorbing state column (H) are greater than zero. The crucial rows in the moneyflows process are F, B, Y.

Where H = additions to money balances, non-bank public and non-bank depository institutions, and leakages due to reserve requirements on time or savings accounts

C_p = planned consumption

I_p = planned investment

C = consumption

I = investment

R = repayment of debt

F = financial savings at non-bank depository institutions

B = time deposits in depository institutions

Y = income

Additions to the public's money balances out of income (the Y,H cell) are the first leakage--a leakage of 20 percent.[15] The B,H cell records the leakage effect of an increase in savings deposits at the expense of checkable deposits. The effect depends on the differential in reserve requirements (Smith, 1978, p. 295; Cohen, 1982c). For example, a reserve requirement of 12 percent against checkable deposits and a 3 percent reserve requirement against time deposits results in a 25 percent leakage of any amount of saving. That is, new loans leading to checkable deposits will decline by the same amount.[16] Finally, cell F,H represents for nonbank institutions an increase in demand deposits equal to 10 percent of their deposit liabilities. The leakage effect is similar to the increase in demand deposits for the nonfinancial sector.

In common with the earlier payments matrix, a weakness of the transition matrix is that it cannot handle the dynamics of moneyflows growth. A realistic description of the money flows process must also allow for changes in the transition probabilities (Smith, 1971, p. 205).

THE CHAPTERS AHEAD

The Theory. The theory of the flow of funds is a theory of the interaction of the real and financial. Inspired by the development of the accounts, it goes beyond the published accounts and focuses on the idea of the accounts. The testing of the theory --the practice--is of course limited by the published accounts.

In succeeding chapters in the theoretical section we develop a flow-of-funds theory using headings which are central to the study of macro-monetary and which permit comparisons with the contemporary literature. We begin with equilibria (Chapter II), and disequilibria (Chapter III) on both a micro- and macro-basis. There are certain difficulties in the interpretation of the means of payment side of the transaction in a flow-of-funds accounting framework. These are considered in Chapter IV, "Money and Banking in the Flow of Funds." Stocks versus flows in Chapter V emphasize the distinction between balance sheet values and balance sheet (flow-of-funds) effects. Finally, in Chapter VI the policy implications of flow-of-funds theory are spelled out.

The Practice. The second part of this monograph deals with applications of the flow of funds. It goes beyond a testing of the theory of the first section because most published applications are based on conventional frameworks. Nevertheless, a major interest is in determining how many of the propositions of a flow-of-funds theory are supported by empirical work. We begin with a comparison of the structure of the United States, British, Canadian, Australian, and Japanese and Yugoslav accounts, the main examples of flow-of-funds accounting (Chapter VII). The use of the accounts for simple model building based on the sector and transaction identities is covered in Chapter VIII. Chapter IX goes beyond identities and introduces regression relationships based on circularity in the flow of funds. In Chapter X, the orientation shifts from sectors to markets and the stock market is analyzed in terms of flows in and out of the market. Chapter XI focuses on the leading portfolio balance models. In Chapter XII, disequilibrium models are considered that offer a more comprehensive treatment of the nonfinancial side. Chapter XIII describes "direct linkage" policy models in which real activity is directly linked to financial variables. Finally, Chapter XIV offers an evaluation of both the theory and practice of the flow of funds.

Notes

1. The language of "debit" and "credit" is superior to the more conventional language of sources and uses of funds since increases in money holdings cannot be considered a "use" of funds, nor can a decrease in money holdings be considered a "source" of funds. The difficulties with the conventional terms becomes apparent later on in the chapter when "credit networks" are discussed. The matter of terminology is considered in detail in Chapter IV, "Money and Banking in the Flow of Funds."
2. Each right-hand term, e.g., ${}_iBP_i$, indicates the allocation of a single source of funds to the use on the left-hand side of the identity and not the product of two separate flows.
3. Our transactions are "simple" transactions involving the exchange of money for one good or the exchange of goods for IOUs (buying "on credit"). In the case of credit transactions it is as if the IOU generated a money inflow which is then spent on the good. In this way, a consistent treatment can be given money and credit transactions.

   "Complex transactions" involve more than two goods (treating money as a good). Examples are rationing where the purchase requires coupons as well as money. In our notation, with coupons represented by B, a rationed purchase would be shown as $({}_iB + {}_iM)\ P_i$ or $({}_iB + {}_iL)\ P_i$ if purchases were financed out of income rather than allowing money balances to run down. In the limited context of consumer choice and using linear-activity analysis, complex transactions have been extensively treated in Wichers (1979).
4. If the output market were treated in grosser fashion, the PP element includes interfirm transactions in intermediate products (an interindustry matrix).
5. "Own" submarkets, when disaggregated, affect prices in the same way as other submarkets. For example, a demand for Treasury bonds financed by the sale of corporate bonds will influence relative prices in the bond market.
6. This "disappearance" is explained in Chapter IV, which traces out the adjustment to an outside disturbance.
7. In Harris's diagrammatics both solutions are found!
8. The Walrasian system is a dual-decision model when there are two markets. Thus an excess supply in one corresponds to an excess demand in the second. When there are more than two markets, however, the Walrasian equation system does not identify intermarket flows.
9. On the other hand, Walras's law tells us that we cannot solve for both the own rate on money balances and the bond rate of interest along with wages and prices with only three independent market equations. An additional relation would have to be introduced, such as making the own rate exogenous or a function of some ceiling rate on time deposits.

10. Model estimation based on sector constraints falls into the general category of allocational models that allocate a given aggregate among its components. Systems of linear consumption expenditures antedated the application of constraints to models of portfolio choice (Barten, 1977; Brox and Maclean, 1983, Chap. 4).
11. I am indebted to James L. Kenkel for this comment on stacking. Estimation techniques will be more extensively discussed in the "practice" section of this monograph. They are relevant here because of their close relationship to the underlying constraints of a flow-of-funds framework.
12. In analogous fashion to the payments matrix, a transactions matrix can be constructed which is limited to the substantive side of transactions. The best-known example of such matrices is the Leontief input-output model. For a pioneering discussion of this matrix, see Richard Stone (1952).
13. While demand deposits and, to a lesser extent, time deposits are a leakage in a moneyflow sense, "checkable" deposits are still active as the medium of exchange. But the use (reduction) in money balances constitutes the money outflow rather than the reverse--the increased holding of deposits. For this reason, unlike the assumption of credit networks, money outflows will not equal money inflows if holdings of money balances change. If they decline, money outflows exceed money inflows. If they increase, money inflows exceed money outflows. This point is further discussed in Chapter IV, "Money and Banking in the Flow of Funds."
14. It is not necessary to add the word "idle" before money balances. An increase in average balances will be a leakage in the sense of not advancing funds regardless of the activity of such balances.
15. This demonstrates a basic asymmetry between saving as seen by the nonfinancial sector and as seen by the depository institution. For the former, it is a use of income; for the latter, it shows up as a compositional change in deposit liabilities, rather than as a transference of purchasing power. (See also Chapter IV below.)

CHAPTER II
EQUILIBRIUM

MARKET EQUILIBRIUM

The Stationary State.

In stationary equilibrium, transactions take place in all of the submarkets of the market matrix. A stationary equilibrium means an absence of both new security issues and net increases in the money stock. A stock of outstanding bonds is assumed as a result of initial financing of business plant and equipment. Similarly, the government or central bank is assumed to supply an original amount of the means of payment. The family life cycle would govern holdings of bonds. They would be bought by those in earlier stages of the life cycle and sold by those in the later stages. In the money market desired money holdings are assumed to equal actual money holdings for all sectors collectively. This is consistent with variation in each transactor's holdings over the payments interval, as transactors bridge the gap between receipts and expenditures by adding to or lowering their money holdings. In terms of the market matrix of Chapter I, bond transactions are LB, BP transactions (buying bonds out of labor income and selling bonds to buy products). When money intermediates, we do not show this as involving the money market. Only in the case of hoarding and dishoarding (which are defined in terms of changes in sector money holdings between time periods) or, in the case of net increases in the money stock, will activity be registered in the money market.

Balanced Growth[1]

The bond market. In balanced growth all submarkets of the matrix are involved. Some reference rate of growth is necessary, and we take this to be the growth rate of output. The borrowing sectors with capital expenditures in excess of current saving are deficit sectors, and the net lending sectors are surplus sectors.[2]

The supply of bonds to buy output (the BP terms in the market matrix) represent the equality of net investment expenditures with the firm's deficit, which in turn is represented by primary security issues. Each bond unit is assumed to pay $1 interest so that B/r (the market rate of interest) represents the nominal value of new issues. New bond issues then are

II.1 $$BP_b/r = P_b - {}_bP$$

where the subscript b denotes business firms. New issues equal planned expenditures less retained earnings (saving).[3] The relation can be expressed in ratio form by introducing the national output (ΣP_i) or Y. Thus

II.2 $$\frac{BP_b}{rY} = \frac{P_b - {}_bP}{Y}$$

Rearranging terms, it can be immediately seen that the issues-income ratio depends on the average propensity to spend out of income $\frac{P_b}{{}_bP}$ and the share of national income received by firms $\frac{{}_bP}{Y}$. That is,

II.3 $$\frac{BP_b}{rY} = \left(\frac{P_b}{{}_bP} - 1\right)\frac{{}_bP}{Y}$$

From the standpoint of households buying bonds the counterpart relation shows that the issues-income ratio depends on consumers' average propensity to consume $(\frac{P_h}{L})$, desired increments in money holdings, $\frac{M_h}{L}$, and the share of national income received by households $(\frac{L}{Y})$. Thus,

II.4 $$\frac{LB}{rY} = \left(1 - \frac{P_h}{L} - \frac{M_h}{L}\right)\frac{L}{Y}$$

These ratios suggest that the distribution of spending relative to the distribution of income between households and business will determine the absolute growth in financial assets. The rate of growth from one year to the next depends on a number of underlying factors, the rate of growth of output, the marginal productivity of investment (the real rental rate on capital)--i--and the market interest rate (r).

The growth rate in the capital stock will be equal to the assumed growth rate in output, n. Investment (requiring financing) will be equal to n times the capital stock, $\bar{K}$. The saving of the firm will be the difference between the return on capital (ignoring dividends), $\bar{K}i$, and the interest payments by the firm $r\bar{B}$, where $\bar{B}$ = stock of bonds.

The new issue ratio can then be stated as:

II.5 $$\frac{BP_b}{rY} = \frac{n\bar{K} - (\bar{K}i - r\bar{B})}{Y}$$

Reformulation of this equation brings out the role of the capital-output ratio--$\frac{K}{Y}$.

II.6 $$\frac{BP_b}{rY} = \frac{(n-i)\ \bar{K}/Y}{1 - r/n}$$

For equilibrium in the bond market, planned issues must correspond to planned purchases by households out of wage income. That is,

II.7 $$\frac{LB}{rY} = \frac{BP_b}{rY}$$

The issues-income ratio will be the greater, the greater is the growth rate of output, the higher the capital-output ratio, and the higher is the market interest rate (r) in relation to the return on capital (i). The latter two variables determine firm saving.

The relation of each of these variables to the issues-income ratio can be illustrated graphically. In Figure II.1, the issues-income is related to the growth rate of output. It is assumed that the capital-output ratio is equal to unity. When the output-growth rate as shown by the A curve equals the real rental rate (.08), the issues-income ratio is zero. At a higher growth rate of output, the issues-income ratio is positive. It becomes negative when the output growth rate falls

FIGURE II.1 RELATION BETWEEN ISSUES-INCOME RATIO AND GROWTH RATE OF OUTPUT

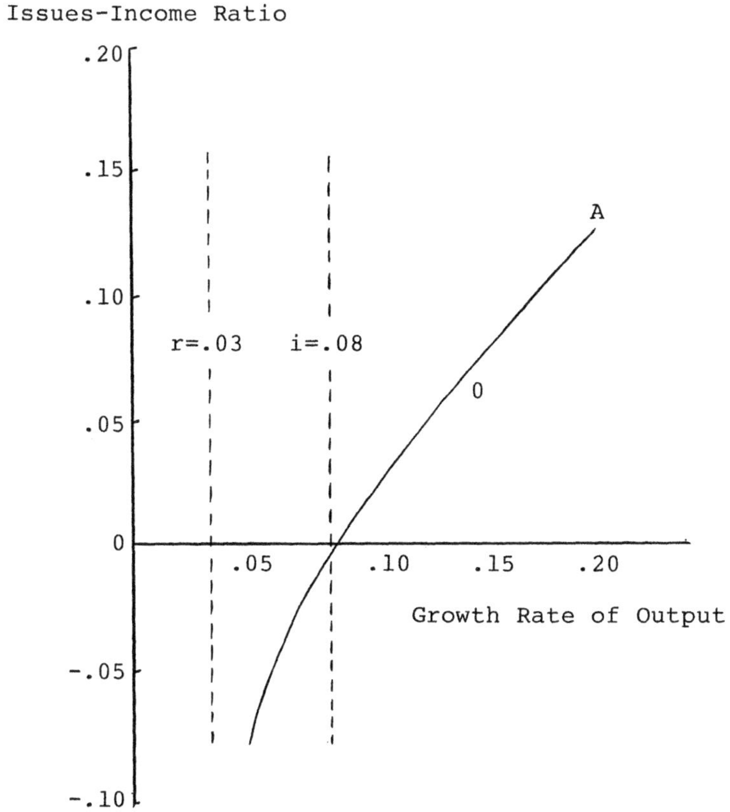

Source: Gurley and Shaw, p. 102.

between the real rental rate and the market rate of interest. Business now has budget surpluses and consumers have budget deficits. Primary issues come from households and not from business firms.

<u>The money market</u>. If we now allow for a steady increase in the money stock, equal to the growth rate in output, government or the central bank has to be introduced. An increase in the money stock is assumed to finance government expenditures.

II.8 $$\frac{g^M}{Y} = \frac{MP_g}{Y}$$

The money increment will be equal to n times the money stock, $\bar{M}$ of the previous period.

II.9 $$\frac{g^M}{Y} = n\bar{M}_{t-1}$$

The incremental demand for money by households (assumed to be the only holders of money balances) will be a function of planned transactions--LB, LP, financial assets $\hat{\bar{A}}$, the market interest rate (r), and the "own" interest rate on money balances, r_m.

II.10 $$\frac{LM_h}{Y} = m(LB, LP, \bar{A}, r, r_m)$$

The equilibrium relation is:

II.11 $$\frac{g^M}{Y} = \frac{LM}{Y}$$

<u>The labor market</u>. The flow demand for labor will be determined by planned output (growing at the rate of n) and by the money wage rate.

II.12 $$\frac{PL_b}{Y} = L_b(Y,W)$$

The flow supply of labor will be determined by planned

expenditures on consumption goods, bonds, money, and by the money wage rate.

$$\text{II.13} \qquad \frac{{}_{h}L}{Y} = L_h(LP_h, LM_h, LB_h, W)$$

In equilibrium,

$$\text{II.14} \qquad \frac{PL_b}{Y} = \frac{{}_{h}L}{Y}$$

The Product Market. The output market can be viewed as the residual market, with output being determined by decisions made in other markets.

$$\text{II.15} \qquad Y = bPPb + bBPb + LPh + gMPg$$

According to our assumption of a rate of growth of "n," flows are growing at this rate in each product submarket.

The Price and Interest Variables. While the submarket functions contain price and interest variables, in a balanced growth situation their market clearing role is obscured by the symmetrical shifts in the demand and supply curves in the chief submarkets. Interest rates, prices, and wage rates stay unchanged as a result of these shifts.

Unbalanced Growth. With a constant growth rate, business firms have chronic deficits and consumers have chronic surpluses (Gurley and Shaw, 1960, p. 114). Deficit rotation depends on business cycles or short-period fluctuations. Business firms are likely to shift from deficits to surpluses in a downturn as earnings increase relative to spending. Consumers may incur deficits as they try to maintain consumption. During the upswing the deficit-surplus wheel twirls again. Unlike balanced growth which has no empirical counterpart, it should be possible to test the notion of rotating deficits and surpluses for households and business.

SECTOR EQUILIBRIUM

The Household Sector. Sector equilibrium turns attention to optimization within a flow-of-funds framework. Now we conceive of the sector evaluating the costs of sources of funds and the benefits from uses of funds. The household sector will be in equilibrium when the marginal costs of (discretionary) sources are all equal and these in turn equal the marginal returns from (discretionary) uses of funds. Maximization can also be stated in present value terms by discounting future returns and costs.

Many of the transactions in the flow of funds involve nondiscretionary variables and are thus outside the optimization process. Financial uses include taxes, debt repayments; financial sources include debt retirement. Financial sources may be nondiscretionary if they depend on the amount of credit made available by lending sectors. The great bulk of nonfinancial expenditures ("necessities") and contractual financial uses, such as insurance premium payments, may be nondiscretionary. For this reason, the number of decision variables may be considerably less than the total number of transaction flows.

A point of departure from previous market analysis in a discussion of sector equilibrium is the introduction of imputations. Internal transactions (imputations) are relevant to the decision-making process. Examples for the household sector are the implicit returns from physical assets, money holdings, and the "cost" (disutility) of earning income.

The Business Sector.[4] We choose the business firm to illustrate in more detail optimal agent behavior in a flow-constrained framework The business firm makes decisions in three major areas--production, investment, and finance. The most comprehensive view of decision-making is in terms of the flow of funds. In an earlier study, the balance sheet constrained the profit function (Vickers, 1968). A flow-of-funds constraint provides more control variables than a stock constraint. In the stock case, financial asset sales (dissaving) have to be netted out against purchases; equity buy-backs against equity issues; debt retirement against debt issuance. The flow version therefore is on a "grosser" basis than the stock version. It is the appropriate dimension for constructing a dynamic optimization model. Now the decision-maker varies the flows of production, investment and finance over time-- allowing for their effects on prices and interest rates. In this way he maximizes the present value of the objective function.

An objective function for a one-period analysis is presented in the appendix to this chapter. In defining the profit function, a wide range of imputed costs and returns have been considered, including revaluation gains and losses. According to the first order conditions, optimization takes place for each decision variable when marginal revenues equal marginal cost. When the decision variable is a use of funds (expenditures on inputs X and Y, increases in net financial assets, money and dividends), the Lagrange multiplier μ is to be interpreted as the shadow price of inputs. When the decision variable is a source of funds (borrowing, sale of equities), μ stands for the marginal return on a dollar of investment.

THE MONETARY LITERATURE

The theory of the flow of funds advanced here expresses finance in the same dimension as real activity. Their interaction takes place across markets and within sectors. The market matrix displays the two-endedness of market transactions. Sector equilibrium requires an equilibrium between a sector's sources and uses of funds. The flow-constrained nature of decision-making is demonstrated in both cases. In equilibrium analysis, the flow-constrained nature of transactions is obscured by the market-clearing process. Decision-making is seen as "price-theoretical," steered and determined by prices. This neglect of the flow-constraints underlying demand and supply is a leading characteristic of the monetary literature.

The Neoclassical Synthesis. We focus on the well-known "neoclassical synthesis" to illustrate departure from a flow-of-funds paradigm.[5] The money market is in stock terms, the product market is in flow terms and "never the twain shall meet."[6] Financial contact between borrowers and lenders and borrowing-spending linkages are both invisible unless one assigns a financial market meaning to IS-LM analysis.[7]

IS-LM analysis can be viewed as an "indirect approach" to finance. In the money market, bonds outstanding are the alternative asset to idle money holdings so that excess demand (in stock terms) in the money market has its mirror-image in excess stock supply in the bond market. If we allow for flows during the adjustment process following a disturbance, money is dishoarded to buy existing bonds (MB) and old bonds are sold to add to money holdings (BM). In the product market, the IS function serves as the mirror-image of the new securities market. The saving function is equivalent to new bond purchases (PB) and investment to new bond issues (BP).

The IS-LM view of the securities market is only possible if we ignore most of the options suggested by the market matrix. Thus, in the money market, we must exclude movements out of idle money balances into the product market and vice-versa (the MP and PM cells in the market matrix of Chapter I). Also, we must exclude movements out of idle money balances into new securities and vice-versa (such hoarding and dishoarding flows are covered by MB and BM). In the product market, options exist beyond the assumed market movements. Saving includes the allocation of income (represented by P and L) to investment, money balances, and to existing securities besides the allocation to new bonds (PP, PM, PB, LP, LM, LB). Similarly, investment cannot be identified with new bond sales since, as already indicated, dishoarding in the money market (MP) is an alternative source of finance, as is retained earnings (PP). Because alternative uses to the proceeds from bond sales exist besides investment--such as additions to money holdings (BM) and possibly outlays on inputs (BL)--the identity between investment and bond sales is further undermined. These restrictions on fund-flows, if IS-LM is to be given a financial market meaning, suggest that we abandon such an effort. While the market matrix reveals that "everything depends on everything else," the proximate determinants of the bond rate of interest will be the demand for and the supply of credit.

Financial Model-Building. Paradoxically, the national income identity of saving equals investment plus the government deficit is still prominent in financial model-building based on the flow of funds.[8] In their famous 1968 "pitfalls" study, William C. Brainard and James Tobin treat investment and the government deficit as financed by the flow of saving (Brainard and Tobin, 1968). This identity also underlines a recent ambitious attempt at model-building closely geared to the Federal Reserve accounts (Backus et al., 1980).[9] Capital outlays are identically equal to the financial saving of households. It is as if the financial data in the Federal Reserve matrix (to be discussed in Chapter VII) has been ignored and only the upper strip (inherited from the national income accounts) had been considered! Even if the financial strip is considered, the temptation is to say that "finance doesn't matter" because "net financial investment" must necessarily be zero over the entire economy. At best, it might be claimed that the lower financial strip shows how saving finances other sector's expenditures. To this extent, the identities underlying the published flow-of-funds accounts are misleading. The level of economic activity and the volume of saving and investment will depend on an outside financial disturbance. Forcing the flow of funds into an IS-LM framework as recent financial modeling does, limits their usefulness for studying real-financial interaction.[10] Finance (the banking system) creates income and wealth rather than being a mere conduit for saving.[11]

Keynes's Finance Motive. Keynes's "finance motive" is an attempt to add BM in the new bond market to the previous money market variables (MB, BM [existing bonds]). New bonds are sold in order to add to transaction balances for prospective investment. But this fails to save the day for IS-LM as the determinant of interest rates. (For one criticism, see Tsiang, 1980.) From the standpoint of the market matrix, the question is whether an increase in investment finance (Keynes's finance motive) is to be treated as a BM or a BP flow. The answer suggested by the matrix is BP. In the bond market there is an increased excess demand for bonds in the money submarket (MB exceeds BM) more or less matched (since other submarkets are involved) by an increased excess supply of bonds in the product submarket (BP exceeds PB). Only when an increase in economic activity ultimately leads to an increase in aggregate transactions will there be an increased demand for money balances (LM + PM). Until transactions demand increases, holders of money balances are "off" their demand curves. In moving equilibrium an excess demand for new money balances in the product and labor submarkets of the money market (PM exceeds MP and LM exceeds ML) match an excess supply of money balances in the bond submarket of the money market (MB exceeds BM).[12]

Patinkin's Contribution. Patinkin's classic work (1965) partly remedied the weaknesses of the neoclassical synthesis. The bond market is treated explicitly rather than as the mirror-image of the money and product markets. He avoids identifying investment and saving flows with new demands and supplies of securities (pp. 272-73). The saving concept is criticized as a nontransaction (p. 270). Moreover, recognition of the central importance of the transaction is found in his discussion of a moneyflows framework and the sector and market identities.[13] In his discussion of the market identity, using Walras's law, the excess demand function for money is equal to the sum of excess demand and/or supply in the labor market, the commodity market and the bond market (p. 227). When the identity is differentiated with respect to real balances, the sum of the marginal propensities to spend out of real money balances on all goods including money is unity.[14] A similar unit-sum identity holds according to Patinkin for marginal propensities to spend out of income. Expressed in terms of the market matrix of Chapter I, the unit-sum identities of Patinkin apply across the "P" and "M" rows of the matrix. What is overlooked in Patinkin's analysis are similar row-identities for the labor and bond markets. Furthermore, the flow-constrained flavor of his introductory treatment is missing in his analysis of equilibrium and the adjustment process. His general equilibrium model simultaneously depicts a flow equilibrium in the product market (with planned output equaling planned investment and consumption) and stock equilibrium in the bond and money markets (Chapter XI). Borrowers again fail to make direct contact with lenders. Spending is not contrained by financial sources.[15] Our contention throughout is that external finance shold be treated conceptually and empirically in expenditure functions on a par with income (internal finance).

Rational Expectations. The rational expectations revolution (see Attfield et al., 1985; Begg, 1982; Shefrin, 1983; Carter and Maddock, 1984) from our standpoint suffers from lack of a transactions framework (Cohen, 1982b, pp. 10-11). Money is reluctantly introduced (Lucas, 1980), and the concept of financial constraint is restricted to agents' beginning-of-period holdings of money balances (see also Kohn, 1981).[16] The phrase "cash-in-advance" is coined to herald the coming of money (Lucas, 1980, p. 203). "Helicopter money" describes its adventitious arrival (Gale, 1982, p. 15). The reductio ad absurdum is adjustment of prices in responses to new information instantaneously without benefit of transactions (Begg, 1982, p. 59).

Lacking a transactions framework, the flow-constraints as necessary conditions for equilibrium are not spelled out. Nevertheless, the R.E. assumption of unbiased and efficient expectations are not inconsistent with the present treatment of equilibrium (except for instantaneous adjustments; see Fisher, 1984, p. 5; Hahn, 1984, pp. 3-4).

BEYOND IS-LM

It is possible to rehabilitate IS-LM analysis and express the money, bond, and product markets in flow equilibrium terms using the familiar two-dimensional diagram.[17] No longer does planned saving signify an automatic flow of funds into investment, nor is investment limited to voluntary saving. The financing part of saving consists of direct investment by surplus sectors and retained earnings of deficit sectors. The nonfinancing elements in saving include increases in the money holdings by both deficit and surplus sectors and the increase in surplus sectors' saving deposits. Beyond the financing by saving, investment is financed by bank borrowing.

The simplest derivation of the bond market curve is to assume that the supply of loanable funds curve is a function of income. Given an increase in income (output) the supply of loanable funds will increase, resulting in a new equilibrium in the bond market at a lower market rate. The "BB" curve will then be a negatively sloping curve in r-y space. It can shift as a result of a shift in the demand for loanable funds (the BB curve shifts to the right) or as a result of monetary dissaving (a shift to the left) (Hosek and Zahn, pp. 59-61).

<u>Equilibrium in the Credit Market</u>. A more complex derivation would explain the demand for credit in terms of investment demand by deficit sectors and their demand for incremental transactions balances in excess of saving (Modigliani and Papademos, p. 126). Thus,

$$\text{II.16} \qquad \Delta L^d = B(r, Y) = I_d(r) - S_d(Y) + \Delta M1_d(r, Y)$$

where the subscript d indicates a deficit sector. Assume now that the total volume of borrowing is given--that it is controlled directly by the monetary authority.[18] Equilibrium is defined by equality of the demand for funds with available loanable funds. The slope of the BB curve will then be determined by the partial derivatives of the borrowing function with respect to income and the interest rate respectively (Modigliani and Papademos, p. 130).

II.17 $$\left.\frac{dr}{dY}\right|_{BB} = -\frac{B_Y}{B_r} = \frac{dS_d/dY - \partial[\Delta M1_d]/Y}{dI_d/dr + \partial[\Delta M1_d]/r}$$

Modigliani and Papademos draw the BB curve as negatively sloping. This implies that the marginal propensity to save of deficit units exceeds the marginal effect of income on their demand for money. Since the denominator of the expression is necessarily negative, the expression as a whole is negative.

The slope of the IS curve is defined by

II.18 $$\left.\frac{dr}{dY}\right|_{IS} = \frac{dS/dY}{dI/dr} = \frac{dS_s/dY + dS_d/dY}{dI_s/dr + dI_d/dr}$$

and is negative.

The investment of surplus sectors (I_s) depends on its opportunity cost. As the institutional lending rate, r, increases, so does the rate paid on savings deposits, the alternative to direct investment. The change in savings deposits is described by

II.19 $$\Delta SD^d = S_s(Y) - I_s(r) - \Delta M1_s(r,Y)$$

This relation introduces the demand for transactions balances by surplus sectors, $\Delta M1_s$.

The IS curve will be steeper than the BB curve, assuming that the response of deficit units to the interest rate relative to response to the change in income (as measured by the BB curve) exceeds that for surplus sectors and thus the population as a whole. In the limiting case when deficit units hold no money balances, the absolute value for II.18 will exceed $dSd/dY / dId/dr$ in II.17. The interest rate relative to the income change has to fall by more in the case of the IS curve in order to maintain equilibrium in the product market. As the marginal effect of income on the demand for money increases, the value of the numerator term in BB declines and BB rotates in a counter-clockwise fashion. The slope of BB turns positive when $\partial[\Delta M1_d]/\partial Y$ exceeds dSd/dY.

Figure II.2 shows the equilibrium relationship for the product and credit markets.

FIGURE II.2
EQUILIBRIUM IN PRODUCT AND CREDIT MARKETS

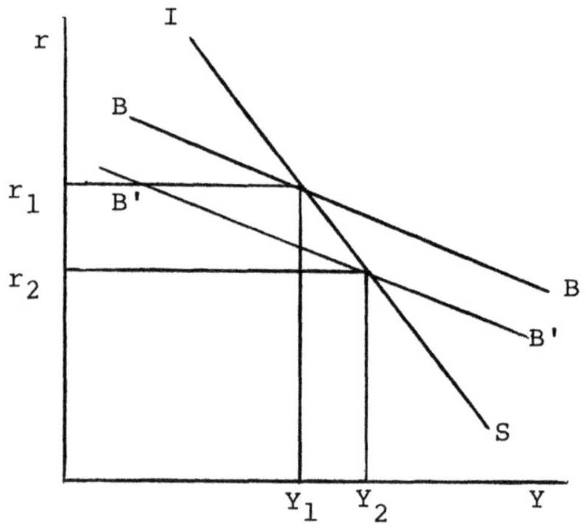

An increase in the amount of borrowing will shift the BB curve downward, occasioning a drop in interest rates and an increase in income.[19]

With the introduction of the bank loan market, deposits become the mirror-image of bank lending and play a passive role. (Reserves and reserve requirements are ignored.) The deposit functions, however, become a limiting factor to income expansion (as discussed below) when a disturbance originates in the product (IS) market. In equilibrium the planned holdings of deposit liabilities will match the asset holdings of financial institutions: $\bar{M}2 = \bar{B}$.[20] The M2 liabilities will include transactions balances M1 and savings deposits SD. In the individual financial markets, the demand for borrowed funds match available credit--$B = \bar{B}$ as already described and the demand for M2--(L2) will equal $\bar{M}2$. The L2 relation follows (Modigliani and Papademos, p. 146).

$$\text{II.20} \qquad \Delta L2(r,Y) = S_s(Y) - I_s(r) + \Delta M1_d(r,Y) = \Delta \bar{M}2$$

We are interested in the slope of the LM2 schedule which defines equilibrium in this market. It is given by

$$\text{II.21} \qquad \left.\frac{dr}{dY}\right|_{LM2} = -\frac{L2_Y}{L2_r} = \frac{dS_s/dY + \partial[\Delta M1_d]/\partial Y}{dI_s/dr - \partial[\Delta M1_d]/\partial r}$$

As in the case of the BB schedule, the LM2 schedule can either be positively or negatively sloping. Since the numerator is necessarily positive and both terms in the denominator are negative, the slope will depend on the absolute value of $\partial[\Delta M1_d]/\partial r$ in relation to dI_s/dr. If the value of dI_s/dr exceeds $\partial[\Delta M1_d]/\partial r$ then the LM2 slope will be negative. This is how Figure II.2 is drawn.

The value of dI_s/dr will affect the elasticity of the IS schedule with respect to the interest rate. The greater the sensitivity of I_s to the interest rate (which means that SD_s responds more positively to the interest rate), the flatter will be the slope of IS. Thus the flatter the slope of LM2, the flatter will also be the slope of the IS schedule.

It is expected that the LM2 curve will be steeper than the BB curve. Comparing (17) and (21), the numerator terms in (21) will exceed the value of the terms in (17). In absolute value the denominator in (21) should be less than in (17) so that the absolute value of the (negative) slope LM2 should be greater than for BB. A similar comparison between (18) and (21) explains why the slope of LM2 is greater than for the IS curve.

In the analysis, with the volume of deposits determined by

the volume of bank lending, either component of deposits--savings deposits (SD) or M1 can be treated as residually determined. We choose to treat M1 in this fashion. The equilibrium interest-rate-income combination will at the same time denote an equilibrium quantity of M1. Instead of the conventional LM1 function, we have a point of equilibrium.[21]

FIGURE II.3 INTRODUCING THE DEPOSIT MARKET

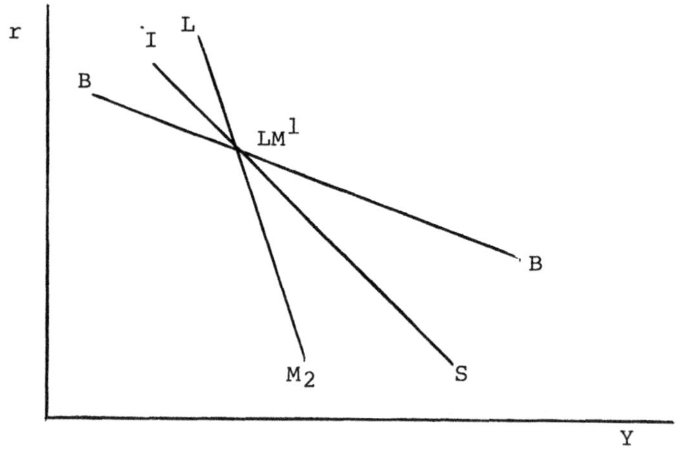

As Modigliani and Papademos point out, an expansion of liabilities just like the expansion of assets will yield a new equilibrium income and interest rate. But the initiative lies with the lending side of financial institutions and not the liability side. M2 is expansionary because it is the other side of the coin--of a process of credit expansion. The flow of credit determines the borrowing and investment of the deficit units. The effect of credit expansion on the interest rate influences the deposit rate and in this way the investment of surplus units. The sum of direct investment by surplus and deficit units and investment financed by banks matches saving in equilibrium. Diagrammatically, the BB and LM2 curves shift to the left and to the right respectively, intersecting the stable

IS curve at a higher value for income and a lower value for the interest rate.[22] The LM1 point shifts downward to coincide with the new equilibrium. Higher transaction requirements and a lower opportunity cost suggest that equilibrium M1 holdings will have increased as a result of the increase in bank credit.

Autonomous Shifts in the IS Function. So far the analysis has focused on the effects of a shift in the BB curve. Now we wish to consider the effects of an autonomous shift in the IS function. Since investment and saving are carried on by both deficit and surplus sectors, the analysis has to distinguish between them. Assume first that deficit sectors plan an increase in investment without any change in planned saving or demand for money balances. The planned increase in investment must be financed by an increase in planned borrowing. Assuming that the credit supply is fixed, this increased demand for credit will cause the BB to shift upward. Assuming equal vertical shifts in both the IS and BB curves, the equilibrium level of income will be unchanged, but interest rates will rise.

A second scenario is to have an autonomous increase in surplus sector investment which is financed by a reduction in planned increases in saving deposits. Now with a given BB, an increase in planned investment (a rightward shift in IS) results in a higher income level, accompanied by a lower market rate of interest. This paradox is explained by the negative BB slope which is flatter than the IS slope. An increase in income generates more internal savings by deficit sectors so that equilibrium in the credit market can only be attained by a lower "r."

In this second scenario, the saving function of surplus sectors has not shifted--only its composition has changed. On the other hand, if there is an autonomous increase in total saving for the purpose of direct investment, the shifts in the saving and investment functions will be offsetting so that the IS curve will not move. An autonomous increase in saving, however, for the purpose of adding to deposits will cause the IS curve to shift to the left.

In both the first and second scenarios the total volume of new credit is fixed by the monetary authority. This creates a problem in the analysis since shifts in the IS function to a new BB-IS intersection should apparently have no effect on the LM2 function: the change in deposits equals the original credit change. This difficulty in the way of a consistent equilibrium analysis suggests that money does indeed matter. When the BB curve shifts upward in response to an upward shift in IS (the first scenario), the LM2 curve will have to tilt in a clockwise fashion to achieve simultaneous equilibrium. In accordance with equation II.21, M demand for deficit sectors ($\partial M1_d/\partial Y$ and $M1_d/\partial r$) will have to become more sensitive to income and interest rates and surplus sectors' investment dI_s/d_r less responsive to the interest rate and their saving (dS_s/dy) more sensitive to income.

In the second scenario (a change in the composition of saving), the LM2 function has to tilt in a counter-clockwise manner so it intersects at the new IS-BB intersection. This requires a diminished sensitivity of money demand on the part of deficit sectors. As II.21 shows, a reduction in $\partial(\Delta M1_d)/\partial Y$ and $\partial(\Delta M1_d)/\partial r$ will flatten the LM2 schedule and make possible the necessary intersection.

In the first case, when the BB curve moves up, the LM1 point drifts upward to a new intersection. At the higher interest rate depositors substitute savings deposits for M1 transactions balances. Assuming the same volume of GNP transactions as before, the velocity of M1 balances will increase. For the second case, the LM1 point has to shift downward to achieve the desired equilibrium. This is accomplished by depositors substituting M1 deposits for savings deposits (the alternative to direct investment as the rate drops).[23] Whether or not M1 velocity increases, depends on the respective increases in Y and M1. What is certain, however, is that the average velocity of M2 deposits will increase.

<u>Financial Saving in the M-P Model.</u> The demand for additional transactions balances and savings deposits (M2) represent

financial saving. Such saving from the standpoint of the banking sector constitutes a leakage. That is, deposits resulting from bank credit do not generate more bank lending. Depositors have no alternative but to hold deposits (neglecting currency drain); their holdings are involuntary or "forced." Deposits are indeed a "hot potato" at least in the short run (Cohen, 1982c).

The Demand for Money and Direct Finance. One remaining scenario is an increase in the demand for money at the expense of direct investment (I_S). Assume first that no attempt is made by firms to replace direct investment with bank credit. The result then is a shifting of IS to the left. The intersection with BB occurs at a higher interest rate and a lower income level. The LM2 curve tilts counter-clockwise to achieve the necessary intersection with the new equilibrium point. The LM1 point moves up. In contrast to the previous scenarios where an autonomous increase in investment resulted in less M1 associated with higher interest rates, now an increase in demand for money will imply higher money holdings. The second possibility is that firms replace equity finance with a demand for bank credit. Since investment plans stay the same and so do saving plans, the IS curve is unchanged; but, as in the first scenario with autonomous shifts in the IS, the BB curve moves up. Output will be higher than when IS shifts to the left, but the interest rate will also be higher. The LM1 point will pass through this new intersection of BB and IS. The LM2 curve will again tilt counter-clockwise and intersect the equilibrium point.[24]

Saving deposits constitute a leakage because of the absence in the M-P model of reserve requirements against deposits. The application of positive but uniform reserve requirements against M1 and M2 would have the same effect. If there are differential reserve requirements against different categories of deposits with lower reserve requirements against saving deposits, leakages will still occur in inverse proportion to the size of this differential, as discussed in the previous chapter. An intention to save in the form of increased saving deposits will be frustrated unless monetary policy compensates for the leakage.

APPENDIX

THE OBJECTIVE FUNCTION

$$\phi = (1 - t)(1 - g)\ f\ (h(X,Y))\ h\ (X,Y) + (1 + \Pi)\ F^n\ m\ (F^n) + \frac{m\ (F^n)\ \overline{F^n}}{\overline{i}}$$

$$+ MON\ n\ (MON) + \frac{n(MON)\ \overline{MON}}{\overline{i}} + DIV\ s(DIV) + f(h(X,Y))\overline{INV} - Xv(X) - Yw(Y)$$

$$- (1 + \Pi)\ D^n z(D^n) - \frac{z(D^n)\overline{D^n}}{\overline{r}} - (1 + \Pi)E^n\ x(E^n) - \frac{x(E^n)\overline{E^n}}{\overline{r}} -$$

$$e(K)\overline{\theta}K + e(K)\ (1 - \overline{\theta})\overline{K} + \mu[DIV + MON + (1+\Pi)F^n$$

$$+ P_k K + gh(X,Y) + (t-1)(1-g)\ f\ (h(X,Y))\ h\ (X,Y) - (1 + \Pi)D^n -$$

$$(1 + \Pi)E^n]\ .$$

GLOSSARY FOR OBJECTIVE FUNCTION

ϕ = profits

t = tax rate

g = fraction of output allocated to inventories.

q (output) = h(X,Y)

where X,Y are "capacity inputs," a term used by Vickers. The term denotes variable inputs X and Y and the fixed capacities with which they work. The use of two capacity inputs allows for differences in capital durability.

P = f(q) = f(h (X,Y))

where P = commodity price

Π = brokerage fees on net financial asset purchases, F^n, borrowing D^n, and equity sales E^n

i_1 = $m(F^n)$

where i_1 = interest return on financial assets

$\bar{i}$ = average interest return

MON = increase in money holdings

i_2 = n (MON) where i_2 is the implicit return on additional money holdings

DIV = dividends

i_3 = s(DIV) where i_3 is the implicit benefit from dividend payments or retentions

γ_1 = v(X) where γ_1 is the cost of input X

γ_2 = w(Y) where γ_2 is the cost of input Y

$\overline{INV}$ = stock of inventories

r1 = z(D^n) where r1 is the interest cost of borrowing

$\bar{r}$ = average interest cost

r2 = x(E^n) where r2 is the implicit interest cost of equities

$\bar{\theta}$ = average depreciation rate on capital stock K in physical units

P_k = e(K) where P_k is the price of capital goods and K is capital expenditures

A bar over a flow variable indicates a stock.

DESCRIPTION OF THE OBJECTIVE FUNCTION

Profits are determined by sales revenues after tax, returns on net asset purchases, revaluation gains on financial assets, the implicit return on additional money balances, revaluation gains on money holdings, the implicit return on dividend payments, revaluation gains on inventory stocks, less the cost of inputs X and Y, borrowing costs, the revaluation losses (gains) on the debt outstanding, equity costs and revaluation losses (gains) on outstanding equities, depreciation expense, plus the revaluation gains on existing physical plant. The profit function is followed by the Lagrange multiplier and the flow-of-funds constraint. Expenditures on capital goods (K_t) and inventories gh(X,Y) are spelled out in the financial constraint.

Notes

1. This section has been strongly influenced by John G. Gurley and Edward S. Shaw, 1960, chapter IV, and Alain C. Enthoven, 1960, pp. 303ff.
2. This terminology is only appropriate when a single financial instrument is involved and a sector is on one or the other side of the market. Otherwise the concepts give the wrong impression. When a sector is on both sides of the market in different financial instruments, surplus-deficit concepts net out increases in financial assets against increases in financial liabilities. The implication is that financial asset acquisition is financed out of borrowing rather than out of saving with only the excess of borrowing over financial saving being available for expenditures. As a result, the impact of borrowing on real markets (for both so-called deficit and surplus sectors) is under-estimated.

   An equally serious objection is the question-begging nature of the classification. It is only after borrowing-lending decisions are made (not before) that sectors fall into one or the other category.
3. Throughout, saving will be regarded as an opening entry in the capital (flow) account of any sector on the sources side and never a uses of funds entry.
4. I am indebted to William Schmalzl for his early collaborative work on this section. Steven Husted has made useful suggestions.
5. The term originates with Paul Samuelson, but his definition is not enlightening. (See Hotson et al., 1976, footnote 13, p. 14.) Most simply, the neoclassical synthesis represents the stretching of the neoclassical framework based on price flexibility to fit (and swallow) Keynesian ideas. A succinct statement is found in Thomas F. Dernburg and Duncan M. McDougall, 1972, pp. 241-42. They show how the same equations can describe neoclassical and Keynesian models but in a different sequence.

   Every modern textbook in macroeconomics, when it integrates the labor market with IS-LM analysis and introduces the real wealth or balance effect as the equilibrating mechanism, is an example of the neoclassical synthesis even though it may avoid this expression. See, for example, Gordon, 1981; Dornbusch, and Fischer, 1981. For additional discussion and criticism of the neoclassical synthesis, see Cohen, 1986, chapter 19.
6. Hicks's unhappiness with his own stock-flow analysis forty-five years later, is documented in his "IS-LM: An Explanation," 1981.
7. One can argue, of course, that assigning a financial meaning to IS is inconsistent with Keynes's original treatment of saving as a leakage setting a limit to the multiplier process initiated by an increase in investment. See the section, "Beyond IS-LM," below.

8. This may be due in part to the "implicit theorizing" of the Federal Reserve flow-of-funds accounts. In 1959 the national income identity became the organizing identity for the published accounts. The evolution of the Federal Reserve accounts will be discussed in a later chapter on the flow-of-funds accounts. See also footnote 11 below.
9. These models are discussed below in Chapter XI.
10. The channeling of saving into investment via financial markets constitutes Tobin's interpretation of the IS schedule. While there are some ambiguities, the LM curve constitutes an asset market model (Tobin, 1969, 1982; Nagatani, 1981, p. 102).
11. The published flow-of-funds accounts in the United States when literally interpreted contribute to the view that deposits are monies advanced to the banking sector. The Federal Reserve flow-of-funds matrix consists of an upper nonfinancial strip derived from the national income accounts and a lower strip describing financial transactions. Lending necessarily equals borrowing in the financial strip and saving necessarily equals investment ("capital outlays") in the upper nonfinancial strip. The temptation is to identify lending with saving and borrowing with investment. In this way, financial markets serve only to channel saving into investment. Tobin and his colleagues give this literal meaning to the flow of funds and thereby distort the dynamic role of banks in credit and money markets.
12. For further discussion, see Chapter IV below.
13. He offers a definitive criticism of "the liquidity trap" in terms of its failure to recognize that an infinite demand for money would have to have its counterpart in infinite holding of some other asset (most likely bonds), pp. 225-26.
14. A nagging question is how the sum is unity when the dollar increase in money balances has to be held by "someone" forcing the sum of the marginal propensities to exceed one. The answer is that unintended money holdings are not counted--they will be spent in a succeeding time period. In succeeding time periods, spending will go on until desired money holdings have increased by one dollar.
15. Douglas Gale (1982), who has been identified by some of his colleagues as the "Patinkin of the 1980s" does not add significant insights to Patinkin's treatment. Gale is mainly interested in Patinkin's discussion of the neutrality of money (Chapter 1). The strand of relevance is the recognition that money relaxes the temporal sequence of budget constraints--money can be carried over and spent in a later period (Chapter 5). The implied flow concept is one of dissaving, and as I point out in Chapter IV, this is a concept that has been inadequately treated in the literature. An enticing section ("borrowing and lending" [5.2]) turns out to be a treatise on the superiority of money over bonds as a medium of exchange!
16. On a recent appraisal of RE's lack of contact with reality, see Zarnowitz, 1985, 558-62, 569-71.

17. An elementary discussion of the bond market in flow terms will be found in William R. Hosek and Frank Zahn, 1977, chapters 4 and 9. An advanced discussion, which has strongly influenced this section and my article, "Beyond IS-LM" (1982b), is found in Franco Modigliani and Lucas Papademos, 1980, pp. 111 ff.
18. Alternatively, we can assume that reserve requirements are imposed against financial institution assets.
19. The BB curve measures flows through financial institutions. Direct lending by surplus sectors--an increase in equity funds, I_s--affects total credit flows and total investment, but not ΔL^d.
20. This "global" view is consistent with individual financial institutions lending on the basis of increases in their deposits.
21. The standard LM1 curve, if incorporated into the diagram, would have a positive slope since the value of the slope is given by

$$-\partial M1/\partial Y \Big/ \frac{\partial M1}{\partial r} = \frac{\partial M1d}{\partial Y} + \frac{\partial M1s}{\partial Y} \Big/ \frac{\partial M1d}{\partial r} + \frac{\partial M1s}{\partial r}$$

If the LM2 curve is positively sloped, it will be steeper than the LM1 curve. The denominator of dr/dY for LM2 is reduced by dI_s/dr while the numerator for LM2 has the extra term dS_s/dY.

The standard interpretation of LM1 is irrelevant here, however, because it assumes a fixed stock of M1 balances. The assumption now is that the demand for M1 balances can be automatically satisfied by shifts out of savings deposits.
22. For a given income level, the rate paid on savings deposits will have to be higher to induce a demand for additional savings deposits, given an increase in total deposits. For a given interest rate, the income level will have to rise for the demand for deposits to match the increase in deposits. This explains the upward (rightward) shift in the LM2 curve when the flow of credit increases.
23. Direct (equity) investment by surplus sectors at the expense of savings deposits will mean that somewhere in the system, M1 holdings will increase without their increase being planned by surplus sectors. If savings deposits are introduced into the functions for deficit sectors, then their substitution of M1 for SD would add another avenue for increases in M1.
24. The reduction of direct finance as a result of an increased demand for money helps to explain the decline in money velocity in 1982 and 1983 (Bharat, 1985). Because of offsetting changes in velocity, M1 becomes a misleading target of monetary policy. As discussed in Chapter VI, however, random disturbances in money demand also make credit targeting unreliable.

CHAPTER III
DISEQUILIBRIUM

The "natural habitat" of disequilibrium theory is the flow of funds. For "quantity constraints" are the essence of disequilibrium economics. In the market clearing model, sectors are on their supply or demand curves. The effective supply and demand values for economic agents are also their notional values. The distinction is between decision-making on the basis of choice-theoretical relations featuring prices and initial endowments where decisions in one market are constrained by planned decisions in a second market and decision-making directly constrained by flows. In the former case, the market dovetails an economic agent's planned sources and uses of funds. In the latter it does not, and disequilibrium prevails.[1]

Given an initial "fixprice" equilibrium, after a disturbance, markets which originally cleared are now quantity-constrained: one or the other side of a given market will be rationed.[2] Thus, for example, in the Keynesian unemployment model featuring an initial decline in notional demand in the product market, sellers are rationed in this market--their notional supply is greater than their effective supply. This leads to rationing in the labor market--labor's effective supply is less than its notional supply. Effective demand in the product market is now determined by the effective supply of labor and effective demand in the labor market by the effective supply of output (which is less than the notional supply). The realized supply (actual transactions) in any market will necessarily equal the effective demand in that market when suppliers are rationed. Similarly, the realized demand in any market will equal the effective supply when demanders are rationed.

Disequilibrium of this kind ("quasi-disequilibrium") follows a disturbance to an initial equilibrium situation. It therefore differs from an original disequilibrium where markets fail to clear (as in the case of credit rationing). It also differs from the case of quantity adjustments to disturbances where markets always clear. We shall deal with four cases of quasi-equilibrium, including the Keynesian model. We shall then discuss credit rationing and quantity adjustments with markets clearing.

The business cycle can be considered a case of financial disequilibrium. Finally, in this connection we discuss the financial instability hypothesis. The framework throughout will be the market matrix introduced in Chapter I.

QUASI-EQUILIBRIUM

The Adjustment Process, Keynesian Model

The characteristics of the Keynesian model, expressed in flow-constrained terms, are the rationing of suppliers in both the product and labor markets. The submarket matrix of Chapter I requires that excess (effective) demand in one submarket have an exact counterpart in excess effective supply in a second submarket; excess effective demand is always zero for all markets combined. This provides a built-in check on the adjustment sequence. In Table III.1, excess effective demand and supply situations in initial and final equilibrium and during two adjustment periods (stages 2 and 3 in the table) are shown for each submarket. The comparative magnitudes of shifts in demand and supply functions during the transitional phases are also suggested.

Down the columns, the table shows the various markets, each broken down into submarkets. Each market can be viewed as consisting of submarkets (the vertical dimension), or each market can be seen as an element of other markets (the horizontal dimension). The submarket of one market (e.g., the product submarket of the bond market) will be the mirror image of a second market (the bond submarket of the product market). Thus an initial excess demand in the bond submarket of the product market corresponds to an initial excess supply situation in the product submarket of the bond market.

Excess demands and supplies for each stage of the adjustment process are summed vertically at the bottom of the table. Each line of this summation is also summed horizontally.

TABLE III.1 THE FIXPRICE ADJUSTMENT PROCESS: KEYNESIAN MODEL

Submarkets \ Markets	Product			Bond			Money			Labor			
	ED or ES	D	S	ED or ES	D	S	ED or ES	D	S	ED or ES	D	S	
Product		PP	PP		PB	BP		PM	MP		PL	LP	
	1. 0			1. ES_1			1. ED_1			1. ED_1			
	2. 0	+	+	2. $ES_2 < ES_1$	0	-	2. $ED_2 = ED_1$	0	0	2. $ED_2 = ED_1$	0	0	
	3. 0	+	+	3. $ES_1 > ES_3 > ES_2$	-	-	3. $ED_3 < ED_2\left(\frac{dS}{dt} < \frac{dD}{dt}\right)$	-	-	3. $ED_3 < ED_2\left(\frac{dS}{dt} < \frac{dD}{dt}\right)$	-	-	
	4. 0			4. $ES_4 < ES_3$			4. $ED_4 < ED_3$			4. $ED_4 < ED_3$			
Bond		BP	PB		BB	BB		BM	MB		BL	LB	
	1. ED_1			1. 0			1. ES_1			1. ES_1			
	2. $ED_2 < ED_1$	-	0	2. 0	0	0	2. $ES_2 = ES_1$	0	0	2. $ES_2 = ES_1$	0	0	
	3. $ED_1 > ED_3 > ED_2$	-	-	3. 0	0	0	3. $ES_3 < ES_2$	+	-	3. $ES_3 < ES_2\left(\frac{dS}{dt} > \frac{dD}{dt}\right)$	-	-	
	4. $ED_4 < ED_3$			4. 0			4. $ES_4 = ES_3$			4. $ES_4 < ES_3$			
Money		MP	PM		MB	BM		MM	MM		ML	LM	
	1. ES_1			1. ED_1			1. 0			1. ES_1			
	2. $ES_2 = ES_1$	0	0	2. $ED_2 = ED_1$	0	0	2. 0	0	0	2. $ES_2 = ES_1$	0	0	
	3. $ES_3 < ES_2\left(\frac{dS}{dt} > \frac{dD}{dt}\right)$	-	-	3. $ED_3 < ED_2$	-	+	3. 0	0	0	3. $ES_3 < ES_2\left(\frac{dS}{dt} > \frac{dD}{dt}\right)$	-	-	
	4. $ES_4 < ES_3$			4. $ED_4 = ED_3$			4. 0			4. $ES_4 < ES_3$			
Labor		LP	PL		LB	BL		LM	ML		LL	LL	
	1. ES_1			1. ED_1			1. ED_1			1. 0			
	2. $ES_2 = ES_1$	0	0	2. $ED_3 = ED_1$	0	0	2. $ED_3 = ED_1$	0	0	2. 0	0	0	
	3. $ES_3 < ES_2\left(\frac{dS}{dt} > \frac{dD}{dt}\right)$	-	-	3. $ED_3 < ED_2\left(\frac{dS}{dt} < \frac{dD}{dt}\right)$	-	-	3. $ED_3 < ED_2\left(\frac{dS}{dt} < \frac{dD}{dt}\right)$	-	-	3. 0	0	0	
	4. $ES_4 < ES_3$			4. $ED_4 < ED_3$			4. $ED_4 < ED_3$			4. 0			
Vertical Σ													Horizontal Σ
	1. 0 $(ED_1^B = ES_1^M + ES_1^L$			1. 0 $(ES_1^P = ED_1^M + ED_1^L)$			1. 0 $(ES_1^B = ED_1^P + ED_1^L)$			1. 0 $(ED_1^P = ES_1^B + ES_1^M)$			1. 0
	2. ES $(ED_2^B < ES_2^M + ES_2^L)$			2. ED $(ED_2^M + ED_2^L > ES_2^P$			2. 0 $(ES_2^B = ED_2^P + ED_2^L)$			2. 0 $(ED_2^P = ES_2^B + ES_2^M)$			2. 0
	3. ES $(ED_3^B < ES_3^M + ES_3^L)$			3. ES $(ED_3^M + ED_3^L < ES_3^P)$			3. ED $(ED_3^P + ED_3^L > ES_3^B)$			3. ES $(ED_3^P < ES_3^B + ES_3^M)$			3. 0
	4. 0 $(ED_4^B = ES_4^M + ES_4^L)$			4. 0 $(ES_4^P = ED_4^M + ED_4^L)$			4. 0 $(ED_4^P + ED_4^L = ES_4^B)$			4. 0 $(ED_4^P = ES_4^B + ES_4^M)$			4. 0

The horizontal sum for each stage is necessarily zero because of the underlying symmetry of the table.

The product market is characterized initially by excess demand in the bond submarket and excess supply in the money and labor submarkets. That is, BP - PM = PM - MP + PL - LP: a demand for output financed by bonds exceeds the supply of output allocated to bond purchase; the allocation of output sales to money holdings exceeds purchases of output financed by reductions in money holdings; the allocation of the proceeds of output to hire inputs exceeds the demand for output financed by the sale of inputs.

We assume that the Keynesian disturbance originates in the bond market with a decline in BP(p), the supply of bonds for the purpose of buying output. We shall assume that the interest rate is not initially affected so that the new BP(p) plans are not modified by a falling interest rate. This decline in BP leads to unintended investment PP which maintains the ex post identity between output and expenditures.[3] That is, PB + PM + PL + PP^I = BP + MP + LP + PP^U where I = intended, and U = unintended investment. Excess supply now exists in the product market. In the second stage of the adjustment process, excess supply persists. Interest rates in the bond market decline due to the decline in the supply of bonds. The effect of lower interest rates is to increase demand in the bond submarket of the product market above its level in the second period (period 3) although it is still below the initial equilibrium level. At the same time (period 3) excess supply is lowered in the money submarket as the leftward shift in MP(p) is assumed to be less than the leftward shift in the PM(p) function.

The shortfall in effective demand (as compared with original notional supply), is responsible for the "income-constrained process." This process is centered on the labor submarket of the product market and the product submarket of the labor market. The response of the business sector to unplanned investment is to decrease its demand for labor (the PL function shifts to the left). Given an initial equilibrium situation in the labor market, the decrease in demand for labor will result in an excess supply situation (based on the initial notional supply). But the "rationing effect" of effective demand in the labor market reduces "effective supply" in that market to the level of effective demand.[4] In each period of adjustment, given a rigid money wage rate, effective supply in the labor market shifts to the left. From the standpoint of the product market, a decline in the effective supply of labor will, in turn, mean a decline in effective demand in the labor submarket of the product market (LP). This decline in turn affects the labor market. Equilibrium is ultimately reached in the product market when the decline in excess effective demand in the bond submarket is compensated for by a decline in excess effective supply in the money and labor submarkets. In the final period, $ED^B = ES^M + ES^L$. Once equilibrium is reached in a given market, I assume that further demand and supply shifts cease.[5] The decline in the money submarket can be traced to a greater decrease in supply of output to add to money balances than the decrease in the demand for output financed by a reduction in money balances. In the labor submarket in a similar way, the supply of output to hire inputs declines by more than the supply of inputs for the purpose of buying output.

Excess effective supply declines in the labor submarket of the product market despite the downward spiral in both business receipts and outlays as households allocate an increasing portion of declining income to consumptions.[6] Such increasing allocations are at the expense of bond purchases and additions to money balances. The substitution of commodities for bonds is encouraged in the second adjustment stage (period 3) by the negative effect of declining interest rates on bond purchases.

Moving over to the column for the bond market we already know about the product submarket since it is the mirror-image of the bond submarket of the product market. That is, an initial excess effective supply in the product submarket is reduced after the disturbance by a reduced supply of bonds (period 2). The resultant decline in interest rates is assumed to have a retarding effect on the decline in excess effective supply in period 3.[7] But the process of decline in bond-financed expenditures continues so that excess supply in the product submarket in the final period is less than in previous periods.

The money submarket cell for the bond market relates these two markets for the first time. As is the case for all money submarkets, we assume that the initial disturbance does not affect the underlying demand and supply curves. Going back to the money submarket of the product market, an initial excess supply situation persisted into the second period. For the money submarket of the bond market an initial excess demand situation also persists into the second period--we assume that the supply of money to buy bonds exceeds the supply of bonds to add to money balances. In period 3, this excess demand diminishes as an increased demand for liquidity, strengthened by a falling interest rate, leads to opposite movements in supply (BM increasing), and demand (MB decreasing) in this submarket. The final cell in the bond market column couples for the first time the labor and bond markets. An initial excess demand situation is reduced beginning in the third period as decreases in the supply of labor to buy bonds exceeds decreases in the supply of bonds to hire labor.

Despite the decline in excess supply in the product submarket, excess supply is assumed to prevail in the bond market in the third period because of the decline in excess demand in the money and labor submarkets. With the assumed stabilization of excess demand in the money submarket after period 3, and a greater decrease in excess supply in the product submarket than the decrease in excess demand in the labor submarket, equilibrium is restored in the bond market in the final period.[8]

The initial situation in the money market is one of excess demand in the product and labor submarkets (business and households add more to money holdings from output and input sales than they reduce money holdings for the purpose of buying outputs and inputs). Excess supply prevails in the bond submarket due to the banking system's purchase of bonds financed by money creation. The initial disturbance in the product market leads to excess demand in the money market in the third period due to the demand for liquidity. This is assumed to reduce sharply excess supply in the bond submarket. The demand for money balances may be somewhat damped by the decline in the "own-yield" on money balances as the supply of money decreases at the same time that the demand for balances increases. What restores equilibrium in the money market is the decline in excess demand in the product submarket, coupled with a less important decline in excess demand in the input (labor) submarket. We can see that a decline in transactions demand for money in the product and labor submarkets is the key to restoring equilibrium in the money market. An increased demand for liquidity is handled in the bond submarket by an increased supply of bonds in exchange for money.

The final market--the labor market--has been examined already via the labor submarkets of the other three markets. Thus, the steady decline in excess supply in the labor submarket of the product market beginning in the third period has its mirror-image in the steady decline in excess demand in the product submarket of the labor market. The bond and money submarkets show declines in excess supply in the third period which continue until equilibrium is reached. Equilibrium obtains when the decline in excess demand in the product submarket falls short of the decline in excess supply in the other two submarkets.

When we look at all markets collectively (the horizontal summation), in all periods the sums of excess demands and supply are zero. In period 2, the disturbance affects only the product and bond markets with excess supply in the former being balanced by excess demand in the bond market. The third period is characterized by excess supply in the product, bond, and labor markets which is balanced by excess demand in the money market. Finally, in period 4 each market clears.

Repressed Inflation

An opposite case to the Keynesian one begins with an increase in demand in the product market, financed by bond sales. We might assume that the government is increasing its spending. Maintaining the fixprice assumptions, the logic of the analysis is to reverse all the signs in the first table, as is done in Table III.2. We now reach a new equilibrium characterized by greater output and employment. In the second period, excess demand in the product market is balanced by excess supply in the bond market. In the third period excess demand prevails in all markets except the money market, which has excess supply. Equilibrium is restored in all markets in the final period as the supply of output catches up with demand in the product market; the demand for bonds catches up with the supply; the demand for money declines to match the supply and finally the demand for labor declines to match the supply.

How then does the literature demonstrate that repressed inflation has similar contractionary effects as the Keynesian Model? (Barro and Grossman, 1971; Muellbauer and Portes, 1979, p. 356). It does so by emphasizing the effect of unsatisfied (rationed) demand in the product market on effective supply in the labor market and vice-versa. Thus, an increase in notional demand in the product market when markets fail to clear results in effective demand being less than notional demand. Frustrated buyers (evidently households) offer less labor in the input market: leisure is preferred to work because of the scarcity of goods. Notional demand for labor is now greater than effective demand, which is limited by the effective supply of labor. The result is a shift in the effective supply of output to the left. The contractionary process continues until the supply of output is consistent with labor supply--that is, until excess effective demand is eliminated in both markets.

The adjustment process for repressed inflation assumes that initially there is excess notional demand in both output and labor markets and thus excess notional demand overall. Overlooked are the bond and money markets.[9] When all markets

TABLE III.2 THE FIXPRICE ADJUSTMENT PROCESS: REPRESSED INFLATION

Markets / Submarkets	Product			Bond			Money			Labor			
	ED or ES	D	S	ED or ES	D	S	ED or ES	D	S	ED or ES	D	S	
Product		PP	PP		PB	BP		PM	MP		PL	LP	
	1. 0			1. ES_1			1. ED_1			1. ED_1			
	2. 0	-	-	2. $ES_2 < ES_1$	0	+	2. $ED_2 = ED_1$	0	0	2. $ED_2 = ED_1$	0	0	
	3. 0	-	-	3. $ES_1 < ES_3 < ES_2$	+	+	3. $ED_3 > ED_2 \left(\frac{dS}{dt} < \frac{dD}{dt}\right)$	+	+	3. $ED_3 > ED_2 \left(\frac{dS}{dt} < \frac{dD}{dt}\right)$	+	+	
	4. 0			4. $ES_4 > ES_3$			4. $ED_4 > ED_3$			4. $ED_4 > ED_3$			
Bond		BP	PB		BB	BB		BM	MB		BL	LB	
	1. ED_1			1. 0			1. ES_1			1. ES_1			
	2. $ED_2 > ED_1$	+	0	2. 0	0	0	2. $ES_2 = ES_1$	0	0	2. $ES_2 = ES_1$	0	0	
	3. $ED_1 < ED_3 < ED_2$	+	+	3. 0	0	0	3. $ES_3 > ES_2$	-	+	3. $ES_1 > ES_2 \left(\frac{dS}{dt} > \frac{dD}{dt}\right)$	+	+	
	4. $ED_4 > ED_3$			4. 0			4. $ES_4 = ES_3$			4. $ES_4 < ES_3$			
Money		MP	PM		MB	BM		MM	MM		ML	LM	
	1. ES_1			1. ED_1			1. 0			1. ES_1			
	2. $ES_2 = ES_1$	0	0	2. $ED_2 = ED_1$	0	0	2. 0	0	0	2. $ES_2 = ES_1$	0	0	
	3. $ES_3 > ES_2 \left(\frac{dS}{dt} > \frac{dD}{dt}\right)$	+	+	3. $ED_3 > ED_2$	+	-	3. 0	0	0	3. $ES_3 > ES_2 \left(\frac{dS}{dt} > \frac{dD}{dt}\right)$	+	+	
	4. $ES_4 > ES_3$			4. $ED_4 = ED_3$			4. 0			4. $ES_4 < ES_3$			
Labor		LP	PL		LB	BL		LM	ML		LL	LL	
	1. ES_1			1. ED_1			1. ED_1			1. 0			
	2. $ES_2 = ES_1$	0	0	2. $ED_2 = ED_1$	0	0	2. $ED_2 = ED_1$	0	0	2. 0	0	0	
	3. $ES_3 > ES_2 \left(\frac{dS}{dt} > \frac{dD}{dt}\right)$	+	+	3. $ED_3 > ED_2 \left(\frac{dS}{dt} < \frac{dD}{dt}\right)$	+	+	3. $ED_3 > ED_2 \left(\frac{dS}{dt} < \frac{dD}{dt}\right)$	+	+	3. 0	0	0	
	4. $ES_4 > ES_3$			4. $ED_4 > ED_3$			4. $ED_4 > ED_3$			4. 0			
Vertical Σ													Horizontal Σ
	1. 0 $(ED_1^B = ES_1^M + ES_1^L)$			1. 0 $(ES_1^P = ED_1^M + ED_1^L)$			1. 0 $(ES_1^B = ED_1^P + ED_1^L)$			1. 0 $(ED_1^P = ES_1^B + ES_1^M)$			1. 0
	2. ED $(ED_2^B < ES_2^M + ES_2^L)$			2. ES $(ED_2^M + ED_2^L < ES_2^P)$			2. 0 $(ES_2^B = ED_2^P + ED_2^L)$			2. 0 $(ED_2^P = ES_2^B + ES_2^M)$			2. 0
	3. ED $(ED_3^B > ES_3^M + ES_3^L)$			3. ED $(ED_3^M + ED_3^L > ES_3^P)$			3. ES $(ED_3^P + ED_3^L < ES_3^B)$			3. ED $(ED_3^P > ES_3^B + ES_3^M)$			3. 0
	4. 0 $(ED_4^B = ES_4^M + ES_4^L)$			4. 0 $(ES_4^M = ED_4^L + ED_4^P)$			4. 0 $(ED_4^P + ED_4^L = ES_4^B)$			4. 0 $(ED_4^P = ES_4^B + ES_4^M)$			4. 0

are considered, in all adjustment periods, excess demands are necessarily zero (whether measured consistently in notional or effective terms). When a demand for extra transactions balances are considered, or the inducement of future consumption via bonds, the contraction in the supply of inputs may not hold. Both output and employment can expand along the lines of Table III.2.[10]

The likelihood that the supply of labor will respond positively to excess demand is heightened by the possibility of liquidating inventories in response to increased demand in the product market. We show this by replacing the positive signs of Table III.1 for the PP cell (upper left-hand corner of Table III.2) with negative signs.

Classical Unemployment

Classical unemployment is voluntary unemployment. The supply of labor in the product submarket shifts to the left at the same time that the demand for output decreases in the labor submarket of the product market.[11] The result is excess effective demand in the labor market and excess effective supply in the output market. Equilibrium is established by a contraction in the effective supply of output.

So far only two markets have been mentioned: the output and labor markets. The money and bond markets are affected when suppliers of inputs simultaneously reduce their demand for money and bonds. Now the impact of a reduced supply of inputs is felt in the other two markets. Excess demand in the input market after the disturbance is balanced by excess supply in the other three markets. Equilibrium is reestablished in financial markets by firms reducing their sale of bonds or in fact retiring bonds. Retiring bonds held by the banking system has the effect of reducing excess supply in the bond and money markets simultaneously.[12]

Underconsumption

Suppose that the demand curve for output financed out of

income (LP) shifts to the left at the same time that the demand for bonds and money shifts to the right (LB and LM). Excess supply now exists in the output market and excess demand in the bond and money markets. The labor market is still in equilibrium. A solution without contraction is possible if firms supplied more bonds to the banking system for the purpose of financing output purchases. This would restore equilibrium in the bond and money markets. Failing that, a deficiency in sales will force firms to reduce their original (notional) demand for inputs until the effective demand for inputs is consistent with the effective supply of output. The resultant excess supply in the labor market would induce a downward spiral similar to the Keynesian case.

CREDIT RATIONING

We have yet to have a disturbance originate in financial markets (bond and money markets). While these markets have been affected in previous cases, the initial disturbance was in the product or labor markets. When prices and interest rates are sticky, for lenders to have the initiative (which is the case now being discussed), credit rationing must prevail. The initial situation in the bond market is an excess notional supply of bonds. One has to assume a "fringe of unsatisfied borrowers" sensitive to changes in planned lending. Assume now an exogenous increase in bond purchases financed by an increase in the money supply. The increase in lending and in borrowing shifts the effective demand curve in the product market to the right, thus reducing the gap between effective and notional values on the demand side. Similarly, in the bond market, the gap between notional and effective supply narrows.

The expansion process proceeds in a conventional way. I assume that the increased demand for output is responded to by an increased supply of output and that simultaneously the demand for inputs is increased to which the input supply responds. The limits to the expansion process are set by equilibrium being reestablished in the money market.[13]

QUANTITY ADJUSTMENT WITH MARKETS CLEARING

A persistent question is why the supply function should respond in a given market to a change in effective demand, as we have consistently assumed in describing the adjustment process. Less explanation is necessary if we were to think of effective supply as a point (rather than a curve) moving along a more or less horizontal line. Instead of a sloping function, the supply function becomes horizontal.

Indeed, such a supply line "makes sense" in a world of price (wage) makers rather than price takers. Suppliers set prices and supply whatever quantities are demanded. The relation between wages and prices is defined by mark-up pricing rules.[14] Markets are in disequilibrium to begin with even if they clear because the clearing is by means of adjustments in quantities rather than by an adjustment in prices (which is the usual sense of market equilibrium). Adjustments in inventories --their involuntary building up or running down, are an essential aspect of disequilibrium (cf. Nagatani, chapter 7).

<u>A Theory of Inflation</u>. The "prices-charged" curves that approach the horizontal in the short-run can shift upward, thus providing a theory of inflation and stagflation (Okun, chapter 6; Weintraub, 1978). Implicit and explicit contracts govern increase in wages. These will be affected by past and expected price changes. The lags in response may be shortened and the magnitude of the response coefficients increased as inflation accelerates. Expectations of higher rates of inflation override episodes of above-normal unemployment explaining the 1975 experience of high inflation rates despite recession. The price curves, since they are primarily based on wages, shift upwards with the wage curves.

FINANCIAL INSTABILITY: THE FLOW-OF-FUNDS CYCLE

Disequilibrium models of another sort are models of financial instability and crises. Underlying the market matrix of Chapter I are sector holdings of real and financial assets and financial indebtedness. Excess demands and supplies in the four markets lead to price and interest changes (markets clear) which affect desired portfolio balance, thus influencing flows in each submarket of the matrix that in turn affect portfolios. As a result, balance sheets are in chronic disequilibrium.

Descriptive studies of the raw data reveals the contours of the cycle (Goldsmith, 1965; Atkinson, 1965). The leading analytical studies are those of Hyman P. Minsky (1975, 1977, 1980, 1982a, 1982b, 1982c, 1985, 1986), Allen Sinai (1975, 1976, 1977, 1980), Sinai and Andrew F. Brimmer (1976), O. Eckstein and A. Sinai (1984), Albert M. Wojnilower (1980, 1985), and Martin H. Wolfson (1984, 1985, 1986a, 1986b).[15] Minsky sees Keynes's General Theory as a theory of financial instability, although admitting that Keynes's account might be "muddled." What is recognizable as Keynesian in Minsky's account is the emphasis on the climate of uncertainty, on "animal spirits."[16] Businessmen's estimates of the future can fluctuate sharply, leading to sharp revisions in their "demand prices" for capital assets. When their balance-sheet position improves, resulting in greater confidence, these features will lead to higher demand prices and greater amounts of external financing (borrowing). But expansion leads to more debt and more cash outflows which are not matched by increased cash inflows. Such financial crises lead to a fall in the demand price of capital assets. When the demand price of capital assets falls below the supply price of such assets, net investment ceases and internal finance is dedicated to rebuilding liquidity.[17]

In Sinai, households and businesses are seen as partially adjusting individual asset (both physical and financial) and liability items in every time period to their desired levels. The stock adjustment process is a complex one, since the flow adjustments toward the desired levels depend on the initial position of the complete balance sheet, with interrelated adjustment paths. The desired levels of assets and liabilities depend on price and interest rate vectors and "noncontrollable" variables such as monetary policy. Most prominently, financial instability is a feature of the business sector whose cash inflows fail to keep pace with cash outflows. Cash inflow declines with a decline in consumer expenditures. At the same time, however, business capital expenditures are increasing as a lagged adjustment to previous levels of sales. The shortage of internal finance produces a "funding gap," necessitating an increased resort to external finance. Higher interest rates induce higher ratios of short-term to long-term debt, and rising external indebtedness increases the cost of debt service. The resulting disequilibrium in the corporate balance sheet, typically aggravated by tight monetary policies and credit crunches, leads to a slowing down in inventory and capital investment and a subsequent building up of corporate liquidity.

Wolfson reviews major theories of financial crises including those of Thorstein Veblen, Wesley Clair Mitchell, Karl Marx, Minsky, Sinai and Albert M. Wojnilower, and Milton Friedman. The latter, however, rejects the credit market perspective taken by Wolfson and other theorists.[18] The conceptual framework developed by Wolfson is applied to five postwar financial crises, beginning with the credit crunch of 1966.

The flow of funds is the indispensable framework for considering the interaction of real and financial variables in the business cycle. The emphasis in these writers on the commercial banking system as the critical institution responsible for variations in the supply of credit is a central feature of what can be called the theory of the flow of funds.[19]

POINTS OF DEPARTURE

Our approach to disequilibrium differs from the vast literature in its consistent treatment of four markets in two-ended "dual decision" fashion, its step-by-step mapping of responses to different kinds of disturbance, and the view that disequilibrium, rather than equilibrium, may be the "natural" order of things. The pioneering work was done by Patinkin (1965, Chapter 13), Clower (1965), and Leijonhufvud (1968). Patinkin demonstrated how the demand for labor was constrained by excess supply in the product market. Clower supplemented this analysis by pointing out the product market is in turn constrained by excess supply in the labor market. Leijonhufvud developed a four-market model based on notional and effective concepts. But his adjustment process is income-constrained rather than flow-constrained, although he begins his analysis of the adjustment process with a decline in expenditures financed by the sale of bonds (Leijonhufvud, Chapters II, III; Cohen, 1974, pp. 261ff). Our description of adjustment went beyond the interaction of the labor and output markets. It demonstrated that in the Keynesian model, in new equilibrium (as well as during the various adjustment stages), the sum of market excess demands equal zero rather than at most being equal to zero as argued by Clower and Leijonhufvud. The reason they give is the existence of excess supply in the labor market when other markets reach equilibrium. This can only be true, however, if supply in the labor market is suddenly interpreted as "notional" rather than "effective" supply.

Disequilibrium After Leijonhufvud. The immense interest in disequilibrium analysis since Leijonhufvud has resulted in two major lines of inquiry both at variance with hydraulic Keynes. On the one hand, quantity constraints (most prominently in theorem-proof format) are introduced into models of utility maximization featuring homogenous households and firms operating only in the product and labor markets. Money and inventories are the typical asset stocks (Barro and Grossman, 1971, 1976; Muellbauer and Portes, 1978; Fisher, 1984; Grandmont, 1982; Malinvaud, 1977; Gale, 1983; Kades, 1985a, 1985b; Laffont, 1985; Benassy, 1976, 1977; Quandt, 1982). A Walrasian equilibrium is achieved by adjustments in parameter values (real money balances, real wages, inventory stocks) in conflict with hydraulic Keynesian.[20]

The second major interest of disequilibrium economics has been with the stickiness of wages and prices. In the search for some rationale, the explanations range from monopolistic price setting (Drazen, 1980; Laffont, appendix 2), to transactions costs (Townsend, 1982; Howitt, 1985; Stiglitz, 1979), to implicit contracts (Azariadis, 1975; Fischer, 1977; Taylor, 1980 Laffont, appendix 1), to coalitions (Olson, 1984). Our interest has been limited to the multiplier adjustment process following a disturbance given sticky prices and wages and so we have ignored this literature.

Rational Expectations. The vast output of disequilibrium literature has coincided with the rational expectations "revolution." Until recently, when rational expectations has turned its attention to fixprice models, this was a paradox because of the R.E. orientation to equilibrium analysis.

Rational expectations has developed its own theories for sticky prices (Taylor, 1985, pp. 409-15). One approach is to assume that prices or wages are fixed in advance by economic agents on the basis of conditional forecasts of demand and supply. The price set is the expected market-clearing price. Monetary policy has an effect on output (even if anticipated) because the monetary authorities have a shorter lead time than do firms in making their pricing decisions. A second approach is to assume that individual agents adjust prices on a staggered or nonsynchronized basis. The "contract" price of the firm is fixed equal to the expected average price of other firms during future periods. This approach produces more realistic (serially correlated) price and output behavior in inflationary periods.

When we move to financial instability theories, however, the differences with a flow-constrained approach are irreconcilable. Rational expectations models of the business cycle are models of rational mistakes (Lucas, 1975; Weiss, 1985). The asymmetric information available to economic agents makes observed money prices misleading indicators of relative price variables. Prices as the key signal are to be contrasted with money flows as the information vehicle in a flow-constrained hypothesis. Without a vector of intertemporal prices, economic agents have to depend on the information provided by moneyflows

(Leijonhufvud, pp. 387-401). Conspicuous by their absence in the rational expectations literature are references to sector cash flows and flows through credit markets.[21]

Keynesian fundamentalism (using Coddington's term), explains expectations in the flow-constrained framework. Uncertainty and animal spirits replace mathematical expected values of the variable in question. That the future is uncertain and unknowable because events are unrepeatable has been Shackle's contribution to the post-Keynesian paradigm (Harcourt, 1981; Shackle, 1961, 1970, 1984).

Notes

1. It should be stressed that the "flow-constrained" concept is itself neutral between equilibrium and disequilibrium situations. Its intent is to insist on the matching of dual-decision flows, whether they are equilibrium or disequilibrium values. In equilibrium analysis, the planned values of flows (based on choice-theoretical variables) match the ex post values. Flow constraints are necessary, but not sufficient. In disequilibrium, the ex post values do not match the notional values. In this case, the flow constraints are both necessary and sufficient. The usual connotation of "flow-constrained" (unless qualified), will be to the disequilibrium case.
2. John Hicks (1974) coined the terms "fixprice" to contrast with the classical "flexprice" approach. Such fixprice equilibria are called non-Walrasian (Kades, 1985, p. 5).
3. Unintended investment increases the stock of inventories. Such inventories will be a critical factor in their own right in prolonging economic slumps. Commodity inventories are the point of departure in a recent macroeconomic model of disequilibrium ("temporary equilibrium") (Nagatani, 1981, chapter 7).
4. Despite the clearing of markets in the realized transactions sense, it is still possible to speak of excess effective supply and demand. When sector B's behavior is constrained in market A by its sales in market B, changes in sales (supply) in market B will affect effective demand in market A. In any time period, effective supply in market A is assumed to be equal to realized supply of the previous period. In this way, a change in effective demand in market A in a given period can cause changes in excess effective supply in that market. A second reason for speaking of excess demand and supply is that the two-endedness of the flows makes possible varying degrees of change on the supply and demand sides of a given submarket. While effective supply in market A may have declined due to a decline in effective demand, suppliers have options as to how much to allocate to other markets. Similarly, demanders in this market have options as to how demand will be financed. In a submarket characterized initially by excess supply, it is possible, despite a decline in effective supply, for excess effective supply to increase as suppliers increase supply destined to finance purchases in a second market and demanders decrease the amount of funds from a second market allocated to this given market.
5. This proviso is necessary, otherwise equilibrium could be marked by continuous shrinkage in markets as decreases in excess demand in one submarket match decreases in excess supply in another submarket.
6. This is consistent with a constant marginal propensity to consume, but the movement to equilibrium will be hastened by an increasing marginal propensity to consume as income falls.

7. We assume more flexibility in interest rates than in prices and wages. The adjustment process could still run its course, however, if interest rates (r) were stable. If an increase in liquidity demand came in the second rather than the third period, as discussed in the next paragraph below in the text the resultant increase in the supply of bonds in the money submarket of the bond market might prevent a decline in interest rates. Assuming that demand and supply shifts are of equal magnitude in subsequent periods, market interest rates would remain the same throughout the adjustment process.
8. Continued decreases in excess demand in the money submarket of the bond market (as banks buy less bonds or the public reduces its money dissaving allocated to buying bonds) would increase the burden of adjustment on the product submarket. Now greater reductions in excess supply in the product submarket of the bond market are required. The counterpart to this is greater reductions in excess demand in the bond submarket of the product market. This in turn entails larger reductions in excess supply in the labor and money submarkets in order for equilibrium to be reestablished in the product market.
9. Because the term "repressed inflation" was coined for a fully monetized system, Janos Kornai (1985) prefers the term "shortage economy" in his extensive writings on East European economies. In the dominant sector--the sector of state-owned firms--transactions are only seemingly monetized and the firm's decisions are not guided by profitability (n. 10, p. 390).
10. It doesn't make any difference to the analysis whether households willingly allocate income to financial saving or whether their frustrated demand for goods "spills over" into financial markets. The "spill-over" concept has been an important part of disequilibrium analysis since Patinkin. In particular, Barro and Grossman have made extensive use of this concept.
11. From the standpoint of the suppliers of inputs, they may consider their decrease in supply as an "upward" rather than a "leftward" shift. They may be seeking higher money wages for the same amount of anticipated employment. Consistent with expected higher incomes, the notional demand for output would shift to the right. With sticky money wages, however, suppliers of inputs quickly learn that income is less than before, and in consistent fashion effective demand necessarily shifts to the left. Whether, then, the supply curve of inputs is perceived as a horizontal or a vertical shift, the effective demand curve for output must decrease.

    Our results differ from Muellbauer and Portes. In their analysis, firms' notional demand for labor is consistent with their notional supply of output (buyers are rationed in the goods market and sellers are rationed in the labor market). As we have interpreted this case, the situation is just the opposite with excess effective demand in the labor and excess effective supply in the output market--firms' notional demands are not realized. If anything, there is consistency in the notional behavior of households. This difference from M-B may arise from our requirement that the dual shifts have to be consistent with each other--a voluntary decrease in the supply of labor is associated with a voluntary decrease in the demand for output.

12. In effect, banks are supplying bonds and demanding money (BM) when bank debt is retired.
13. This process is discussed further in the next chapter.
14. Two recent studies which support the notion of horizontal effective supply functions with respect to prices, are Arthur M. Okun, 1981, and Robert J. Gordon, 1981b. See also Jacob Cohen and James L. Kenkel, 1980. The pioneering studies of mark-up pricing are those of Weintraub (1958, 1959, 1978).
15. Closely related to the financial instability thesis is "post-Keynesian short-period theory" (see Eichner and Kregel, 1975; Foreman, Groves, and Eichner, 1985). The post-Keynesian paradigm fits readily into our flow-constrained framework and fleshes out the behavioral relations underlying a flow-of-funds theory.
16. Alan Coddington (1983) refers to the uncertainty feature as "fundamentalist" Keynes. The flow-constrained (multiplier) aspect of Keynes is called "hydraulic" Keynes.
17. Minsky's work has inspired various models of his theories (Weise and Kraft, 1981; Taylor and O'Connell, 1985; Lavoie, 1986-87). The most rigorous attempt--that of Taylor and O'Connell--converts Minsky's theory into a portfolio balance model. While capturing the choice-theoretical aspects of investment decision-making in Minsky, the role of business cash flow in generating the crisis is not modeled or even mentioned. Closer to the spirit of Minsky, although the crisis itself is not modeled, is Lavoie's "little" four-equation model. An investment boom inevitably leads to an increase in the leverage ratio, a proxy for financial fragility. In terms of our notation, Lavoie provides the variables explaining $\dot{P}B$, where the dot indicates a time derivative (his equation 5, p. 261). The crisis itself as described by Minsky and Wolfson can be depicted as a scramble for liquidity ($\dot{B}M$), at the same time that the banking system is retrenching (MB is declining).
18. Wolfson finds little support for Friedman's theory of financial crises based on erratic control of the money supply by the Fed (Wolfson, 1986b, 182-87). Similarly, Bernanke's study (1983) argues that a sharp decline in credit was more responsible for the decline in output in the Great Depression than the relatively small decline in the money stock.
19. Overlooked by Wolfson and other writers is the work of Harold G. Moulton in the 1930s. His is literally a flow-of-funds theory. Bank credit makes possible an

expanding flow of funds through consumption channels and at the same time additional funds for the construction of new capital goods (1935, esp. Chapter VIII).

20. I criticize in Chapter V the universal treatment of real money balances as the deus ex machina that restores equilibrium in macro-monetary models.

21. A significant exception is the application of rational expectations to financial modeling in the United Kingdom in a flow-of-funds framework. Financial forecasts of flows and prices incorporate expectations in accordance with an R.E. hypothesis (London Business School, 1983, 1985). See Chapter VIII below.

CHAPTER IV
MONEY AND BANKING IN THE FLOW OF FUNDS

CASH-OR-EQUIVALENT ACCOUNTING

The treatment of money in previous chapters may seem to violate the logic of flow-of-funds accounting. The idea of banks creating money to finance their bond purchases runs counter to the notion that holders of money balances advance funds to the bank sector. Certainly, the advancing of funds is a valid interpretation of increments in money being a "source of funds" for the banking system and "uses of funds" for holders of money. Morris A. Copeland, in his pioneering moneyflows study (1952, esp. chapters 13 and 14), distinguished three classes of transactors--those whose cash balances are increasing, those who are borrowing from the banks (the "loans and securities class"), and as an intermediary between them, the banks themselves. When cash balances are increasing, there is a "two-step moneyflow" from the cash balances class via the bank to the loans and securities class. A one-step moneyflow applies when the loans and securities class is identical with the cash balances class. In such a case, cash balance holders are advancing funds to the bank sector at the same time that the bank sector is advancing funds to cash balance holders. Such moneyflows are "equal and synchronous." The same theme is found in later studies by J. G. Gurley and E. S. Shaw (1955, 1956, 1960), James Tobin (1963), Tilford C. Gaines (1963), and Lyle E. Gramley and Samuel B. Chase, Jr. (1965).

Copeland interpreted the banking sector accounts as "cash-or-equivalent funds" accounts. In such an interpretation, moneyflows means flows of "resources" or "values."[1] A source of funds is any transaction which increases the "resources" or "values" of the sector and a use of funds is any transaction which applies resources or values. Increases in the means of payment by the bank sector are then "sources of funds" because they increase the "resources" of the bank sector. The bank and nonbank sectors simultaneously advance funds to each other; the acquisition of money by nonbank sectors advances funds ("resources") to the bank sector at the same time that the bank sector advances resources to nonbank sectors by the acquisition of earning assets. This same kind of "cash-or-equivalent" account approach underlies the argument of the other authors cited.[2]

It is only by employing broad concepts such as "funds" or "resources," that one is able to speak of equal and opposing flows between the bank and nonbank sectors. The anomaly of nonbank sectors increasing their holdings of the means of payment at the same time that they advance these "funds" to the banks is self-evident.

The Demand for Money. The public's demand for money determines the total money stock. This offshoot of the "cash-or-equivalent" accounting approach defines the "New View" of the money supply process. The "New View" (see Gramley and Chase), stresses the price-theoretical behavior of the public. The key idea is portfolio balance--a substitutionary relationship between money, securities, and time deposits. When the interest rate falls on securities or time deposits, the amounts demanded of currency and demand deposits will increase. Take, for example, the case of an open market purchase. The growth in both demand and time deposits is not the result of an increase in the quantity of deposits that banks are willing to supply, but of an enlarged public demand to hold them due to falling security rates (Gramley and Chase, pp. 1287-88).

The demand for demand deposits is drawn as a positively sloping curve with respect to the (implicit) yield on demand deposits (as in our own analysis). The supply of demand deposits is assumed to be perfectly elastic at some implicit rate of interest (e.g., free servicing of checks). This differs from our own assumption of a negative slope. Banks will supply more demand deposits in financing their asset purchases the lower the implicit/explicit costs of such deposits. The quantity of deposits supplied in their analysis depends on the willingness of the public to hold deposits. Since this is true for each and every bank in the system, the constraint on bank deposits and thus on bank asset holdings is based on the public's desire to hold bank deposits. Gramley and Chase provide a demand-pull interpretation of demand deposits.[3]

CASH-FUNDS ACCOUNTING

A cash-funds form of account emancipates us from the cash-or-equivalent point of view. "Funds" are now restricted in meaning to the means of payment. Sources of funds are those transactions occasioning an increase in a transactor's money holdings (for nonbank sectors), and decreases in the total means of payment (for the bank sector). Uses of funds would refer to transactions that cause a sector's holdings of the means of payment to decrease (nonbank sector), or cause total means of payment to increase (for the bank sector).[4] The "funds" items is not itself a source or use transaction. "Sources" and "uses" and the means of payment entry are all subsumed under the more generic headings of "credits" and "debits." For example, increases in the means of payment are a credit item for the bank sector, a debit for the nonbank holder. An increase in bank reserves is a debit for the bank gaining reserves, a credit for the bank losing reserves.

If demand deposits are not monies advanced, then they are not debt. This leaves only the alternative of treating them as a product, albeit a special kind of product (Cohen, 1957; Pesek and Saving, 1967, 1968). A more positive argument for the commodity treatment is that demand deposits yield a return for their services as a medium of exchange. Demand deposits can be considered to be the capitalized value of these services (Harris, pp. 37-38).

Increments in the means of payment now appear on the product side of the bank income account. On the expense or allocations side, there will be a corresponding charge to some liability reserve account, such as "additions to reserve for return of the means of payment." This reserve account will appear on the credit side of the bank flow-of-funds statement in the place of demand deposits. Alternatively, demand deposits can be replaced by "liability for servicing demand deposits." Assuming that the value of the medium of exchange function is measured by servicing costs, this liability item will correspond to the present value of these services--i.e., the dollar value of demand deposits.[5]

Money and the Real Balance Effect

The effect of this treatment of demand deposits on the bank balance sheet is that demand deposit holdings by the non-bank private sector do not "cancel out" against deposit liabilities of the bank sector when these two sectors are consolidated. From the standpoint of defining money balances, this offset (of deposit holdings against deposit liabilities) seems to be the crucial one rather than the better known offset of bank purchase of primary securities (loans) against demand deposit holdings in the private nonbank sector account. This offset is the basis of distinguishing inside money from outside money (Gurley-Shaw, 1960, chapter 4; Harris, chapter 3).

Pesek and Saving argued that inside money was indistinguishable from outside money and should be included in the wealth effect (1967). Patinkin (1969) took exception to this position. P-S bring on Patinkin's attack by mistakenly allocating demand deposits to a bank's net worth. Inside and outside money are part of real balances without necessarily contributing to the net worth (wealth) of the private sector. The substitution of a reserve account for deposit liabilities meets the objection of Patinkin at the same time that real balances can be preserved intact. The key issue is whether holdings of money balances should be offset by bank loans. Bank loans outstanding may be one of the many variables influencing monetary dissaving (the operational real balance effect discussed below in Chapter V), but there is no more reason to offset them against sector holdings of money balances than any other asset or liability item.[6]

MICRO- VS. MACRO-VIEWS

The commodity view of the means of payment solves the long-standing paradox posed by the micro- and macro-views of the banking system. This paradox was stated more than sixty years ago in Phillips's pioneering study: while deposits were the offspring of loans, individual bank loans are the offspring of deposits (Phillips, 1924, p. 64). Until the 1960s the monetary literature focused on the macro-view by refining and expanding Phillips's "textbook multiplier" (Brunner, 1961; Burger, 1971; Rasche, 1972). The "New View" of the money supply process as already discussed took the micro-view with the demand for demand deposits determining both the money stock and the collective ability of banks to make loans.

Each bank in the banking system, according to the money as commodity view, produces money. Demand deposits as described by Pesek are "sold" or "rented" with an "instant repurchase [of currency] clause." The bank buying reserves pays for them by selling primary demand deposits. The bank acquiring earning assets pays for them by selling derivative demand deposits. From this standpoint, it is misleading to use expressions such as "a deposit of funds" or a bank "attracting deposits." The so-called depositor is either selling reserves or supplying assets for which he receives payment in demand deposits.

The Equivalence of Models

The resolution of the micro-macro paradox still leaves unanswered the respective influence of demand and supply on money stock determination. Substitution possibilities on the demand side cannot be denied. The difficulties in theorizing are highlighted by a simple model of the reserve and money market. Demand-side and supply-side theories are equally consistent with this model (for this model see Cohen, 1984a, 340-41).

The choice among theories seems to depend on which market we wish to emphasize--the reserve or money market. But more markets may be involved and their introduction should give a less ambiguous view of the money supply process. What is called for is a generalized framework with the spotlight on the bank credit and product markets and which is constructed in such a way that it captures the two-endedness of market transactions. While "general," the analysis is not necessarily an "equilibrium" one. An important feature of the succeeding discussion will be disequilibrium in the money market when the interest rate is the "own interest rate" on checkable deposits.

A GENERALIZED FRAMEWORK

The key equations for the bank loan and money markets are (Cohen, 1984, p. 342):

$$\text{IV.1} \qquad MB = MB\,(\overset{+}{r_i},\ \overset{-}{r_m},\ \overset{+}{1/r_b},\ \overset{-}{q},\ \overset{+}{R})$$

$$\text{IV.2} \qquad BP + BL = BPBL\,(\overset{+}{r_e},\ \overset{-}{1/r_b},\ \overset{+}{r_n},\ \overset{+}{p},\ \overset{+}{Y},\ \overset{+-}{EXP})$$

$$\text{IV.3} \qquad MB = BP + BL$$

$$\text{IV.4} \qquad LM + PM = LMPM\,(\overset{-}{r_i},\ \overset{+}{r_m},\ \overset{-}{r_s},\ \overset{-}{r_e},\ \overset{+}{Y})$$

$$\text{IV.5} \qquad MB - (LM + PM) = \lambda MB$$

Where the additional symbols are:

Y = GNP

r_i = return on time deposits

r_s = return on nonbank claims

r_e = return on equities

r_n = expected rate of return on investment

q = average reserve ratio

λ = speed of adjustment coefficient

The disturbances that we emphasize originate on the borrowing side of the bank loan market. The BP and BL functions in response to changes in Y or EXP (expectational) variables shift to the right or the left. Business and households borrow to buy output or to hire inputs. This shift in the demand for funds shows up in the MB equation as a change in the yield on loans (r_b) leading to a change in the flow of bank credit financed by money creation. Equation IV.3 states the equilibrium condition in the bank loan market ignoring other elements in the row and column of the transactions matrix of Chapter I. This emphasis on the bank loan market is a striking feature of recent model building (Modigliani and Papademos, 1980; Judd and Scadding, 1981, 1982; Goodfriend, 1982).

If we picture the checkable deposit market in r_m - M space, with the supply of deposits downward sloping and the demand for deposits upward sloping with respect to the own (implicit-explicit) interest rate, r_m, the counterpart to an increase in bank loans in the bank loan market is an increase in the supply of derivative deposits in the deposit market.

A fundamental misunderstanding is that the seller of bonds is demanding additional money balances. This is the Gramley-Chase identity--the demand for money is the other side of the sale of securities to the bank. The credit market transaction, however, has to be distinguished from the deposit market transaction. The borrower borrows to spend in the product market--the relevant term on the supply side of the bond market is the BP term of the matrix.[7]

I assume that the implicit and/or explicit yield on money balances is set by the banks and is not affected by an increase in the supply of demand deposits. In terms of the transactions matrix, transactors are "off" their demand curves for incremental money balances until the demand for increased money balances matches the new supply. Balances are involuntarily held at the end of one transaction period until the beginning of the next. In successive periods, transactors dishoard involuntarily held money balances. A dishoarding curve now replaces the original money supply curve. It shifts to the left in succeeding periods as money holdings are added to permanent money balances. Finally, (assuming a one-shot increase in the money supply), when the money market is in equilibrium, all entries will disappear in the submarkets of the money market and the money submarkets of the other three markets. That is, in equilibrium, the supply and demand for incremental money balances is zero. The supply and demand curves in the money market all intersect at a single point on the "own-rate of interest" axis.[8]

Disequilibrium Money. As shown in equation IV.5, the immediate result of bank lending is an excess supply of money balances at the prevailing own rate of interest. The increase in actual balances exceeds the desired increase (described in equation IV.4) by some fraction of the initial change in deposits.[9] An expansionary disturbance can be represented by the following sequence, MB → BP + BL → LM + PM. The monetary disturbance is shown by the first term--money creation to finance the purchase of bonds. Bond sales finance output directly or indirectly via the hiring of inputs. The money leakage is represented by the final terms--the allocation of income from inputs or product sales into money balances. In this framework, expansion takes place until desired money holdings (in response to increased transactions or changes in relative yields) match the initial disturbance. That is, "leakages" into money balances along the way set a limit to the ultimate expansion and define the value of the income multiplier (Cohen, 1982a, p. 16, n. 41). Desired money balances will decline with movements into depository liabilities such as time deposits.[10]

The expansion process assumes response of producers to increases in demand. If producers fail to raise prices or output, this will accentuate disequilibrium in both the output and deposit markets (Tucker, 1971). If interest rates are sticky, the spillover into the bond market will fail to depress interest rates sufficiently to absorb undesired balances (Artis and Lewis, 1976, pp. 167-76).

Disequilibrium money may also originate on the demand side of the money market. Corporations faced with a "cash flow" problem--finding their cash receipts to be less than anticipated --will use income to build up cash balances (Sinai, 1976). In terms of the transactions matrix, PM and BM replace PP and PL flows. Liquidity crises are dramatic cases of disequilibrium money.

Deposit supply as a shock precipitating disequilibrium money has been elaborated in a recent money market model (Judd and Scadding, 1981). Bank loans have deposits as a byproduct. Changes in credit demand are not necessarily equal to changes in deposit demand (p. 28). The public ends up holding deposits only because this is a necessary part of accepting the credit it wants.[11]

The notion of disequilibrium money has been contested by William H. White (1981). "Buffer-stocks" of money are not likely with prevailing cash balance management techniques, ability to repay bank debts, the use of overdraft accounts, and the depressing effect of excess cash holdings on market interest rates.[12] The response might be that households and small corporations face relatively large transactions costs relative to the benefits of holding exactly the desired amount of money.[13] This results in "loosely managed" portfolios (Judd and Scadding, 1981, p. 28; Judd, 1982, n. 15, pp. 17-18). The empirical results of the J-S model support the hypothesis that deposit supply shocks associated with changes in bank credit force the public off their (equilibrium) demand curve for transactions deposits (Judd and Scadding, 1981, 1982).

DEFINING MONEY

In the discussion of money as bank product, I have assumed that transaction deposits are meant. A price-theoretical approach leads to the dictum that in equilibrium all assets must yield their holder the same return, abstracting from risk. The implicit yield on demand deposits measured by bank costs is close to the going market rate (Pesek, 1976, p. 872). As soon as an asset pays the market rate, e.g., time deposits, it ceases being money and becomes bank debt (P-S, 1967, chapter 5). The argument follows from the equilibrium assumption: when the explicit rate equals the market rate, then the value of money-debt as a medium of exchange must have fallen to zero and the asset ceases to be money (1967, p. 118). In the case of assets such as savings and loan shares, where additional services are offered such as freedom from interest-rate risk, default risk, perfectly divisible denominations, their "partial" moneyness depends on an excess of the market rate over the value of these services plus the explicit returns on saving and loan shares (1967, pp. 121-23).

How then do we handle today's transactions accounts which perform both a medium of exchange function and earn interest? It certainly seems arbitrary to apportion transactions between money (product) and debt on the basis of some ratio of interest paid to the estimated market rate of interest.[14] On the other hand, holders of NOW accounts do not turn them over as fast as demand deposits. They must regard these holdings in part as savings. The Federal Reserve for a time calculated an "adjusted M-1B" which subtracted estimated saving transfers from M-1B (see Thomas D. Simpson et al., 1981). This could be the basis for defining money.[15] Now the yield on money becomes not only the cost of the services provided by banks, but also an explicit yield.[16] Banks and other financial institutions, in order to attract reserves or interest-earning IOUs, offer an explicit yield (equivalent to a negative service charge). In today's financial world shift-adjusted checkable deposits are the money commodity and the appropriate "repurchase reserve" should equal such deposits.

POINTS OF DEPARTURE

Ironically, a flow-of-funds theory albeit inspired by the social accounts must resist a "social accounting" view of the means of payment. To this end, we have interpreted the flow-of-funds accounts as "cash funds" accounts. This approach is necessary to capture the dynamics of the banking system. Treating depository institutions as financial intermediaries (as pointed out in Chapter II) obscures the self-finance of banks in a fractional reserve system.

The cash funds accounting view advocated here rejects inside-outside money. The social accounting interpretation mistakenly sees the banking system as advancing funds to borrowers at the same time that cash balance holders are advancing funds to the banks. Treating transactions deposits as a bank product breaks this simultaneity. Checkable deposits are the creation of banks whether viewed from the standpoint of the banking system or the individual bank.

The money supply process is best analyzed in the context of a general equilibrium framework based on the two-endedness of market transactions. In the short run, transactions deposits are determined in the bank credit market. As a consequence, disequilibrium obtains in the money market. In the long run, substitution into bank liabilities, adjustments in nominal income and interest rates bring the demand for money into balance with the supply of money.

Notes

1. In fact, Copeland wrote moneyflows as one word rather than two to distinguish his accounting from "cash funds" accounting. The fear that this was not explicit enough led the Federal Reserve to adopt the terminology of "flow of funds." See Cohen (1972), p. 15.
2. One author has sarcastically spoken of the humble borrower being converted into a proud lender by this approach. Boris P. Pesek, 1976, p. 878.
3. It is conceded that "ultimate capacity limits" exist for demand deposits and time deposits, but that they are said to depend on extreme conditions. Thus, the capacity limit for demand deposits is reached when currency held by the public, excess bank reserves, and public holding of time deposits are all zero (p. 1389).

   Paradoxically, theorists identified with the "post-Keynesian view" who see the demand for credit as determining the money stock may appear to support the New View (see Moore, 1983, 1984a, 1984b). The supply of money schedule is pictured as horizontal so that demand deposits are at the initiative of the nonbank public ("banks stand ready to receive deposits on demand at their administered deposit rates") (Moore, 1984b, p. 106). The assumed lender-of-last-resort function of the central bank resolves the inconsistency. The central bank can never quantity-constrain bank reserves or the money stock without abrogating its role as the financial system's provider of ultimate liquidity. Thus, reserves are the result rather than the cause of movements in demand deposits.

   Whether one takes the conventional multiplier approach, or the post-Keynesian view, both are consistent with a flow-constrained approach to money and banking. Either reserves induce bank lending leading to deposits or the demand for credit leads to deposits and reserve accommodation. In contrast, for the New View variations in demand deposits are the result of substitution on the basis of interest rates. Equilibrium in the reserve market determines interest rates and the swap of bank deposits for bank-held securities without any constraining effect of reserves on deposits (see Cohen, 1984a, and below).
4. The means of payment may be viewed as a source of funds in the accepted cash funds sense when an increase in demand deposits is associated with an increase in reserves for the individual bank. Our objection here would be the lack of symmetry--the increase in demand deposits is not a use of funds for the depositor.
5. Treating demand deposits as bank product resolves the unsatisfactory treatment of the banking sector in the national income accounts. It is only by a complex imputation procedure that the Department of Commerce is able to assign a positive income originating to the bank sector. Now, all compensation of bank employees and corporate

profits before taxes can be included in national income originating in the banking industry (Cohen, 1957, p. 428; Pesek, 1976, p. 868).

The New View, coupled with a completely deregulated banking system would in theory resolve the imputation problem. Treating a bank deposit as a share in a mutual fund administered by the bank (a possible interpretation of the New View), and bank deregulation (including payment of interest on reserves, abolishing legal reserve requirements, and permitting interest payments on demand deposits) would result in bank service charges being equal to the cost of services provided by banks and equality in the interest rates on deposits and on loans and advances (Rymes, 1985). It is the absence of these equalities that explains the bank imputation problem.

6. The uncritical acceptance in the literature that in the aggregate, bank loans have a negative effect on uses of funds corresponding to the positive effect of money balances ignores both the varying importance of bank loans and money balances in individual transactor balance sheets and the influence of the remaining asset and liability items on monetary dissaving.
7. This is also the basis for criticizing Keynes's so-called "finance motive" which has the borrower adding to his money balances (Cohen, 1982b).
8. The theoretical significance of such an equilibrium is that it makes sense of "Say's law." As was shown earlier in Chapter I, money "cancels out" in "octuple entry" transactions between pairs of economic agents at unique prices. Say's world is indeed a world of price determinacy. Money demand is "there," but invisible in a world of mutual exchanges. Say's law (identity)-- $\Sigma p_n^d(x_n^s - x_n) = 0$--is less general than Walras's law-- $\Sigma p_n(x_n^d - x_n^s) = m^s - m^d$. But it is consistent (in equilibrium) with the excess demand for money being identically zero--$m^s - m^d = 0$.
9. Disequilibrium in the deposit market can also be measured by constructing demand and supply functions of the money market and taking minimum of demand and supply estimates as the desired value. A model for Switzerland generated excess demand and supply values that tested successfully against extraordinary financial events such as the large-scale nonsterilized exchange-rate intervention by the Swiss National Bank in the first and fourth quarters of 1978 (Buttler, Frei, and Schips, 1986, p. 66).
10. Depending on the relative cost of supplying money versus supplying other claims, banks may initiate the shift from checkable deposits to liabilities by increasing the supply of liabilities. This is what is meant by "liability management."
11. J-S substitute the commercial paper rate for the own-rate

of interest in the deposit market. The deposit supply curve is positively sloping because an increase in the commercial paper rate results in the public substituting commercial paper for nondeposit liabilities. Transactions deposits, as a result, replace nondeposit liabilities. (For a similar discussion, see Jonson, 1976, p. 506.)

12. In White's survey of the disequilibrium literature, money demand stock adjustment models are classified as equilibrium models. Presumably this is justified because the lagged terms reflect the costs of adjustment so in that sense short-run equilibrium exists. Nonetheless, stock adjustment and distributed lag models have a clear connotation of disequilibrium--that desired holdings of money depart from actual holdings.
13. Another response might be that retirement of bank debt (money being returned for bank assets) will be countered by banks, if necessary, acquiring open-market securities.
14. Similarly, index numbers of monetary quantities based on rates of turnover of elementary monetary assets (see Berkman 1980; Kopcke, 1986, 9-11) are necessarily arbitrary. Moreover, the index number approach fails empirically to establish a closer relationship between the money concept and the GNP, its stated purpose (Kopcke, 1986).
15. Shift-adjusted M-1B failed to capture current saving flows into checkable deposits whose source is demand deposits. These too should be removed from estimates of money as the means of payment. At the present time, both M-1A and M-1B are defined as M1.
16. Pesek and Saving's emphasis on the noninterest-bearing characteristics of demand deposits has been called a "red herring" (Laidler, 1969, p. 513).

CHAPTER V
THE DEGREE OF NETNESS: STOCKS VS. FLOWS

The rationale of the flow of funds is to solve for expenditures by solving for the elemental flows which add up to such expenditures. Thus it solves for an expenditure identity:

$$P = PP + BP + LP + MP$$

In "real terms, $\frac{P}{p} = \frac{PP}{p} + \frac{BP}{p} + \frac{LP}{p} + \frac{MP}{p}$ where p = price level. The "BP" term is broad enough to include the sell-off of financial assets in addition to increases in financial liabilities. Similarly, the MP term embraces monetary dissaving in addition to money creation by the banking system. Dissaving can be identified by the subscript dis. Thus, $P = PP + BP + BP_{dis} + MP + MP_{dis}$.

In practice, we could not expect to solve the market matrix for the necessary elemental flows. Obviously, the information needed to identify all submarket flows, disaggregated further by sector, and to specify all the submarket functions makes solution of the matrix an impossible task. The question then is, when stock variables are introduced into functional relationships explaining expenditures, as is ordinarily done, do they succeed in capturing the effect of borrowing and dissaving?

FLOW-FLOW VS. STOCK-FLOW

The problem in the use of stocks to explain flows is that it results in a higher degree of netness. The relation between stocks and flows is shown in the following identity:

$$\bar{B}_t - BP + LB = \bar{B}_{t+1}$$

An initial stock of bonds, $\bar{B}_t$ for an individual sector is depleted by the selling-off of bonds to finance expenditures (BP) and subsequently built up out of income (LB). If the flows are offsetting, then the stock of bonds is unchanged at the end of the period as compared with the beginning. The use of the stock variable will fail to reflect the influence of dissaving on expenditures. The choice of initial versus closing values of the stock becomes relevant in the case of a change in the level. Closing values are a better proxy for the flow effect than initial values. Thus, borrowing will be reflected in rising debt levels over the period. Dissaving on the other hand will be reflected in declining asset values. But closing stock values by themselves are still an inadequate measure of changes in stocks.[1] And beginning stocks cannot be ignored because plans to change the level of stocks may be a function of beginning stocks. How to reconcile the dependence of expenditures on changes in stocks with the dependence of plans to change the level of stocks on beginning stocks is the challenge. Reconciliation requires a two-equation approach to expenditure functions. We apply this analysis first to Patinkin's real balance effect.

PATINKIN'S REAL BALANCE EFFECT

On the coefficient of the stock variable in conventional expenditure functions rests the burden of capturing its flow-effect. We begin with Patinkin's well-known "real balance effect" where the M/p variable in the following equation is meant to measure this effect (Patinkin, 1965, chapters IX-XII *passim*).

V.1 $$E = F\ (Y, r, M/p)$$

where E = expenditures

Y = real income

M/p = the stock of real money balances

One has to identify the point of time at which real balances are being measured. The beginning of the period is customarily chosen. This is questionable, however, if the intent is to measure dissaving during the subsequent time period. The expected positive relationship between the stock variable and expenditures may be due to the effect of real balances on spending out of income rather than a dissaving effect. A better proxy for dissaving is end-of-year stock values. Now a negative relation with expenditure is consistent with dissaving over the time period.

At best money balances are a poor proxy for monetary dissaving--the negative changes in such balances. Monetary dissaving can be influenced by many other variables besides the stock of money assets. The drawing down of money balances, for example, can be the result of changes in the payments structure, the market rate of interest, the implicit and/or explicit return on money, expectations, and capital market imperfections (IMP).[2] One might suggest the following equation as the "missing equation" in macro-monetary theory. Now initial money balances are the appropriate monetary variable. Plans to dissave during the ensuing period will be related to beginning holdings.

$$\text{V.2} \qquad \frac{MB_{dis}}{p} + \frac{MP_{dis}}{p} = f\left(Pay,\ r_b,\ r_m,\ EXP,\ IMP, \frac{\overline{M}_{t-1}}{p}\right)$$

subject to the limitation that

$$\frac{MB_{dis}}{p} + \frac{MP_{dis}}{p} \leq \frac{\overline{M}_{t-1}}{p}$$

Both the expenditure and dissaving equations have to be considered in estimating the full effect of real balances on expenditures.[3] That is,

$$\text{V.3} \qquad \frac{\frac{\partial P}{p}}{\frac{\partial \overline{M}}{p}} = \frac{\frac{\partial P}{p}}{\frac{\partial MP_{dis}}{p}} \cdot \frac{\frac{\partial MP_{dis}}{p}}{\frac{\partial \overline{M}}{p}}$$

The expression on the right-hand side, rather than the direct relation between money balances and expenditures on the left-hand side, is the way to estimate the full real balance effect. The "proximate" real balance effect is the influence of real balances on dissaving (the second term on the right-hand side of

V.3). Similar second terms can be written for the other terms in the monetary dissaving equation, suggesting that interest rates, etc., exert their own effects on expenditures via their effect on monetary dissaving.[4]

Stock-Adjustment Models. Stock-adjustment models are appropriate for explaining the financial flow variables which then enter the expenditure equations as explanatory variables. Thus, we could formulate monetary dissaving as a function of desired money holdings and lagged money holdings with the difference modified by the speed of adjustment. It would not be appropriate, however, to treat expenditure functions in this way since the desideratum is a flow-flow (flow-constrained) relationship.[5]

Interest Rates and Monetary Dissaving. The adjustment process in the neoclassical model illustrates the influence of the interest rate on monetary dissaving. The proximate real balance effect, as defined above, plays a secondary role in this process. I shall assume a once-for-all increase in investment demand due to technological change, financed by the sale of bonds (Patinkin, 1965, p. 269). Unlike Patinkin, we cannot ignore the labor market. Patinkin assumes an instantaneous adjustment in money wages given a change in prices so that a condition of perpetual equilibrium prevails in the labor market. Had Patinkin's analysis satisfied both flow-of-funds and value-theoretical criteria, he could not have avoided a discussion of the labor market.[6]

In response to the disturbance, curves shift in the relevant submarkets and subsequently they shift in response to income changes and also in response to the changes in the wage-price relationship. In the period of the disturbance, the volume of physical output is given so that increased demand in the output market is reflected solely in prices.

In a moneyflows framework, the product-market identity is preserved by the transfer of money holdings from the household sector to the business sector. The household sector buys bonds with money balances, the business sector uses the proceeds to buy output from other members of the business sector so that the money balances of the business sector show a net increase. (In terms of the market matrix MB = BP = PM.) Thus, BP + LP + MP = PB + PL + PM with BP on the demand side of the product market equalling PM on the supply side of the market. The reason for the shift in money balances is the higher market interest rate due to the increased supply of bonds in the product submarket of the bond market. In diagrammatic terms, BP (1/r) shifts to the right in the product submarket of the bond market with the excess supply in the product submarket now corresponding to the excess demand in the money submarket at a higher interest yield.

Following the disturbance, the higher money income of the business sector leads to an increased demand for labor (a rightward shift in PL[W] in the product submarket of the labor market). The higher price level in the product market leads to higher reservation prices for labor in the product submarket of the labor market (the LP[W] curve shifts upward). The effect is a higher money wage bill for the same volume of employment. At the same time, the PL(p) curve shifts to the left in the labor submarket of the product market reflecting higher money wage costs. The income effect of higher wages simultaneously causes the LP(p) curve to shift to the right in the labor submarket of the product market. This increase in LP(p) replaces the once-for-all increase in BP of the first period. The price-constrained and flow-constrained shifts in the product and labor markets thus are responsible for an expanded circular flow of money payments in the labor and product markets. The money balances initially shifted to the business sector serve as the means of payment for an increased volume of money transactions.

It is the substitution effect of higher interest rates on household portfolios that leads to the release of money balances and in this way to higher levels of moneyflows and prices. This effect of higher interest rates on monetary dissaving is to be distinguished from the proximate "real balance effect" of real balances on monetary dissaving. Defined in this way, Patinkin's real balance effect plays its role in the adjustment process by inducing the leftward shift of the MB(1/r) function. The decline in household money balances and the higher price level causes $\frac{\bar{M}}{p}$ to fall and monetary dissaving (MB(1/r)) to decline. In final equilibrium (the only adjustment stage assuming tatonnement) the shift in MB(1/r) to the left eliminates excess demand in the money submarket of the bond market. The remaining money submarkets similarly show zero excess demand in stationary equilibrium. In the bond market an excess (flow) supply of existing bonds in the product submarket of the bond market will now correspond to excess demand in the labor submarket at the new higher level of yields. Assuming an absence of both new security issues and net increases in the money stock, some sectors in each time period will be offering outstanding bonds in exchange for products while households will finance their purchases of existing bonds out of income.

When the real balance effect is defined as the product of two partial derivatives, as in V.3, it has the side benefit of omitting real balances from the expenditure function. The problem of real balances interacting with other variables is avoided. This problem is most prominent in connection with the income variable. Variations in real balances might affect the extent to which income is used to finance expenditures. What is identified as a real balance effect may really be an effect exerted on the marginal propensity to consume out of current income (i.e., LP may be confused with MP). Both the LP and real balance variables should appear in the dissaving function, where their interaction can help explain this variable.

WEALTH AND DEBT EFFECTS

What has been said about real money balances applies to wider magnitudes such as liquid assets, all financial assets, or wealth (net worth) (Modigliani, 1971; Tobin and Dolde, 1971; Tobin, 1980, pp. 57-80).[7] Now BP_{dis} and PP_{dis} are the relevant terms in the expenditure equation. The first term indicates the sell-off of nonmonetary financial assets, the second the sell-off of tangible assets. When these variables are used in expenditure equations, the missing equations are intermediate equations explaining the sell-off of such assets.

The limitation of the wealth variable carry over to its proxy permanent income (M. Friedman, 1957). Permanent income (or any income averaging concept) suggests a gap between current income and expenditures--a gap that has to be filled in by estimates of dissaving and/or borrowing. Permanent income instead of, or perhaps along with, wealth deserves a place in intermediate dissaving functions.

On the other side of the balance sheet, the missing equation is one relating borrowing to a series of explanatory variables, one of which will be the debt of the sector. A good example is consumer credit. What influences consumer spending is the gross extension of credit. It is this variable that belongs in expenditure equations. "Consumer credit outstanding" is a poor proxy for such flows because the stock of consumer credit reflects net changes--gross extensions less repayments. Unless credit extensions finance repayments, net extensions and thus the level of consumer debt will understate the impact of credit on consumer spending. Another way of putting this is that the volume of consumer debt could stay the same and yet the impact of consumer borrowing could vary. Assume, for example, that extensions and repayments both doubled, consumer debt would stay the same and yet consumer spending would increase. Borrowing (as for dissaving) requires its own equation with beginning debt as one of the explanatory variables.

The interpretation of balance sheet variables in expenditure equations is ambiguous even if they are significant (see, e.g., Mishkin, 1977). The borrowing that finances expenditures will cause end-of-period debt levels and expenditures to be correlated. Similarly, dissaving may affect both asset levels and expenditures in a systematic way. The rejoinder might be that this interpretation is not consistent with a negative sign for the debt variable and a positive sign for financial assets (as in Mishkin's equations). But in this case the expenditure effect of debt and financial assets measured as they are at the beginning of the period (p. 132)--could be spending out of income. High beginning debt values could discourage such spending and higher beginning asset values encourage spending out of income. Borrowing and dissaving as influences on expenditures are still being ignored.[8]

THE OPTIMAL DEGREE OF GROSSNESS

The significance of finance is obscured by the use of stock values. So-called real balance effects, wealth effects, and indebtedness effects are flow-of-funds effects and require that the flow be made explicit in expenditure functions. To make such flows endogenous, they have to be explained by equations of their own.

It is not enough to use the net change in assets in expenditure equations. The flow-of-funds effect is more than the first difference in stock values. "Pluses" and "minuses" in asset change are to be sharply distinguished. Dissaving is limited to the minus change which, for estimation purposes, are to be treated as positive values in both dissaving and expenditure functions.

The more detailed are asset and liability categories in financial accounts, the greater will be the harvest of "minus" values signifying dissaving and the greater will be the magnitude of positive borrowing flows. So a flow-of-funds approach has a bias in favor of financial detail (on the various gradations of grossness in financial accounts, see Mendelson, 1962). In terms of our dual-decision framework, any netting of transactions presupposes a linkage between markets that may be in error. A key instance is the description of sectors as deficit-surplus sectors. Such a designation offsets increases in financial liabilities against increases in financial assets. The questionable implication is that borrowing in the first instance finances the acquisition of financial assets.

Notes

1. A flow-equilibrium in markets is formally equivalent to an end-of-period stock equilibrium (Harris, chapter 16). Thus a flow equilibrium can be written as

$$\Delta B_T^D = \Delta B_T^S \text{ where T stands for the period as a}$$

whole.
Plans of lenders and borrowers can also be expressed as:

$$\Delta B_T^D = (B_{t+1}^D - B_t)$$

$$\Delta B_T^S = (B_{t+1}^S - B_t)$$

where t and t+1 stand for the beginning and end of the period. The flow equilibrium can now be written in terms of stocks as:

$$B_{t+1}^D = B_{t+1}^S$$

This solution is irrelevant for variables that are strictly flows, such as current consumption. More importantly, it demonstrates equivalence of stocks and flows only in terms of the left-hand variables in demand and supply analysis. It does not demonstrate that flows and stocks provide equivalent explanations of expenditure flows.

2. Willem H. Buiter (1983, p. 47), has pointed out the importance of capital market imperfections in constraining dissaving. In the abstract, an inability to trade future income for present assets is a market imperfection inhibiting dissaving.
3. The superiority of dissaving over stocks in expenditure equations may be challenged on the grounds of the endogeneity of dissaving--its dependence in part on stocks. This endogeneity is taken care of in a two-equation model: first expenditures are explained by dissaving and then dissaving is explained with assorted arguments including financial stocks.
4. Higher interest rates would induce dissaving to buy bonds. Bond sales in turn finance expenditures.
5. The distinction between flow-of-funds (flow-constrained) models and stock adjustment models has been brought out in a study of company financing. "Pride of place" is given to flow-flow relationships in explaining financial behavior rather than adjustment to some optimal balance sheet (Bain, Day, and Wearing, 1975). Although in this model nonfinancial expenditures are exogenous and financial flows endogenous, the contrast between the two approaches still holds.
6. For a similar criticism, cf. Clower, 1965, p. 112, including note 1.

7. Tobin and Dolde distinguish between wealth and liquidity constraints. The latter is equivalent to a borrowing constraint (Hayashi, 1985, p. 183; Chapter XII below).
8. Elsewhere, Mishkin has estimated borrowing in a stock-adjustment equation but has not used this variable in expenditure functions (Mishkin, 1976).

CHAPTER VI
POLICY IMPLICATIONS

An effective monetary policy involves stability in two linkages: the linkage between the target and economic activity ("predictability") and the linkage between the target and the policy instrument ("controllability"). The flow-of-funds framework singles out financial flows as having a closer relationship to final expenditures than interest rates or the money stock.[1] Interest rate changes do not predict changes in nominal income because such variation may either signal movements in the same or opposite direction. It depends on whether or not interest rate changes are due to shifts on the demand side of credit markets or the supply side. In the case of a positive relation between interest rates and nominal income, sums raised in credit markets may be going up (indicating no policy restraint) at the same time that interest rates are going up (signaling restraint). The relationship between money and nominal income is similarly unstable. The evidence is in the search for ever wider M_i categories.[2] More controversial is the question of controllability. The chapter will explore the strengths and weaknesses of money and credit targeting from the standpoint of both linkages.

In this chapter additional financial markets will be introduced so the "transmission mechanism" can be analyzed in detail. I have added markets for equities (E), deposits other than demand deposits in commercial banks (T), deposits in financial intermediaries (F), currency (C), and bank reserves (R).

CONTROLLABILITY

We begin by tracing the effects of a tighter money policy implemented by reducing the rate of growth in bank reserves via open market purchases (RB in Table VI.1). Bank reserves will either be directly affected if the open market transaction involves the commercial banks directly (RB = BR), or indirectly affected as the nonbank sector converts its bond sales to the

Supply \ Demand	$P(p)$	$E(r_e)$	$L(W)$	$B(\frac{1}{r})$	$T(r_t)$	$F(r_s)$	$M(r_m)$	$C(r_c)$	$R(r_f)$
$P(p)$	PP	PE	PL	PB	PT	PF	PM	PC	PR
$E(r_e)$	EP	EE	EL	EB	ET	EF	EM	EC	ER
$L(W)$	LP	LE	LL	LB	LT	LF	LM	LC	LR
$B(\frac{1}{r})$	BP	BE	BL	BB	BT	BF	BM	BC	BR
$T(r_t)$	TP	TE	TL	TB	TT	TF	TM	TC	TR
$F(r_s)$	FP	FE	FL	FB	FT	FF	FM	FC	FR
$M(r_m)$	MP	ME	ML	MB	MT	MF	MM	MC	MR
$C(r_c)$	CP	CE	CL	CB	CT	CF	CM	CC	CR
$R(r_f)$	RP	RE	RL	RB	RT	RF	RM	RC	RR

TABLE VI.1 ADDING FINANCIAL MARKETS

central bank into checking accounts (BR = RM). The effect of a reduced rate of growth of reserves will be to shift the bank MB function to the left. The commercial banks will plan to buy less bonds (the IOUs of borrowers), which they pay for by crediting the accounts of borrowers. Assuming that banks can borrow at the discount window, borrowings will go up, offsetting the decline in the rate of increase in unborrowed reserves. (In terms of the market matrix this would be a shift to the right in the bank supply of bonds in exchange for reserves [BR].)

The key submarket in the transmission process is the bond submarket of the product market. It is here via the BP flow that monetary policy makes contact with the product market. This flow will be reduced as a result of the bond market clearing at a higher level of interest rates.[3] With a lag in the adjustment of the bank loan rate to its desired level, credit rationing will take place with an immediate effect on planned investment expenditures (Tucker, 1968). A restrictive monetary policy in this way exerts an income effect along with an interest rate effect.

We assume that the "own-rate" of interest on M1 balances stays unchanged and that the interest return on currency holdings are zero. Depending on the substitution elasticities, the incremental demand for money balances will decline. Movements into open market securities (MB) will moderate interest rate increases.

If yields on time deposits (T) and intermediary claims (F) rise, there will be increased MT, CT, MF, CF flows. Higher interest yields brought on by a tight monetary policy have "slippage" effects. Slippage can also operate through trade credit. Inter-firm lending may offset a tight money policy by encouraging liquid firms to channel trade credit to less liquid firms, thus increasing the activity of money balances. (In terms of the submarket flows, MB $\rightarrow$ BP, where B now represents trade credit.)

<u>Controlling Money</u>. The money multiplier is a convenient way to

assess controllability. The coefficients of the multiplier may move in the desired direction, reinforcing policy actions or they may change in an offsetting direction. Such slippage undermines controllability.

The standard multiplier formula is:

$$m = \frac{1 + k}{(r + f)\ (1 + t + g) + k} \tag{VI.1}$$

where k = currency/checkable deposit ratio

r = average reserve ratio

f = ratio of free reserves to checkable deposits; free reserves equal excess reserves minus borrowing from the Federal Reserve

t = ratio of time deposits to checkable deposits

g = ratio of Treasury deposits to checkable deposits $(\frac{T}{D})$

The traditional money multiplier (m) has reserves (R) or the monetary base (B) as the multiplicant:

$$M = mR \text{ or } M = m_1B \tag{VI.2}$$

Assuming stability of the multiplier, control of the monetary base implies control of the money stock. This stability has been argued in various studies (Balbach, 1981; Burger, 1972; Burger, Kalish, and Babb, 1971; Hoffman, 1979; Johannes and Rasche, 1979, 1981; Hafer, Hein, and Kool, 1983). Our interest is in determining whether the induced changes in the coefficients threaten or reinforce policy intentions. The focus is on interest rate disturbances. The interest rate effects will be reinforcing if holders of M1 shift into time deposits. The negative income effect will reduce the transactions demand for money balances also reinforcing restrictive policy. I assume that desired free reserves do not fall to offset the decline in the value of the multiplier.

Controlling Credit. In constructing a credit multiplier transaction accounts are again the numeraire as additional asset categories are introduced. The denominator specifies reserve leakages as before, and the numerator specifies credit flows involving both direct and indirect finance.

VI.3 $$m_{cr} = \frac{1 + k + t + g + d + s + o + u}{(r + e)(1 + t + g) + k + r^{1}\alpha d}$$

Where the additional parameters are:

d = money market mutual funds (MMMF) as a proportion of checkable deposits

s = life insurance and pension reserves as a proportion of checkable deposits

o = nonreservable open market securities acquired by the private nonfinancial sector as a proportion of checkable deposits

u = nonreservable foreign lending as a proportion of checkable deposits

= percentage of MMMF held in reservable liabilities of depository institutions (CD's)

r^1= reserve requirements against CD's

Unlike monetary targeting, restrictive credit targeting will induce slippage effects as shifts take place from high-reserve to low-reserve assets to nonreservable assets in response to higher market interest rates. From the standpoint of the response of the multiplier coefficients, money is more controllable than credit.

THE SAVING LEAKAGE

Instead of increased flows into T and F being financed by dishoarding (MT), (MF), they may be financed out of income (L). From the standpoint of households, these flows are LT and LF flows made at the expense of expenditures in the product market (LP). An important asymmetry, however, is that the increase in time deposits is seen by depository institutions as MT, MF flows (Cohen, 1982b). From the institutional standpoint there is no difference between an act of dishoarding (MT), (MF), and an act of saving (LT), (LF). Assuming as the polar case that reserve requirements were uniform against checkables and time deposits, the depository system could not finance new investment. The act of saving via time deposits and intermediary claims in these circumstances is a leakage. A substitution of time deposits for direct lending to nonfinancial sectors (an LB = BP flow) will have the same leakage effect.

It is only because reserve requirements are at most three percent against time deposit components of M2 that the saving leakage is not significant at the present time. More relevant under the present institutional structure are shifts within M1. Thus an act of saving that takes the form of a NOW account will constitute a leakage. A paycheck is being transferred from old M-1B (the employer's account) to old M-1B. Since reserve requirements are a uniform 12 percent, with unchanged monetary targeting depository institutions do not have an increased capacity to lend.[4]

The Federal Reserve's "shift-adjusted" M1-B concept allowed for funds flowing into transactions balances from non-transaction sources (Simpson, 1981). The intent was to measure bona fide transactions balances for purposes of targeting the money supply. Since nontransaction sources refer to other asset holdings rather than to current saving, the adjustment failed to allow for shifts within M1. Simultaneous declines in narrow money (old M-1A) were ignored even though this decline is symptomatic of an intention to save. Without an increase in total credit, such plans will be frustrated. The saving leakage is a compelling argument for targeting total credit flows rather than monitoring transactions balances.

<u>The Proximate Target</u>. In controlling external finance, will the central bank be better advised to aim at total reserves, or the monetary base? In terms of the expanded matrix, if the public unexpectedly increases its holdings of currency on balance by cashing in demand deposits (MC > CM), this will lead to a reduction in reserves as depository institutions secure currency from the central bank (MC = RC). Since random cash drains will have

a disproportionate effect on bank credit, focusing on total currency and reserves (the monetary base) has its drawbacks. The attractiveness of base money is its controllability. By its control over assets, the central bank is able to control its liabilities. Ignoring other factors of change in the monetary base, $B_{fed} = R + C$. Such control, however, as suggested above, does not guarantee the control of credit. A better target would be total reserves.

Since 1979, the Federal Reserve has in fact been targeting total reserves, although the implementation procedure changed after 1982. Before 1982 nonborrowed reserves were set with the anticipated flexibility in borrowed reserves. Thereafter borrowed reserves were targeted with the anticipated flexibility being in nonborrowed reserves (Gilbert, 1985). But the targeting of reserves has had money rather than credit as the intermediate target.

PREDICTABILITY

Predictability depends on a stable relation between total credit flow and aggregate demand.[5] The distribution of saving and investment and "fluff" are two factors that might affect this relationship.

<u>Saving-Investment Patterns</u>. The credit target will be affected by saving-investment distributions. The greater the saving done by nonbusiness sectors, the greater will have to be the flow of credit to transfer such saving to the business sector (Lindbeck, 1973; Chapter II above). Similarly, a changing distribution of saving-investment within the business sector will affect desired credit targets.

<u>The "Fluff" in Moneyflows</u>. The policymaker has to allow for the changing importance of technical transactions or "fluff" in targeting credit flows (Copeland, 1952, chapter 10). Fluff fits into the BB cell of the market matrix. The use of credit in financing takeovers (Gilbert and Ott, 1985), or the increase in

"financial layering," e.g., the introduction of money market funds, contribute to an increase in such transactions.[6] (On financial layering, see Goldsmith, 1958, 1969, 1982, 1985). Over the liquidity cycle, long-term borrowing may be used in varying proportions for spending versus the building-up of liquidity (Sinai, forthcoming; Minsky, 1975, chapters 3-6).

Reverse Causality. On theoretical and possibly empirical grounds (see Chapter XIII below), we can argue for the linkage between credit and nominal income. But reverse causality may be responsible. A planned increase in economic activity (perhaps signaled by lagged GNP) increases the demand for credit which in turn leads to central bank support of the government securities market. Stability in the linkages may demonstrate passive rather than discretionary central bank behavior (Davis, 1979; Cohen, 1975; Cohen and Schmalzl, 1974; McMillin and Beard, 1980; Moore, 1983, 1984a, 1984b).

An Overall Comparison. With reserves, R, as the instrument, M1 the intermediate target, and nominal income, Y, the objective, controllability involves the relation

VI.4 $$M = mR$$

and predictability the relation

VI.5 $$Y = vM$$

or with substitution,

VI.6 $$Y = vmR$$

With external finance as the intermediate target the relations can be written:

VI.7 $EXF = v_e mR$

VI.8 $Y = cEXF$

and

VI.9 $Y = c\ v_e mR$

The parameter v_e stands for the turnover in credit markets of the increase in the money stock induced by R. It is a nonbank credit multiplier. Greater stability can be assumed for the EXF relation in comparison with the M relation because of the compensating effects of variations in m and v_e. A decline in m due to higher interest rates will be offset by increases in v_e. The stability of c as compared with v is based on the dual decision to borrow for spending purposes. Ultimately, the relative stability of the functions is an empirical question.

SELECTIVE CONTROLS

Policy effects on the flow of credit have been studied so far assuming indirect controls. Now I wish to study the effect of selective (direct) controls on total credit, its allocation, and on output. Selective controls can apply to the credit side of institutional financial statements or the debit side. Interest rate ceilings or differential reserve requirements on liabilities are examples of credit side restrictions. On the asset side, differential reserve requirements, in the place of requirements on liabilities, down payment and maturity terms can be used to allocate credit.

The theoretical analysis of selective controls requires a more complex study of substitution possibilities. Instead of a single aggregated "bond market," we must now visualize a series of financial markets--markets for government bonds, markets for corporates, markets for mortgages, markets for business loans, markets for consumer credit, etc. The intent of controls is to limit borrowing by a given sector in a given financial market for the purpose of making expenditures in a designated product market, i.e., the amount of $B_{ij}P_k$ transactions (where i stands for the individual sector, j for the individual financial instruments, and k for specific kinds of expenditures). For example, the purpose of consumer credit controls is to restrict expenditures on consumer goods, usually consumer durables. For controls to be successful, the assumed close relationship between a particular instrument and a particular kind of spending has to be insensitive to three possible kinds of substitution: financial substitution, capital expenditure substitution, and substitution between internal and external finance.

The first kind of substitution refers to substituting a second source of finance for the restricted source. The elasticity of substitution with respect to credit terms for the ith sector can be defined as $\partial B_{ij}/B_{ij} / \partial B_{im}/B_{im} \Big/ \partial c_j/c_j / \partial c_m/c_m$ (where j identifies the first instrument, m the second, and C stands for credit terms). Because of financial substitution, the effectiveness of selective controls cannot be gauged by study of the restricted financial market. While the proximate success of credit restriction will depend on high supply and demand elasticities in this market, such elasticities might measure the ease of substituting a second kind of credit for the controlled credit.[7] Paradoxically, then, the greater the selective reduction of credit, the less might be the effectiveness of controls in restraining expenditures. The possibilities of financial substitution are enhanced if the would-be borrower has liquid assets which he can dissave. Financial dissaving should be considered an alternative source of finance.[8]

The second kind of substitution, capital expenditure substitution, refers to several expenditures being substitutes in the utilization of a given source of funds, e.g., the use of mortgage credit for consumer credit purposes. Credit restriction in this case may merely graze the intended target.

Substitution of income (internal finance) for borrowing may also thwart the selective control of expenditures. If the interest, however, is in the control of expenditures in general, such substitution becomes a virtue rather than a weakness of direct controls. To the extent that saving out of current income is encouraged and capital expenditures become more dependent on such saving, the aggregate demand for credit is curtailed and inflationary financing is reduced. (See also Chapter XII below).

Interest Rate Ceilings. When interest rate ceilings are imposed on deposit liabilities, substitutability might promote the intended allocation. Thus, regulation Q on time deposits in commercial banks was meant to encourage savings in institutions specializing in mortgage finance.[9] At the same time such ceilings pushed the commercial banks into expanding their liability management.

Interest rate ceilings at a time of monetary stringency promote disintermediation. They have the effect, then, of increasing the total flow of funds, thus inducing "slippage" in credit control.

MINIMIZING INCOME VARIANCE

In the fashion of the classic Poole model (Poole, 1970), I return to the predictability linkage by comparing credit versus M1 targeting in r-Y space (Figure VI.1). The effect on nominal GNP of random disturbances provides an additional criterion for choosing an intermediate target. The simplifying assumption is that M1 provides the sole means of payment and is used exclusively for this purpose. Disturbances are initially limited to the product market (the IS function). Unlike the Poole model which was not concerned with the financing side, our comparison requires that disturbances have a financing counterpart. Both the credit and money market functions react to disturbances in the product market.

When credit flows are targeted it is assumed in this analysis that total credit and not just bank credit can be controlled by the policymaker.[10] Assume a random shift in investment by deficit sectors. Excess demand or supply in the credit market

FIGURE VI.1 TARGETING M1 VERSUS CREDIT

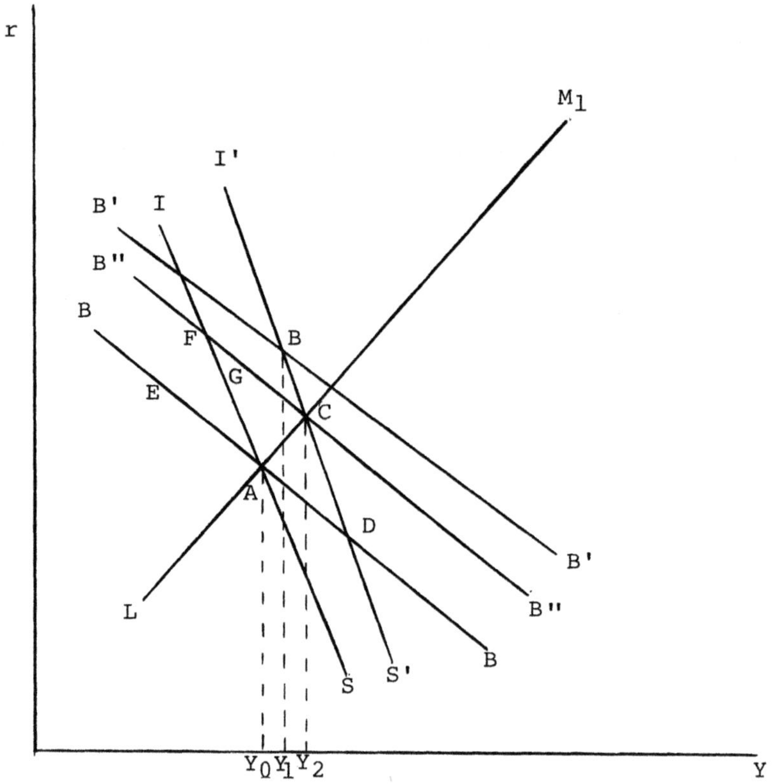

generated by this shift (as discussed previously in Chapter II), will cause the BB curve to shift in the same direction as the IS curve. Targeting credit so as to stabilize the income level will have the effect of offsetting the initial shift in IS and will tend to stabilize nominal GNP at Y_0.

Figure VI.1 has been drawn so that a planned increase in investment results in some increases in income (the movement is from A to B). The vertical shift in IS exceeds the shift in BB. This is explained by deficit sectors husbanding their cash balances ($\partial[\Delta M1_d]/\partial Y$ decreases and $\partial[\Delta M1_d]/\partial r$ increases in value and by the steepening of the IS curve with an assumed increase in income sensitivity of deficit saving (ds_d/dY in II.18). Given that $\partial[\Delta M1_d]/\partial r$ now exceeds dI_s/dr in II.21, the LM2 function (not drawn) turns positive and tilts clockwise, intersecting B'B' and I'S' at B. As in previous analysis (Chapter II) with M1 holdings at the discretion of depositors, money market equilibrium is represented by a point at B.

Suppose on the other hand that M1 is being targeted. Reserve controls are applied only to the money stock. The focus is now on the LM1 curve. The same shifting of IS will have more of a destabilizing effect on nominal GNP because movements to a new intersection with the LM1 function at C will be to the right of B. The explanation is a lesser movement in the BB curve (B"B") than when credit is being targeted. The supply of credit expands as financial institutions engage in "liability management" to finance an increased volume of credit.[11]

So far it has been assumed that increased investment is at the behest of deficit units. In the less likely case of surplus units financing investment by reducing asset holdings (savings deposits) the movement under credit targeting will be to point D, signifying the largest expansion in nominal GNP (see the related discussion in Chapter II). The M1 increase and downward movement in the LM1 curve that this implies cannot take place under M1 targeting, however, without the cooperation of the monetary authorities.[12] More reserves are required if M1 liabilities are to replace low reserve liabilities. Now money targeting is superior to credit targeting. The cost of credit will increase as a result of monetary control and the BB curve will move towards B"B" and intersection with LM1 at C.

Now we turn to disturbances originating in the money market. Again second market impacts have to be considered. Assume an increase in the demand for money balances financed out of savings deposits. Under credit targeting, the original equilibrium stays at A. The IS curve does not shift because saving and investment plans are unaffected. Equilibrium point A now denotes an increased quantity of M1. Under M1 targeting, however, the LM1 curve will shift to the left, say to an intersection at G. Now only if the central bank is accommodative will the LM1 curve stay put, maintaining the original equilibrium at A.

The final possibility was anticipated in Chapter II. The increased demand for M1 is now at the expense of direct finance (the case discussed by Trehan). Assume first that under credit targeting this results in a leftward shift in IS. The new equilibrium will be to the left of A as suggested by point E. At this point, the money market will also be in equilibrium with higher interest rates and reduced Y. (M1 holdings may not have increased because reduced investment and income mean lower demand for transactions balances.) In the second subcase, investment plans are maintained and equity finance is replaced by resort to the credit market. Depending on the increased pressure in the credit market and the resultant movement in BB, the equilibrium may lie above and to the left of E, or to the right and below E. Assuming B" B" to be the new curve, the new equilibrium will be at F.

Under monetary targeting, substitution of money demand for direct finance will mean a movement of IS to the left to point E, if the LM1 curve shifts the same distance as in the case of substitution for savings deposits. The results are then similar for both types of targeting. In the second subcase, assuming IS stays unchanged, and LM1 shifts the same distance to the left, G would be a possible equilibrium point lying to the right of the credit targeting equilibrium of F.

The circumstances favoring either credit or money targeting are summarized below (Table VI.2). In essence, in the five cases examined, credit targeting has the advantage when shifts in the product market are at the initiative of deficit units and shifts in the money market involve savings deposits. On the other hand, money targeting seems to have the advantage when shifts in IS originate with surplus units and when money demand shifts result in the substitution of bank credit for equity finance. A case can be made for interest-rate targeting when money demand shifts but IS does not (2.b.ii). Equilibrium could be maintained at A by converting LM1 into a horizontal function.

DOES MONEY STILL MATTER?

The theory of the flow of funds leads to the flow of credit as the intermediate target for monetary policy. There are difficulties in the control of credit because of the slippage effects of higher interest rates on the flow of funds. Predictability of the effect of credit on nominal income is influenced by the sector distribution of saving and investment, by fluff, and by the possibility of "reverse causality." When random disturbances in the product and money markets are considered, money targeting (using simplified assumptions) may have as many successes as credit targeting.

A preference for targeting credit as opposed to targeting M1 must assume that IS shifts in the product market are due to deficit units and that money demand shifts come out of savings deposits. These are empirical issues that will be taken up in Chapter XII. The implications of the more realistic assumption that depository (bank) institution credit is being targeted rather than total credit flows must also be considered.

TABLE VI.2

COMPARING THE VARIANCE IN INCOME (Y) UNDER CREDIT AND M1 TARGETING

Disturbance	Credit Targeting	M1 Targeting
1. Product Market		
a. Shift in IS, deficit units	Y stabilized*	Y less stable
b. Shift in IS, surplus units	Y not stabilized	Y stable*
2. Money Market		
a. Money Demand Shift via savings deposits	Y stabilized*	Y less stable
b. Money Demand Shift via direct finance		
i. IS function shifts	Y unstable	Y unstable
ii. IS function does not shift	Y unstable	Y possibly more stable*

*indicates superiority

Notes

1. Targeting credit aggregates has been criticized because of their "inevitable, definitional correlation with nominal income." (Batchelor, 1981, p. 83.) Since a theoretical framework exists for demonstrating how disturbances in credit markets are transmitted to nominal income, this criticism is more of a tribute to the credit linkage than a valid objection.
2. In addition to the conference volume Monetary Targets (1981), which discusses experience in six countries, a U.S. conference volume, Controlling Monetary Aggregates III (1980), reflects increasing doubts about monetary targeting. For the downgrading of M1 after 1982 see Cohen 1986, chapter 12. See also Chapter XIII below.
3. This flow-constrained approach to aggregate expenditures can be reconciled with a "value-theoretical" approach expressed in terms of prices. The effect of higher interest rates is to reduce the schedule of demand prices of new investment relative to the schedule of supply prices. Investment decisions made on the basis of equality of demand and supply prices will have to be consistent with the sector's income and borrowing constraint (Minsky, 1975, chapters 3-6).

   Tobin's well-known "q-ratio" has similar properties. It compares the market value of physical assets as measured by equity prices with their replacement cost. In his analysis, investment falls off when equity values fall below replacement cost.
4. The vast literature on financial repression emphasizes the adverse economic effects of below equilibrium real interest rates on LDCs. Since the market referred to is the bank deposit market, the analysis ignores the saving leakage effect. See Cohen, 1982a, "The Myth of Indirect Finance," pp. 11-12.
5. The empirical evidence is discussed in Chapter XIII below.
6. In Chapter V a high degree of grossness was recommended for analytical purposes. For policy purposes, it is necessary to know whether the credit-nominal income ratio is changing because of factors such as fluff.
7. As in the case of tax incidence, we can assume that the impact of credit restriction is either on the lender or the buyer. Reserve requirements on the lender would affect the supply curve; credit terms would affect the demand curve. No matter which curve does the shifting, the greater the elasticities of supply and demand, the greater the impact of credit controls on the restricted source.
8. Tobin and Dolde have distinguished between wealth-constrained and liquidity-constrained households. Credit controls have more effect on the latter than on the former because of the greater dependence of liquidity-constrained households on borrowing (Tobin and Dolde, 1971).
9. This effect was later offset by similar ceilings on savings institutions with only a small interest

differential allowed between them.

10. Reserve requirements are assumed to be imposed on bank assets. Credit targeting is still possible, however, (as evidenced by so-called "monitoring" beginning in 1982) if reserve requirements are imposed on bank liabilities.
11. Liability management implies lower or zero reserve requirements on nonmonetary liabilities as compared with M1. We thus depart from the simplifying assumptions of Chapter II where either reserve requirements were assumed to be uniform across all bank liabilities or were assumed to apply uniformly to bank assets.
12. I assume no reduction in desired holdings of existing money balances so this second factor in a downward movement is ruled out.

CHAPTER VII
THE FLOW-OF-FUNDS ACCOUNTS

An Idealized Set of Accounts

The theory of the flow of funds discussed in previous chapters was inspired by the published accounts. Nevertheless, the theory has a life of its own independent of the statistical accounts. The theory suggests an idealized set of accounts which is not necessarily embodied in the published accounts.

The theoretical framework was organized around the market matrix. Each cell can be considered a submatrix of intersectoral transactions with the columns and rows consisting of institutionally defined sectors--households, unincorporated business, corporate business, financial institutions, government, and the rest of the world.

As Table VII.1 shows for two sectors only, the matrix of Chapter I can be seen as a single submatrix in a matrix of intersectoral flows. The newly introduced subscripts to the previous market symbols show the sectors involved in the various transactions. The matrix is so arranged that the rows show planned sources of funds for the row sector and planned uses of funds for the column sectors. Thus, for example, the symbol PL_{ch} indicates that the business sector planning to purchase inputs supplied by households and to finance its planned purchases by the planned sale of output. If there are corresponding plans by households to sell labor and buy outputs (LP_{hc}) then both markets will be in equilibrium without the involvement of other markets. More realistically, all elements of the matrix will be simultaneously involved. Of special interest is the (PP_{cc}) element which when expanded constitutes a matrix of interindustry flows.

This is an idealized set of accounts because statistical data is not available on a two-ended basis. Three types of two-ended information are implied: from-whom to-whom knowledge of intersectoral flows, source-use linkages within the sector

TABLE VII.1

AN IDEALIZED FLOW-OF-FUNDS ACCOUNTING SYSTEM

HOUSEHOLDS (H) AND BUSINESS (C)

	H				C			
H	PP_{hh}	PB_{hh}	PL_{hh}	PM_{hh}	PP_{ch}	PB_{ch}	PL_{ch}	PM_{ch}
	BP	BB	BL	BM	BP	BB	BL	BM
	LP	LB	LL	LM	LP	LB	LL	LM
	MP	MB	ML	MM	MP	MB	ML	MM
C	PP_{hc}	PB_{hc}	PL_{hc}	PM_{hc}	PP_{cc}	PB_{cc}	PL_{cc}	PM_{cc}
	BP	BB	BL	BM	BP	BB	BL	BM
	LP	LB	LL	LM	LP	LB	LL	LM
	MP	MB	ML	MM	MP	MB	ML	MM

The "stock representation is in terms of the "$\overline{B}$" and "$\overline{P}$" values where the bars depict stocks.[1] Consolidated rather than combined statements are assumed. In this way, intrasector claims can be neglected. Net worths are indicated by "N."

Households	
$\overline{P}$	$\overline{B}_{ch}$
$\overline{B}_{hc}$	N_h

Business	
$\overline{P}$	$\overline{B}_{hc}$
$\overline{B}_{ch}$	N_b

and dual-market identification of transactions. An idealized accounting system further assumes that all transactions can be analyzed on an institutionally defined basis. Production data, however, is on an establishment-commodity basis as opposed to a company classification. Reconciling company and commodity establishment data by linkage studies might be a way out but so far nothing has been accomplished in terms of the fundamental criteria: allocating financial flows on an establishment basis.[2]

<u>The UN System of National Accounts.</u> With all these limitations in mind, the closest to an idealized set of accounts becomes the integrated set of accounts proposed by the UN Statistical Office (United Nations, 1968).[3] These accounts are still a great distance from current statistical practice.[4]

The SNA Matrix. The integrated SNA accounts in symbolic form are shown in Table VII.2. This table has 28 rows and columns and has submatrices in 82 of the cells.[5]

Opening assets are the first of seven sections to the matrix. Across row 1 are locally issued financial assets held by institutional sectors (T1.23) and the rest of the world (T1.24). Tangible assets in row 2 (T2.23) are shown only for resident sectors since by definition when such assets are owned by the rest of the world they are treated as financial assets. Similarly, foreign assets are uniformly treated as financial assets for resident institutional sectors. Down the first column are shown sector financial liabilities--domestic (T23.1) and foreign (T24.1).[6] Column 2 shows domestic (T23.2) and foreign (T24.2) net worths. The latter is positive when the rest of the world has net claims on the country in question.

The flow accounts begin with production which is subdivided into accounts for commodities and activities (industries, producers of government services, private services), to household goods and services and to inventories and capital formation. Commodity taxes are allocated to these outputs in row 4. Activities in rows 5-7 are identified by their commodity

TABLE VII.2 A SYMBOLIC REPRESENTATION OF THE SNA

				1	2	3	4	5	6	7	8	9	10	11	12	13	14
Opening assets		Financial assets	1														
		Net tangible assets	2														
Production	Commodities	Commodities, basic value	3					$T_{3.5}$	$T_{3.6}$	$T_{3.7}$	$T_{3.8}$						
		Commodity taxes, net	4					$T_{4.5}$	$T_{4.6}$	$T_{4.7}$	$T_{4.8}$						
	Activities	Industries	5			$T_{5.3}$	$T_{5.4}$										
		Producers of government services	6			$T_{6.3}$					$T_{6.8}$	$T_{6.9}$					
		Private services: domestic service and producers of private n-p services	7			$T_{7.3}$					$T_{7.8}$		$T_{7.10}$				
Consumption	Expenditure	Household goods and services	8														$T_{8.14}$
		Government purposes	9														$T_{9.14}$
		Purposes of private n-p bodies	10														$T_{10.14}$
	Income and outlay	Value added	11			$T_{11.3}$	$T_{11.4}$	$T_{11.5}$	$T_{11.6}$	$T_{11.7}$							
		Institutional sector of origin	12											$T_{12.11}$			
		Form of income	13												$T_{13.12}$		$T_{13.14}$
		Institutional sector of receipt	14											$T_{14.11}$		$T_{14.13}$	
Accumulation	Increase in stocks	Industries	15														
		Producers of government services	16														
	Fixed capital formation	Industries	17														
		Producers of government services	18														
		Producers of private non-profit services to households	19														
	Capital Finance	Industrial capital formation, land, etc.	20														
		Capital transfers	21														
		Financial assets	22														
		Institutional sectors	23	$T_{23.1}$	$T_{23.2}$												$T_{23.14}$
Rest of the world: current and capital transactions			24	$T_{24.1}$	$T_{24.2}$	$T_{24.3}$			$T_{24.6}$		$T_{24.8}$					$T_{24.13}$	
Evaluation		Financial assets	25														
		Net tangible assets	26														
Closing assets		Financial assets	27														
		Net tangible assets	28														
				1	2	3	4	5	6	7	8	9	10	11	12	13	14

(Table VII.2 continued)

				15	16	17	18	19	20	21	22	23	24	25	26	27	28
Opening assets		Financial assets	1											$T_{1.25}$	$T_{1.26}$		
		Net tangible assets	2											$T_{2.25}$			
Production	Com-modi-ties	Commodities, basic value	3	$T_{3.15}$	$T_{3.16}$	$T_{3.17}$	$T_{3.18}$	$T_{3.19}$					$T_{3.24}$				
		Commodity taxes, net	4	$T_{4.15}$		$T_{4.17}$	$T_{4.18}$	$T_{4.19}$					$T_{4.24}$				
	Activi-ties	Industries	5														
		Producers of government services	6														
		Private services: domestic service and producers of private n-p services	7														
Consumption	Expendi-ture	Household goods and services	8										$T_{8.24}$				
		Government purposes	9														
		Purposes of private n-p bodies	10														
	Income and outlay	Value added	11									$T_{11.23}$					
		Institutional sector of origin	12														
		Form of income	13										$T_{13.24}$				
		Institutional sector of receipt	14														
Accumulation	In-crease in stocks	Industries	15						$T_{15.20}$								
		Producers of government services	16									$T_{16.23}$					
	Fixed capital formation	Industries	17						$T_{17.20}$								
		Producers of government services	18									$T_{18.23}$					
		Producers of private non-profit services to households	19									$T_{19.23}$					
	Capital Finance	Industrial capital formation, land, etc.	20									$T_{20.23}$					
		Capital transfers	21														
		Financial assets	22									$T_{22.23}$	$T_{22.24}$				
		Institutional sectors	23							$T_{23.21}$	$T_{23.22}$			$T_{23.25}$	$T_{23.26}$	$T_{23.27}$	$T_{23.28}$
Rest of the world:		current and capital transactions	24							$T_{24.21}$	$T_{24.22}$		$T_{24.24}$	$T_{24.25}$	$T_{24.26}$	$T_{24.27}$	$T_{24.28}$
Evaluation		Financial assets	25									$T_{25.23}$	$T_{25.24}$				
		Net tangible assets	26									$T_{26.23}$					
Closing assets		Financial assets	27									$T_{27.23}$	$T_{27.24}$				
		Net tangible assets	28									$T_{28.23}$					
				15	16	17	18	19	20	21	22	23	24	25	26	27	28

Source: U.N., A System of National Accounts, 1968, opp., p. 32.

composition in column 3. While T3.5 represents the submatrix of inputs or commodities into industries, T5.3 represents the distribution of commodities by the industries producing them.

"Consumption" is divided into two parts--consumption expenditure and income and outlay. The inputs for household goods and services as shown in column 8 originate in the production sector (rows 3, 4, 6, 7) and include resident expenditures abroad (T24.8). Row 8 shows the allocation of household goods and services to final consumption by institutional sectors (T8.14) and to expenditures by nonresidents in the domestic market (T8.24).

By means of the income and outlay accounts, the value added in production--compensation of employees, operating surplus, consumption of fixed capital, indirect taxes--is assigned to the institutional sectors in which the value added originates and subsequently allocated to the sector of receipt of income. First in row 11, value added is assembled from the production sectors. T11.3 and T11.4 stand for import duties, T11.5, 6, 7 measure value added for industries, government, and nonprofit services. The submatrix T11.23 signifies depreciation which is assigned to institutional sectors with a negative sign. By means of T12.11, value added once assembled is assigned to institutional sectors--nonfinancial enterprises (corporations and quasi-corporate), financial institutions, general government, households, and private nonprofit institutions. In T13.12 compensations of employees and operating surpluses arising in institutional sectors are classified by component forms of income. For example, compensation of employees is split into wages and salaries and employees' contributions to pension funds (SNA, 1968, p. 34). "Current income transfers" are added to previous income categories in T13.14 and T13.24.[7] "Current income transfers" (they are not included in value added) are paid out by institutional sectors now defined as sector of receipt (row and column 14). T13.14 would show, for example, the amounts paid out in property income. On the income and outlay account of institutional sectors, this amount appears on the "outgoing" side. "Incomings" on this account show up in the next row ("institutional sector of receipt") in the T14.13 matrix. In T14.11 indirect taxes net paid to general government are recorded.

The accounts for accumulation consist of accounts for capital formation and for capital finance. Capital formation as shown in lines 15-19 is further subdivided into "stocks" (inventories) and fixed capital formation. Since the capital formation accounts are classified by industry (rows 15, 17), whereas the capital finance accounts are classified by institutional sector (line 23), "dummy" transactions are necessary to intermediate between the two types of classification and avoid an industry times sector interaction in the capital accounts. Thus capital formation by industries in rows 15 and 17 is absorbed by the dummy account "industrial capital formation" (T15.20 and T17.20) and then purchased by institutional sectors via their capital finance account (T20.23). The dummy account here plays the same role as "value added" that assembled factor payments originating in production. Dummy accounts are not necessary for producers of government services (rows 16 and 18) and for producers of private nonprofit services to households (row 19) since they are already defined on an institutional basis. Capital formation is assigned directly to these sectors. Capital transfers (row 21) show no entries. They are defined as unrequited transfers, e.g., investment grants, which are not considered by the recipient as adding to his current income or by the payer as reducing his current income (SNA, 1968, p. 131). The column entry (T23.21) records net receipts of capital transfers by institutional sectors.

The net acquisition of financial assets by institutional sectors (T22.23) and by the rest of the world (T22.24) are next. The flow entries in row 23 for institutional sectors include saving which is shown as a transaction between institutional sectors (T23.14). Thus, saving is an "outgoing" on the income and outlay account for institutions and an "incoming" in their capital finance account (SNA, 1968, tables 2.8, 2.11, pp. 25, 27). Net issues of financial liabilities by institutional sectors are shown in submatrix T23.22.

On the row, T24.1 for the rest of the world records their financial liabilities held by resident institutional sectors at the beginning of the period. The next submatrix T24.2 contains a single number, the net worth of the rest of the world at the beginning of the period. This will be the difference between financial assets held by the rest of the world and its financial liabilities. T24.3 stands for imports of commodities measured at c.i.f. values. T24.6 and T24.8 respectively show direct expenditures abroad by the producers of government services (e.g., military expenditures) and final consumption expenditures abroad by resident households. In T24.13 gross receipts of income by the rest of the world are shown. Net receipts of capital transfers and net issues of financial liabilities by the rest of the world are in the next two matrices. The balance of payments surplus is recorded in the T24.24 matrix. Assuming separate treatment of current and capital account transactions (as is done in the more detailed Table 2.1), a single figure would be entered at the intersection of the capital row and current column.

The next two submatrices deal with the revaluation section of the accounting system and stand for the revaluation of financial liabilities issued by the rest of the world (T24.26). Revaluations reflect changes in the market value of assets and liabilities. Finally, closing liabilities and net worth for the rest of the world are given in the last matrices of row 24.

In the revaluations row number 25, the first submatrix shown (T25.23) revalues financial assets held by institutional sectors. The second matrix revalues financial assets held by the rest of the world (T25.24). In the next row, T26.23 stands for the revaluation of net tangible assets. In the second last row, which is one of the two rows describing closing assets, final holdings of financial assets by institutional sectors (T27.23) and by the rest of the world (T27.24) are shown. In the final row, closing net tangible assets are recorded by institutional sector (28.23).

The SNA matrix has been described in detail because it represents an idealized set of transactions or flow-of-funds accounts. From this perspective, the published flow-of-funds accounts are a partial set of transactions accounts, limited principally to the submatrices shown in rows 22 and 23 under "capital finance" and to closing balance sheets (row and column 27). We begin our review of the best-known accounts with the U.S. Federal Reserve accounts.

U.S. FEDERAL RESERVE ACCOUNTS

The Summary Matrix. The Federal Reserve flow-of-funds accounts are the first and best known of all the national accounts.[8] The basic structure is illustrated in a sample matrix (Table VII.3).

The matrix constitutes a breakdown by sector of the capital (saving and investment) account of the national income and product accounts. Unlike its early intentions, the flow of funds have become an elaboration of the national income accounts (Cohen, 1972, p. 16; Federal Reserve, 1980, pp. 27-31).

In Table VII.3, transactions categories are shown across the rows, sectors down the columns. The flow-of-funds saving and investment concepts are modifications of the NIP concepts, the principal modification being the inclusion of consumer durables in the FOF definitions (Federal Reserve, 1980, Table 4, p. 27). Saving for each sector is arrived at by subtracting its outlays for consumption or operating expenses (the latter apply to business and government) from current income receipts (which, for the government sector, would largely be taxes).

Capital outlays equal the sector's physical investment (housing, consumer durables, plant and equipment, inventories). Saving and capital outlays are equal for the entire economy including the rest of the world sector. This equality of saving and capital outlays over all sectors which is a major tenet of the income and product accounts, is our first identity. Thus, saving (179 plus -18 plus 5 plus 4) equals 170, which equals capital outlays 170.

TABLE VII.3 AN ABBREVIATED FLOW-OF-FUNDS TABLE WITH NUMERICAL VALUES

(Hypothetical data; billions of dollars)

Transaction Category	Private domestic non financial sec.		Government Sector		Financial intermediaries sector		Rest of world sector		Totals		Memo: domestic totals	
	Dr	Cr	Dr	Cr	Dr	Cr	Dr	Cr	Dr	Cr	Dr	Cr
Nonfinancial:												
1. Saving		179		-18 [10]		5		4 [-4]		170		166 [174]
2. Capital outlays	170		--		--		--		170		170	
Financial:												
3. Net financial investment	9		-18 [-10]		5		4 [-4]		0		-4 [4]	
4. Total financial uses and sources (5+6)	69	60	5	23 [15]	70	65	11 [3]	7	155 [147]	155 [147]	144 [144]	148 [140]
5. Deposits at financial intermediaries	50		3			55	2		55	55	53	55
6. Loans and securities	19	60	2	23 [15]	70	10	9 [1]	7	100	100	91	93

Source: Based on Board of Governors of the Federal Reserve System, Introduction to Flow of Funds (Washington, DC 1975), Table 1, p. 3.

The saving for the rest of the world (4) reflects the net value of transactions between the rest of the world and the domestic economy. This value tells us that the U.S. domestic economy was making four billion less financial investment in the rest of the world than the latter was making in the U.S. domestic economy. If we exclude the positive saving of the rest of the world, we arrive at the domestic total (in the last column) which consequently will be 4 billions lower, or $166 billion.

A second identity underlying the matrix is the equality of credits (sources of funds) and debits (uses of funds) for each sector. Alternative totals can be estimated depending on the degree of netting (the extent to which credit and debit values are offset against each other). For example, on a gross basis, total financial uses for the private domestic nonfinancial sector would be 69 which, added on to capital outlays, gives a total of 239. This total is equal to saving (179) plus financial sources (60). If financial sources are offset against financial uses in line four to give net financial investment of 9, this amount plus capital outlays of 170 equal 179, which is the smaller amount of sources of funds via saving. Capital outlays plus net financial investment equal saving, both on the sectoral and aggregate level.

The saving-investment identity for individual sectors differs from the saving-capital outlay identity for all sectors combined (the first identity). Now net financial investment must be added on to a sector's capital outlays in order for the identity with saving to hold for the individual sector. For all sectors, net financial investment is zero, as can be seen by totaling the values across line three. Thus, for all sectors, saving equals capital outlays (the initial identity).

Lines five and six of the table spell out the lender-borrower characteristics of each sector. The nonfinancial sector, for example, was a net lender but at the same time it was a borrower via loans and securities of 60. This borrowing is offset against the total of financial uses, of deposits at financial intermediaries (50) and loans and securities (19).

Unlike the nonfinancial sector, which subtracts only current outlays from income in estimating saving, for the government sector the prevailing accounting practice is to subtract all outlays. The deficit of 18 (saving = -18) shown for the government sector thus overstates the "true" deficit since some government outlays deserve to be treated as capital outlays (highway construction, new government buildings, for example). Corresponding to negative saving of -18 for the government is -18 of net financial investment. Thus the underlying sector identity holds.

Despite its deficit position, the government lends directly (line six) and indirectly via financial institutions (line five). Its total borrowing (including borrowing to finance the deficit) exceeds its lending, thus explaining the negative overall value of -18.

The saving (5 billion) of the next sector, financial intermediaries, makes it possible for them to lend 5 billion more than they borrow (70-65). Finally, the rest of the world sector, like the government sector, acquires financial assets in excess of its surplus (saving) as shown in lines five and six.

The equality of sources and uses across financial transaction rows (lines five and six and summary row four) are a third category of identities. This identity follows from a financial debit being a corresponding credit on another sector's account. In an overall sense, taking all sectors together (considering them as one huge sector) finance "cancels out." Financial uses and sources would be internal to this consolidated sector, so they lose their character as financial claims. Zero net financial investment for all sectors combined as shown in the second last "total" column, line three, is another way of seeing that finance "disappears." As emphasized in the earlier theoretical chapters, this downgrades the importance of finance.

"Net financial investment" is a key line for checking on the accuracy of any flow-of-funds matrix. Whether we begin with financial flows (below line 3) and work up to line 3, or begin with nonfinancial flows and work down, one should secure the same answer for this row.

A good way of seeing the interrelationship of sectors and their transactions is to change one of the cell values in the matrix. It will quickly be discovered that many more cell values have to be changed if the constraints are to be satisfied. Changing a cell value will throw a transaction and sector balance out of kilter, requiring compensating adjustments along the transaction row, and down the column sector, which in turn will lead to other transaction and sectoral adjustments.[9]

Direct vs. Indirect Finance. The data in the sample matrix can be arranged to show total funds raised in credit markets in terms of direct and indirect sources of funds.[10] The table begins with the funds raised by nonfinancial sectors. These amount to $92 bns. with 70 constituting indirect borrowing. Direct borrowing of 22 is determined residually. Funds advanced by the nonfinancial sector (section II of Table VII.4), include 22 of direct lending and 65 of indirect lending. Indirect lending is 5 less than indirect borrowing of 70 from financial sectors since 5 of indirect lending by financial intermediaries is financed by saving.

"Funds advanced" by financial intermediaries in III are indirect (70). They exceed their indirect borrowing by the amount of intermediary saving of 5 shown in (IV).

The Summary Matrix for 1984. A summary flow-of-funds matrix for 1984 is given in Table VII.5. In addition to much more detail, both for sectors and transactions, the summary matrix differs from the model matrix by a discrepancy row and column.[11]

In this way, unaccounted entries in transaction rows and sector columns are absorbed. Since errors show up equally down the columns and across the rows, the sum of sector discrepancies equals the sum of transaction discrepancies (see the lower right-hand corner of the matrix). Discrepancies are defined in

TABLE VII.4

ESTIMATING DIRECT AND INDIRECT FINANCE ($ bns.)

Line				
1.	[ℓ.6]	I.	Funds Raised by Nonfinancial Sectors	92
2.	[ℓ.1-ℓ.3]		Direct Borrowing (Credit Market Borrowing)	22
3.	[ℓ.4] = ℓ7		Indirect Borrowing	70
4.	ℓ.1 - ℓ13	II.	Funds Advanced by Nonfinancial Sectors	87
5.	ℓ.2		Direct Lending	22
6.	ℓ 7 - ℓ13		Indirect Lending	65
7.	[ℓ.4]	III.	Funds Advanced by Financial Intermediaries	70
8.	[ℓ.4]		Indirect Lending	70
9.	[ℓ.4] + [ℓ.1]	IV.	Funds Raised by Financial Intermediaries	70
10.	[ℓ.4]		Indirect Borrowing	65
11.	[ℓ.5]		Deposits at Financial Intermediaries	55
12.	[ℓ.6]		Loans and securities (credit market borrowing)	10
13.	[ℓ1]		Saving	5

Note: Bracketed line references are to Table VII.3. Other line references are to lines in table.

TABLE VII.5 THE U.S. FLOW-OF-FUNDS MATRIX, 1984 ($ bns.)

	1	2	3	4	5	6	7	8	9	10	11	12	
	PRIVATE DOMESTIC NONFINANCIAL SECTORS								FOREIGN SECTOR		U.S. GOVERNMENT		
	HOUSEHOLDS		BUSINESS		STATE & LOCAL GOVERNMENTS		TOTAL						
	U	S	U	S	U	S	U	S	U	S	U	S	
1 GROSS SAVING		514.4		366.9		8.4		889.7		33.9		-192.9	1
2 CAPITAL CONSUMPTION		280.4		301.8				582.2					2
3 NET SAVING (1-2)		234.0		65.1		8.4		307.5		33.9		-192.9	3
4 GROSS INVESTMENT (5+11)	562.3		319.6		7.3		889.2		29.3		-202.0		4
5 PVT CAPITAL EXPENDITURES	400.4		339.7				740.1				-7.8		5
6 CONSUMER DURABLES	279.8						279.8						6
7 RESIDENTIAL CONSTRUCTION	108.2		24.1				132.2						7
8 PLANT AND EQUIPMENT	12.4		321.4				333.7						8
9 INVENTORY CHANGE			-13.5				-13.5						9
10 MINERAL RIGHTS			7.8				7.8				-7.8		10
11 NET FINANCIAL INVESTMENT	161.9		-20.1		7.3		149.1		29.3		-194.2		11
12 FINANCIAL USES	363.1		121.0		45.8		529.9		65.3		12.1		12
13 FINANCIAL SOURCES		201.2		141.1		38.4		380.7		36.0		206.3	13
14 GOLD & OFF. FGN. EXCHANGE									*	.5	2.7		14
15 TREASURY CURRENCY												.5	15
16 CHECKABLE DEPOSITS & CURR.	43.1		-2.4		-3.5		37.2		1.6		-8.1		16
17 U.S. GOVERNMENT											-8.1		17
18 FOREIGN									1.6				18
19 PRIVATE DOMESTIC	43.1		-2.4		-3.5		37.2						19
20 SMALL TIME & SAVINGS DEP.	214.2				5.3		219.5				-.5		20
21 MONEY MARKET FUND SHARES	-44.1						-44.1						21
22 LARGE TIME DEPOSITS	-15.3		16.6		-8.8		-7.5		.5				22
23 FED. FUNDS & SECURITY RP'S			11.2		3.0		14.3						23
24 FOREIGN DEPOSITS			4.8				4.8			3.0			24
25 LIFE INSURANCE RESERVES	8.0						8.0					.2	25
26 PENSION FUND RESERVES	136.2						136.2					14.1	26
27 INTERBANK CLAIMS									20.1				27
28 CORPORATE EQUITIES	6.0			28.3			6.0	28.3	5.4	4.0			28
29 CREDIT MKT. INSTRUMENTS	70.9	190.4	24.2	124.3	47.7	37.6	142.8	352.3	27.1	18.9	9.7	186.6	29
30 U.S. TREASURY SECURITIES	39.4		5.0		31.1		75.5		16.9			186.7	30
31 FEDERAL AGENCY SECURITIES	2.8		*		10.0		12.8				-	*	31
32 STATE & LOCAL GOVT. SECUR.	42.3	11.4	.7	9.4	.6	36.5	43.5	57.3					32
33 CORPORATE & FOREIGN BONDS	-9.2			16.0			-9.2	16.0	4.9	3.8			33
34 MORTGAGES	-.1	112.6		63.1	6.0		5.9	175.7			1.2	-.1	34
35 CONSUMER CREDIT		59.8	7.8				7.8	59.8					35
36 BANK LOANS N.E.C.		3.4		23.4				26.7		4.9			36
37 OPEN-MARKET PAPER	-4.1		10.7	-1.6			6.5	-1.6	5.4	6.0			37
38 OTHER LOANS		3.3		13.9		1.1		18.3		4.3	8.5		38
39 SECURITY CREDIT	2.4	8.4					2.4	8.4	-	-			39
40 TRADE CREDIT		1.8	54.6	37.2		.8	54.6	39.8	-1.1	.2	3.8	3.0	40
41 TAXES PAYABLE				5.8	1.9		1.9	5.8			3.7		41
42 EQUITY IN NONCORP. BUS.	-66.4			-66.4			-66.4	-66.4					42
43 MISCELLANEOUS	8.0	.6	12.0	11.9			20.0	12.5	11.8	9.4	.7	2.0	43
44 SECTOR DISCREPANCIES (1-4)	-47.8		47.3		1.0		.5		4.6		9.1		44

TABLE VII.5 continued

	13	14	15	16	17	18	19	20	21	22	23	24	
	FINANCIAL SECTORS												
	TOTAL		SPONS. & MTG.	AG. POOLS	MONETARY AUTHORITY		COMMERCIAL BANKING		PVT. NONBANK FINANCE		ALL SECTORS		
	U	S	U	S	U	S	U	S	U	S	U	S	
1 GROSS SAVING		20.2		1.5		.5		14.3		3.9		751.0	1
2 CAPITAL CONSUMPTION		13.2						10.1		3.1		595.4	2
3 NET SAVING (1-2)		7.0		1.5		.5		4.2		.8		155.5	3
4 GROSS INVESTMENT (5+11)	32.2		.9		.5		23.0		7.8		748.7		4
5 PVT. CAPITAL EXPENDITURES	19.1						15.2		4.0		751.4		5
6 CONSUMER DURABLES											279.8		6
7 RESIDENTIAL CONSTRUCTION	*								*		132.2		7
8 PLANT AND EQUIPMENT	19.2						15.2		4.0		352.9		8
9 INVENTORY CHANGE											-13.5		9
10 MINERAL RIGHTS													10
11 NET FINANCIAL INVESTMENT	1[illegible].0		.9		.5		7.8		3.9		-2.8		11
12 FINANCIAL USES	555.3		68.4		9.4		148.4		329.0		1162.5		12
13 FINANCIAL SOURCES		542.2		67.6		8.9		140.6		325.1		1165.2	13
14 GOLD & OFF. FOR. EXCHANGE	-2.1				-2.1						.5	.5	14
15 TREASURY CURRENCY	.7				.7						.7	.5	15
16 CHECKABLE DEPOSITS & CURR.	7.2	39.5	.2			13.0	2.2	15.9	4.8	10.6	37.9	39.5	16
17 U.S. GOVERNMENT		-6.7				-1.3		-5.3			-8.1	-6.7	17
18 FOREIGN		1.6				*		1.6			1.6	1.6	18
19 PRIVATE DOMESTIC	7.2	44.5	.2			14.3	2.2	19.7	4.8	10.6	44.4	44.5	19
20 SMALL TIME & SAVINGS DEP.	-1.3	217.7						130.0	-1.3	87.8	217.7	217.7	20
21 MONEY MARKET FUND SHARES		-44.1								-44.1	-44.1	-44.1	21
22 LARGE TIME DEPOSITS	-11.1	-18.1						-52.3	-11.1	34.2	-18.1	-18.1	22
23 FED. FUNDS & SECURITY RP'S	9.5	24.0	-2.3					10.2	11.8	13.9	23.8	24.0	23
24 FOREIGN DEPOSITS	-1.8								-1.8		3.0	3.0	24
25 LIFE INSURANCE RESERVES		7.8								7.8	8.0	8.0	25
26 PENSION FUND RESERVES		122.2								122.2	136.2	136.2	26
27 INTERBANK CLAIMS	-4.6	14.4			-1.0	-3.6	-3.6	18.0			15.5	14.4	27
28 CORPORATE EQUITIES	56.4	35.5					*	.7	56.4	34.8	67.8	67.8	28
29 CREDIT MKT. INSTRUMENTS	463.4	85.2	69.8	67.8	10.9		136.1	8.4	246.6	9.0	643.0	643.0	29
30 U.S. TREASURY SECURITIES	94.3		-.8		12.6		45.5		36.9		186.7	186.7	30
31 FEDERAL AGENCY SECURITIES	55.0	67.8	-.4	67.8	-.7		.7		55.4		67.8	67.8	31
32 STATE & LOCAL GOVT. SECUR.	13.8						3.9		10.0		57.3	57.3	32
33 CORPORATE & FOREIGN BONDS	32.8	8.6					3.9	4.9	28.8	3.6	28.4	28.4	33
34 MORTGAGES	168.6	*	76.8				29.2		62.5	*	175.6	175.6	34
35 CONSUMER CREDIT	51.9						22.7		29.2		59.8	59.8	35
36 BANK LOANS N.E.C.	31.4	-.2			-		31.4			-.2	31.4	31.4	36
37 OPEN-MARKET PAPER	8.5	16.0	.4		-1.1		-1.4	3.5	10.6	12.6	20.4	20.4	37
38 OTHER LOANS	7.1	-7.0	-6.1	-					13.2	-7.0	15.5	15.5	38
39 SECURITY CREDIT	9.8	3.8									12.2	12.2	39
40 TRADE CREDIT	2.0						2.4		7.4	3.8	59.2	43.0	40
41 TAXES PAYABLE		*						-.1	2.0	.1	5.7	5.8	41
42 EQUITY IN NONCORP. BUS.											-66.4	-66.4	42
43 MISCELLANEOUS	27.3	54.3	.7	-.2	1.0	-.5	11.3	9.9	14.4	45.1	59.8	78.3	43
44 SECTOR DISCREPANCIES (1-4)	-11.9		.7		-		-8.7		-3.9		2.3		44

TABLE VII.5 continued

		25 DISCR. U	26 NATL. SVG. & INV.	
1	GROSS SAVING		717.1	1
2	CAPITAL CONSUMPTION		595.4	2
3	NET SAVING (1-2)		121.6	3
4	GROSS INVESTMENT (5+11)	2.3	722.2	4
5	PVT. CAPITAL EXPENDITURES	-.5	751.4	5
6	CONSUMER DURABLES		279.8	6
7	RESIDENTIAL CONSTRUCTION		132.2	7
8	PLANT AND EQUIPMENT		352.9	8
9	INVENTORY CHANGE		-13.5	9
10	MINERAL RIGHTS			10
11	NET FINANCIAL INVESTMENT	2.8	-29.3	11
12	FINANCIAL USES	2.8	36.0	12
13	FINANCIAL SOURCES		65.3	13
14	GOLD & OFF. FGN. EXCHANGE			14
15	TREASURY CURRENCY	-.2		15
16	CHECKABLE DEPOSITS & CURR.	1.5		16
17	U.S. GOVERNMENT	1.4		17
18	FOREIGN			18
19	PRIVATE DOMESTIC	.1		19
20	SMALL TIME & SAVINGS DEP.			20
21	MONEY MARKET FUND SHARES			21
22	LARGE TIME DEPOSITS			22
23	FED. FUNDS & SECURITY RP'S	.3		23
24	FOREIGN DEPOSITS			24
25	LIFE INSURANCE RESERVES			25
26	PENSION FUND RESERVES			26
27	INTERBANK CLAIMS	-1.1		27
28	CORPORATE EQUITIES			28
29	CREDIT MKT. INSTRUMENTS			29
30	U.S. TREASURY SECURITIES			30
31	FEDERAL AGENCY SECURITIES			31
32	STATE & LOCAL GOVT. SECUR.			32
33	CORPORATE & FOREIGN BONDS			33
34	MORTGAGES			34
35	CONSUMER CREDIT			35
36	BANK LOANS N.E.C.			36
37	OPEN-MARKET PAPER			37
38	OTHER LOANS			38
39	SECURITY CREDIT			39
40	TRADE CREDIT	-16.2		40
41	TAXES PAYABLE	.1		41
42	EQUITY IN NONCORP. BUS.			42
43	MISCELLANEOUS	18.4		43
44	SECTOR DISCREPANCIES (1-4)	2.3	-5.1	44

Source: Federal Reserve, Flow-of-Funds Section (Washington, D.C., 1985) terms of sources minus uses and listed under uses. The discrepancies for the individual sectors and overall are based on the difference between gross saving and gross investment. The latter equals capital outlays and net financial investment. Discrepancy entries reflect various kinds of statistical errors and various kinds of inconsistencies: in valuation bases, in timing, in classification of transactions and omissions of pertinent transactions or transactors from the accounts (Federal Reserve, 1955, p. 372).

Discrepancies are shifted when an entry is calculated as the residual in the account. The residual will be allocated to a sector for which specific data are inadequate. This explains why the discrepancy for the household sector is large. Since there is little direct information on the activities of consumers as such, the data is derived residually by deducting particicipation of other groups from control totals or by using and adjusting the records of the other parties to the transaction (Federal Reserve, 1955, p. 54). The household discrepancy is thus the final resting place for data inconsistencies throughout the system (Federal Reserve, 1980, p. 47).

The statistical discrepancies in the flow-of-funds accounts have been subjected to regression analysis. Each "endogenous" sector discrepancy was made a function of "exogenous" transaction discrepancies (Hendershott, 1977, appendix E). The effort was not deemed to be very successful (Hendershott, 1977, p. 360). Among his strongest results as pointed out by De Leeuw (1984, p. 21), were the relations between household and nonfinancial business discrepancies and the errors and omissions category of the rest of the world.

The alternative approach is to regress sector discrepancies on lagged values of the dependent variables and lagged values of the overall discrepancy. This approach has proven quite successful in a study of U.S. and Canadian discrepancies (Cohen and Husted, 1985). Introducing interest-rate differentials, trade flows, and the level of international investment into rest of the world discrepancy equations greatly improved estimation results for both countries.

The Fed publishes detailed flow-of-funds and financial asset and liabilities tables by sector and by instrument. In 1982 for the first time complete sector balance sheets for the private sectors of the economy were published. Estimates of tangible assets and land were combined with financial assets and liabilities to produce measures of net worth (Federal Reserve, October 1982; October 1985). The U.S. also pioneered the development of seasonally adjusted quarterly accounts (Federal Reserve, November 1962).

Integrated Economic Accounts for the United States. A promising recent development is the expansion of the national income and product accounts (NIPA) along the lines of the institutional sectoring of the flow of funds.[12] The potential is there for the elaboration of current accounts similar to those found in the pioneering Federal Reserve 1985 study. Consistent with our theorizing about the flow of funds, the Ruggles emphasize the primary function of the NIPA is to provide a framework for displaying the interactions of different sectors (enterprises) (Ruggles and Ruggles, November 1982, p. 44). Market transactions and nonmarket imputations are clearly distinguished in the accounts. The decision on classifying a transaction as actual or imputed depends on how the transactors view it (May 1982, p. 9). The proposed modification of the accounts makes it possible for the national accounts to serve as a framework for both macro and micro data.[13] This will lead to extensive disaggregation of the accounts by institutional sector. While sector saving figures are acknowledged as lacking a transactions content, nevertheless, the concept plays a major role in their economic interpretation of the accounting data (Ruggles and Ruggles, May 1982, pp. 49-53).

As compared with the SNA accounts, an advance in the integrated economic accounts (IEA) is the attempt to treat production along enterprise rather than along strictly establishment ("functional") lines. What is lacking, however, is an interlocking of the accounts by means of a summary matrix. For example, the capital and current accounts are shown separately. This obscures their obvious "togetherness" (see comments of Taylor, May 1982, pp. 68-69). The edifice of an integrated accounting system can be better appreciated when the bricks are in place than when they are laid out separately.

THE CANADIAN ACCOUNTS

National transactions accounts for Canada (later called the financial flow accounts) were presented for the first time as part of a study on financing economic activity in Canada, 1946-1954.[14] In this pioneering study the summary matrix tables included detail on current nonfinancial transactions. The published matrix now begins as with the U.S. accounts with saving and capital outlays. Statistics Canada prepares financial flow accounts on a quarterly basis and publishes partial year-end balance sheets.[15] In 1986 full balance sheets were published for the first time (Statistics Canada 1986).

Canada alone of all the major producers of flow of funds assigns this function to its chief statistical agency without involving the central bank. This causes problems because of conflicts with data prepared by the Bank of Canada--besides having a longer lag. The Bank of Canada has begun to take a serious interest in the flow of funds. It would be hoped that Statistics Canada and the Bank of Canada would ultimately prepare a single set of financial accounts.

The financial matrix for 1984 features 13 sectors (Table VII.6). Unincorporated business, unlike the U.S. breakdown, is part of the personal (household) sector. A single entry form of accounts is followed as compared with the double entry form for the U.S. The financial transaction stub has to be repeated twice--once for assets and once for liabilities. The discrepancy column ("residual error of estimate") contains only three entries. They carry over to the flow-of-funds accounts the discrepancy in the Canadian national income and expenditure accounts. On the assumption that each series is equally

TABLE VII.6 CANADIAN FINANCIAL FLOWS MATRIX, 1984, ($ bns.)

Category		Sector: I&II. Persons and Unincorp'd Business	III. Non-financial Private Corporations	IV. Non-financial Government Enterprises	V. The Monetary Authorities	VI.1 Chartered Banks	VI.2 Near-Banks
		Millions of dollars					
1100	Gross Saving	51242	24257	2104	6	621	219
1101	Residual Error of Estimate, NIEA	...	...	...	...	...	...
1200	C.C.A. and Misc. Valuation Adjustments	12436	22719	2708	6	149	66
1400	Net saving	38806	1538	-604	...	472	153
1500	Non-Financial Capital Acquisition	13044	27609	12691	6	452	315
1501	Residual Error of Estimate, NIEA	...	...	...	...	...	...
1600	Gross Fixed Capital Formation	15736	37118	12877	6	452	204
1700	Value of Physical Change in Inventories	437	-10014	-244	...	...	...
1800	Net Purchases of Existing Assets	-3129	505	58	...	-	111
1900	Net Lending or Borrowing (1100-1500)	38198	-3352	-10587	-	169	-96
2000	Net Financial Investment (2100-3100)	36162	-3998	-8365	-3	456	-97
2100	Net Increase in Financial Assets	38484	10880	3048	-2030	-3964	14418
2210	Official International Reserves	...	...	...	-666	...	...
2310	Currency and Deposits	9449	-1103	562	...	723	1384
2311	Currency and Bank Deposits	-1791	-2632	576	...	1276	491
2312	Deposits in Other Institutions	9839	352	101	...	...	280
2313	Foreign Currency and Deposits	1401	1177	-115	...	-553	613
2321	Consumer credit	-22	-49	...	...	237	56
2322	Trade	...	1624	329	...	...	...
2330	Loans	...	664	708	105	-5164	788
2340	Government of Canada Treasury Bills	1146	1346	46	-2820	1462	1035
2350	Finance and Other Short Term Paper	2196	404	-45	-	-223	2606
2410	Mortgages	250	391	18	...	-5392	7234
2420	Bonds	5943	-39	-49	1277	71	921
2430	Life Insurance and Pensions	14330	...	...	...	...	...
2510	Claims on Associated Enterprises	...	6709	27	-	4701	261
2520	Stocks	2516	286	170	...	-738	-51
2530	Foreign Investments	192	-198	-	...	93	40
2610	Other Financial Assets	2484	845	1282	74	266	144
3100	Net Increase in Liabilities	2322	14878	11413	-2027	-4420	14515
3210	Official International Reserves	...	...	...	...	...	...
3310	Currency and Deposits	...	...	...	-50	-5121	10818
3311	Currency and Bank Deposits	...	...	...	-50	-1940	...
3312	Deposits in Other Institutions	...	...	...	...	...	10815
3313	Foreign Currency and Deposits	...	...	...	...	-3181	3
3321	Consumer Credit	-193	...	...	...	...	...
3322	Trade	2677	-800	225	...	...	...
3330	Loans	-3541	2261	1521	...	105	-433
3331	Bank Loans	-1941	20	919	...	...	-89
3332	Other Loans	-1600	2241	602	...	105	-344
3340	Government of Canada Treasury Bills	...	...	...	...	...	...
3350	Finance and Other Short Term Paper	1	503	-87	...	...	2383
3410	Mortgages	3342	1337	-2	...	...	2
3420	Bonds	36	2838	5277	...	769	-367
3430	Life Insurance and Pensions	...	...	...	...	...	...
3510	Claims on Associated Enterprises	...	4741	3392	-2012	-	619
3520	Stocks	...	3805	-61	...	817	382
3530	Foreign Investments	...	...	...	...	...	...
3610	Other Liabilities	...	193	1148	35	-990	1111
4000	Discrepancy (1900-2000)	2036	646	-2222	3	-287	1

(Table VII.6 continued)

	Sector: VII. Insurance Companies & Pension Funds	VIII. Other Private Financial Institutions	IX. Public Financial Institutions	X. Federal Government	XI. Other Levels of Government and Hospitals	XII. Social Security Funds	XIII. Rest of the World	XIV. Residual Error of Estimate	Total
	Millions of dollars								
	55	169	-417	-19078	7070	3786	-1910	-93	68031
	...	...	...	...	...	...	...	-93	-93
	55	21	6	1046	5100	...	...	...	44312
	-	148	-423	-20124	1970	3786	-1910	...	23812
	1096	117	305	1456	9740	-	1107	93	68031
	...	...	...	...	...	...	...	93	93
	112	58	492	1350	9280	...	...	...	77685
	...	...	-	74	-	...	...	...	-9747
	984	59	-187	32	460	...	1107	...	-
	-1041	52	-722	-20534	-2670	3786	-3017	-186	-
	-1041	52	-964	-21100	-4797	3850	-155	-	-
	13131	1236	4031	-801	8751	3850	5871	...	96905
	...	...	...	...	...	...	...	...	-666
	896	234	369	-740	191	...	-5524	...	6471
	755	-4	64	-635	-16	...	112	...	-1804
	107	109	305	-	147	...	-1	...	11239
	34	159	-	-105	60	...	-5635	...	-2964
	210	-625	...	...	...	...	...	...	-193
	6	131	33	38	119	...	...	...	2280
	19	-1531	1114	320	281	...	1570	...	-1126
	861	1361	138	-	323	...	127	...	5025
	546	-314	133	7	-7	...	-1001	...	4302
	1457	-420	818	-30	428	...	-	...	4754
	5945	1260	1059	8	4673	2724	12092	...	35885
	...	...	...	...	...	...	...	...	14330
	301	902	61	469	2137	1052	-694	...	15926
	1931	-53	250	128	369	...	-368	...	4440
	673	-33	-	1	-	...	...	...	768
	286	294	56	-1002	237	74	-331	...	4709
	14172	1184	4995	20299	13548	-	6026	...	96905
	...	...	...	...	...	...	-666	...	-666
	...	77	347	186	...	...	214	...	6471
	...	...	...	186	...	...	...	...	-1804
	...	77	347	-	...	...	...	...	11239
	...	...	...	...	...	...	214	...	-2964
	...	...	...	...	...	...	...	...	-193
	7	9	13	-18	167	...	...	...	2280
	26	-104	24	-46	9	...	-948	...	-1126
	27	-407	-61	17	3	...	-3652	...	-5164
	-1	303	85	-63	6	...	2704	...	4038
	...	...	...	5025	...	...	...	...	5025
	...	-661	320	...	1843	...	...	...	4302
	52	9	12	...	2	...	-	...	4754
	...	256	1526	14297	...	...	...	...	35885
	14062	288	...	-20	...	...	...	...	14330
	-123	-1620	2164	124	130	...	6542	...	13957
	18	1448	-	...	...	...	...	...	6409
	...	...	...	...	...	...	768	...	758
	130	1482	389	751	144	...	116	...	4709
	-	-	242	566	2127	-64	-2862	-186	-

Source: Statistics Canada, *Financial Flow Accounts*, First Quarter 1985 (Ottawa, responsible, the error is split between gross saving (category 1100) and nonfinancial capital acquisition (1500). The sum of these errors (the third entry) yields the overall statistical discrepancy in the financial accounts.

Individual sector discrepancies are the difference between two different estimates of net lending or borrowing, one derived from nonfinancial (capital) transactions (category 1100 minus category 1500) and one derived from the detail on financial transactions--net financial investment (category 2000). This discrepancy is equivalent to subtracting nonfinancial capital acquisition (line 1500) and net financial investment (line 2000) from gross saving (line 11). When the value is positive it indicates that recorded credits exceed recorded debits: debits have been underestimated or credits overestimated. A negative value indicates the reverse--an excess of recorded debits over recorded credits--credits have been underestimated or debits overestimated. The same interpretation of the sign of the sector discrepancy applies to the U.S. accounts.

In contrast to Canada, in the U.S. accounts net financial investment (net lending or borrowing) is calculated in one way only, as the difference between financial uses and sources. While both accounts assume the sector identity of gross saving equaling gross investment which in turn equals capital outlays and net financial investment, the Canadian accounts initially assume that there is no statistical discrepancy in arriving at net lending and borrowing and then correct for this assumption by the second calculation (net financial investment). The U.S. accounts, on the other hand, allow the sector discrepancy to originate in the difference between gross saving and gross investment. This conceptual difference, however, doesn't affect estimation of the sector discrepancy which will be the same in both cases. Both approaches can be expressed in the following sector identity: Detailed lending minus detailed borrowing equals net financial investment equals net lending equals gross saving minus capital outlays. A discrepancy between net financial investment and net lending in the Canadian case will correspond exactly to the discrepancy between saving and the sum of capital outlays and net financial investment in the U.S. case.

Giving the identity arbitrary values,

$$\underset{L-B}{200\ 100} = \underset{NFI}{100} \neq \underset{NL}{200} = \underset{GS}{300} - \underset{CO}{100}$$

Under either approach, the sector discrepancy is 100. Thus under the Canadian method, NL - (L-B) equals 100. Under the U.S. method the discrepancy equals GS - (CO - NFI) equals 100.

Over all sectors, the U.S. statistical discrepancy reflects both the discrepancy in the national income accounts (see line 5 in Table VII.5, col. 25) and the discrepancy in net financial investment. In the Canadian accounts, in contrast, financial transaction debits and credits are forced into balance so that net financial investment is zero. The overall discrepancy is confined to the discrepancy between capital expenditures and gross saving in the national income and expenditure accounts. As a consequence, Canadian and U.S. economic accountants looking at the same data would come up with different measures of overall discrepancy.[16]

The Canadian accounts rate the quality of the data on the basis of letter grades--A is good, B is fair, and C is poor. The poorest data are for persons and unincorporated business, local governments, and hospitals. The best data are for financial institutions and the central government.

THE AUSTRALIAN ACCOUNTS

The Reserve Bank of Australia maintains the flow-of-funds accounts on a regular basis beginning with the fiscal 1953/54 year (see, e.g., Statistical Bulletin Supplements and occasional paper, 1979). The summary flow-of-funds matrix for 1983/84 is given in Table VII.7. In similar fashion to the Canadian accounts a single column is used for each sector with incurrence of liabilities being listed separately below acquisition of financial assets. Sector statistical discrepancy is calculated in the Canadian way as the difference between net lending (1.4) and

TABLE VII.7 SUMMARY MATRIX, AUSTRALIA

FINANCIAL FLOWS

1982 83 (PRELIMINARY) — $ million

	Reserve Bank	Other Banks (Consol.)	Life Off & Pension Funds	Other Financial Groups	C'wealth Govt	State & Local Govts	Corp Trading Enterp	Households	Rest of World	Discrep	TOTAL
A. Capital formation and saving											
1. Gross saving	79	666	718	1 376	-959	5 468	4 561	17 753	6 708	—	36 370
2. Gross capital formation											
stocks	—	—	—	27	249	276	-2 515	-539	—	—	-2 502
fixed capital	13	400	939	859	2 285	11 106	10 300	10 631	—	—	36 533
3. Capital transfers	—	—	—	—	278	98	-178	-198	—	—	0
Statistical adjustment	—	—	—	—	—	—	—	—	—	-2 339(a)	-2 339
4. Net lending (+) or borrowing (-)	66	266	-221	490	-3 771	-6 012	-3 046	7 859	6 708	-2 339	0
B. Financial account											
5. Acquisition of financial assets											
Bank deposits, notes and coin	-12	-76	57	743	112	361	726	1 956	94	—	3 961
Savings bank deposits	—	—	—	—	—	—	—	4 961	—	—	4 961
Advances of trading banks	—	1 792	—	—	—	—	—	—	—	—	1 792
Other advances	-26	3 253	441	2 666	1 064	221	—	—	4 903	—	12 522
Commonwealth government securities	-1 299	1 604	743	666	-120	-100	593	1 933	791	-102	4 709
Local and semi-governmental securities	—	371	758	569	—	—	—	1 438	1 569	—	4 705
Shares and deposits in co-operatives, etc	—	—	—	—	—	—	—	2 859	—	—	2 859
Ordinary and preference shares	—	320	1 273	316	—	—	—	-1 249	1 082	—	1 742
Debentures, notes and deposits	—	619	-29	441	-26	-20	800	1 354	340	—	3 479
Net contributions to life insurance, etc	—	—	—	—	—	—	—	753	-38	—	715
Interest on life and superannuation funds (imputed)	—	—	—	—	—	—	—	3 312	—	—	3 312
Trade credit: debtors	—	—	152	321	50	50	520	547	-59	—	1 581
Asset formation abroad											
gold, foreign exchange, etc	2 460	-342	—	—	—	—	—	—	—	—	2 118
other	—	18	—	—	286	—	394	269	—	—	967
Other claims	-125	3 471	175	2 447	—	—	—	-2 027	370	—	4 311
TOTAL	998	11 030	3 570	8 169	1 366	512	3 033	16 106	9 052	-102	53 734
6. Incurrence of liabilities											
Bank deposits, notes and coin	943	2 978	—	—	40	—	—	—	—	—	3 961
Savings bank deposits	—	4 961	—	—	—	—	—	—	—	—	4 961
Advances of trading banks	—	—	-145	-111	2	-89	395	1 740	—	—	1 792
Other advances	—	184	—	-135	—	1 051	6 980	4 442	—	—	12 522
Commonwealth government securities	—	—	—	—	4 709	—	—	—	—	—	4 709
Local and semi-governmental securities	—	—	—	—	505	4 200	—	—	—	—	4 705
Shares and deposits in co-operatives, etc	—	—	—	2 859	—	—	—	—	—	—	2 859
Ordinary and preference shares	—	132	—	549	—	—	1 061	—	—	—	1 742
Debentures, notes and deposits	—	—	68	3 211	—	50	150	—	—	—	3 479
Net contributions to life insurance, etc	—	—	715	—	—	—	—	—	—	—	715
Interest on life and superannuation funds (imputed)	—	—	3 312	—	—	—	—	—	—	—	3 312
Trade credit: creditors	—	—	67	1 148	—	—	366	—	—	—	1 581
Liabilities incurred abroad											
gold, foreign exchange, etc	—	—	—	—	—	—	—	—	2 118	—	2 118
other	—	—	—	—	—	—	—	—	967	—	967
Other claims	-11	2 668	—	141	-68	—	1 581	—	—	—	4 311
TOTAL	932	10 923	4 017	7 662	5 188	5 212	10 533	6 182	3 085	—	53 734
7. Financial surplus (+) or deficit (-)	66	107	-447	507	-3 822	-4 700	-7 500	9 924	5 967	-102	0
8. Difference (line 4 — line 7)	—	159	226	-17	51	-1 312	4 454	-2 065	741	-2 237	0
9. Net lending (+) or borrowing (-)(line 4)	66	266	-221	490	-3 771	-6 012	-3 046	7 859	6 708	-2 339	0

(a) Reflects the "statistical discrepancy" in the *Australian National Accounts* and other errors and omissions.

Source: Reserve Bank of Australia, Financial Flows, Bulletin Supplement (April 1985), p. 17.

financial surplus (1.7) based on detailed lending and borrowing.

THE JAPANESE ACCOUNTS

The Bank of Japan prepares the Japanese accounts (annual special papers; historical, 1978; and the Japanese Financial System, 1978). As shown in Table VII.8, for 1984, they are limited to financial transactions for nine elementary sectors but without saving-investment data. The double entry format is similar to the U.S. The line for financial surplus-deficit (line f) incorporates the statistical discrepancy. In addition to the transactions accounts, balance sheet accounts are prepared for the end of the year. The Bank of Japan began publishing accounts in 1954. The annual special paper offers a detailed summary of each sector's surplus-deficit behavior. The changes in the flow of funds and in sector surplus-deficit positions as a result of financial liberalization have recently been analyzed by a western author (Cargill, 1986).

THE UK ACCOUNTS

The first push toward developing official UK flow-of-funds accounts was given by the Radcliffe Committee report of 1959. They concluded that "monetary changes must be seen against a wider background of changes affecting the flow of funds to different parts of the economy" (Bank of England, 1978, p. 11). The accounts were also influenced by the U.S. flow-of funds accounts.

The annual matrix and quarterly tables (for 1963) were first published in 1964. Three different presentations were prepared initially--one by the Bank of England in the Quarterly Bulletin and two by the Central Statistical Office. The latter were published in National Income and Expenditure (the "Blue Book") and in monthly Financial Statistics. In April 1981 the three presentations moved to a more or less common format. (On details of their historical evolution, present structure, and a reliability rating of the data, see Alford, chaps. 2, 3, and Appendix 1.) The Bank of England matrix for 1984 is reproduced in Table VII.9. Since 1978, the main development in the UK financial accounts has been the progress toward sector balance

TABLE VII.8 FINANCIAL TRANSACTIONS ACCOUNTS FOR 1984, JAPAN (¥ bil.)

		Financial Institutions		The Bank of Japan		Private Financial Institutions		All banks		Other financial institutions		Public Financial Institutions		Central Government		Public Corporations & Local Authorities		Corporate Business		Personal		Rest-of-the-World		Total	
		A	L	A	L	A	L	A	L	A	L	A	L	A	L	A	L	A	L	A	L	A	L		
A	**Deposits to the Bank of Japan**	172	172		172	164		133		31		8												172	A
B	**Currency**		1,487		(a) 2,101	626		358		267		−11						148		1,339				1,487	B
C	**Demand Deposits**		4,512				4,684		2,778	−607	1,299	110	−62			25		1,909		2,577				4,512	C
D	**Time Deposits**		21,307				13,871		6,764	−267	6,839		7,436			283		3,198		17,824				21,307	D
D_2	**CDs**		2,622				2,708		2,425	21	304	85				342		2,273		7				2,622	D_2
E	**Non-resident Yen Deposits & Foreign Currency Deposits**		3,792				3,792		2,926		865													3,792	E
F	**Government Current Deposits**		2		2									2										2	F
G	**Trusts**		5,180				5,180	198		963	6,342					86		1,378		3,715				5,180	G
H	**Insurance**		9,326				6,545				6,545		2,780							9,326				9,326	H
I	**Securities**	22,762	9,776	(b) 2,239		14,904	8,480	2,260	3,201	12,643	5,278	5,618	1,296	−599	12,281	180	3,066	1,546	4,128	7,341		1,414		29,252	I
J	Short-term Government Securities	2,376		2,296		0.1				0.1		79		−2,231	(c) 123	47				881				123	J
K	Medium/long-term Government Bonds	9,507		−56		5,391		412		4,979		4,172		1,631	12,157	20								12,157	K
L	Local Government Bonds	748				299		−163		462		449					756	750		12		510		756	L
M	Public Corporation Bonds	2,806	1,161	−0.3		2,295		429		1,866		511	1,161			−1	2,206			324				3,368	M
N	Bank Debentures	1,950	3,986			1,662	3,986	456	3,061	1,206	925	288								1,829				3,986	N
O	Industrial Bonds	690				586		−130		716		103							857	118				857	O
P	Stocks	4,268	145			4,254	145	1,239	61	3,015	84	13				115		641	1,850	476		−833		1,996	P
Q	Securities Investment Trust	414	4,268			414	4,268	18		396	4,268							154		3,699				4,268	Q
R	Bonds in Foreign Currency		213				79		79				134		−0.1		102		1,420			1,736		1,736	R
S	**The Bank of Japan Loans**	−299	−299	−299			−299		−816		516													−299	S
T	**Call Money**	523	523			523	523	−951	1,482	1,474	−959													523	T
U	**Bills Bought & Sold**	1,180	1,180	200		980	1,180	119	1,513	860	−333													1,180	U
V	**Loans**	35,858				26,962		21,121	114	10,129	4,174	8,896			589		5,496		20,766		9,005			35,858	V
W	Loans by Private Financial Institutions	26,962				26,962		21,121	114	10,129	4,174						952		19,437		6,572			26,962	W
X	Loans by Public Financial Institutions	8,896										8,896			589		4,543		1,329		2,433			8,896	X
Y	**Trade Credit**																	13,128	9,143		3,985			13,128	Y
Z	**Deposits to Trust Fund Bureau**		3,479										3,479	3,479										3,479	Z
a	**Gold & Foreign Exchange Reserves**	…		…										…									434	434	a
b	**Foreign Trade Credits**	−322	−269			−322	−269	−322	−269									1,179	−784			−784	1,126	71	b
c	**Foreign Direct Investment**																	1,411	−4			−4	1,411	1,407	c
d	**Other Foreign Claims & Debts**	8,173	5,870			7,426	5,870	4,134	5,880	3,291	−10	747					−5	3,570	376			6,534	12,538	18.780	d
e	**Other**		−4,622	137			−1,003		1,051		−2,055		524	238			−113	−2,317		−1,323				−4,736	e
f	**Financial Surplus or Deficit (−)**		4,006												−9,749		−7,524		−6,198		27.817		−8,350	—	f
g	**Total**	68,048	68,048	2,277	2,277	51,263	51,263	27,053	27,053	28,808	28,808	15,454	15,454	3,121	3,121	918	918	27,427	27,427	40.808	40.808	7,160	7,160	147,483	g

Source: Bank of Japan, Flow of Funds in the Japanese Economy in 1984. Special Paper No. 185 (Tokyo, Japan, August 1985), p. 21.

TABLE VII.9 FLOW-OF-FUNDS MATRIX UNITED KINGDOM (£ mns.) 1984

	Line	Central government	Local authorities	Public corporations	Public sector	Monetary sector	Other financial institutions	Industrial and commercial companies	Personal sector	Overseas sector(a)	Residual error
Capital account											
Saving	1	- 399	+ 845	+2,380	+2,826	+1,669		+6,679	+2,496	-1,052	
Taxes on capital and capital transfers	2	- 386	- 181	+ 141	- 426	- 53		+ 87	+ 392	—	
less											
Gross fixed capital formation at home	3	- 624	- 770	-2,067	-3,461	-1,653		-4,277	-3,173		
Increase in value of stocks and work in progress	4	- 20		- 7	- 27	- 1		- 122	+ 49		
Financial surplus+/deficit-	5	-1,429	- 106	+ 447	-1,088	- 38		+2,387	- 236	-1,052	+ 47
Changes in financial assets and liabilities											
Assets increase+/decrease-											
Liabilities increase-/decrease+											
Notes and coin	6	- 773		—	- 773	+ 590	—	+ 27	+ 256	- 100	
Market Treasury bills	7	+ 101	—	+ 61	+ 162	+ 31	+ 9	- 92		- 110	
British government securities	8	-1,820	+ 1	+ 20	-1,799	- 468	+1,938	+ 1	+ 449	- 121	
National savings	9	- 929	- 1	- 14	- 944		+ 8	+ 58	+ 878		
Certificates of tax deposit	10	- 25		- 31	- 56	+ 21	+ 43	- 23	+ 15		
Net government indebtedness to Banking Department	11	+ 185			+ 185	- 185					
Northern Ireland central government debt	12	+ 24			+ 24	- 18	—	—	- 6		
Government liabilities under exchange cover scheme	13	+ 18	- 2	- 16	—						
Other public sector financing:											
Non-marketable debt	14.1	- 163		+ 164	+ 1	- 1	—				
Short-term assets	14.2		+ 20	—	+ 20		- 17	- 7	+ 4	—	
Issue Department's transactions in commercial bills	15	+ 176			+ 176			- 176			
Government foreign currency debt	16	—			—	—				—	
Other government overseas financing	17	+ 93			+ 93					- 93	
Official reserves	18	- 129			- 129					+ 129	
Local authority debt											
Temporary	19.1	- 169	+ 606	- 237	+ 200	- 36	- 38	- 58	- 64	- 4	
Foreign currency	19.2		- 38		- 38	—	—			+ 38	
Sterling securities	19.3	—	- 14	—	- 14	+ 16	+ 23		- 22	- 3	
Other sterling debt	19.4	+ 844	- 469	- 10	+ 365	- 291	+ 24	- 9	- 88	- 1	
Public corporation debt											
Foreign currency	20.1			- 135	- 135	+ 185	—			- 50	
Other	20.2	- 122	- 12	- 267	- 401	+ 409	- 4	—	+ 6	- 10	
Deposits with banks											
Sterling sight	21.1	+ 187	+ 30	+ 64	+ 281	-2,142	+ 356	+1,763	- 445	+ 187	
Sterling time	21.2	+ 34	+ 57	- 167	- 76	-2,357	+1,423	- 28	- 151	+1,189	
Foreign currency	21.3	+ 1	+ 4	- 66	- 61	-6,696	+ 295	+1,630	- 198	+5,030	
Deposits with building societies	22					+ 318	-4,516	+ 191	+4,012	- 5	
Bank lending (excluding public sector)											
Foreign currency	24.1					+5,777	- 334	+ 521	- 34	-5,930	
Sterling	24.2					+2,904	+ 29	-1,103	- 901	- 929	
Credit extended by retailers	25			+ 10	+ 10			+ 168	- 178		
Identified trade credit											
Domestic	26.1	- 1		+1,116	+1,115			- 637	- 478		
Import and export	26.2	- 34		+ 3	- 31		—	+ 34		- 3	
Loans for house purchase											
Building societies	27.1						+2,785		-2,785		
Other	27.2	+ 1	- 23	+ 43	+ 21	+ 703	+ 51		- 775		
Other public sector lending	28	- 7	+ 1	+ 7	+ 1		—	- 4	+ 10	- 7	
Other lending by financial institutions	29			—	—		+ 563	- 316	- 247		
Unit trust units	30						- 202		+ 202		
UK company securities	31	- 11		+ 8	- 3	+ 161	+ 411	- 54	- 746	+ 231	
Overseas securities	32	—		—	—	+ 724	+ 746	+ 114	+ 5	-1,589	
Life assurance and pension funds	33	- 61			- 61		-3,825		+3,886		
Miscellaneous domestic instruments	34	—		—	—	—	- 141	+ 103	+ 38	—	
Direct and other investment abroad	35					- 77	+ 33	+1,020		- 976	
Overseas direct and other investment in the United Kingdom	36					- 53	- 78	- 55		+ 186	
Miscellaneous overseas instruments	37	+ 165		+ 3	+ 168		+ 55	- 554		+ 331	
Accruals adjustment	38	+1,311	-1,198	- 8	+ 105	+ 290	- 279	- 11	- 105		
Financial transactions	39	-1,104	-1,038	+ 548	-1,594	- 195	- 642	+2,503	+2,538	-2,610	
Balancing item	40	- 325	+ 932	- 101	+ 506	+ 799		- 136	-2,774	+1,558	+ 47

(a) It has not been possible to incorporate in this table the revised balance of payments estimates which were released in June

Source: Bank of England, Quarterly Bulletin (June 1985), p. 243.

sheets (Pettigrew, 1980; Great Britain, HM Treasury and CSO, 1981).

The UK accounts are used to explain key financial indicators such as the public sector borrowing requirement (PSBR) and the monetary aggregates--M1, M3 and domestic credit expansion (DCE) (See Chapter VIII below for forecasting uses).[17]

A Zero-Sum Matrix

A unique feature of the UK accounts is the identifying of single-column sector entries with a plus (change in assets) and a minus (change in liabilities). While the Canadian and Australian accounts also have a single column of entries, increases in both assets and liabilities are shown with a plus sign, requiring repetition of the financial rows for both assets and liabilities. The manipulative potential of the zero-sum matrix for quadruple-entry arithmetic has been appreciated by Alford who devotes most of his book to working out the permutations.[18]

Several modifications are still required to convert the UK matrix to a zero-sum format. The capital account (saving, capital expenditures) has to be dropped and the matrix must begin with the financial surplus (net financial investment) row.[19] The plus-minus entries in the conventional format must be reversed: increases in financial assets are to be shown with a minus and increases in financial liabilities with a plus.[20] An error column and row complete the matrix.

Alford devotes two chapters to error entries in the UK accounts and the extent of data revisions (chapters 6 and 7). Alford is for explicit error entries; "attributions" to the cells of the matrix table are risky. Unfortunately there seems to be little payoff from his matrix manipulation. While macro-disturbances can be portrayed in neat quadruple-entry form (pp. 97-103), this is just as well done in a source-use format (see Chapter VIII below). Moreover, a zero-sum matrix has an information cost. Saving and capital outlays have to go and the sector entry for a given financial category has to be net rather than gross (both source and use entries being possible in non-zero frameworks).

THE YUGOSLAV ACCOUNTS

Yugoslavia has since the late 1950s prepared flow-of-funds accounts organized according to a Marxist socialist economy. They are produced by the central bank on an annual basis. The flow-of-funds accounts for 1985 are shown in Table VII.10. "OALs" (economic sector) includes two subsectors: one being "organizations of associated labor." It includes transactions of organizations of associated labor in the economic sector (socialist enterprises), their internal banks, working communities of banks, and other financial organizations. "Self-managed communities of interest for material production and housing" is the second subsector. In 1977 organizations engaging in financial and other services previously shown in the noneconomic sector, "other organizations" were included in the OAL sector. At the same time, a number of activities were transferred to "other organizations." These include self-managed communities of interest in the field of communal activities, education, health, culture, and other activities outside "material production" and public organizations not included in other institutional sectors. "Other socio-political communities" represents the activities of government on the nonfederal level (e.g., republican, provincial, and communal authorities). "Unclassified" comprised unidentifiable transactions and errors and omissions.[21] "Distribution of social product" under "1. Nonfinancial transactions" refers to income flows. Sector tables presenting time series of transactions involved are also provided. In addition to the matrix of flows, a matrix of end-of-year stocks is regularly prepared (see Quarterly Bulletin of the Bank, October 1986).

The National Bank of Yugoslavia is now preparing comparative flow-of-fund accounts for all countries covered by IMF, International Financial Statistics. A relatively simplified structure of institutional sectoring has been adjusted to the statistical information available in the country pages of this

TABLE VII.10 YUGOSLAVIA, FLOW-OF-FUNDS ACCOUNTS, 1983

	OALs /economic sector/						Federal government		Other socio-political communities		Other organizations		Households	
	Total		Self-managed communities of interest		Total									
	U	S	U	S	U	S	U	S	U	S	U	S	U	S
I. NON-FINANCIAL TRANSACTIONS														
1. Current transactions														
Purchase and sale of goods and services	29032352	38119565	167193	607049	29199545	38726614	225370		414886		737519	504808	4716918	1377914
Disburtion of social product	6647169		55850		6703019		1682186	2209750	1214507	1802524	1557267	2197093	593784	5214085
Non-financial transfers				38198		38198	87825					49627		90000
Other receipts and expenditures, net errors and omissions		124056	319640		195584		195937		62856			29659		1106280
Gross savings		2564100		102564		2666664		18432		110275		486401		2477577
2. Investment	4125700		46220		4171920		4903		25363		180481		607500	
Fixed assets	1101500		46220		1147720		4903		25363		180481		535500	
Stocks	3024200				3024200								72000	
Financial surplus or deficit	1561600			56344	1505256			13529		84912		305920		1870077
II. FINANCIAL TRANSACTIONS														
1. Financial surplus or deficit	1561600			56344	1505256			13529		84912		305920		1870077
2. Money	98482	40	15024		113506	40	27807		51072		105496		274047	
a/ Currency	12918				12918								211583	
b/ Giro and current accounts	85564	40	15024		100588	40	27807		51072		105496		62464	
3. Other liquid assets	303844	330615	13518		317362	330615		-34	10811	-22	186285	-2574	292808	
a/ Other sight deposits	-369	128628			-369	128628			-29		138512		88869	
a1/ Time deposits	75227	39334	7410		82637	39334			1033		21566		203952	
b/ Restricted deposits	60126	-44	5085		65211	-44			10025		20347		-12	
c/ Short-term securities	108472	79039	-1		108471	79039		-34	-6	-22		-2969	-9	
d/ Pooled resources	60388	83652	1024		61412	83658			-212		5860	395	8	
4. Non-liquid assets	272306	149151	989	148	273295	149299	1945	2314	1217	56	5762	1144	308525	
a/ Time deposits and other long-term assets	65019	13877	530		65549	13877			83		623		244869	
a1/ Long-term deposits for housing and communal development	11607	304	809		12416	304	1945		1162		1353		63652	
b/ Long-term securities	ti 58081	-6838		2	58081	-6836		2316	-415	51		-14	4	
c/ Bank funds	39214	1509	691		39905	1509					1112			
d/ Pooled resources	98385	140299	-1041	146	97344	140445		-2	387	5	2674	1158		

(Table VII.10 continued)

	Financial institutions: Monetary system: Total		National banks		Basic and asociated banks		Other financial organizations		Rest of the world		Unclassified		T o t a l	
	U	S	U	S	U	S	U	S	U	S	U	S	U	S
I. NON-FINANCIAL TRANSACTIONS														
1. Current transactions														
Purchase and sale of goods and services									4154300	4670696	841327		39448538	45280032
Disburtion of social product								74633	730076	29532		953222	12480839	12480839
Non-financial transfers									90000				177825	177825
Other receipts and expendizures, net errors and omissions											681562		1135939	1135939
Gross savings								74633	274148		569667		843815	5833982
2. Investment													4990167	
Fixed assets													1893967	
Stocks													3096200	
Financial surplus or deficit								74633	274148		569667		2349071	2349071
II. FINANCIAL TRANSACTIONS														
1. Financial surplus or deficit								74633	274148		569667		2349071	2349071
2. Money		591552		265510		326042	18903		761				591592	591592
a/ Currency		224501		224501									224501	224501
b/ Giro and current accounts		367051		41009		326042	18903		761				367091	367091
3. Other liquid assets	-31775	763710	-1336	347696	-30439	416014			316204				1091695	1091695
a/ Other sight deposits		98355		205		98150							226983	226983
a1/ Time deposits		270230		324		269906			376				309564	309564
b/ Restricted deposits		411443		347160		64283			315828				411399	411399
c/ Short-term securities	-32446	-4	-1336		-31110	-4							76010	76010
d/ Pooled resources	671	-16314		7	671	-16321							67739	67739
4. Non-liquid assets	41120	368044	-109	-3470	41229	371514		111066		1			631864	631864
a/ Time deposits and other long-term assets		250520		-8582		259102		46727					311124	311124
a1/ Long-term deposits for housing and communal development		80224		2058		78166							80528	80528
b/ Long-term securities	-3802	-936			-3802	-936		59287					53868	53868
c/ Bank funds		38943		2586		36357		565					41017	41017
d/ Pooled resources	44922	-707	-109	468	45031	-1175		4427		1			145327	145327

(Table VII.10 continued)

	OALs /economic sector/ Total		Self-managed communities of interest		Total		Federal government		Other socio-political communities		Other organizations		households	
5. Short-term credits	3159397	3977632	25058	-2654	3184455	3974978		380	-7963	28	53074	7335		27822
a/ Bank credits	421221	1190647		-2654	421221	1187993		380		28		7335		7486
b/ Trade credits														
d/ Credits from/liabilities to users	2701236	2745500	22085		2723321	2745500					42515			20336
of socially-owned resources	36940	41485	2973		39913	41485			-7963		10559			
6. Long-term credits	102019	519318	115	1568	102134	520886	-75	13488	31700	3827	-21107	3024		164314
a/ Bank credits	72979	441339		1568	72979	442907		13488		3827		3024		164314
c/ Credits from/liabilities to users of socially-owned resources	29040	77979	115		29155	77979	-75		31700		-21107			
8. Short-term foreign currency transactions	90787	66710	21		90808	66710			-160	4	10406	12335	451025	
a/ Gold and foreign exchange													35000	
b/ Bilateral balances														
c/ Foreign currency accounts														
d/ Short-term credits														
e/ Foreign currency deposits of and credits to residents	78236	97999	21		78257	97999			-160		-1563	2921	420099	
f/ Other claims and liabilities	12551	-31289			12551	-31289				4	11969	9414	-4074	
9. Long-term foreign currency transactions	5012	1275897		-681	5012	1275216				-2128	617	13349	735808	
b/ Securities														
c/ Long-term credits		376633				376633								
d/ Foreign currency deposits of and credits to residents	5012	899264		-681	5012	898583				-2128	617	2190	735808	
e/ Other claims and liabilities												11159		
11. Transactions between financial organizations	442562	500765			442562	500765								
a/ Dinar transactions														
aa/ Short-term	283791	321468			283791	321468								
ab/ long-term	158771	179297			158771	179297								
b/ Foreign currency transactions														
aa/ Short-term														
ab/ Long-term														
12. Unclassified, errors and omissions	412041	377922			412041	377922		56368						
a/ Short-term	409575	378959			409575	378959								
b/ Long-term	2466	-1037			2466	-1037		56368						
12a. The 1983 devaluation effect	750000				750000		56368							
a/ External transactions	750000				750000									
b/ Domestic transactions							56368							
13. Increase in financial assets and liabilities	5636450	7198050	54725	-1619	5691175	7196431	86045	72516	86677	1765	340533	34613	2062213	192136

(Table VII.10 continued)

	Financial institutions													
			Monetary system											
	Total		National banks		Basic and associated banks		Other financial organizations		Rest of the world		Unclassified		Total	
5. Short-term credits	757451	224	42670		724781	224	14550	800					4011567	4011567
a/ Bank credits	767451		42670		724781		14550						1203222	1203222
b/ Trade credits													2765836	2765836
d/ Credits from/liabilities to users of socially-owned resources		224				224		800					42509	42509
6. Long-term credits	542837	1424	18351		524486	1424	10881	-201	40884	492			707254	707254
a/ Bank credits	543843		18351		525492		11230			492			628052	628052
c/ Credits from/liabilities to users of socially-owned resources	-1006	1424			-1006	1424	-349	-201	40884				79202	79202
8. Short-term foreign currency transactions	621842	796389	235804	18592	386038	777797			311410	591757	-18136		1467195	1467195
a/ Gold and foreign exchange	414591		143024		271567					449591			449591	449591
b/ Bilateral balances	63688	-59286	63688	-59268					-59268	63688			4420	4420
c/ Foreign currency accounts	73063	127506	22470	23220	50593	104286			127506	73063			200569	200569
d/ Short-term credits	5415	57115		11623	5415	45492			57115	5415			62530	62530
e/ Foreign currency deposits of and credits to residents	100920	496633		37940	100920	458693							597553	597553
f/ Other claims and liabilities	-35835	174403	6622	5077	-42457	169326			186057		-18136		152532	152532
9. Long-term foreign currency transactions	948564	2121829	12562	465143	936002	1656868			1757025	38760			3447026	3447026
b/ Securities	768		307		461					768			768	768
c/ Long-term credits	20398	1380076		465143	20398	914933			1756709	20398			1777107	1777107
d/ Foreign currency deposits of and credits to residents	898645	741437			898645	741437							1640082	1640082
e/ Other claims and liabilities	28753	316	12255		16498	316			316	•17594			29069	29069
11. Transactions between financial organizations	146117	148897	413629	1079430	2427567	1764546	165913	65624			113025	152331	867617	867617
a/ Dinar transactions														
aa/ Short-term		11763	238065	191643	421554	479739	-1494	35004			85938		368235	368235
ab/ long-term		110047	67429	17687	184725	344514	167407	30620				6214	326178	326178
b/ Foreign currency transactions														
aa/ Short-term	146117			863881	1211777	201779						146117	146117	146117
ab/ Long-term		27087	108135	6219	609511	738514					27087		27087	27087
12. Unclassified, errors and omissions	1422139	1442006	279083	389148	1143056	1052858	66374	24759			8461	7960	1909015	1909015
a/ Short-term	1365930	1438054	222715	389148	1143215	1048906	66374	16906				7960	1841879	1841879
b/ Long-term	56209	3952	56368		-159	3952		7853			8461		67136	67136
12a. The 1983 devaluation effect	1775780		1561395		214385					2069422	1319422	1832148	3901570	3901570
a/ External transactions	692554		692554							2069422	1319422	692554	2761976	2761976
b/ Domestic transactions	1083226		868841		214385							1139594	1139594	1139594
13. Increase in financial assets and liabilities	6234075	6234075	2562049	2562049	6367105	6367105	276621	201988	2426284	2700432	1422772	1992439	18626395	18626395

Source: National Bank of Yugoslavia, Quarterly Bulletin (October 1986), following page 23.

publication.

First used primarily for monetary analysis, flow-of-funds accounts have been increasingly used for monetary planning. In 1967 they became the institutionalized model for monetary planning. Projection of changes in money supply, bank credit and the creation of reserve money by the National Bank of Yugoslavia are based on the accounts. The model of monetary planning has made it possible to plan monetary policy consistent with the real (nonfinancial) economic planning. The positive experience in monetary planning has stimulated recently a complex financial model based on these accounts (see also Dimitrijevic, 1969, 1975).

OTHER COUNTRY ACCOUNTS

At a special session on the uses of flow-of-funds tables held by the Group of Financial Statisticians in 1978, sixteen countries were represented (OECD, Committee on Financial Markets, 1978). In addition to the countries already summarized, seven countries regularly publish financial flow accounts--Belgium, Finland, France, Germany, Italy, Norway, and Austria.[22] With the exception of France, these countries also prepare data on levels. Four other countries in attendance did not at that time have any financial accounting--Denmark, the Netherlands, Switzerland, and Spain. From the oral statements and written submissions at this conference, it appears that in the majority of participating countries, flow-of-funds tables are not used for monetary and financial analysis. The reason is the problems of working with the flow of funds. These include the absence of theoretical foundations, the precedence given to analysis based on the monetary aggregates, the complexity of the flow-of-funds accounts, the delay in compiling them, the lack of quarterly tables and long time series, and the defects in the data. On the latter score are included inadequate coherence with "real" accounts, the poor quality of the information collected on certain sectors (e.g., households, enterprises), the absence of gross data, the absence of data on levels. Where the tables are used by government, the principal use is as a basis for financial forecasts.

In contrast, the OECD secretariat is an active user of flow-of-funds statistics for current analysis. It has set up indicators of households' financial behavior, of corporate finance, and of government financing in order to assess financial developments (OECD, 1978, p. 4). One OECD staff paper written in 1977 is quite optimistic about their potential usefulness. The flow-of-funds identities provided useful information for policymakers in analyzing the effects of a succession of economic shocks in the first half of the 1970s (Dudler and Chouraqui, 1977).

THE OECD publishes extensive flow-of-funds data. They appear in two of the three series comprising Financial Statistics: in Financial Accounts of OECD Countries and Non-financial Enterprises Financial Statements.[23] The latter shows balance sheets, statement of income and change in net worth, and sources and uses of funds for member countries. The coverage may either consist of the entire nonfinancial sector or components. The financial statements are not integrated into the system of national accounts nor are they compatible with the main flow-of-funds series--Financial Accounts of OECD Countries. The matrix for Germany is reproduced below (Table VII.11), comparing 1967 and 1984. Similar statements are found for Canada, Spain, United States, France, Italy, Netherlands, United Kingdom, Sweden, Japan, Finland, and Yugoslavia.

Financial transactions are organized in the OECD tables according to liquidity beginning with gold, acquired SDRs, net position in the IMF, in row 9 down to long-term loans (row 18). No statistical adjustment is shown although one appears in a "model" OECD table.[24] A second general table summarizing funds raised and supplied in credit markets is also published. It is similar to one appearing monthly for the U.S. in the Federal Reserve Bulletin.

A brief summary table (Table VII.11) compares leading features of the main accounts discussed in the chapter.

TABLE VII.11 FLOW OF FUNDS MATRIX, GERMANY, 1967, 1984

ary unit: billion DM.

	Financial institutions - Institutions financières								General Government			
	Banking institutions - Système bancaire				Others - Autres				Administrations publiques			
	Central Bank / Banque centrale		Banks / Banques		Insurance companies / Compagnies d'assurances		Building and loan associations / Caisses d'épargne-construction		Government authorities / Autorités gouvernementales		Social Security funds / Administrations de Sécurité sociale	
	a		*b*		*c*1		*c*2		*d + e*		*f*	
	S	U	S	U	S	U	S	U	S	U	S	U
	S			U								
19												
ross saving	2.63			—	0.08	—	0.30	—	18.91	—	—	0.86
ross physical investment	—			1.30	—	0.71	—	0.04	—	18.54	—	0.33
apital transfers (net)	—			0.08	—	0.45	—	—	—	6.08	—	0.07
otal	**2.63**			**1.38**	**0.08**	**1.16**	**0.30**	**0.04**	**18.91**	**24.62**	—	**1.26**
et financial saving	—	**0.14**	—	**1.12**	**1.08**	—	—	**0.26**	**5.71**	—	**1.26**	—
inancial assets	—	0.36	—	47.68	—	6.50	—	3.10	—	10.25	—	- 1.12
ndebtedness	0.22	—	46.57	—	7.58	—	2.84	—	15.96	—	0.14	—
old, acquired SDRs, position in the IMF, CUs	—	- 1.08	—	—	—	—	—	—	—	—	—	—
xchange holdings of the Bundesbank	0.09	1.48	—	—	—	—	—	—	—	—	—	—
ash and other sight deposits	0.96	—	9.83	—	—	0.13	—	0.15	—	0.84	—	0.18
ther deposits with banks	—	—	27.59	—	—	0.77	—	0.52	—	5.69	—	- 1.94
.1. Time deposits	—	—	*9.02*	—	—	*0.77*	—	*0.52*	—	*5.05*	—	*- 2.04*
.2. Savings deposits	—	—	*18.57*	—	—	—	—	—	—	*0.64*	—	*0.10*
oney market paper	1.37	- 1.36	- 0.01	6.83	—	—	—	0.02	4.24	- 0.15	—	0.12
ort-term bank loans	—	1.22	—	7.07	—	—	- 0.01	—	0.96	—	0.06	—
ade credits	—	—	—	—	—	—	—	—	—	—	—	—
onds	—	1.22	9.12	11.70	—	1.83	—	0.01	4.01	0.22	—	- 1.27
ares	—	—	0.08	- 0.32	0.03	0.34	—	—	—	0.37	—	—
ong-term loans	—	- 0.93	0.04	24.53	—	3.43	- 0.03	2.40	5.19	—	0.08	—
.1. Banking institutions	—	*- 0.93*	—	*24.53*	—	—	*- 0.03*	—	*4.52*	—	*0.08*	—
.2. Insurance companies	—	—	—	—	—	*3.43*	—	—	*0.53*	—	—	—
.3. Building and loan associations	—	—	*0.04*	—	—	—	—	*2.40*	*0.14*	—	—	—
unds placed with insurance companies	—	—	—	—	7.36	—	—	—	—	0.03	—	—
unds placed with building and loan associations	—	—	—	0.07	—	—	2.88	—	—	0.04	—	—
thers	—	—	0.12	—	0.19	—	—	—	- 0.04	3.22	—	0.18
tersectoral claims and liabilities	- 2.20	- 0.21	- 0.21	- 2.20	—	—	—	—	1.61	—	—	1.61
19												
ross saving	22.07			—	7.61	—	1.19	—	32.86	—	—	0.18
ross physical investment	—			6.30	—	3.21	—	0.17	—	42.79	—	1.25
apital transfers (net)	—			0.02	—	0.56	—	—	—	27.41	—	2.01
otal	**22.07**			**6.32**	**7.61**	**3.77**	**1.19**	**0.17**	**32.86**	**70.20**	—	**3.44**
et financial saving	—	**1.95**	—	**13.79**	—	**3.84**	—	**1.02**	**37.34**	—	**3.44**	—
nancial assets	—	9.27	—	162.86	—	42.63	—	5.11	—	10.05	—	- 3.38
debtedness	7.31	—	149.07	—	38.79	—	4.09	—	47.39	—	0.07	—
old, acquired SDRs, position in the IMF, CUs	—	0.63	—	—	—	—	—	—	—	—	—	—
change holdings of the Bundesbank	1.63	- 2.69	—	—	—	—	—	—	—	—	—	—
ash and other sight deposits	2.32	—	17.02	—	—	0.74	—	- 0.02	—	0.26	—	0.27
her deposits with banks	—	—	83.11	—	—	15.58	—	- 0.39	—	9.25	—	- 2.52
.1. Time deposits	—	—	*61.68*	—	—	*15.58*	—	*- 0.39*	—	*9.00*	—	*- 2.52*
.2. Savings deposits	—	—	*24.43*	—	—	—	—	—	—	*0.25*	—	—
oney market paper	0.22	0.01	0.10	- 4.93	—	—	—	—	- 6.29	0.06	—	—
ort-term bank loans	—	2.26	—	36.17	0.12	—	1.36	—	- 0.18	—	0.04	—
ade credits	—	—	—	—	—	—	—	—	—	—	—	—
nds	—	- 3.46	34.16	26.48	—	12.01	0.39	- 0.07	34.70	0.83	—	- 0.70
ares	—	—	1.26	2.30	0.35	1.87	0.12	0.01	—	0.67	—	—
ng-term loans	—	—	0.02	99.82	0.07	12.43	1.98	5.58	16.42	—	0.03	—
.1. Banking institutions	—	—	—	*99.82*	*0.06*	—	*1.95*	—	*13.57*	—	*0.03*	—
.2. Insurance companies	—	—	—	—	—	*12.43*	*0.03*	—	*2.91*	—	—	—
.3. Building and loan associations	—	—	*0.02*	—	*0.01*	—	—	*5.58*	*- 0.06*	—	—	—
nds placed with insurance companies	—	—	—	—	37.63	—	—	—	—	0.05	—	—
nds placed with building and loan associations	—	—	—	- 0.12	—	—	0.26	—	—	- 0.05	—	—
hers	—	—	0.88	—	0.62	—	—	—	2.96	- 1.04	—	- 0.21
ersectoral claims and liabilities	3.15	12.51	12.51	3.15	—	—	—	—	- 0.21	—	—	- 0.21

orandum Item:

— Allocations of SDRs (not included in the table): nil.

Discrepancies in the totals are due to rounding.

(Table VII.11 continued)

Non-financial enterprises / Sociétés non financières				Households / Ménages		Rest of the world / Reste du monde		TOTAL		
Except housing / A l'exception du logement		Housing / Logement								
g^1		g^2		h		i		j		
S	U	S	U	S	U	S	U	S	U	
67										
52.75	—	12.94	—	37.73	—	—	10.80	125.34	11.66	1. Épargne brute
—	56.51	—	36.25	—	—	—	—	—	113.68	2. Investissements réels bruts
2.57	—	9.35	—	—	5.80	0.56	—	12.48	12.48	3. Transferts en capital (nets)
55.32	**56.51**	**22.29**	**36.25**	**37.73**	**5.80**	**0.56**	**10.80**	**137.78**	**137.78**	**4. Total**
1.19	—	**13.96**	—	—	**31.93**	**10.24**	—	**33.45**	**33.45**	**6. Épargne financière nette**
—	18.95	—	0.28	—	33.75	—	4.64	—	124.39	7. Placements financiers
20.14	—	14.24	—	1.82	—	14.88	—	124.39	—	8. Endettement
—	—	—	—	—	—	- 1.08	—	- 1.08	- 1.08	9. Or, DTS acquis, position au FMI, I
—	—	—	—	—	—	1.48	0.09	1.57	1.57	10.1. Avoirs en devises de la Bundesbank
—	6.21	—	0.28	—	2.09	—	0.92	10.79	10.79	10.2. Numéraire et autres dépôts à vue
—	4.40	—	—	—	17.68	—	0.46	27.59	27.59	11. Autres dépôts auprès des banques
—	*4.10*	—	—	—	*0.32*	—	*0.30*	*9.02*	*9.02*	*11.1. Dépôts à terme*
—	*0.30*	—	—	—	*17.36*	—	*0.16*	*18.57*	*18.57*	*11.2. Dépôts d'épargne*
- 0.55	0.15	—	—	—	—	0.53	- 0.03	5.58	5.58	12. Titres du marché monétaire
1.95	—	0.11	—	0.16	—	5.06	—	8.29	8.29	13. Prêts bancaires à court terme
0.90	3.00	—	—	—	—	3.00	0.90	3.90	3.90	14. Crédits commerciaux
1.66	0.08	—	—	—	2.34	0.45	- 0.89	15.24	15.24	15. Obligations
1.73	1.03	0.07	—	—	1.15	1.42	0.75	3.33	3.33	16. Actions
8.97	—	12.28	—	1.19	—	1.72	—	29.44	29.44	18. Prêts à long terme
7.70	—	*8.57*	—	*1.04*	—	*1.72*	—	*23.60*	*23.60*	*18.1. Système bancaire*
1.26	—	*1.50*	—	*0.15*	—	—	—	*3.43*	*3.43*	*18.2. Compagnies d'assurances*
0.01	—	*2.21*	—	—	—	—	—	*2.40*	*2.40*	*18.3. Caisses d'épargne-construction*
—	1.12	—	—	—	6.19	—	0.02	7.36	7.36	• Fonds confiés aux compagnies d'assu
—	0.03	—	—	—	2.74	—	—	2.88	2.88	• Fonds confiés aux caisses d'ép construction
5.48	2.41	1.27	—	0.48	1.55	2.30	2.42	9.78	9.78	20. Divers
—	0.51	0.51	—	—	—	—	—	- 0.29	- 0.29	• Créances et engagements intersector
84										
164.96	—	15.29	—	146.15	—	—	16.38	390.13	16.56	1. Épargne brute
—	209.57	—	110.28	—	—	—	—	—	373.57	2. Investissements réels bruts
22.61	—	41.86	—	—	36.92	2.45	—	66.92	66.92	3. Transferts en capital (nets)
187.57	**209.57**	**57.15**	**110.28**	**146.15**	**36.92**	**2.45**	**16.38**	**457.05**	**457.05**	**4. Total**
22.00	—	**53.12**	—	—	**109.23**	**13.93**	—	**129.83**	**129.83**	**6. Épargne financière nette**
—	56.94	—	1.20	—	119.11	—	60.85	—	464.64	7. Placements financiers
78.94	—	54.32	—	9.88	—	74.78	—	464.64	—	8. Endettement
—	—	—	—	—	—	0.63	—	0.63	0.63	9. Or, DTS acquis, position au FMI,
—	—	—	—	—	—	- 2.69	1.63	- 1.06	- 1.06	10.1. Avoirs en devises de la Bundesbanl
—	3.55	—	1.20	—	6.04	—	7.31	19.34	19.34	10.2. Numéraire et autres dépôts à vue
—	11.68	—	—	—	39.24	—	10.25	83.11	83.11	11. Autres dépôts auprès des banques
—	*11.78*	—	—	—	*18.49*	—	*9.73*	*61.68*	*61.68*	*11.1. Dépôts à terme*
—	*- 0.10*	—	—	—	*20.75*	—	*0.52*	*21.43*	*21.43*	*11.2. Dépôts d'épargne*
- 0.63	0.12	—	—	—	- 0.63	0.62	- 0.62	- 5.98	- 5.98	12. Titres du marché monétaire
16.83	—	2.80	—	3.21	—	14.24	—	38.42	38.42	13. Prêts bancaires à court terme
3.55	12.66	—	—	—	—	12.66	3.55	16.21	16.21	14. Crédits commerciaux
1.57	10.84	—	—	—	26.73	15.74	13.89	86.56	86.56	15. Obligations
4.47	0.77	0.08	—	—	0.70	4.15	4.10	10.42	10.42	16. Actions
28.28	—	50.64	—	6.75	—	13.67	—	117.83	117.83	18. Prêts à long terme
24.36	—	*40.69*	—	*5.66*	—	*13.52*	—	*99.82*	*99.82*	*18.1. Système bancaire*
4.25	—	*3.97*	—	*1.09*	—	*0.19*	—	*12.43*	*12.43*	*18.2. Compagnies d'assurances*
- 0.33	—	*5.98*	—	—	—	*- 0.04*		*5.58*	*5.58*	*18.3. Caisses d'épargne-construction*
—	2.15	—	—	—	35.30	—	0.13	37.63	37.63	• Fonds confiés aux compagnies d'assu
—	0.04	—	—	—	0.16	—	0.22	0.26	0.26	• Fonds confiés aux caisses d'ép construction
24.87	14.16	- 0.16	—	- 0.08	11.56	15.77	20.39	44.86	44.86	20. Divers
—	0.97	0.97	—	—	—	—	—	16.42	16.42	• Créances et engagements intersector

Source: OECD, Financial Accounts, 1985, Part 2, pp. 18-19.

TABLE VII.12

COMPARING FLOW-OF-FUNDS ACCOUNTS

Country	Flow Accounts Annual	Flow Accounts Qtly	Levels Annual	Levels Qtly	Detailed Sector Coverage	Detailed Transaction Coverage	Non-Financial Data	Sector Statistical Discrepancy
Australia	✓		Limited		✓	✓	✓	✓
Canada	✓	✓	✓			✓	✓	✓
Japan	✓		✓		✓	Limited	*	None
U.K.	✓	✓	✓		Limited	✓	✓	✓
United States	✓	✓	✓		✓	✓	✓	✓
Yugoslavia	✓		✓		✓	✓	✓	None

*Nonfinancial data available in the summary matrix published by OECD for most member countries.

APPLICATIONS

We shall restrict applications of the flow of funds in succeeding chapters to studies which exploit the underlying constraints of the accounts. The extensive mining of the flow of funds as a data base does not suffice. We begin with models based on the transaction and sector identities, proceed to self-contained circular flow models, apply a flow-constrained analysis to the stock market and discuss successively portfolio balance, disequilibrium and policy models.

Notes

1. The nomenclature of "flow-of-funds accounts" encompasses stock or balance sheet values in addition to the obvious flow values. The term "financial accounts" has been preferred by one author, one reason being its embracing data on total balance sheet positions (Dorrance, 1978, n. 5, p. 165).
2. See, e.g., U.S. Department of Commerce, Bureau of the Census, Enterprise Statistics, part 3, "Link of Census Establishment and IRS Corporation Data," 1958, 1963, and 1967.

   The promising work of the Ruggles suggests a strong interest in efforts to analyze the activities of individual establishments in terms of their contribution to saving of firms and the relation of savings to capital formation at the establishment level (Ruggles, November 1982).
3. For a useful summary of the conference that preceded the UN publication, see Helen Stone Tice, March 1967. A recent special issue of the Review of Income and Wealth, Series 32 (June 1986) is devoted to a review of the structure of the SNA. A European System of Integrated Accounts (ESA) presents the Commission of the European Communities version of the UN accounts. While calling for additional input-output information and providing more detail on income distribution and redistribution, it lacks the matrix formulation of the UN accounts (Luxemburg, 1980, 2nd ed.).
4. For the small movement toward implementation since 1968, see United Nations Economic and Social Council, Report of the Secretary-General (July 21, 1982).
5. A more detailed table (Table 2.1 following p. 18 of SNA, 1968), using numbers for illustrative purposes, consists of 88 rows and columns.
6. There is an obverse relationship between market (transaction) and sector which might help to understand the source-uses of funds structure underlying row and column 1. The financial instruments detailed in row one are sources of funds for financial markets and uses of funds for institutional sectors and the rest of the world as shown in the entries for columns 23 and 24. Going down column 1, the liabilities of these sectors are uses of funds from the standpoint of financial markets.
7. "Forms of income" are detailed in Table 2.1 of the SNA in rows 38 to 50. "Current income transfers" account for lines 42 to 50.
8. The early version of the accounts with considerable nonfinancial data covers the period 1939-1955. The revised version in the annual series begins in 1946. The quarterly adjusted and seasonally adjusted series begin with 1952.

   For a brief history, see Cohen, 1972, pp. 14ff; Taylor, 1973; and Hillabold, 1983. For a discussion of the structure of the accounts, see Kendrick, 1971, chapter 9; Federal Reserve, 1980.

9. Table 3 above illustrates these adjustments. The bracket figures are original figures found in Introduction to Flow of Funds. They suggest that saving by the rest of the world was negative which is a misleading picture of today's world. By changing the figures for the government deficit (-18 instead of -10), at the same time that rest of the world saving was increased by 8 (from -4 to +4), adjustments in the cells were reduced to a minimum. The change in one cell requires a change in at least three other cells--one on the transaction row and two down the sector columns. "Loans and securities" were adjusted for the government and the rest of the world sectors, from 15 to 23 and 1 to 9, respectively.

The "conjectural variations" associated with changing one cell of the matrix have been worked out mathematically in Alford (1986, pp. 90-93). This important study of the flow of funds is further discussed in connection with the UK accounts.

10. "Funds raised in credit markets" in a regularly published table in the Federal Reserve Bulletin are also analyzed by sector and instrument.

11. For a detailed discussion of discrepancies, see Federal Reserve, 1980, pp. 26, 46-47; Federal Reserve, 1955), appendix A, pp. 371-77; Hendershott, 1977, appendix E, pp. 353-361.

12. The entire May 1982 issue of the Survey of Current Business was devoted to the Ruggles's "Integrated Economic Accounts for the United States, 1947-80," and comments. In the November issue the Ruggles replied to these comments. Extensive sample accounts covering current and capital transactions, balance sheets with revaluations are provided for 1969-1980.

13. Three conference papers reviewing the United Nations SNA (Review of Income and Wealth, June 1986, pp. 127-212), deal extensively with the possibilities of linking macro accounts with the underlying micro data. The proposed modifications in the accounts should lead to more micro-simulated models of the economy. The pioneering model is that of Orcutt et al., 1961. The most recent study has been authored by Bennett and Bergmann, 1986. The latter represents an advance on the earlier simulation study by testing the predictive power of the model. The authors consider the predictions to be "remarkably good, despite obvious weak spots" (p. 102).

14. William C. Hood, 1958. The accounts at the end of the volume were prepared by L. M. Read, S. J. Handfield-Jones, and F. W. Emmerson.

15. Financial Flow Accounts (Catalogue 13- 002). A summary volume showing annual flows and year-end financial assets and liabilities 1961-1979 has also been published (Catalogue 13-563 Occasional).

16. This corrects an original impression that Canadian and U.S. accountants would come up with the same measure of overall discrepancy (Cohen and Husted 1985a, p. 213). Our error was due to the treatment of the residual error of estimate as the handiwork of the financial accountants rather than the inherited and accepted error from the Canadian national income and expenditure accounts.
17. The Quarterly Bulletin also features frequent articles on the flow of funds (see e.g., Bank of England, 1966, 1967, 1969, 1977).
18. The pitfall models of the "Yale School" make use of a similar zero-sum matrix. See Chapter IX below. On the textbook level, it is found in G. Smith (1982, chapters 1, 16).
19. Another unique feature of the UK accounts pointed out by Alford is that saving and capital formation include capital gains (Alford, pp. 22-23).
20. Alford feels that it is necessary to defend the reversal of signs by concocting a "purchasing power" interpretation of debit and credit entries. Thus persons acquire purchasing power (plus entry) by disposing of money and simultaneously dispose of this purchasing power (minus entry) by acquiring another asset (p. 10). And elsewhere we are told to treat the concept of purchasing power as a form of meta-money: "It is as if the buyer of Z uses money to acquire meta-money and uses the meta-money to acquire Z . . ." (p. 15). One could just as sensibly argue that a reduction of money holdings is a loss of purchasing power and the acquisition of an asset denotes an increase in purchasing power. The statement that debits will be denoted by a minus and credits as a plus (as is routinely done in balance of payments analysis) would have sufficed.
21. The definition of individual sectors is spelled out in the October 1984 Quarterly Bulletin of the Bank, pp. 21-23. The architect of the accounts, Dr. Dimitrije Dimitrijevic, retired general manager of the Research Department, of the National Bank of Yugoslavia, has written a monetary theory text based on the financial accounts (Monetarna Analiza [Belgrade, Yugoslavia, 1981]). I am greatly indebted to Dr. Dimitrijevic for suggestions.
22. Flow-of-funds accounts have been prepared regularly for Austria since 1970. They are published in Monatsberichte des Österreichischen Institute fur Wirtschaftsforschung. See No. 7/1984, No. 4/1985, and No. 4/1986. An earlier study covered the 1960-1977 period (Mooschlechner and Nowotny, 1980). I am indebted to Professor Nowotny and Dr. Mooschlechner for this information.
23. The third series is Financial Statistics Monthly, which covers security issues in international and domestic financial markets and interest rates.
24. OECD, Financial Statistics, Methodological Supplement, 1981, p. 170.

CHAPTER VIII
SIMPLE MODEL BUILDING: THE SECTOR AND TRANSACTION IDENTITIES

DEFICIT-SURPLUS ANALYSIS

The simplest kind of model building focuses on the sector and transaction identities of the flow of funds. For each sector, gross investment equals gross saving (apart from discrepancy) but when gross investment is decomposed into net financial investment and capital outlays, each sector will either show a surplus or a deficit. An excess of final product expenditures over receipts from the gross national product or an excess of investment over saving ($I_i - S_i > 0$), indicates that a sector is a deficit sector and is exercising an expansionary effect on the economy A reverse situation ($S_i - I_i > 0$) identifies a sector as a surplus sector, one which is exerting a damping effect on the economy. Alternatively, a deficit sector can be defined as one experiencing a net money inflow from financial transactions ($L_i - A_i > 0$) and a surplus sector as one experiencing a net money outflow from financial transactions ($A_i - L_i > 0$). Combining these two points of view indicates the underlying assumptions of surplus-deficit analysis about real-financial linkages. A deficit sector is one which converts financial sources into final product expenditures ($L_i - A_i = I_i - S_i$).

The weakness of straight surplus-deficit analysis is the equality of surpluses and deficits for the economy as a whole. This makes it impossible to say which sector is expansionary or deflationary. One sector's surplus is as much responsible for a second sector's deficit as the other way around.[1]

One way of overcoming this difficulty is to maintain that a deficit sector is responsible for other sectors' surpluses and to single out the responsible deficit sector. The "New Cambridge" school of British economists in the 1970s argued that the overseas sector surplus (balance of payments deficit) varied directly with the public sector deficit (Johnson, 1977, pp.

250-51; Alford, 100-01). The same argument has been repeated recently (Congdon, 1982). Congdon begins with the identity:

Overseas sector net financial investment (NFI) = public sector's NFI + private sector's NFI

When the overseas sector's NFI is positive, a country is running a current account deficit. Congdon dismisses the private sector current account deficit as a balance of payments problem between "consenting adults." This leaves the public sector current account deficit which is equal to the financial deficit less sales of public sector debt to the domestic private sector (including money creation). From this identity it follows that the external deficit can be reduced in only two ways--by reducing the budget deficit or by increasing domestic sales of public sector debt. Other measures such as restricting imports must fail.[2]

A more comprehensive Keynesian identity was employed to reach the same conclusion (Eltis, 1976). Keynesian policies can be described in terms of the following sector surpluses and deficits.

$$\left(\begin{matrix}\text{government}\\ \text{expenditure}\end{matrix} - \text{taxation}\right) \equiv \left(\begin{matrix}\text{private}\\ \text{saving}\end{matrix} - \begin{matrix}\text{private}\\ \text{investment}\end{matrix}\right) + (\text{imports} - \text{exports})$$

Assume that government expenditure is increased by 3,000 dollars and taxes reduced by 3,000. Assume further that as a result of the expansion in national income, saving and tax revenues rise equally and both rise by $3000. The net reduction in taxes is zero as a result and the private saving of $3000 finances the increase in government expenditure. The error in Keynesian thinking, however, is to ignore the expansionary effect of national income on private investment. If we assume that private investment rises by 3,000, the identity only balances if the deficit in the balance of payments (the difference between imports and exports), rises by 3,000. The budget deficit is responsible for the balance of payments deficit (Eltis, pp. 4-5).

The contemporary concern with the U.S. current account deficit at a time of record public sector deficits has resulted in the same causal interpretation being given to the identity. The current account balance is seen as turning negative as the total government deficit began to rise (see, e.g., Lawrence and Litan, 1985, 6-7; Krugman, 1983, 123-24; Cohen, 1984b; Branson, 1985). The assumed causality does not always hold, however. A large public sector deficit in 1975 coincided with positive U.S. net foreign investment (Dornbusch, 1980, pp. 17-24).

Bulls, Bears, and Sheep. The previous causal interpretation can be avoided by working with the first differences of surpluses and deficits and assuming that a sector has more discretion over its real uses of funds than its real sources. In this way, Copeland develops a three-part classification of bulls, bears, and sheet (1952, pp. 259ff). Active sectors whose real uses of funds are increasing faster than real sources of funds are bulls ($\Delta I > \Delta S$, $\Delta I > 0$); bears are active sectors whose real uses of funds are decreasing faster than real sources of funds ($|\Delta I| > |\Delta S|$, $\Delta I < 0$); sheep are sectors whose sources are changing by a greater amount than their uses ($\Delta I / \Delta S < 1$). If sheep are distinguished as "inflationary" and "deflationary," (those whose real uses are increasing and decreasing respectively), the classification becomes four-fold. In the place of four sectors, the number can be expanded to eight if we distinguish between decreases and increases in surpluses and deficits.[3] Such analyses have been little used since Copeland's application of his classification to the 1936-42 period in the United States. Several reasons can be suggested. The ex post nature of the analysis rules against its use in forecasting. The fact that a sector is a bullish sector may not be an indication as to future behavior. Moreover, bullish or bearish behavior may not be correlated with movements in the GNP.[4] One can also question its basic premise: that discretion for changes in external finance lies with the borrower and never with the lender.[5]

Nevertheless, it is interesting to identify nonfinancial sectors as bulls, bears, and sheep. The following table uses a four-fold classification for the U.S. based on changes in GNP expenditures and in net financial investment.

Bulls: $\Delta \overset{+}{E}$ $\Delta \overset{-}{NFI}$ Inflationary Sheep: $\Delta \overset{+}{E}$ $\Delta \overset{+}{NFI}$

Bears: $\Delta \overset{-}{E}$ $\Delta \overset{+}{NFI}$ Deflationary Sheep: $\Delta \overset{-}{E}$ $\Delta \overset{-}{NFI}$

The most dynamic sector is seen to be the rest of the world with only two years of "sheepish" behavior. More cases of bearishness are found here than for any other sector. The household sector is the leading passive sector with expenditures generally going along with increases in income (inflationary sheep). The leading bullish sector is business followed by both levels of government. While households and business do not rotate their surplus-deficit positions as suggested by Gurley and Shaw (see Chapter II), there is evidence that they do indeed move in opposite directions. Increases in household surpluses accompany increases in business deficits and decreases in household surpluses accompany decreases in business deficits. The correlation 1949-1984 in the annual series for net financial investment is -.765. It declines to -.478 in the quarterly unadjusted data.[6]

FINANCIAL MARKET IDENTITIES

Instead of sectoral identities, financial market forecasters have made use of the financial transaction identities both for individual markets and for financial markets in the aggregate. Thus,

$$\sum_{i=1}^{m} A_{ij} = \sum_{i=1}^{m} L_{ij}$$

where A and L indicate lending and borrowing respectively and j indicates a series of market instruments. On the basis of forecasts of demand supply and the market identities, financial

TABLE VIII.1 BULLS, BEARS, AND SHEEP, 1950-81

	1950	51	52	53	54	55	56	57	58	59	60	61	62	63	64	65	66
Households	IS	IS	BL	BL	BL	BL	IS	IS	IS	BL	IS	IS	IS	IS	IS	IS	IS
Nonfinan. Business	BL	IS	BR	IS	BR	BL	BL	BR	BR	BL	BL	BR	BL	BL	BL	BL	BL
States & Loc.	BL	IS	BR	IS	BR	BL	BL	BL	BL	IS	IS	BL	IS	IS	DL	IS	IS
U.S. Govt.	BR	BL	BL	BL	BR	BR	DS	BL	BL	BR	BR	BL	IS	IS	BL	IS	BL
Rest of World	BR	BL	BR	BR	BR	BL	BL	BL	BR	BR	BL	BL	BR	BL	DL	BR	BR

	67	68	69	70	71	72	73	74	75	76	77	78	79	80	81	TOTALS BL	TOTALS BR	TOTALS IS	TOTALS DS
Households	IS	BL	BL	IS	BL	IS	IS	IS	IS	BL	BL	IS	IS	IS	IS	10	0	22	0
Nonfinan. Business	BR	BL	BL	DS	IS	IS	BL	BL	BR	BL	BL	BL	IS	BR	BL	18	8	5	1
States & Loc.	BL	BL	BL	IS	BL	IS	IS	IS	IS	IS	IS	BL	IS	BL	IS	13	2	17	0
U.S. Govt.	BL	IS	BR	DS	BL	IS	IS	BL	BL	IS	IS	IS	IS	BL	BL	14	6	10	2
Rest of World	BR	BR	BR	BL	BR	DS	IS	BR	BL	BR	BR	BR	BL	BL	BL	13	17	1	1

BL - Bulls
BR = Bears

IS = Inflationary Sheep
DS = Deflationary Sheep

Source: Federal Reserve Flow of Funds Accounts.

flow, and market clearing rates of interest have been predicted (Cohen, 1972, p. 3; Ronk, 1981; Bankers Trust, 1984).

Bankers Trust Forecasting. The following table illustrates the Bankers Trust Company use of the financial market identity for forecasting purposes (see Table VIII.2). "Funds raised" (by sectors) are the uses of funds from the standpoint of financial market. "Funds supplied" by lenders describes the supply of funds (sources of funds) side of the market. Similar tables were prepared by Bankers Trust for individual financial markets.[7]

What is known for certain is that ex post, credit demanded will equal credit supplied. The forecast is concerned with ex ante values. If ex ante demand exceeds ex ante supply at current interest rates, the forecast will be that the gap will be closed by higher interest rates. Early in 1984 interest rates were expected to clear the market when $586 billion of funds were demanded and supplied about $60 billion more than 1983. A firming trend was predicted for 1984 interest rates because of tight monetary policy and an unprecedented fiscal environment (substantial government borrowing) (Bankers Trust, 1984, p. 11). In retrospect the forecast of higher interest rates turned out to be correct, but borrowings were greatly underestimated (Federal Reserve, 1985, p. 3).

The composition of sources of funds has also been taken as a clue to future interest rate movements. The amount of noninstitutional funds supplied signals varying degrees of tightness in financial markets (Cohen, 1972, p. 6; Ronk, 1981). Greater dependence on a residual sector (households, personal trusts, nonprofit organizations and the rest of the world) heralds rising interest rates.[8]

Long-Term Forecasting. Financial market forecasts whether short run or long run take as their starting point a projection of the "real economy"--spending, income, and saving of the various sectors--(Shuford, 1977; Wachtel, 1981b). The real economy is then

TABLE VIII.2
PROJECTION OF FUNDS RAISED AND SUPPLIED, 1984, BANKERS TRUST

	1977	1978	1979	1980	1981	1982 (est.)	1983 (proj.)
FUNDS RAISED							
Investment funds	186.4	219.1	235.7	232.2	191.7	198.5	214.3
Short-term funds	100.5	123.8	137.3	81.8	120.6	55.0	63.4
U.S. Government and budget agency securities, privately held	51.5	46.8	29.9	75.7	78.0	151.7	191.5
Total uses	338.5	389.7	403.0	389.7	390.3	405.2	469.2
FUNDS SUPPLIED							
Insurance companies and pension funds							
Life insurance companies	29.4	33.7	33.6	33.9	38.0	40.8	44.3
Private noninsured pension funds	16.5	16.0	15.9	20.8	21.5	25.2	26.6
State and local retirement funds	13.9	14.3	19.4	23.4	23.2	29.4	31.5
Fire and casualty insurance companies	19.3	19.2	17.5	14.4	12.7	12.6	14.0
Total	79.1	83.2	86.5	92.6	95.4	108.0	116.4
Thrift institutions							
Savings and loan associations	61.3	56.7	51.5	42.1	23.8	18.6	44.0
Mutual savings banks	11.7	8.6	4.8	5.3	−.2	−.5	6.2
Credit unions	8.2	8.3	2.0	−2.2	.8	1.2	5.0
Total	81.2	73.6	58.3	45.2	24.4	19.3	55.2
Investment companies	3.4	5.2	22.4	22.5	72.9	51.7	47.1
Other financial intermediaries							
Finance companies	19.4	20.9	24.1	11.8	22.6	3.8	9.1
Mortgage companies	3.7	2.6	−1.4	2.8	.2	−2.6	1.7
Real estate investment trusts	−2.4	−1.1	−1.0	−.7	−1.1	−.8	−.5
Total	20.7	22.4	21.7	13.9	21.7	.4	10.3
Commercial banks	89.9	125.9	120.3	100.5	108.7	96.0	107.3
Business							
Business corporations	14.9	9.6	24.9	14.8	8.2	9.8	15.9
Noncorporate business	.5	1.4	1.8	.5	2.7	1.3	1.7
Total	15.4	11.0	26.7	15.3	10.9	11.1	17.6
Government							
U.S. Government	2.0	3.1	6.2	6.9	4.3	2.4	2.9
Federally sponsored agencies	2.9	13.8	19.8	18.0	14.0	13.3	10.0
State and local general funds	8.9	11.5	8.1	14.9	14.4	18.7	21.2
Total	13.8	28.4	34.1	39.8	32.8	34.4	34.1
Foreign investors	42.2	40.4	−3.2	28.2	21.9	27.3	30.5
Individuals and others	21.6	47.1	86.4	69.2	58.9	80.9	81.4
Total gross sources	367.2	437.3	453.2	427.2	447.7	429.1	499.9
Less: Funds raised by financial intermediaries							
Investment funds	11.2	9.2	10.0	8.2	−1.1	4.1	6.4
Short-term funds	11.5	14.5	16.7	5.2	28.4	2.6	9.5
Federally sponsored agency securities, privately held	6.0	23.9	23.6	24.1	30.1	17.2	14.8
Total	28.7	47.6	50.3	37.5	57.4	23.9	30.7
Total net sources	338.5	389.7	403.0	389.7	390.3	405.2	469.2

<u>Source</u>: Bankers Trust, 1984:T1

linked in judgmental forecasts to broad financial aggregates. Initial projections are made of individual financial markets and demand and supply brought into balance by an iteration process (see Wachtel, 1981b, pp. 604-05, for the 1985 projection of the supply and demand for funds expressed as percentages of GNP). For each financial instrument demand equals supply. Over all sectors total financial uses equal total sources. For each sector the excess of financial uses over sources equals net financial investment which sums to zero over all sectors.

The failure to work back from financial markets to the real economy detracts from the original purpose of the Shuford-Wachtel enterprise--to determine the likelihood of a future capital shortage. Since the real flows are assumed and not revised, this seems to be a question-begging procedure. Financial flows are made consistent with projections of saving and capital outlay projections.

The Bank of England. While the accuracy of Bank of England forecasts cannot be assessed, the procedure has been spelled out in considerable detail (Bain, 1973, pp. 1078-81; Hewitt, 1977). The flow-of-funds (financial transactions) matrix discussed in Chapter VIII is rearranged for forecasting purposes as shown in Table VIII.3. The aim is to zero in on the policy targets of public sector borrowing requirements and the monetary aggregates.

The exercise consists of four separate but related forecasts: world economic prospects; output and expenditure at constant and current prices; external capital movements; and domestic financial flows (Hewitt, p. 188). Real and financial variables do not interact directly in an integrated forecasting model as is the case at the Fed (see below). The starting point for the financial forecast is the national income forecast of surpluses and deficits (line 5 of Table VIII.3). The matrix is organized to focus on the "public sector borrowing requirement" (line 34). The preceding lines, 6-33, sum up to this figure (L8,799). The separate forecast of external capital flows

TABLE VIII.3 U.K. FLOW OF FUNDS IN 1975/1976: FORECASTING MATRIX

£ millions

	Line	Central government	Local authorities	Public corporations	Overseas	Persons	Industrial and commercial companies	Banks	Other financial institutions	Unallocated
Capital account										
Receipts +, payments –										
Saving	1	– 1,977	2,057	1,682		11,464	9,425	460		
Capital transfers (net)	2	– 409	20	332		– 252	401	– 92		
Fixed investment	3	– 1,332	– 4,005	– 4,193		– 3,210	– 6,917	– 1,621		
Stockbuilding	4	– 55	–	– 625		– 614	– 2,567	– 50		
Financial surplus/deficit	5	– 3,763	– 1,928	– 2,804	1,204	7,388	342	– 1,303		864
								200	1,503	
Financial transactions										
Receipts –, payments +										
Government lending	6	3,914	– 1,150	– 2,120	– 594	– 9	– 168		127	
Lending by public corporations (other than for house purchase)	7			97	– 86		– 11			
Trade credit (net) extended and received by public corporations	8			24		– 322	298			
Accruals adjustments etc. (see notes)	9	957	40	– 675		– 29	– 213	– 33	– 47	
Deposits with:										
Building societies	10					4,488	29		– 4,517	
Savings banks	11					221			– 221	
Hire-purchase companies etc.	12				179	– 1	50		– 228	
Life assurance and pension funds	13					4,783			– 4,783	
Unit trust units	14					101			– 101	
Company borrowing through hire purchase	15						14		– 14	
Borrowing through hire purchase for consumption	16			– 4		– 79	73		10	
Loans for house purchase:										
Building societies	17					– 3,042			3,042	
Other (excluding banks)	18		462	228		– 748			58	
Lending to central government by public sector pension funds	19	– 277							277	
Loans and mortgages by other financial institutions	20					7	– 27		20	
UK private investment overseas	21				– 1,355		1,355			
Overseas investment in UK private sector	22				2,523		– 2,531		8	
External liabilities and claims banking adjustment (see notes)	23				– 746		727	19		
Capital issues	24						– 1,360	– 299	– 303	
Other company and overseas securities	25	367	–	107	– 134	– 1,271	532	[a] – 29 [b] – 10 [c] 78	2,322	
Banks' foreign currency claims on deposits with non-residents	26				810			– 810		
Banks:										
Foreign currency lending for investment overseas	27						– 145	320	– 175	
Other bank lending in foreign currency to private sector	28					60	– 345	273	12	
Bank lending in sterling	29				– 432	– 12	476	96	– 128	
Domestic foreign currency bank deposits Sterling bank deposits	30 31	102	50	103	– 389	914	869	– 50 – 2,409	32	
Subtotal	32	5,063	598	– 2,240	554	5,061	– 377	– 2,854	– 4,609	

(Table XIII.3 continued)

	Line	Central government	Local authorities	Public corporations	Overseas	Persons	Industrial and commercial companies	Banks	Other financial institutions	Unallocated
Unidentified	33	*- 27*	*- 8*	*- 60*	*- 553*	*1,311*	*- 419*	*- 321*	*- 787*	*864*
Public sector borrowing requirement	34	- 8,799	- 1,322	- 504	1,203	1,016	1,138	3,375	3,893	
Treasury bills	35	517			- 517					
British government stocks	36	59			- 59					
Direct borrowing by central government	37	84			- 84					
Reserves etc. (= currency flow)	38	- 1,170			1,170					
Borrowing by local authorities and public corporations	39		4	- 697	693					
External finance	40	510	4	- 697	1,203					
Notes and coin	41	463				233	230			
National savings	42	496				496				
Certificates of tax deposit	43	4				- 10	6			
British government stocks	44	- 3,827				590	130		3,107	
Treasury bills	45	- 808					506		301	
Northern Ireland central government debt	46	- 18				- 35	17			
Local authority short-term debt	47		381	1		- 144	19		- 257	
Other local authority debt	48		- 659	1		- 102	28		790	
Public corporations' debt (pension funds etc.)	49		- 43	109		- 12	- 5		- 49	
Issue Department transactions in commercial bills	50	263					263			
Other Issue Department transactions	51	234	- 234							
Non-banks	52	- 5,601	- 55	109		1,016	1,138		3,893	
Banks	53	- 2,688	- 771	84				3,375		

nil or less than £½ million.

Notes

PSBR (borrowing) = line 34 (CG + LA + PC) = £ - 10,625 million.

Sterling DCE = lines 25b + 29 + 53 (banks) + line 40 (overseas) + line 41 (persons + ICCs) = £5,127 million.

Change in sterling M_3 = line 31 (CG + LA + PC + persons + ICCs + OFIs) + line 41 (persons + ICCs) + line 30 (banks) = £2,483 million.

DCE (old definition) = lines 25b + 28 + 29 + 53 (banks) + line 40 (overseas) + line 41 (persons + ICCs) = £5,400 million.

Change (increase -) in banks' non-deposit liabilities = lines 33 5 + 24 + 25a + 9 (banks) = £ - 882 million.

Government lending (line 6) includes CG refinance of export credit.

Line 9: the national income accounts record items (such as payments of VAT) as they accrue, the financial accounts as they are actually paid. This adjustment reconciles the respective figures.

Line 23: this is an adjustment to reconcile differences of coverage etc. between figures of UK banks' net external liabilities as used in the balance of payments accounts and those used in the financial accounts.

The entry for 'banks' on line 25 ('other company and overseas securities') comprises:

[a] mainly banks' take-up of shares of own subsidiaries;

[b] banks' take-up of shares of non-banks;

[c] banks' take-up of overseas shares (sterling and foreign currency).

<u>Source:</u> Hewitt, p. 196

provides estimates of external financing of the public sector (lines 35-40).

Lines 10-25 detail the largest domestic flows within the nonbank private sector. On the basis of these flows and the sources and uses of funds statements of this sector, purchases of various forms of public sector can be estimated (summarized in line 34 and 52 and detailed in lines 41-51). Net bank finance of the public sector (line 53) can then be calculated as a residual which reflects UK practice in public financing (Hewitt, p. 192). From bank asset information sterling bank deposits (line 31) can be simultaneously determined from banks' nondeposit liabilities (see notes to table) and from domestically held foreign currency deposits (line 30). As detailed in the notes, it is then possible to calculate and forecast the key monetary aggregates.

The Bank appears to rely more extensively than the Federal Reserve on econometric estimation, e.g., predictions of the money stock based on demand-for-money equations or forecasts of new security issues using the Bank's econometric relations. The problems faced by the forecaster because of psychological intangibles--the state of market confidence and market expectations--are stressed (Hewitt, p. 190). Judgments become "precarious."

The London Business School. The London Business School Centre for Economic Forecasting began forecasting financial flows in 1983 and publishing them quarterly in Financial Outlook. They are based on forecasts of income and expenditure produced by the main LBS model. (For an updated version of this model, see London Business School, February 1985). Table VIII.4 reproduces ex post estimates for 1982/83 and projections for two forecast years, 1983/84 and 1986/87. The discrepancy is buried in a residual asset account. Despite this residual asset account, the authors deride "dustbin" techniques where the asset and sector represented by the last row and column act as a residual.[9] The LBS financing flow model purports to eliminate the residual by forecasting asset prices that clear asset

TABLE VIII.4 SUMMARY NAFA AND FINANCIAL FLOWS

£ billion

	Personal sector	ICCs	Overseas	Banks B.Socs and finance houses	Pension Funds, Ins.Cos, Unit and Invt. Trusts	Public sector
1982/3						
Savings	21	17	−5	4		5
Less Investment	−9	−16	–	−5		−13
Gives Net acquisition of financial assets (NAFA)	11	1	−5	0	−2	−8
Acquisition (+) and disposals (−) by type of asset: (1)						
Broad Money: bank and Building Society deposits and notes and coin	16	1	4	−22	0	0
Loans by banks, Building Societies and by finance houses etc:	−20	−2	−3	25	0	0
Long term assets – gilts etc, equities, debentures and National Savings:	0	0	1	−1	6	−5
Foreign currency assets:	0	2	−6	0	4	−1
Inflows to pension funds and other assets including unidentified:	15	0	−2	−1	−13	−1
1983/4						
Savings	17	25	0	2		6
Less Investment	−11	−20	–	−6		−14
Gives Net acquisition of financial assets (NAFA)	6	4	0	0	−3	−8
Aquisition (+) and disposals (−) by type of asset: (1)						
Broad Money: bank and Building Society deposits and notes and coin	15	6	3	−23	0	−1
Loans by banks, Building Societies and by finance houses etc:	−21	−1	−2	22	0	2
Long term assets – gilts etc, equities, debentures and National Savings:	0	−1	2	2	7	−10
Foreign currency assets:	0	2	−2	−1	2	0
Inflows to pension funds and other assets including unidentified:	13	0	0	0	−14	0

(Table VIII.4 continued)

					1986/7		
	Savings	21	33	0	2		17
Less	Investment	−15	−30	−	−8		−20
Gives	Net acquisition of financial assets (NAFA)	6	3	0	0	−6	−3
Acquisition (+) and disposals (−) by type of asset: [1]							
	Broad Money: bank and Building Society deposits and notes and coin	16	4	3	−25	1	−1
	Loans by banks, Building Societies and by finance houses etc:	−22	−4	−1	25	0	3
	Long term assets – gilts etc, equities, debentures and National Savings:	−5	0	1	0	9	−6
	Foreign currency assets:	−1	4	−5	0	1	0
	Inflows to pension funds and other assets including unidentified:	19	0	0	1	−19	0

(1) Increase in assets or reduction in liabilities shown positive; reduction in assets or increase in liabilities shown negative.

Because of the National accounts residual error, the net acquisitions of financial assets do not always sum precisely to zero. The sum of unidentified financial transactions, included in the last row, is equal and opposite to the residual error. Net acquisition of financial assets is not precisely equal to savings less investment--it also includes net capital transfers.

Source: LBS *Financial Outlook*, 1983, p. 3.

markets. Something has to "give" in the forecast if interest rates and quantities in financial markets are inconsistent with the government's target interest rate on "gilts" (pp. 32-35). While this leads to ex ante forecasts without row discrepancy, it would be absurd to expect that residual errors will not be prominent in the ex post magnitudes.

The LBS forecasting model goes beyond financial market identities by econometric estimation of financial asset demands. The forecasting model deserves a second classification then, as a portfolio balance model. The modeling of expectations is noteworthy also because users of the model are allowed to choose between rational, exogenous, and adaptive expectation forming regimes (LBS, 1985, p. 155).[10] Evaluations to date of the effectiveness of LBS modeling are guarded (Alford, 78).

BALANCING THE MATRIX

Federal Reserve The full discipline of the flow of funds can be used to forecast real and financial flows. Let us say that fixed estimates are made for five of the eight entries of a two-sector two-transaction matrix as shown in Table VIII.5. The forecaster may base them on judgment or on functional relationships that are not part of the model. Thus, if the forecaster takes I_1, S_1, A_1, I_2, S_2 as initially given, he can automatically estimate L_1, A_2, L_2 from the balanced matrix. After initial estimation by "successive approximations" on the basis of "plausibility" and "reasonableness" he can vary all the values to achieve a balanced matrix. This is the forecasting technique at the Fed (Cohen, 1972, p. 3; Taylor, 1963).[11] Initially, the nonfinancial flows (saving, capital outlays), are forecast by the Fed national income forecasting unit. Financial flows are then projected on the basis of the real flows. An iterative process is followed with the real projection modified in the light of the financial forecast, and so on. Unfortunately, the Federal Reserve has never published the "log" on any of its forecasts. The one paper where detailed flow-of-funds statements are presented works out the financial implications of a Data Resources Incorporated (DRI) income and product projection rather than demonstrating an iterative adjustment in real and financial flows (Taylor, 1974).

TABLE VIII.5 A SCHEMATIC FLOW-OF-FUNDS TABLE

	Sector 1		Sector 2	
	Dr(Uses)	Cr(Sources)	Dr(Uses)	Cr(Sources)
Transactions:				
1 "Real"	I_1	S_1	I_2	S_2
2 "Financial"	A_1	L_1	A_2	I_2

AN INTEGRATED TWO-COUNTRY MATRIX

The attraction of merging the flow-of-funds matrices of two countries is that it adds an additional constraint in forecasting real and financial flows. Barring statistical discrepancy, the bilateral balance of payments of one country should be the mirror image of the bilateral balance for the second. When converted to subsectors of each country's rest of the world sector (the second subsector will be the "rest" of the rest of the world), the reciprocal relationship still holds. For example, if Canada is recorded with positive gross saving in the U.S. matrix, then the U.S. will be recorded with negative gross saving in the U.S. subsector of the Canadian rest of the world sector.

Such a matrix has been the basis of a joint forecast of Canadian-U.S. flow of funds for 1985 (Cohen and Husted, 1985a; 1985b). The forecast was limited to key aggregates--gross saving, capital outlays, increases in financial assets and liabilities for twelve Canadian and eight U.S. domestic sectors, plus two subsectors of the rest of the world for each country. Initial values of the cells were based on autoregressive estimates using one- or two-year lags in the annual data. Unlike the London Business School, sector statistical discrepancy was deemed inevitable and was itself forecast by autoregressive techniques with outside variables being introduced for the bilateral rest of the world subsectors. Depending on the "reasonableness" of the discrepancy forecast (looking at past historical data), they replaced residual estimates. In such a case, the effect was to constrain the sum of debits and credits for the remaining cells.

There is an additional advantage in joint estimation. Certain cell values, representing monetary and fiscal policy, can be taken as exogenous and their effects on the remaining cell values can be studied by regression techniques. Thus, we tested the hypothesis that U.S. disturbance variables exerted more effect on the Canadian endogenous cell values than similar Canadian disturbances (Cohen and Husted, forthcoming).

Notes

1. The "special papers" of the Bank of Japan provide an extensive analysis of sector surpluses and deficits on an annual basis. They suffer from this inability to provide a causal explanation. (See, e.g., Bank of Japan, 1985)
2. The author points out the irony of the Cambridge Economic Policy Group recently showing enthusiasm for import controls when it runs counter to the New Cambridge School theory of the mid-1970s (Congdon, p. 14).
3. Thus, in J. Tinbergen and D. B. J. Schouten (1955), decreases in surpluses and increases in deficits are reflationary and inflationary respectively. Similarly, on the contractionary side, increases in surpluses are disinflationary while decreases in deficits are deflationary. On this basis, bulls could be reflationary and inflationary, bears disinflationary and deflationary, and sheep would fall into all four categories
4. Still, when percentage changes in nominal GNP were related to the frequency of bulls, bears, and inflationary sheep, ("deflationary sheep" was dropped because of high correlation with the other predictor variables), bulls and inflationary sheep have the expected positive sign and are significant at the 5% level over the 1951-1981 period.
5. An apportionment procedure can be used, however, for estimating the "financial" contribution of a lending sector. See Cohen, 1972, pp. 6-7; Cohen and Grodzins, 1963.
6. An earlier study shows considerable rotation on an individual transactor basis (Goldsmith, 1969, 418-426). A study of 565 larger American corporations 1952-63 indicates that almost one-half had rotation ratios lying between 0.3 and -0.3, "indicating a considerable alternation of years with financial surplus and years with financial deficit" (p. 424). The rotation ratio is defined as the ratio of the arithmetic to the absolute sum of the subperiods' surpluses and deficits (p. 419).
7. Publication of Credit and Capital Markets ceased with the 1984 projection.
8. I am told that Sally Ronk steered the Bankers Trust projections (which were originally her handiwork) toward an emphasis on interest rate forecasts. Other economists at the bank have thought that too great an emphasis was placed in the annual publication on interest rates and not enough on "where the money was coming from" say, to finance business uses of funds. Projection of resources and uses of funds by sector should have received the primary emphasis.
9. It is not clear from the discussion whether a residual error of estimate column and row is meant or whether some identifiable asset and sector receives all the "rubbish" from elsewhere in the system.
10. Initially, only rational expectations were modeled according to the initial issue of Financial Outlook. Markets were assumed to form their expectations by "using a model

like the LBS one" (p. 34). Expectations are seen as self-fulfilling. The emphasis on rational expectations is not surprising since the research director of the center at the time was David K. H. Begg.

11. The Federal Reserve prefers the milder term "projections" to the word "forecasts" (Taylor, 1963, p. 254).

CHAPTER IX
FLOW-FLOW MODELS

Self-sufficient models of the flow of funds go beyond the constraints of simple identities. One type developed by Stone (1966) is a "financial input-output" model. Programming models are a closely related class. A third category can be described as a model of circular flow.

FINANCIAL INPUT-OUTPUT MODELS

Investment as Disturbance. Stone's first financial input-output model can be thought of as a simple Keynesian-type model in which investment plays the role of exogenous disturbance. Continuing the previous notation (Chapter VIII, Table VII.5) for the two-sector model, we have the following relationships:

IX.1 $S_1 = aL_1$

IX.2 $S_2 = I_1 + I_2 - S_1$ (Identity)

IX.3 $A_1 = bL_1 + bL_2$

IX.4 $A_2 = (1 - b)L_1 + (1-b)L_2$ (Identity)

IX.5 $L_1 = cA_2$

IX.6 $L_2 = A_2 + I_2 - S_2$ (Identity)

The three independent identities are supplemented by three structural relationships. The saving (income) of sector 1 is a fixed proportion of increases in its liabilities (equation 1). The increases in financial assets of the first sector are proportionally related to the increases in liabilities of both sectors (equation 3). (I assume combined rather than netted sector accounts so that intrasector transactions are recorded in the accounts.) Finally, the increase in liabilities of the first sector has a fixed relationship with the increases in financial assets of the second sector (equation 5). The six relations are sufficient to solve for S_i, A_i, and L_i, given the I values.

Saving as Disturbance. Alternatively, a model can be formulated with saving the generating force and the remaining variables endogenously determined. Thus, in the place of (1), (3), (4), and (5), we now have

IX.1A $I_1 = aA_1$

IX.3A $L_1 = bA_1 + bA_2$

IX.4A $L_2 = (1-b)A_1 + (1-b)A_2$ (Identity)

IX.5A $A_1 = cL_2$

Stone goes beyond these formulations by suggesting that both saving and investment could be exogenously determined and, in addition, sectors could follow their "preferred portfolio patterns." What would now have to give is the quantity and composition of financial claims issued by the various sectors. Under certain conditions, an empirical solution could be reached by means of the RAS technique (Stone, 1963 and Stone, 1966, pp. 24-25). In a second version, saving and investment could be independently determined, sectors could follow their preferred patterns of liabilities, and the composition of portfolios could be made to give to assure a balanced set of accounts.

The Cambridge Financial Interdependence Model. The Stone investment model has been applied to the British capital accounts (Stone and Roe, 1971; Bain, 1973; Roe, 1973). Assuming that each investing sector finances new investment by issuing liabilities in a fixed proportion and any given sector always holds the same share of any given financial claim, then a change in real assets (investment) generates consistent balance sheet values for each sector. The matrix multiplier can be written as:

$$(I_{jj} - A^*_{jk}\, L^*_{kj})^{-1}$$

where A^*_{jk} denotes the n x m coefficients matrix for "k" asset holdings (k = 1...m) by "j" sectors (j = 1...n), and L^*_{kj} represents the corresponding matrix for liabilities.

Using this matrix multiplier, £1000 of real investment by the personal sector, for example, as shown in Table IX.1, would lead to an increase of £1,116 in the sector's total asset holdings. The rationale of this excess over £1000 of real investment is that the personal sector will borrow (e.g., mortgage or consumer credit). This leads to an increase in the assets of lenders which must be matched by an equal increase in liabilities which will be held as someone's assets (Stone and Roe, pp. 17-18; Roe, p. 417).

TABLE IX.1 THE MATRIX MULTIPLIER
$(I_{jj} - A_{jk}{*}L_{kj}{*})^{-1}$ for 1962
(All elements multiplied by 1,000)

Financing Sector \ Investing Sector	Persons	Financial Institutions	Nonfinancial Companies	Government
Persons	1,116	1,000	761	1,217
Financial Institutions	104	1,324	409	649
Nonfinancial Companies	39	202	1,244	322
Government	32	104	243	1,282

Source: Roe, p. 417.

When the matrix multiplier is premultiplied by the coefficient matrix $L_{kj}{*}$ the total increase in financial assets for each sector can be broken down by specific financial classes. A basic conceptual difficulty is that the model is based on balance sheet values. It is therefore assumed that investment will be financed by each sector in the proportions suggested by the balance sheet statements (as represented by the $L_{kj}{*}$ matrix) and that these will be distributed in fixed proportions among asset portfolios (constancy of $A_{jk}{*}$).[1] When the pattern of new investment by the various sectors departs from the distribution of existing tangible assets, the pattern of asset holdings will no longer be consistent with the balance sheet

A_{jk}^* and this matrix will have to be adjusted (Bain, p. 1073).[2]

The instability of input-output coefficients in the sphere of production due to changes in relative prices, technical innovation, etc., is well known. This instability is compounded in the financial realm by the greater importance of the price (interest rate) element (Stone and Roe, pp. 20-21). It is not surprising, then, that the coefficients for 1962 and 1966 were found to be sharply at variance with each other (Bain, p. 1074; Roe, p. 419).[3]

PROGRAMMING MODELS

Programming models differ from financial input-output models by maximizing an objective function subject to the financial constraints imposed by a flow-of-funds framework. Three studies can be cited (Stone, 1970; Thore and Vardal, 1974; Correa, 1977). The most interesting study is the second mentioned because of its empirical content and implications for financial disequilibrium; the Correa study has the virtue of integrating the nonfinancial and financial sectors. The Stone model is unique in taking account of borrower and lender risk.

Thore and Vardal's "mathematical programming of a credit network" has its point of departure in Thore's earlier work on credit networks (see Chapter I above). The objective function is the sum of the profit functions of six Norwegian financial institutions for the year 1971. The arguments in these functions are the markets rates for assets and liabilities as of January 1, 1971. The institutional setting, the legal framework and current banking and monetary policy provide a hundred mathematical restrictions (p. 449). The linear program solves for the combined portfolios of the six institutions. The duals to the selected constraints (e.g., liquidity rules set by the Monetary and Credit Act of 1965) reveal whether or not they are binding. In addition to the global solution based on given interest yields, a so-called decomposed or decentralized solution solves for market clearing ("corrected") interest rates.

These measure the departure from given yields (as of January 1, 1971) for open market instruments if these markets are to clear. The relevant interest rates are for portfolio items participating in "coupling" relations. These refer to transactions in government securities (Treasury bills and bonds). Since the corrected interest rates are higher than actual rates, in a decentralized setting (where couplings are recognized), higher interest rates would be necessary to induce financial intermediaries to arrive at portfolio decisions which would clear the markets. This denotes an excess supply (of securities) situation in these markets. The smallness of the correction (less than one percent) is due to institutional requirements in buttressing the demand for securities. These constraints (e.g., supplementary reserve requirements) relieve pressure on financial markets. The programming model has planning implications. The model can be solved for alternative sets of policy so the authorities can evaluate the effects of contemplated action, e.g., changing reserve requirements or imposing ceilings on borrowing abroad (p. 449).

CIRCULAR FLOW MODELS[4]

Financial input-output models of the Stone and Roe variety have a serious shortcoming. Investment no matter what the amount is always assured of finance. The A_{jk}^* and L_{kj}^* matrices guarantee it. (It also follows from the fixed relationships in the simple Stone investment model above.) It can be argued that any increase in investment requires a new outside source of finance--one that is not automatically explained by investment. An increase in borrowing precedes an increase in investment. What makes this possible is money creation and/or monetary dissaving. The following model replaces investment as the shock variable with monetary disturbances. The circularity of nonmonetary flows are now spelled out by linking sector uses of funds with their sources of funds which in turn are linked with the uses of funds of other sectors.

The basic model takes the following form:

IX.7 $E_1 = a_1 + b_1L_1 + c_1DIS_1$

IX.8 $A1 = a2Y1 + b2L1 + c2DIS1$

IX.9 $E2 = d_1Y2 + e_1L2 + f_1DIS2$

IX.10 $A2 = Y2 + L2 + DIS2 - E2 - F2$ (Identity)

IX.11 $Y1 = jE1 + kE2$

IX.12 $Y2 = E1 + E2 - Y1$ (Identity)

IX.13 $F1 = Y1 + L1 + DIS1 - E1 - A1$ (Identity)

IX.14 $F2 = DIS1 + DIS2 - F1$ (Identity)

IX.15 $L1 = mA1 + nA2$

IX.16 $L2 = qA1$

where the additional symbols are

E = nonfinancial (real) expenditures

Y = income

DIS_i^M = reductions in sector money holdings (monetary dissaving)

F_i = increase in sector money holdings (positive values only)

F_i and DIS_i^M represent two independent time series constructed from an initial time series--"increase in money holdings." The positive values of the initial time series together with the value of zero in the place of the original negative values of the time series constitute the F_i variable. The negative values of the initial time series have their signs reversed and when zero values replace the original positive values, this new series becomes the DIS_i^M variable. Both F_i and DIS_i^M are relevant to each sector's behavior since an exogenous act of monetary dissaving will be followed by each sector building up its money balances in response to income changes. This disaggregation of a single time series into two, shows how the "grossness" of the flow of funds can be pushed further for purposes of model building. The monetary dissaving variable converts velocity as a ratio into a flow.

The first four equations express real expenditures and financial asset increases as a function of income (internal finance), borrowing, and monetary dissaving. The model is closed for real flows by equations IX.11 and IX.12. The internal finance of one sector is explained in terms of the real spending of both sectors. The F_i equations solve for increases in sector money holdings in terms of the first sector identity and the money market identity. Equations IX.15 and 16 explain each sector's borrowing in terms of other sectors' lending. Given DIS_i^M, the model has sufficient relations to solve for E_i, Y_i, L_i, and F_i.

Such a model with modifications has been tested in a five-sector U.S. model covering the years 1946-1958 (Cohen, 1963). Instead of limiting dissaving to monetary saving, dissaving is more exhaustive, including nonmonetary financial asset dissaving (DIS_1, DIS_2, DIS_4, DIS_5). Federal government borrowing (G_3) is introduced as an exogenous variable and increments in the money stock (M_4) are an additional exogenous variable in the financial sector.[5] Each sector has two "from-what-to-what" equations linking its real uses and financial uses respectively with the sector's real and financial sources of funds and two "from-whom-to-whom" equations linking income and financial sources (borrowings) with the uses of the same and other sectors (Cohen, 1963, Table 2).[6]

The stability of the complete model was tested for by inserting 1959 and 1960 values for all the exogenous variables and noting how well the equation system forecasts simultaneously the ex post values of the endogenous flows. The model was at its best in predicting expenditures (E_i) values and at its worst in predicting the A_i (financial asset) values. The stability of relationships linking sector expenditures and its consumption and investment components to income and external finance is a persistent finding, offering a flow-constrained hypothesis its greatest empirical support (see also Fand, 1959; Gurley and Shaw, 1957; Cohen, 1957, 1961, 1968, 1970, 1986, chapter II; Cohen and Kenkel, 1980; Cohen and Kenkel, 1986).

Financial Multipliers

The chief analytical use of the model lies in its ability to reveal the interrelations of financial and real flows for a multisector economy. These interdependencies are best seen if we analyze the multiplier effects of the "shock" variables. The multipliers of the circular flow model are "financial" multipliers. Using the reduced form of the model, partial derivatives for each sector's expenditures and financial asset purchases were estimated with respect to changes in the financial disturbance variables. In Table IX.2 we show the multiplier values for each of the exogenous variables with respect to each sector's real uses of funds.[7] The inverse elements underlying the multipliers have also been shown in the table. Each element of the inverse matrix shows the effect on a row variable of a change in the predetermined variable (shown above the columns) assuming that the change in the predetermined variable was sufficient to cause an initial change of one dollar in the dependent variable in each of the equations in which the predetermined variable occurs. For example, the inverse element of 5.39 in the DIS_1 column and E_1 row of the table signifies that a change in dissavings sufficient to increase E_1 initially by one dollar will ultimately via the interdependencies of the system increase E_1 by 5.39 dollars. When this amount is multiplied by the coefficient of the DIS_1 variable, 1.33 (the actual increase in DIS_1) we secure the multiplier for DIS_1 with respect to E_1 via the E_1 equation--7.17. Similarly, estimates for the impact of DIS_1 via the A_1 equation can be calculated. Adding the two multipliers 7.17 and .59 together gives us the value of 7.76, which is the total multiplier effect of consumer dissavings on consumer real uses.

With an absence of lags in the equation system, the

TABLE IX.2 SELECTED MULTIPLIER VALUES, CIRCULAR FLOW MODEL

Real uses of funds \ Disturbance variable	DIS_1: Coefficient in E_1 equation 1.3291	Coefficient in A_1 equation .1534	Multiplier	DIS_2: Coefficient in E_2 equation 1.2370	Coefficient in A_2 equation .2704	Multiplier	G_3: Coefficient in E_3 equation .4600	Coefficient in A_3 equation -.1044	Multiplier
E_1*	5.3917 **	3.8707		4.3917	8.8707		4.3917	3.8707	
	7.1661 +	.5938 =	7.7599	5.4325 -	1.0466 =	4.3859	2.0202 -	.4041 =	1.6161
E_2	.8222	.7604		1.8222	.7604		.8222	.7604	
	1.0928 +	.1166 =	1.2094	2.2540 -	.2056 =	2.0484	.3782 -	.0794 =	.2988
E_3	1.9488	1.5034		1.9488	1.5034		2.9488	1.5034	
	2.5902 +	.2306 =	2.8208	2.4107 -	.4065 =	2.0042	1.3564 -	.1569 =	1.1995
E_4	.00009	- .0008		.00009	- .0008		.00009	- .0008	
	.000119 -	.000122 =	- .000003	.0001 +	.0002 =	.0003	.00004 +	.00008 =	.0001
E_5	.7428	.5891		.7428	.5891		.7428	.5891	
	.9873 +	.0904 =	1.0777	.9189 -	.1593 =	.7596	.3417 -	.0615 =	.2802
E	8.9056	6.7229		8.9056	6.7229		8.9056	6.7229	
	11.8365 +	1.0313 =	12.8678	11.0162 -	9.1984		4.0966 -	.7019 =	3.3947

*Flow-of-funds sectors as indicated by subscripts are:
1. Consumer and nonprofit organizations (later defined as the household sector)
2. Business (farm, noncorporate nonfinancial, corporate nonfinancial)
3. Government (federal, state and local)
4. Financial (commercial banking and monetary authorities, nonbank financial)
5. Rest of the world

See sources to Cohen, 1963, Table 2, for details on the definition of variables.

**Underlined terms are elements of the inverse matrix.

Real uses of funds \ Disturbance variable	DIS_4: Coefficient in A_4 equation 1.4233		DIS_4: Multiplier	M_4: Coefficient in A_4 equation 1.2697		M_4: Multiplier	DIS_5: Coefficient in E_5 equation 1.8646		DIS_5: Coefficient in A_5 equation -1.4130	DIS_5: Multiplier	Total
E_1	3.8707			3.8707			4.3917		3.8707		
	5.5092	=	5.5092	4.9146	=	4.9146	8.1888	-	5.4693	2.7195	26.9052
E_2	.7604			..7604			.8222		.7604		
	1.0823	=	1.0823	.9655	=	.9655	1.5330	-	1.0745	.4585	6.0629
E_3	1.5034			1.5034			1.9488		1.5034		
	2.1398	=	2.1398	1.9089	=	1.9089	3.6337	-	2.1243	1.5004	11.5826
E_4	- .0008			-.0008			.00009		-.0008		
	- .0011	=	-.0011	-.0010	=	-.0010	.0002	+	.0011	.0013	-.0004
E_5	.5891			.5891			1.7428		.5891		
	.8385	=	.8385	.7480	=	.7480	3.2497	-	.8324	2.4173	6.1213
E	6.7229			6.7229			8.9056		6.7229		
	9.5687	=	9.5687	8.5360	=	8.5360	16.6054	-	9.4994	7.1060	50.6716

<u>Source</u>: Cohen, 1963, table insert, pp. 164-65.

multipliers are instantaneous multipliers summarizing long-run multiplier effects. When compared with typical Keynesian multipliers of the long-run type, they are quite "large." Comparable multipliers to the Keynesian multipliers are those given in the E row of Table IX.2. These multipliers measure the total effect on all sectors' real uses of a given increase in an exogenous flow variable.

The reasons for the larger magnitudes lie in the different sizes of the disturbance variables and in differences in the definition of expenditures. In circular flow multipliers of the kind discussed here, the disturbance variables dissaving, money creation or public borrowing will be smaller in magnitude than changes in autonomous investment or in government expenditures or exports, the predetermined transaction variables of Keynesian analysis. At the same time, the change in "real uses" will include expenditures not found in gross national product estimates. As the real uses functions are constructed in the present model, both imports and exports are counted in estimating the effect of autonomous disturbances. U.S. imports are reflected in the E_1-E_4 functions and U.S. exports in the rest of the world's E_5 equation. Stated in terms of leakages, the marginal propensities to save, to pay taxes, and to import in the Keynesian model are replaced with the smaller-valued marginal propensities to add to cash, to holdings of federal obligations or to holdings of dissaved assets.

It is clear from the table that the largest multiplier values are typically associated with the consumer sector. Along the row one must attribute this to the elements of the inverse matrix. The increases in E_1 per dollar of disturbance are larger than the increases for other E_1 variables. Behind these large inverse elements lie certain key regression coefficients in the consumer sector equations. The coefficient for Y_1 in the real sources equation (Cohen, 1963, equation 4, table 1, p. 158), indicates that an amount equal to 71 percent of any increase in real uses (no matter where it originates) will in turn become sources for the consumer sector and thus a basis for further spending. While any increase in financial spending (A) increases L_1 by only 25 percent of such spending (as indicated by the coefficient of R in the fifth equation of Table 1), a dollar increase in L_1 will result in an increase of $1.57 in real uses.

The larger multipliers down the DIS_1 column as compared with other columns must be attributed to the size of the DIS_1 coefficient in the Y_1 and L_1 equations. These are applied uniformly to all the inverse elements in this column. Both row and column influences combine in the first cell of the table to provide the largest single multiplier. The table indicates that financial sector dissavings (the DIS_4 column) exert a series of multiplier effects next to those of consumer dissavings. Next in importance is the impact of business dissavings. Money creation is seen to exert less of a multiplier effect than dissavings by any of these three sectors. For the business, government, and rest of the world sectors, the multiplier effects of the exogenous variables in their E_i equations are offset by the negative effects of these variables in the A_i equations.

Some of the exogenous variables can be considered to be "policy variables" capable of control. This is true of increments in the money supply--the target of central banking policy --and federal public marketable borrowing which is part of federal fiscal policy. The multiplier values then have some implications for policymaking. If we estimate the likely amount of change in financial dissavings and make certain equilibrium assumptions, the amount of compensatory action necessary can be immediately estimated. The multipliers along the E row of Table 4 indicate that consumer dissavings have potentially the greatest disequilibrating effect followed by those for the financial, business, and rest of the world sectors in that order. Compensatory action through monetary policy would be considerably more effective than debt policy (for the same amount of increase in the exogenous variables) as revealed by the respective multipliers of 8.5 and 3.4 for M and G in the E row. Nor can it be argued that given a preference for public expenditures, federal borrowing is superior to monetary policy. Because of its effects on tax sources and endogenous financial sources, a dollar increase in monetary liabilities will generate a larger increase in public expenditures (E3) than a dollar increase in public borrowing.

By emphasizing the exogenous character of financial dissavings, the model underscores the problems associated with public policymaking. In the present institutional setting at least, free access to financial markets means that holders of financial assets can secure spendable funds more or less at will. This may make it very difficult in practice to forecast disturbances. It is also possible that sector dissaving may be influenced by public policy, thus frustrating attempts at control. For example, monetary restraint ordinarily directed at the financial sector may be offset by the latter's selling-off of financial assets. This has been true in the past as shown by the negative correlation coefficient for DIS5 and M of .8148 over the sample period.[8]

CIRCULAR FLOW MODELS IN AN OPEN ECONOMY

The linking of uses to sources of a sector and the sources to other sector uses has been attempted in an extensive model geared to explaining equilibrium in the balance of payments (Georgiadis, 1964). The basic macro-model not counting the detailed import equations consist of 207 equations covering eight flow-of-funds sectors--consumer, corporate business, farm, federal government, state and local, commercial bank, insurance, and rest of the world. The behavior equations are in logarithmic form.

It is shown that the model can be solved simultaneously given the exogeneity of the government sectors (alternatively, the corporate or consumer sector could be treated exogenously). It is also demonstrated that the model can generate a cycle by introducing lags in the equations of the rest of the world sector.

The contribution of the study is to impose sector equilibrium as a prerequisite for equilibrium in the balance of payments. The sources of funds of the rest of the world are linked to uses of funds of the domestic sectors and the uses of funds of the rest of the world are determined by its sources of funds. In turn, the uses of funds of the rest of the world influence the sources of funds of domestic sectors. In contrast, it is pointed out that Nurkse and Meade criteria for equilibrium in the balance of payments can be satisfied when the economy as a whole is in disequilibrium (p. 174). The model is an untested one: it is experimental and exploratory "in every respect" (p. 171). Its complexity is seen as discouraging any further work.

Notes

1. The fixed proportions of assets has two dimensions--a fixed percentage of the kth asset held by the jth sector and a fixed proportion of the kth asset in total asset holdings including tangible assets.
2. Stone is aware of this difficulty and has suggested ways around it (Bain, p. 1073).
3. My own negative results from testing the Stone investment model for the U.S. are described in my 1972 article, p. 5. Attention is also drawn there to Fry's work (1969) simulating financial planning in Turkey on the basis of the Stone models.
4. This section is based largely on my 1963 paper.
5. For the banking sector, money creation replaces monetary dissaving and will be represented by the symbol "M." In their present form, equations 1-3 are underidentified. How this can be handled, is discussed in my 1972 article, p. 8, no. 15.
6. Exogenous financial flow variables in the circular flow model can be brought within the model by additional equations consistent with the two-stage estimation described in Chapter V and exemplified in the stock market model (Chapter X) and also in direct linkage models (Chapter XIII). For a formal statement of the extended model see Cohen, 1972, 8-9.
7. No effort was made to constrain the sum of sector coefficients for a given source of funds to one in the "from-what-to-what" equations or similarly to constrain the sum of a use of funds variable in the from-whom-to-whom equations.
8. Negative relationships between these variables may have other explanations as well, however. The year 1946 perhaps provides the best example. In that year, when there was substantial retirement of bank-held federal debt, reductions in net demand deposits did not represent the application of monetary restraint by the Federal Reserve, nor were the accompanying reductions in bank assets evidence of discretionary dissaving.

CHAPTER X

A STOCK MARKET MODEL[1]

The flow-constrained strategy applied to intra- and intersectoral behavior can be applied to individual markets. The source-constraints limit financial asset purchases (in the case of a financial market) and "use" constraints explain funds raised in a given market in terms of the planned allocation of these funds. In effect, a market is being analyzed from the "outside" rather than the "inside." In the case of the stock market, the purchase of equities is initially explained by sources of funds in outside markets and the issuance of securities by the corporate business sector is related to the allocation of proceeds to other markets. Subsequently, the second-market flows are explored in their own equations.

There has long been an interest in identifying flows in and out of the stock market. Whether funds that flowed into the market stayed there was a major controversy of the 1920s. The controversy was summarized and evaluated in a famous study by Fritz Machlup (1940), who argued that the funds that flowed in also flowed out (Cohen, 1965; Cohen and L'Esperance, 1965). Machlup admitted to a lack of empirical evidence. What is most relevant in his study is his interest in identifying flows into and out of the market.[2]

<u>The Taxonomy of Stock Market Flows</u>. Spelling out the implications of the market matrix of Chapter I, net purchases of equity securities in the stock market must be financed from the sale of currently produced or second-hand economic goods, from the sale of newly created financial assets (IOUs), from the sale of existing IOUs in other markets (financial dissaving), by running down money balances or by money creation. Net sales in the stock market must show a corresponding amount of purchases in other markets. For the market as a whole, the inflow of funds must equal the outflow of fund plus the net change in money balances arising from stock market transactions. The accompanying matrix

(Table X.1) is similar to the market matrix in Chapter VI. As before, the matrix columns represent the demand side of a market; the rows, the supply side. Besides the equities market denoted by E, the matrix includes the other (nonmonetary) financial assets market (0), the product market (P), the bank loan market (L), and the market for money balances (M).

TABLE X.1 A MATRIX OF FINANCIAL MARKET FLOWS

Supply Side of Market \ Demand Side of Market	Equities	Other Assets	Product	Bank Loans	Cash Balances
Equities	EE	EO	EP	EL	EM
Other Assets	OE	OO	OP	OL	OM
Product	PE	PO	PP	PL	PM
Bank Loans	LE	LO	LP	LL	LM
Cash Balances	ME	MO	MP	ML	MM

The bank loan submarket is unique in representing both a particular sector and a particular category of transactions. We shall interpret the demand for equities in the bank loan submarket (LE) as indicating the purchase of equities by the nonbank public financed by its sale of assets to the banking sector (including but not confined to IOUs with stocks as collateral).[3] On the supply side of the bank loan submarket, EL would indicate the supply of equity securities by the nonbank public for the purpose of acquiring assets held by the banking sector (including retirement of their IOUs to the banking sector).

The identities underlying the matrix are also equilibrium relations, given the assumption that market prices are market-clearing prices. Under these conditions, supply and demand aggregated over all submarkets are equal in the equities market. This means that excess supply (positive or negative) in the individual submarkets is consistent with overall equilibrium in the equity securities market, as shown in Figure X.1.

FIGURE X.1 THE EQUITIES MARKET

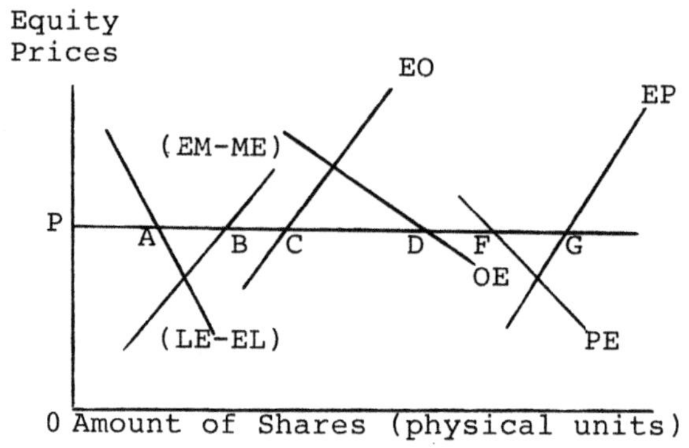

The average price of common stock is plotted on the vertical axis and the units of common stock are represented on the horizontal axis. To escape arbitrariness, shares are defined in terms of a fixed dividend, a $1.00 dividend denoting one share. The three submarkets, moving to the right in the figure, are the money submarket, the other assets submarket, and the product submarket. The excess demand in the other assets submarket (the CD distance) is drawn to equal the sum of the excess supplies in the other two submarkets (AB + FG). In drawing the demand and supply functions, the conventional assumptions as to slopes were made.[4]

Estimating Fund Flows in the Stock Market. Several strategies present themselves for estimating the flow of funds. Closest to the theory would be the identification of two-ended flows in the individual submarkets by means of a single statistical time series, which is then functionally related to a series of explanatory variables. Such knowledge is hard to come by, and the time series selected must be arbitrary. Moreover, in some earlier work, it proved impossible to explain stock market prices in terms of submarket demands and supplies (Cohen, 1965; Cohen and L'Esperance, 1965).

Instead, a two-stage strategy has been followed. First, the second-market flows are identified. Once identified the second market flows are ultimately subjected to analysis, using a variety of regressors. The sectors on the buying side of the stock market are limited to the household and insurance sectors (the latter sector includes life insurance companies, other insurance companies, and private pension funds). In the household sector, direct and indirect purchases are distinguished, the latter being its purchases of investment company shares. Direct purchases are estimated by subtracting investment company issues from total household equity purchases. On the supply side of the market, only equity issues by the nonfinancial corporate sector were considered.

Purchases of corporate stock by the household and insurance sectors are identified with a second market by being linked with sources of funds variables. Since stock purchases are uses of funds, their financing may result either from receipts (internal or external finance), reduced expenditures, or through financial portfolio adjustments which make funds available by the sell-off of assets. The explanatory variables are thus constrained to be positive if they appear on the sources of funds side of the sector account and negative if they appear on the uses of funds side.

In symmetrical fashion, on the supply side of the stock market, to be identified as a second market flow, net corporate issues are required to have a positive relationship with corporate uses of funds and a negative relationship with increases in financial liabilities. The latter relationship suggests the use of corporate stock sales for debt retirement purposes. We went beyond these constraints because of important complementary or substitute relations between other sources of funds variables and new security issues. Thus, corporate cash flows and corporate bond issues are included in the equation for corporate stock issues because of their obvious relevance to sales of new equities (see equation 4 of the model in Table X.2 and data directory, Appendix).[5]

A further departure from the strict logic of the dual-decision process is to permit the relationships between submarket flows to be lagged relationships. Thus, the supply of equity securities issued by the corporate sector is linked to future corporate expenditures on plant and equipment and residential construction (equation 4). On the demand side of the equities market, household purchases are linked to earlier values of personal income (equation 2). The use of lagged relationships means that ultimate sources or uses are considered along with same-period sources or uses despite a connection between them. It is possible that personal income may lead to the possible build-up of money balances (equation 7) and subsequently to the running down of these balances as reflected in the importance of the money balance variable in equation 2 of the model. Similar linkages between final and immediate uses may apply on the supply side of the equities market. It is possible, for example, that increases in other financial assets (OFA), a current financial use in equation 4, may be the source of funds for later capital expenditures, also in this equation.

Once the second market is identified in the four dual-decision equations, the remaining sixteen equations of the model explain these second-market flows. The one second-market flow not traced back in this fashion is "other financial assets," because of its miscellaneous character. These sixteen equations consist of fourteen structural equations and two identities. In the first identity, corporate gross cash flow is defined as corporate profits plus inventory valuation adjustment plus capital consumption allowances (equation 14). In the last equation, the identity shows that the demand and supply variables in the first four dual-decision equations plus a residual flow equal flows in the stock market. The equations have been estimated by both OLS and TSLS methods.

<u>Characteristics of the Model</u>. The dual-decision functions are

TABLE X.2 THE FLOW-OF-FUNDS MODEL 1953:I--1969:III

A. The Dual-Decision Functions

										$\bar{R}^2$	$\overline{SEE}$	D.W.
OLS	1a.	$DSP_h =$	1.901 (9.111)[1]	$- .061PT_h$ (2.620)	$- .101CD_h$ (2.631)	$- .082DD_h$ (2.635)	$- .079SA_h$ (2.205)			.786	.494	1.495
TSLS	1b.	$DSP_h =$	1.990 (7.702)	$- .208\hat{PT}_h$ (.970)	$- .162\hat{CD}_h$ (3.244)	$- .022\hat{DD}_h^2$ (.428)	$- .040\hat{SA}_h$ (.730)			.676	.608	1.529
OLS	2a.	$ISP_h =$	$-.489$ (3.156)	$+ .020PY_{-2,h}$ (6.898)	$- .037DD_h$ (2.981)	$- .403IPF_h$ (4.802)	$- .111DSP_h$ (2.086)			.677	.230	1.718
TSLS	2b.	$ISP_h =$	$-.190$ (.873)	$+ .009PY_{-2,h}$ (4.666)	$- .057\hat{DD}_h$ (2.920)	$- .125\hat{IPF}_h$ (1.378)	$- .218\hat{DSP}_h$ (2.444)			.616	.251	1.700
OLS	3a.	$DSP_{ins} =$	$-.133$ (1.036)	$+ .539NIL_{ins}$ (10.786)	$- .271GS_{ins}$ (3.323)	$- .767MOR_{ins}$ (6.671)				.868	.182	1.937
TSLS	3b.	$DSP_{ins} =$	$-.126$ (.819)	$+ .550\hat{NIL}_{ins}$ (9.307)	$- .195\hat{GS}_{ins}$ (1.801)	$- .827\hat{MOR}_{ins}$ (6.060)				.876	.177	2.243
OLS	4a.	$NSI_{corp} =$	1.107 (7.062)	$- .115CF_{-1,corp}$ (4.911)	$+ .170CB_{-1,corp}$ (2.811)	$+ .088PLE_{+2,corp}$ (2.800)	$+ .197RC_{+4,corp}$ (2.526)	$+ .107OFA_{corp}$ (3.168)		.380	.315	1.434

B. Household Second-Market Functions

										$\bar{R}^2$	$\overline{SEE}$	D.W.
OLS	5a.	$PT_h =$	-3.624 (3.714)	$+ .160PY_h$ (19.292)						.849	2.264	1.639
TSLS	5b.	$PT_h =$	-3.783 (4.061)	$+ .162\hat{PY}_h$ (20.384)						.863	2.159	1.576
OLS	6a.	$CD_h =$	-1.758 (5.043)	$+ .123PY_h$ (43.130)	$+ 1.338S_2$ (5.783)	$+ 2.599S_4$ (11.006)				.968	.779	1.649
TSLS	6b.	$CD_h =$	-1.828 (5.425)	$+ .124\hat{PY}_h$ (44.773)	$+ 1.271S_2$ (5.695)	$+ 2.840S_4$ (12.471)				.970	.751	1.493
OLS	7a.	$DD_h =$	.719 (.423)	$+ .204PY_h$ (4.075)	$- .686i_{tb}$ (2.360)	$- 1.966i_{td}$ (2.822)	$- .231\overline{DD}_{-1,h}$ (3.282)	$+ 2.524S_3$ (5.002)	$+ 3.568S_4$ (7.605)	.725	1.355	2.192
TSLS	7b.	$DD_h =$	$-.155$ (.094)	$+ .183\hat{PY}_h$ (3.630)	$- .712i_{tb}$ (2.364)	$- 1.696i_{td}$ (2.413)	$- .198\overline{DD}_{-1,h}$ (2.845)	$+ 2.859S_3$ (5.927)	$+ 4.130S_4$ (9.478)	.713	1.387	2.111
OLS	8a.	$SA_h =$	$-.205$ (.364)	$+ .047PY_h$ (9.667)	$- 1.468(i_{tb} - i_{td})$ (7.011)		$- 1.476S_3$ (4.081)			.658	1.287	.890
TSLS	8b.	$SA_h =$	$-.220$ (.391)	$+ .047\hat{PY}_h$ (9.703)	$- 1.469(i_{tb} - i_{td})$ (7.032)		$- 1.465S_3$ (4.058)			.659	1.284	.893
OLS	9a.	$PY_h =$	$-.423$ (.481)	$+ .199GNP$ (133.810)						.996	2.030	1.691
OLS	10a.	$IPF_h =$	$-.344$ (2.836)	$+ .029\hat{PY}_h$ (28.732)		$+ .613S_2^*$ (7.869)				.930	.277	2.131
TSLS	10b.	$IPF_h =$	$-.350$ (3.034)	$+ .029PY_h$ (30.259)		$+ .578S_2$ (7.796)				.937	.264	2.089

C. Insurance Sector Second-Market Functions

OLS	11a.	$NIL_{ins} = .181\,(2.116) + .016PY_h\,(22.682) - .141S_2\,(2.483) + .227S_4\,(3.901)$		.892	.192	1.497
TSLS	11b.	$NIL_{ins} = .177\,(2.035) + .016PY_h\,(22.347) - .150S_2\,(2.601) + .258S_4\,(4.379)$		.889	.194	1.515
OLS	12a.	$GS_{ins} = 1.165\,(3.091) - .419(i_m - i_{gb})\,(3.125) - .005STP\,(2.605) - .340S_2\,(5.501)$		.361	.220	1.705
OLS	13a.	$MOR_{ins} = -.165\,(.912) - .971(i_{cb} - i_m)\,(14.490) + .648(i_{gb} - i_m)\,(7.038) + .105COM_{-1,\,ins}\,(2.713) + .121S_4\,(3.746)$		.804	.112	1.049

D. Corporate Sector Second-Market Functions

	14a.	$CF_{corp} = PROF_{corp} + CCA_{corp}$ (identity)				
OLS	15a.	$CB_{corp} = .283\,(.921) + .428PLE_{+2,\,corp}\,(5.747) + .579RC_{+1,\,corp}\,(3.931) - .188CF_{corp}\,(3.390)$		.717	.538	1.376
TSLS	15b.	$CB_{corp} = .459\,(1.470) + .478PLE_{+2,\,corp}\,(6.222) + .629RC_{+1,\,corp}\,(4.316) - .227CF_{corp}\,(3.946)$		.731	.524	1.509
OLS	16a.	$PLE_{corp} = -12.473\,(7.478) + .062\left[\frac{CU_{-1} + CU_{-2}}{2}\right]_{mfg}\,(3.569) + .053[SAL_{-1} - SAL_{-4}]_{mfg+tr}\,(6.057) + .097SAL_{-3,\,mfg+tr}\,(21.377) - .634i_{cb,-3}\,(2.534)$				
		$+ 1.579S_2\,(10.073) + 1.162S_3\,(7.406) + 1.775S_4\,(11.295)$		.988	.451	1.114
OLS	17a.	$RC_{corp} = -.880\,(8.451) + .001GNP\,(7.323) + .160[i_{cb} - i_{cp}]_{-3}\,(3.718) + .999S_2\,(16.050) + .978S_3\,(15.666) + .377S_4\,(5.946)$		.864	.181	1.301
OLS	18a.	$PROF_{corp} = -11.783\,(7.092) + .019GNP\,(41.008) + .180CU_{mfg}\,(10.126) - .036\,(1.917)\,\frac{\left[\frac{1}{2}CU_{-2} + \sum_{i=3}^{3} CU_{-i} + \frac{1}{2}CU_{-4}\right]_{mfg}}{4} + 1.227S_2\,(5.560)$				
		$+ .410S_3\,(1.858) + 1.137S_4\,(5.072)$		.967	.643	.917
OLS	19a.	$CCA_{corp} = -6.664\,(40.871) + .035K_{corp}\,(84.719)$		.991	.240	.214
	20a.	$RES = NSI_{corp} - DSP_h - ISP_h - DSP_{ins}$ (identity)				

1. T-ratios in parentheses below regression coefficients.
For description of variables see data directory in Appendix 1.
2. Values of the independent endogenous variables as estimated in the first round of TSLS estimation.

Source: Cohen and Miller, 1973, table 2, pp. 74-95

quite successful in describing the sources of funds for stock purchases. Direct stock purchases of the household sector (equation 1) are seen to be financed by reductions in alternative uses of funds--personal tax payments, consumer durable expenditures, additions to demand deposits, and savings accounts. (The significance of all these variables except for consumer durables declines substantially in two-stage least-squares estimation.) Indirect purchases by households (equation 2) are influenced positively by lagged personal income and negatively by changes in demand deposits, flows into insurance and pension fund reserves, and direct stock purchases. The insurance sector's purchases (equation 3) are strongly influenced by inflows of funds (NIL_{ins}) and by a substitute relation with government security and mortgage purchases. In contrast to the satisfactory $\bar{R}^2$ on the demand side of the market, net corporate stock issues (equation 4) are less satisfactorily explained in terms of flows, although each of the five explanatory variables--cash flows (negative relation), corporate bonds, plant and equipment expenditures, residential construction expenditures, and increases in a miscellany of financial assets (positive relations) --have high t-ratios according to standard statistical tests.[6]

In section B of Table X.2, the household second-market functions push back the explanation of the independent-flow variables in the household dual-decision functions. Many of these variables are related to other flow variables--personal taxes are closely related to personal incomes, (equation 5); personal income in turn is related to GNP (a) consumer durables to personal income, (6) and insurance and pension fund payments to personal income, (10). "Choice-theoretic" variables make their appearance in the demand deposit and savings account equations (7, 8) with the Treasury-bill rate and time-deposit rate both having the expected negative effect on demand-deposit flows and their differential having the same negative effect on savings accounts. In addition, the stock of demand deposits influences demand-deposit flows.

For the second-market functions of the insurance sector

purchases, personal income and seasonal factors explain net increases in financial liabilities. Interest-rate differentials including the mortgage, government bond, and corporate bond rates are significant variables in the government security and mortgage equations.

In the second-market functions for the corporate sector, decisions to issue corporate bonds (equation 15) are influenced in a positive way by the same variables that influence the issuance of corporate stock--planned capital expenditures and same-period cash flow. Cash flows equal corporate profits and capital-consumption allowances (equation 14). The latter depend on the size of the capital stock (equation 19) and the former on the GNP, current and past capacity utilization, and a seasonal term. Increases in GNP can be identified with increases in business output, while increases in capacity utilization result in the decline of fixed unit costs and, thus, in increases in profits. The lagged capacity-utilization term represents the lagged adjustment of money wages to changes in capacity utilization so that the negative coefficient of this variable is consistent with expectations (Evans, 1969, pp. 274-80).

The plant and equipment and residential construction equations make use of anticipation and modification (realization) variables (Evans, pp. 95-105). The anticipation variables are typically lagged more than several quarters in line with the observed lag between capital appropriations and actual expenditures. In the PLE equation (16), five-quarter lagged values of sales and the corporate-bond rate constitute the anticipation variables. The realization variables modify initial plans, implying a relatively short lag before actual expenditures are made. The capacity utilization term and the four-quarter sales accelerator represent the modification variables.

In the RC equation (17), the lagged interest-rate differential is the anticipation variable, and GNP is the modification variable. If the corporate bond rate is viewed as a representative long-term rate and the commercial-paper rate as a representative short-term rate, the prevalence of monetary stringency will cause the short-term rate to rise above the long-term rate leading to financing problems (Evans, pp. 188-97).

<u>The Reduced Form of the Model.</u> The multiplier matrix of the model provides a convenient way of discussing the linkages between the stock market and disturbance variables (see Cohen and Miller, table 3, p. 78). The exogenous variables can be classified as "real" and "financial" market variables. The real variables include PY-2, CF-1, PLE+2, RC+4, GNP, the CU variables, the SAL variables, and the capital stock 1C. The financial variables include the CB-1, OFA, DD-1, STP, COM-1, and the interest-rate variables. The financial variables, except for the stock market price index (STP), refer to the money and other assets markets of the initial market matrix (Table X.1). On the demand side of the market, interest rates and their differentials are the leading disturbance variables. For example, household purchases respond to decreases in the demand for money triggered through increases in the Treasury bill-rate and the time deposit rate and the differential in these rates. On the other hand, the supply of equity securities issued by the corporate sector has its closest relation with the product market via cash flow and expected capital expenditures.[7]

Implications for the Study of Financial Markets

The outside-inside analysis of the stock market suggests that two-stage approach can be applied to markets as well as to sectors. First, sectoral flows in and out of a given market are related to other sectoral flows. Choice-theoretical variables in second-stage equations then explain the right-hand flow variables in the first-stage analysis.

APPENDIX

Description of Variables	Symbols	Sources
A. Household Sector (persons as members of households plus personal trusts and nonprofit organizations serving individuals)		
1. Direct stock purchases: seasonally unadjusted, quarterly rates in billions of dollars (total stock purchases less indirect stock purchases	DSP_h	Board of Governors of the Federal Reserve System, *Flow-of-Funds Accounts*
2. Indirect stock purchases: shares of stock issued by open-end investment companies, seasonally unadjusted, quarterly rates in billions of dollars	ISP_h	Ibid.
3. Personal taxes: seasonally unadjusted, quarterly rates in billions of dollars	PT_h	Ibid.
4. Consumer durable expenditures: seasonally unadjusted, quarterly rates in billions of dollars	CD_h	Ibid.
5. ΔDemand deposit and currency holdings: seasonally unadjusted, quarterly rates in billions of dollars	DD_h	Ibid.
6. ΔSavings accounts: commercial bank time deposits plus savings and loan company shares plus mutual savings bank deposits, seasonally unadjusted, quarterly rates in billions of dollars	SA_h	Ibid.
7. Personal income: seasonally unadjusted, quarterly rates in billions of dollars	PY_h	Ibid.
8. Life insurance and pension fund reserves: changes in policy reserves against private and U. S. government life insurance policies, quarterly rates in billions of dollars, seasonally unadjusted	IPF_h	Ibid.
9. One-quarter lagged stock of demand deposit and currency holdings: seasonally unadjusted, quarterly rates in billions of dollars	$\overline{DD}_{t-1,h}$	Ibid.
10. Treasury bill rate: quarterly averages of monthly figures, percent	i_{tb}	Various issues of *Federal Reserve Bulletin*
11. Effective rate on passbook savings deposits at commercial banks, percent	i_s	Charlottle Scott, Chicago Federal Reserve Bank, as found in "Housekeeper No. 106," Fed. Res.-MIT-Penn Econometric Model Data Directory
12. Gross National Product: seasonally adjusted, quarterly data at annual rates, billions of dollars	GNP	National Income Accounts, as found in "Housekeeper No. 48," Fed. Res.-MIT-Penn Econometric Model Data Directory
13. Seasonal dummy variables representing the second, third, and fourth quarters, respectively	S_2, S_3, S_4	
B. Insurance Sector (life insurance companies plus other insurance companies plus private pension funds)		
1. Direct stock purchases: seasonally unadjusted, quarterly rates in billions of dollars	DSP_{ins}	Board of Governors of the Federal Reserve System, *Flow-of-Funds Accounts*
2. Net increase in liabilities: seasonally unadjusted, quarterly rates in billions of dollars	NIL_{ins}	Ibid.
3. U. S. government security purchases: seasonally unadjusted, quarterly rates in billions of dollars	GS_{ins}	Ibid.
4. Investment in mortgages on 1- to 4-family nonfarm residential properties: seasonally unadjusted, quarterly rates in billions of dollars	MOR_{ins}	Ibid.
5. Long-term government bond rate, quarterly averages of monthly figures, percent per annum	i_{gb}	Various issues of *Federal Reserve Bulletin*
6. Mortgage rate, percent	i_m	*Federal Reserve Bulletin*, as found in "Housekeeper No. 104," Fed. Res.-MIT-Penn Econometric Model Data Directory

Description of Variables	Symbols	Sources
7. One-quarter lagged new mortgage commitments of life insurance companies: seasonally adjusted, quarterly rates in billions of dollars	$COM_{t-1,\,ins}$	Federal Reserve Board, Capital Markets Section, as found in "Housekeeper No. 11," Fed. Res.-MIT-Penn Econometric Model Data Directory
8. Standard and Poor's Stock Price Index: 1941-43 = 10, quarterly averages of monthly figures	*STP*	Various issues of *Federal Reserve Bulletin*
C. Corporate Sector (private nonfinancial and nonfarm corporations)		
1. Net stock issues: seasonally unadjusted, quarterly rates in billions of dollars	NSI_{corp}	Board of Governors of the Federal Reserve System, *Flow-of-Funds Accounts*
2. Cash flow: undistributed corporate profits plus inventory valuation adjustment plus CCA: seasonally unadjusted, quarterly rates in billions of dollars	CF_{corp}	Ibid.
3. Corporate bond issues: seasonally unadjusted, quarterly rates in billions of dollars	CB_{corp}	Ibid.
4. Undistributed corporate profits plus inventory valuation adjustment: seasonally unadjusted, quarterly rates in billions of dollars	PRO_{corp}	Ibid.
4a. Capital consumption allowances: seasonally unadjusted, quarterly rates in billions of dollars	CCA_{corp}	Ibid.
5. Plant and equipment expenditures: seasonally unadjusted, quarterly rates in billions of dollars	PLE_{corp}	Ibid.
6. Residential construction expenditures: seasonally unadjusted, quarterly rates in billions of dollars	RC_{corp}	Ibid.
7. Other financial assets: nonlife insurance claims plus miscellaneous financial transactions plus foreign currency holdings plus direct investment abroad less Eurobond issues plus unallocated claims, seasonally unadjusted, quarterly rates in billions of dollars	OFA_{corp}	Ibid.
8. Corporate Aaa bond rate: quarterly averages of monthly figures, percent	i_{aa}	*Federal Reserve Bulletin*, as found in "Housekeeper No. 91," Fed. Res.-MIT-Penn Econometric Model Data Directory
9. Capacity utilization in manufacturing, 1967 = 100, quarterly averages of monthly figures	*CU*	Various issues of *Federal Reserve Bulletin*
10. Total manufacturing and trade sales: seasonally adjusted, quarterly totals of monthly figures in billions of dollars	*SAL*	Various issues of the *Survey of Current Business*
11. Commercial paper rate, quarterly averages of monthly figures	i_{cp}	*Federal Reserve Bulletin*, as found in "Housekeeper No. 88," Fed. Res.-MIT-Penn Econometric Model Data Directory
12. Stock of corporate business structures and durables: billions of dollars	*K*	Calculated according to identities found in "Housekeeper Nos, 18, 30, 34, and 35," Fed. Res.-MIT-Penn Econometric Model Data Directory
D. Other Sectors		
1. Residual stock market flows: open-end investment company stock issues plus commercial bank and rest-of-world issues minus purchases by state and local employee retirement funds, mutual savings banks, finance, n.e.c., and rest of world, seasonally unadjusted, quarterly rates in billions of dollars	*RES*	Board of Governors of the Federal Reserve System, *Flow-of-Funds Accounts*

Source: Cohen and Miller, 1973, pp. 80-82

Notes

1. This chapter depends heavily on Cohen and Miller, 1973.
2. The absorption of funds by bank-financed mergers is a contemporary version of the earlier debate (see Berry, 1984, p. 6). While Berry makes the same argument that funds are not absorbed by mergers, his argument overlooks the "transfer" versus "exhaustive" character of the initial bank loan. There may be merit in the criticism that bank loans are unproductive since the initial bank loan does not finance an "exhaustive" expenditure--that is, one entailing primary inputs. It is true that stockholders being bought out have spendable income but an analogy exists to the comparative "real" effects of government spending on goods and services versus the first round effects of transfer payments.
3. In practice, only loans with securities as collateral are classified by banks as security loans. Considerable possibilities for error thus exist because so-called nonpurpose loans not subject to margin requirements may in fact be used for stock market purposes although excluded from the security loan statistics. Other types of collateral may also be the basis for playing the market, further weakening the security loan category as a measure of stock market financing.
4. Quantities are here in physical units rather than in dollar amounts as in Chapter I.
5. On the demand side of the equities market, parallel treatment would have required identifying equity purchases by the household and insurance sectors with sources of funds showing a negative sign and uses of funds showing a positive sign. In this way, it would have been possible to test for complementarities among equity purchases, debt retirement, and other uses of funds. The strength of the demand equations made such an extension less pressing than on the supply side of the market.
6. The difficulties in fitting a satisfactory corporate-equities equation are not uncommon. W. H. Locke Anderson, for example, conceded an inability to fit such a relationship (1964, pp. 42-43). Similar problems have been acknowledged by the Bank of England (Hewitt, 1977). The better results secured by the Bosworth-Duesenberry model, as discussed in the next chapter are illusory.
7. Dynamic multipliers besides the impact multipliers discussed above have been estimated by another author (Edgar, 1977). They sum up the impact and all the interim multiplier effects of the lagged endogenous variables. His results indicate that the total impact of the decrease in demand for money on direct and indirect stock purchases by the household sector is lessened as the public adjusts to the initial interest shocks in later periods. (The exogenous shock is assumed to continue into succeeding quarters.) In the corporate sector, the influence of expected capital expenditures is increased

substantially. The model also implies that as GNP and corporate fixed assets increase, external corporate financing declines.

Unfortunately, Edgar's analysis is marred by his interpretation of the one-quarter lagged stock of house

hold demand deposit and currency holdings ($\overline{DD}_{t-1,\ h}$)

as a lagged endogenous flow variable. Only two of the three lagged endogenous variables he incorporates in his dynamic analysis are legitimate ($CF_{t-1,c}$ and $CB_{t-1,c}$).

CHAPTER XI
PORTFOLIO BALANCE MODELS

INTRODUCTION

Portfolio balance models go beyond the self-contained relationships of previous chapters. Now "choice-theoretical" variables are introduced in the first (and only) estimating stages. The a priori constraints now are also applied more consistently. Adding-up constraints apply to both the quantity variables and to the price variables. Symmetry constraints are imposed on the cross-effects of interest rates and speeds of adjustment in the financial asset equations. Dynamic portfolio adjustments must be consistent over all asset-liability items: movements to equilibrium in one asset require accommodating movements in other assets.

Portfolio balance models in the flow of funds succeeded earlier financial model-building which focused on the bank reserve and money markets. Once a key short-term interest rate was determined in these markets, term-structure relationships solved for longer term rates. (For a brief summary of these models, see Hendershott, 1977, chapter 2; Guentner, 1978, chapter 2). The interest rate then provided the linkage with the real economy.[1] Flow-of-funds portfolio balance models, on the other hand, emphasize the credit markets and approach them in demand and supply terms. This is the central feature of such models although some attention is given to linkages with the real economy. The disequilibrium models of the next chapter are distinguished by their greater emphasis on nonfinancial behavior.

We shall deal in this chapter with three leading models--Bosworth-Duesenberry, Hendershott, and the "pitfall" models of Yale.

THE BOSWORTH-DUESENBERRY MODEL

This is the first comprehensive flow-of-funds model tied to the theory of portfolio balance (Bosworth and Duesenberry,

1973). The deficits and surpluses of five major nonfinancial sectors provide the basic framework as shown in equation 1.

XI.1 DEFB + DEFGF + DEFGSL + DEFFOR - SURH - STAT = 0

The deficits of business, federal, and state and local governments, and the foreign sector are equivalent to household savings (SURH) plus the statistical discrepancy. Financial sectors with their small surpluses are ignored.

The typical equation for the nonfinancial sector is a stock adjustment equation. The underlying theory is that the sector has a desired stock of assets and liabilities with portfolios determined on the basis of yields, liquidity, riskiness, and investor preferences. Adjustments are not instantaneous for reasons of investment inertia, transactions costs, and uncertainty. As a result the period flows are partial adjustments to the desired long-run portfolio. The typical equation for desired stocks takes the following form:[2]

$$\text{XI.2} \quad A_i^* = a_i + \sum_j b_{ij}(r_j W) + c_i W + \sum_k d_{ik} \cdot X_k.$$

The desired stock of each asset or liability depends on a vector of interest rates r scaled by wealth; a wealth constraint W and other factors X.

The partial stock adjustment equation then takes the form:

$$\text{XI.3} \quad \Delta A_i = \sum_j \lambda_{ij} [A_j^* - A_{j-1}] + \gamma_k \cdot Z$$

In addition to lagged stocks of other assets, this equation adds a disturbance term, Z.

<u>A Priori Constraints</u>. The BD study is not scrupulous in adhering to the a priori constraints. Including the same set of right-hand variables in each equation as required results in a rapid proliferation in the number of coefficients to be

estimated. According to the authors, the result is multicollinearity, a risk of spurious correlations and highly inefficient estimates (BD, p. 65). A simultaneous-estimation approach (Hendershott's stacked equations) is also rejected. Errors in specification can ruin all the estimates.

Doubts can also be expressed about applying symmetry conditions to the matrix of interest rate coefficients. Time series data measure the total response in the demand for an asset to a change in expected yields. This total response is a gross substitution effect since it includes both a net substitution effect (holding constant the income and wealth effects of a yield change) and the income and wealth effect. Since these effects may differ for the ith and jth securities, there is no reason for the net substitution effect to be symmetrical. Unless these effects are assumed to be negligible, the condition $\frac{\partial A_j}{\partial R_i} = \frac{\partial A_i}{\partial R_j}$ cannot be satisfied (Guentner, p. 73; Silber, pp. 12-15).

As a result, the authors have opted for a more eclectic approach. Their pragmatism shows up in residual estimation, e.g., the business sector's money holdings, and in the ad hoc way that key interest rates are determined. In the case of Treasury bills, three-to-five year U.S. bonds and corporate bonds, the household demand equations have been dropped. Instead, the rates are normalized to the left-hand side. Quantities residually absorbed by households (after allowing for security supply and demand of other sectors) are on the right-hand side (BD, pp. 70- 71). There are serious problems, however, with this procedure. The household demand for short-term credit market instruments has been normalized twice--once to determine the three-month Treasury bill rate and once to determine the three-to-five year U.S. bond rate (equations H5, H6, in BD, pp. 133-34); (Guentner, p. 23; Hendershott, pp. 66-68). Finally, presence of the 3-5 year U.S. rate in the Treasury bill rate (H5) and corporate bond rate (H7) equations gives them the appearance of term-structure relations.

The BD model distinguished among four categories of financial assets: deposit accounts, negotiated loans, liquid marketable securities and income-yielding long-term market assets. Such disaggregation is obviously superior to the homogenizing of interest-bearing assets in the bank-reserve model. Nevertheless, much diversity still remains within the last two categories. The short-term long-term distinction blurs over such obvious factors as differences in tax treatment, substantial differences in risk of default, nonexistent to sparse to excellent secondary markets, and legislatively induced "preferred habitats" resulting from legal restrictions on financial institutions (Guentner, p. 36).

The BD model consists of 110 linear equations fitted by ordinary least squares. These include expenditure equations and 25 equations for the determination of wage and price-level changes. We pay special attention to the financial equations of the business, household, and commercial bank sectors (BD, pp. 123-129).

The Business Sector. The business sector constitutes the major deficit sector during the 1965.1-70.2 period covered by BD. The debt equations beginning with A3 (p. 121) are functions of the deficit to which they contribute (suggesting simultaneous equation bias). Interest rates are scaled by the size of the cumulative business deficit. Expectational theories make plausible the "wrong" signs of interest rate variables. When short-term interest rates move up rapidly, corporate long-term borrowing is deferred but brought forward when rates decline (A4). In consistent fashion, short-term borrowing (A3) replaces long-term borrowing when short-term rates increase.

The high R^2 for the borrowing equations might belie the previously mentioned difficulties in fitting such equations (Chapter X). But to a considerable degree, however, the results are illusory. The interest rate and similar "price" variables are swamped by stock and flow variables which are either lagged values of the dependent variables or by definition include the dependent variables (e.g., the deficit variables). Flow variables that would make more "sense" would be plans to spend, to refund obligations, or to add to liquid asset holdings. More variables are called for such as the STKRET (corporate stock retirement variable) in the corporate bond equation (A4, p. 121).

The change in liquid asset holdings (A7, p. 122) has its chief explanation in a residual variable derived from the cumulative deficit and from the lagged value of the dependent variable. Interest rates play a larger role in the open market paper component of short-term debt (A8a, p. 122), and the time deposit (A9.a, p. 122) and short-term market instruments (A9.b, p. 122) components of liquid assets.

<u>The Household Sector</u>. In the household sector the stock of financial assets is the scale variable magnifying the influence of interest rates. The analysis of assets is confined to deposit accounts. A choice-theoretical solution dominates with the household sector showing sensitivity to own-interest rates and interest-rate differentials. A great number of the coefficients are estimated outside the regression analysis ("constr" below the coefficient). In this sector the symmetry constraint is imposed on the interest rate variable. The RSL-RTD differential (savings and loan deposit rate--time deposit rate) is constrained to have the same impact on savings and loan deposits as it does on time deposits (equations E3 and E5, p. 125). Similarly, the savings bank deposit-time deposit rate differential shows the same coefficient in both of these equations (E4 and E5).

<u>Commercial Banks</u>. The importance in flow-of-funds theory of the bank credit market finds empirical expression in the BD model. Banks are portrayed as demanders of assets. By adding equations from other sectors one can deduce the determinants of the money supply but only as a memo item.

Great weight is placed in the BD model on the "tension" between the demand for business loans and the passive supply of funds--the potential supply of deposits given reserve requirements and the volume of unborrowed reserves (equation F7, p. 127). The underlying hypothesis is that for reasons of long-term profit maximization, banks will attempt to accommodate the business customers' demand for loans (BD, pp. 67-68). When the Fed fails to provide enough reserves the pressure of excess loan demand is passed to the rest of the market through bank sales of securities or bank issues of additional short-term liabilities (see equations F10, F11, F13, F14, p. 128).[3] At the same time, free reserves (FR) are reduced as a result of excess loan demand. The $FRNEG_{-1}$ term in equation F8 reflects Federal Reserve pressure to limit bank borrowing. When system free reserves are negative (net borrowed reserves), this is followed by a retirement of member bank borrowing as shown by the negative sign of the $FRNEG_{-1}$ term (BD, pp. 68-69).

The emphasis placed on business loan demand in the BD model suggests more of a flow-constrained interpretation of bank behavior than a choice-theoretical one. Interest rates play a subordinate role in bank portfolio decisions.

Real-Financial Linkages. BD are eloquent protagonists of flow-of-funds modeling. Conventional money market models homogenize the bond market (BD, p. 46-51). This narrow approach, it is pointed out, is incapable of handling the diversity of financial markets that business, state, and local government, the federal government, depend on (pp. 74-75). Expenditures are mainly flow-constrained (automobiles, durable goods, nondurables and services (A1-A3, p. 137), and residential construction (A8, p. 138). Except for residential construction where mortgage finance is the key variable, the flow constraints are income variables. Mixed flow and price (interest-rate) constraints characterize business investment, nonresidential and residential construction (A6, A7, A8, p. 138).

Simulation Results. Flow-of-funds models are most frequently put to the test by means of simulation rather than by tracking the historical data or ex ante forecasting.[4] Some policy variable is shocked above or below its historical value and the results are compared with a control solution of the model.[5] The 1973 BD model is shocked by an increase in unborrowed reserves, federal purchases of goods, and mortgage purchases by the Federal National Mortgage Association. In a later presentation, four additional simulations focus on the 1969 period of tight money (BD, 1974). Ceiling rates on deposits other than CDs and on CDs are raised in the first two simulations. The third experiment holds Eurodollar loans at 1968 levels. The fourth simulation examines the effect of constraining FNMA purchases.

The resultant flow-of-funds effects generally accord with prior expectations. One unexpected result of the increase in unborrowed reserves might be the shift into long-term financing despite the sharp fall in the short-term interest rates. This is due to the expectations structure underlying equations A4 and A3 for the business sector. Because of interest-inelastic expectations, reversals in upward and downward movements in short-term rates are anticipated.

The authors regard the decline in open market rates as one of the most surprising results of the simulation of interest rate ceilings. It follows, however, from estimating household security purchases as a residual. Open market rates are positively related to these quantities (equations H5, H6, H7, BD, 1973, pp. 133-34). The increased flow of funds into deposits when ceilings are raised reduces the size of the residual and in this way dampens open market rates. BD see changes in the composition of financial assets, because of differences in interest elasticities and because of time lags, as exerting an aggregate demand effect. This is a major rationale of flow-of-funds financial models. But their discussion of FNMA operations (1973) is taken by Meltzer as evidence that such compositional changes have no aggregative effect (Meltzer, 1974, p. 362). Because data disaggregation is costly, Meltzer calls for a reallocation of resources from collection and processing of data on the flow of funds to improved statistics on the money stock (p. 363)!

The BD model has also been criticized for slurring over the distinction between real and nominal rates and bypassing considerations of anticipated inflation (Goldfeld, p. 358). One might add to this the sense of unreality that the analysis conveys because of its "givens." For example, an increase in unborrowed reserves generates federal government surpluses because its expenditures are "largely exogenous" (BD, p. 77).

THE HENDERSHOTT MODEL[7]

The Hendershott model differs in many respects from the BD model. While BD divide primary securities into two broad groups, negotiated loans and marketable securities, Hendershott (H) divides primary securities into longs and shorts. Hendershott's treatment of financial institutions is more extensive (Hendershott, 1977, chapter 5). The model is estimated on quarterly flow-of-funds data 1957-71 as compared with the semiannual model of BD covering 1965-70. Three methodological differences are to be stressed. Hendershott enforces the balance sheet constraints and interest symmetry (Hendershott, 1977, chapter 4). Second, the expenditure variables are exogenous in Hendershott whereas they are endogenous in the BD model. Third, Hendershott abandons the stock-adjustment format.

For comparative purposes, we feature the same sector equations--business, households, and commercial banks. Hendershott's empirical results are reproduced because of their faithfulness to the underlying constraints.

The Household Sector. The equations for the household sector are given in Table XI.1, where

FA = financial assets

CG_e = equity capital gains

CC = consumer credit and bank loans

PL = policy loans

MOR = home mortgages

SAV = personal savings

CDUR = consumer durable expenditures

TABLE XI.1

HOUSEHOLD TOTAL FINANCIAL ASSET PURCHASES AND ISSUES OF CONSUMER CREDIT, POLICY LOANS, AND MORTGAGES

	SAV	$CDUR$	$HOUS$	$Rmor{*}HOUS$	CSV	CG_e^a	$\Delta(Rcp{*}SCSV)$	R^2	DW	SEE
$\Delta FA - CG_e$	.972 (.022)	−.195 (.075)	−.164 (.045)	−.068 (.057)	−.264 (.089)	−.195 (.017)	.00077 (.00011)	.97	1.51	0.686
$-\Delta CC$	—	−.463 (.066)	−.161 (.038)	−.065 (.048)	−.283 (.061)	.101 (.011)		.86	1.97	0.421
$-\Delta PL$	.004 (.004)	—	—	−.081 (.008)	−.081 (.013)	.012 (.002)	−.00077 (.00011)	.87	1.22	0.065
$-\Delta MOR$	.024 (.024)	−.342 (.056)	−.675 (.036)	.214 (.044)	−.372 (.076)	.082 (.016)		.86	1.36	0.400
** Σ	1	- 1	- 1	0	- 1	0	0			

Note: Interest rates are measured in percentage points and dollar magnitudes are in billions of dollars. The numbers in parentheses below the regression coefficients are standard errors.

[a] Eighteen-quarter distributed lag.

[b] Five-quarter distributed lag.

** I have added this row.

Source: Hendershott, 1977, p. 82.

HOUS = housing expenditures
CSV = contractual saving
SCSV = stock of contractual saving
Rcp = the commercial paper rate
Rmor = the difference between the current mortgage rate and the average during the previous two years

The adding-up constraints are satisfied as shown in the summation row. The dependent variables are flow-of-funds variables. The sources equal uses identity will only be satisfied if the interest rate change affects both sides of the identity equally. So when the coefficients in the sources of funds equations (ΔCC, ΔPL, ΔMOR) are subtracted from the coefficients for the uses of funds (ΔFA - CG_e), the sum is zero in the interest rate columns (Rmor*HOUS, [Rcp*SCSV]). While capital gains are a source of funds variable, their past (distributed lag) effect will be zero, exerting an allocational effect similar to interest rates. The coefficients for saving sum to unity. Those for uses of funds variables (CDUR, HOUS, CSV) add up to minus unity. The coefficients down the columns have to be interpreted in the light of the signs of the dependent variables. Thus, for example, -.161 in the HOUS column indicates a positive relation with changes in consumer credit ΔCC.

The empirical results are in accord with theoretical expectations. First, we look down the columns. Ninety-seven percent of SAV (as measured by the first coefficient in the SAV column) is allocated to financial assets. To a slight extent such saving reduces borrowing (the negative relation with PL and MOR). Consumer durable expenditures (second column) are financed by a reduction in financial assets, by consumer credit (almost half of expenditures are financed in this way), and by mortgage credit (a third). Similarly, new housing expenditures (column 3) are financed in the same three ways with mortgages accounting for two-thirds of the financing. The results indicate the fungibility of money. Money borrowed on a chattel mortgage, ostensibly to buy a car, may be used to finance housing. Similarly, money borrowed presumably to finance housing (on the basis of a mortgage loan) may go into consumer durables. The cushioning role of financial asset holdings is also noteworthy. Initially built up out of saving, they can later be used to finance capital expenditures as shown by the negative coefficients of CDUR and HOUS in the first row. The fungibility of money and saleability of financial assets again dramatize the problems faced by monetary policy either in applying selective credit controls or general controls. Selective controls can be circumvented by using an acceptable collateral or funds can be had for any spending whatsoever by selling off financial assets. The coefficients for the final flow-of-funds variable, CSV, show that contractual saving is financed by reductions in other financial assets and by increased borrowing.

The Rmor*HOUS column measures the effects of higher mortgage interest rates. The substitution effects of higher rates result in less financial asset acquisition (as current spending on housing is increased out of current or past saving), more consumer credit borrowing, more policy loans, and, as expected, less mortgage borrowing.[8] The commercial paper rate scaled by the stock of contractual saving (Rcp*SCSV) has the expected positive effect on policy loans. Substituting the 1971 value for the stock of contractual saving, if the commercial paper rate advances by one percentage point, then over the space of three quarters, policy loans will go up by $500 mn. The proceeds in turn are invested in financial assets (shown by the coefficients of Rcp*SCSV in the financial asset equation).[9]

Finally, the capital gains variable (CG_e) indicates that past capital gains, embodied in financial assets, will be liquidated (by the selling-off of financial assets) and used to repay mortgages, consumer credit, and, to a lesser extent, policy loans. The coefficients indicate that a past dollar of capital gains in equities results in twenty cents being devoted to such retirement in any quarter.

Looking across the rows gives an explanation of each of

the dependent variables. We see first that the change of financial assets (with capital gains netted out) are primarily explained by personal saving. The signs of the remaining variables except for the commercial paper rate are negative. More capital expenditures lead to less financial saving as households substitute real outlays for financial claims. Higher mortgage rates lead indirectly to less financial saving as households are encouraged to finance expenditures internally. The more contractual saving (CSV), the smaller the additions to "discretionary" financial assets represented by FA. Past capital gains CG_e become part of the stock of financial assets and are then used to repay past indebtedness (Hendershott, p. 79).[10] This explains the negative effect of this variable on increase in financial assets.

The remaining equations describe the liability functions. The pattern is for borrowing to be related chiefly to the real expenditures suggested by the borrowing instrument but also to be affected by contractual saving and interest rates. Financial sources are constrained by real uses in Hendershott (in contrast with uses being constrained by borrowing in the circular flow model).

Breaking Down Financial Assets. Financial asset purchases have been subdivided in Hendershott into four categories--money, savings accounts (commercial and mutual savings bank deposits, large negotiable certificates of deposit, savings and loan and credit union shares), short-term securities (commercial paper and Treasury bills), and long-term securities (equities and corporate, state and local, and federal government long-term debt) (Hendershott, pp. 84-94). The first finding is that net sources of funds (saving less expenditures on durables, housing and contractual saving) go largely into interest-bearing assets with only one-fifth going into money holdings. One quarter later half of the increase in money holdings is shifted largely into saving accounts. Capital gains go into short-term assets and reducing liabilities with the latter adjustment process taking longer than the asset adjustment.

Runoffs of certificates of deposit (CDs) when interest rates reach ceiling levels are shifted into open-market securities, two-thirds of which are short-term, one-third long-term. Changes in the yields on savings accounts induce rapid movements out of money. Thus, the money elasticity with respect to the savings account rate is -.43 as compared with -.05 with respect to the short-term (commercial paper) rate. Similarly, interest rate substitutions between saving accounts and open market securities have low values. Moreover, the adjustment process takes longer than in the case of money. Policy loans in response to higher short-term rates are invested in short-term security holdings. When mortgage rates are high, households reduce their mortgage borrowing and liquidate their savings accounts.

Finally, an increase in income increases transactions balances and reduces the demand for open-market securities. The elasticity of transactions balances with respect to income is estimated to be .30.

The Business Sector. Hendershott has reversed the signs on the dependent variables in this sector as compared with the household sector. Financial asset purchases are entered negatively and financial sources are entered positively (Table XI.2). As a result the exogenous uses of funds down the columns enter all the equations positively--they are financed by security issues or asset liquidation. (Lagged miscellaneous assets do not have current financing and for this reason $MISC_{-1}$ is treated in the same way as the interest rate variables.)

The empirical analysis (going down the columns) shows that fixed investment is largely financed by long-term debt issues. Inventories and trade credit are financed by short-term debt (mainly bank loans), liquidation of short-term assets and money holdings. Residential construction in process has mortgages as its chief source of financing.

The business sector matches the maturity structure of its sources and uses. Such matching minimizes the interest and

TABLE XI.2

ESTIMATES FOR THE AGGREGATE FINANCIAL CATEGORIES, BUSINESS SECTOR

		$FIXI$	$INV + \Delta TC$	$MISC^e$	$MISC^e_{-1}$	CF	ΔPTL	$\Delta(RcpTFA^e)$	$\Delta(RsvbTFA^e)$	$\Delta(Rcp - Rsvb)TFA^e_{-1}$
	$-\Delta MON^d$		.175 (.083)	.220 (.076)	−.121 (.073)	−.022 (.023)		.00192 (.00161)	.0155 (.0050)	
XI.	$-\Delta SVB^d$					−.012 (.007)			−.0155 (.0050)	.00461 .00135)
XI.1	$-\Delta B^d$		.290 (.099)	.396 (.090)	.121 (.073)	−.171 (.024)	−.554 (.102)	−.00192 (.00161)		−.00461 (.00135)
XI.	ΔS^e	.113 (.077)	.535 (.066)	.379 (.072)		−.152 (.015)	−.446 (.102)			
XI	ΔL^e	.887 (.077)		.005 (.110)		−.643 (.081)				
**	Σ	1	1	1	0	−1	−1	0	0	0

		$\Delta(Rcp - Rsvb)TFA^e_{-2}$	CDD	Δy_b	Rcor*	LIQ	R	DW	SEE
XI.1..	$-\Delta MON^d$			−.0732 (.0152)			.55	2.16	.629
XI	$-\Delta SVB^d$	.00348 (.00135)	−.133 (.037)	.0169 (.0111)			.60	1.50	.524
XI	$-\Delta S^d$	−.00348 (.00135)	.133 (.037)		.070 (.018)	−.062 (.194)	.76	2.07	.312
XI	ΔS^e			.0471 (.010)	.080 (.018)	−.931 (.194)	.79	2.14	.826
I	ΔL^e			.0092 (.0188)	−.150 (.025)	.993 (.349)	.96	1.69	1.060
**	Σ	0	0	0	0	0			

Note: Dollar magnitudes including the standard error of estimate (SEE), are in billions of dollars and interest rates are in percentage points.

**I have supplied the "adding-up" rows.

Source: Hendershott, p. 108.

Where

MON^d	= change in money holdings, business sector
SVB^d	= savings accounts
S^d	= short-term securities
S^s	= short-term loans
L	= long-term loans
FIXI	= fixed investment
INV + TC	= inventory investment and net trade credit purchases
MISC*	= miscellaneous assets less miscellaneous liability items
CF	= cash flow
PTL	= change in profits tax liabilities
TFA^d	= total financial assets
Rsvb	= interest return on savings accounts
CDD	= certificate of deposit dummy variable
Yb	= change in gross business product
Rcor*	= expected corporate bond rate: $= (Rcor - \frac{1}{n}\sum_{i=1}^{n} Rcor_{-i})\,Z$ where Z = net financing required
LIQ	= liquidity variable: $= \left[\frac{S^s}{TFA} - \frac{1}{m}\sum_{i=1}^{m}\left(\frac{S^s}{TFA}\right)_{-i}\right]_{-1} Z$

transactions costs of financing and it also makes the financing and interest more certain for long-term investment Permanent short-term borrowing requires having to renew loans periodically. On the other hand, long-term borrowing for short-term purposes entails expensive flotation costs. Substitution between financial and nonfinancial uses takes place for inventories and trade credit. Money holdings and short-term assets are disposed of as these assets are acquired (or vice-versa).

On the sources of funds side, linkages exist between gross internal funds ("cash flow") and financial sources of funds. "Total internal funds" converts undistributed profits into a cash flow measure by adding to profits imputed expenses (mainly capital consumption allowances) and subtracting paper profits from inflated prices of inventories--(inventory valuation adjustment).[11]

The strong negative relationship with long-term borrowing indicates that cash flow is a closer substitute for long-term borrowing than with short-term borrowing. Cash flow is viewed by the firm as a long-run source of funds having to be supplemented by long-term borrowing when it declines (Hendershott, p. 100). A positive linkage between cash flow and financial assets is also in evidence from the empirical estimates.

The change in profit tax liability is a "quasi-cash flow" item. It increases the cash flow temporarily as funds are retained for tax payment purposes. Such funds are invested in short-term assets (such as government securities) or used to retire short-term debts. Changes in gross business product have their greatest effect on money holdings. The liquidity variable measures illiquidity due to a rising ratio of short-term debt to total financial assets. The response is a substitution of long-term for short-term debt.

The interest rate variables display the expected relationships with financial assets and liabilities. For assets the signs are negative for other rates and positive for own rates of interest. An increase in the corporate bond rate encourages short-term borrowing at the expense of long-term borrowing and the holding of short-term assets.

Long-Term Sources of Funds. It is possible to divide the long-term category into commercial-type mortgages, term loans (loans exceeding a year in maturity), corporate equity and corporate bonds. Cash flow now is seen as a substitute for the long-term sources of corporate stock and corporate bonds (Hendershott, p. 113, table 7-8, p. 114). The liquidity variable affects corporate bonds positively--more long-terms are issues when short-term debt exceeds desired levels. An additional variable--stock market prices--helps to explain the issuance of corporate stock in the place of corporate bonds. More corporate stock will be issued the higher are market prices with the proceeds possibly being used to retire long-term debt.

Commercial Banking Sector. The regression results are given in Table XI.3:

TABLE XI.3

COMMERCIAL BANK PURCHASES AND ISSUES

	$\Delta[DD(1-d)]$	$\Delta[DD(1-d)]_{-1}$	SAV^*	$\Delta[SVP(1-t)]$	$\sum w\Delta[SVP(1-t)]_{-i}$
ΔS	.7766894	−.1367014	.8343997	.55921655	−.4211137
ΔL	.183447 (.101558)	.122440 (.108496)	.132164 (.148710)	.423785 (.115812)	.240688
ΔMOR	.0033088 (.0152613)	.0142614 (.0168853)	.0334363 (.0222354)	.00462545 (.0137310)	.1804257
$-ISS$	.0365548 (.0788508)	—	—	.0123730 (.0606051)	—
** Σ	1	0	1	1	0

	X	$INV - IVA$	$\Delta[(Rcp - Rcor)T]$	R	DW	SEE
22 ΔS	.522388	.3905405	.00395717 (.00159253)	.608	1.27	2.00
ΔL	.194651 (.128968)	−.0493965 (.144767)	−.00395717 (.00159253)	.819	1.13	1.46
ΔMOR	—	—		.877	0.91	0.17
$-ISS$	.717039 (.097238)	−.341144 (.108937)		.633	1.96	1.27
** Σ	0	0	0			

Note: Interest rates are measured in percentage points and dollar magnitudes are in millions of dollars. SEE is in billions of dollars.

**I have supplied the "adding-up" rows.

Source: Hendershott, p. 124.

Where

ΔS = change in shorts (includes U.S. governments, consumer credit, bank loans n.e.c., open-market paper, security credit)

ΔL = change in longs (U.S. and state and local government, nonhome mortgages, term loans)

ΔMOR = change in home mortgages

ΔISS = change in controlled issues = Δ[CD (1-c)] + Δ[LFB(1-f)] where CD = large negotiable certificates of deposit with reserve requirements of c

LFB = liabilities to foreign branches with reserve requirements of f

Δ DD(1-d) = change in demand deposits with reserve requirements of d

SAV* = surplus plus residual items (see Hendershott, n. 5, p. 119)

Δ SVP = change in savings accounts with reserve requirement of t

X = Δ [CD (1-c)] when CDD $\neq$ 0 (the CD rate ceiling is binding) X = 0 when CDD = 0. CDD = dummy variable.

INV-IVA = business inventories less inventory valuation adjustment

The exogeneity of demand deposits in Hendershott is in contrast to the ignoring of the money stock in Bosworth-Duesenberry. The interpretation of demand deposits as "moneys advanced" to the banking sector also differs sharply from the treatment of the money stock in our dual-decision framework.[12] In common with the BD model is the emphasis on business demand for funds. The business inventory variable influences this demand, as does the spread between the commercial paper and corporate bond rate. An increase in the short-term rate relative to the long rate leads to expectations of lower future rates thus inducing increased short-term bank borrowing in the present.

The results of experimenting with the interest rate variable aside from this case were disappointing. It was thought that banks would expand their footings if the return on assets increased relative to the cost of liabilities. But various measures of the yield spread never worked as expected (p. 123). Relative yields are found to have little influence on asset portfolios.

The model compares the paths taken by demand and time deposits. Time deposits go more largely into longs and mortgages than was the case for demand deposits. In the following quarter after an inflow of demand deposits into shorts, the purchase of shorts still constituted nearly two-thirds of the total inflow (p. 123).[13] Source-use linkages dominate the effect of interest rates in explaining bank allocations. More emphasis on linkages with expenditures (e.g., consumer credit for consumer durable spending, mortgage lending for home purchases would strengthen the explanation of bank portfolio behavior (Hendershott, pp. 128-29).

Simulation Results.

Testing the Model. More than half of the Hendershott study is devoted to testing the model's forecasting ability and to simulation exercises. Part III, "The Viability of the Flow-of-Funds Model," deals with the ability of the model to explain and forecast interest rates and security flows. He pits the flow-of-funds model (a 48-equation version) against the bank reserves model (which he describes in detail in appendix C). For the in-sample control simulation (1966.1-1971.4), the FF model was better at predicting levels (most notably the corporate bond rate) and the BR model changes (particularly the commercial paper rate). Out-of-sample (1972.1-1972.4), the FF model did better with the corporate rate (both levels and changes) and the BR model did better with the commercial paper rate and the home mortgage rate. While analytically inferior, the simpler term structure format of the BR model would seem to have the better record.

The FF model has its own analytical weaknesses. Because nonfinancial expenditures are exogenous, there is no feedback from interest rates to planned outlays and thus to borrowing. Introducing the conventional investment function would take care of the relationship with interest rates. A linkage between planned investment and recourse to credit markets is still lacking, however. As discussed in our theoretical chapters, the analytical solution is a dual-decision formulation where the dependent variable defines plans to spend financed by borrowing. In terms of the notation previously used, BP flows would be explained by a series of variables including interest rates.[14]

Policy Simulations. The major policy simulations (based on an extended 59 equation version) are summarized in Table XI.4. The first disturbance shows that both short-term and long-term interest rates are increased by one billion of open market sales or an equivalent increase in legal reserve requirements (one-time changes). In the second simulation, debt management operations (a reverse of "operation twist" of 1961-62) cause long-term interest rates to increase and short-terms to decrease but in the long-run (after four years), there is zero effect as compared with the preshock situation. Raising the ceiling on nonbank savings accounts by a half a percentage point (the third case) substantially increases the flow of funds to thrifts and their demand for mortgages. This lowers the mortgage rate and stimulates housing outlays. In the long run, however, the impact on housing outlays is zero. Raising the ceiling for banks in addition to nonbanks has similar effects. In contrast to Bosworth-Duesenberry, who emphasize the contractionary effect of deposit ceilings, Hendershott regards the binding ceilings of 1967-1969 as appropriate for stabilization (p. 211). A change in the mix of policy, however, with open-market sales offsetting higher ceilings would have improved the trade-off between inflation and unemployment. Industries with output close to capacity would have been restrained and residential construction encouraged.

In chapter 15, "A Tax Cut: Crowding Out, Pulling In, and All That," Hendershott makes a sharp detour from his underlying

TABLE XI.4

POLICY AND REFORM SIMULATIONS

Disturbance	Interest Rate Effect		Output Effect	
	S.R.	L.R.	S.R.	L.R.
1. Open Market Sale or Increase in Legal Reserves	+	+		
2. Debt Management Operations	s.t. -	0		
FR holdings of s.t. securities +, l.t.-	l.t. +	0		
3. Deposit Rate Ceilings				
a. Raising ceiling on nonbank savings institutions	-	-	(housing) +	0
b. Raising ceiling banks and nonbanks	-	-	+	0
4. Tax Cut				
a. Financed by short-terms	l.t. -	l.t.-	+	+
	s.t. +	s.t.+		
b. Financed by long-terms	l.t. +	l.t.+	-	-
	s.t. +	s.t.+		
5. Increase in FSCA holdings of Home Mortgages (1969)	mtge rate -	mtge rate -	(housing) +	0
	s.t. +	s.t.+		
6. Freezing FSCA Purchases (1965 level)	Mtge-bond spread	+	housing (cumulative)	-

Source: Hendershott, Chapters 14-18.

approach. An extended IS-LM framework (Hendershott, p. 214), is used to work out the impact of a tax cut in a two-security, multisector model (fourth shock). This focus on the money market suggests a retreat from flow-of-funds modeling. The interest-rate effect of a tax cut (financed by borrowing) depends on the relative strengths of the "debt management effect" (a change in the maturity composition of the debt) and the "intermediation effect" (tax saving allocated to bank deposits). With the long-term rate on the vertical axis, the former pushes the LM curve to the right, the latter to the left with interest-lowering and raising effects respectively.

The simulation results in Table XI.4 support the analysis. When the tax cut is financed by short-terms (4a), long-term interest rates fall and short-terms rise.[15] Higher short-term rates when the financing is by long-terms (4b) is explained by a rising demand for a fixed stock of legal reserves when households direct part of their tax saving to commercial bank deposits. The results are in contrast to bank reserve models (such as the FMP model--later the MPS model) based on an extreme form of the expectations hypothesis (maturities do not matter).

The output effects from short-term borrowing are due to increased consumption and investment spending (when not all of the tax cut is invested in financial assets). Because of the effects of higher long-term rates on investment, the output effects are negative in 4(b). Diagrammatically, such output effects take the form of shifts in a vertical IS curve. The endogenizing of nonfinancial expenditures is another major departure from Hendershott's FF model.[16]

Next, Hendershott evaluates federal housing policies aimed at expanding the supply of mortgage credit (the fifth shock). An increase in federally sponsored credit agencies' (FSCA) purchases of home mortgages has the expected effect of lowering the mortgage rate and because of FSCA financing by means of short-term issues, short-term rates stiffen. There is a short-run positive effective on housing outlays. Finally, freezing FSCA purchases at their 1965 level demonstrates that without such purchases the spread between the yields on home mortgages and bonds increases. The results, however, differ from the BD model which finds only a small and temporary increase in the mortgage rate as a result of a restriction in FSCA holdings. Additional simulations are performed in chapter 17 on the potential impact of the Financial Institutions Act of 1975 (which was never passed).

Subsequent to the 1977 model, Hendershott has continued to simulate a number of policy issues using a revised version of his model. These issues include the impact of deposit rate ceilings on the housing market (Hendershott, 1977b, 1979); the effect of liability management on commercial bank asset portfolios (Hendershott and Winder, 1979); the reasons for the growth in home mortgage debt, 1964-78 (Hendershott and Hsieh, 1980); and, finally the likely consequences of reforms in the tax-exempt market (Hendershott, 1980).

"PITFALL" MODELS

Wealth Models. The Brainard-Tobin pitfalls article (1968) has spawned a number of empirical studies of portfolio adjustment, the most important being the 1980 article by the same authors in collaboration with Backus and Smith. Despite the study's title, "A Model of U.S. Financial and Nonfinancial Economic Behavior," the emphasis is on financial behavior without any empirical linkage being forged with the real sector. One anticipates problems when such linkages are attempted. The model will have to face the same challenge as the Bosworth-Duesenberry and Hendershott models in integrating spending (investing) behavior with financial market flows. The interpretations of the accounts as a detailing of the savings-investment identity means that saving is synonymous with lending and investment with borrowing (Backus-Smith-Tobin, 1980, table 1, p. 264). Such identification as pointed out in an earlier chapter ignores most of the dual decisions involving saving and investment.

The 1980 empirical model differs from the Bosworth-Duesenberry and Hendershott studies by incorporating multivariate stock adjustments as described in the 1968 paper. The adjustment of every asset has to be consistent with the adjustment of every other asset. For example, the speed with which a discrepancy between desired and actual holdings of bonds is eliminated depends on the speed of adjustment of some counterpart asset. The speed of adjustment will be more rapid if the bond disequilibrium is the counterpart of a discrepancy between desired and actual holdings of cash than if it is the counterpart of a discrepancy in mortgage holdings. Secondly, the same variables responsible for partial adjustment of one asset must explain offsetting adjustments in other assets, assuming total wealth is given (p. 275).

The original pitfalls table is reproduced below to illustrate the adjustment behavior of the public.[17] The diagonal (bracketed) terms for "deviation from desired stocks" indicate the period adjustment to disequilibrium in each of these four markets. Other values in each column indicate matching discrepancies in the remaining markets and in the market for equities (V). For example, when desired demand deposits exceed actual demand deposits by one unit, the adjustment coefficient is .30 (hypothetical values). Consistent behavior requires offsetting adjustments totalling .30 in the other four markets.[18] The change in a given asset is estimated across the rows. For example, the period change in demand deposits is .84 with all of saving going initially into this asset. Summing up all the rows the change in assets equals 2, the amount of saving and capital gains.

Stated formally, asset changes for the public $\Delta X_i(t)$ are determined as follows:

$$\Delta X_i(t) = X_i(t) - X_i(t-1) = \Sigma_j \alpha_{ij} [X_j^{**}(t) - X(t-1)] + B_i H(t) + \gamma_i K(t-1) \Delta p(t)$$

TABLE XI.5 ADJUSTMENT BEHAVIOR OF PUBLIC

ADJUSTMENT BEHAVIOR OF PUBLIC

Coefficient of:	Deviation from Desired Stocks				Changes in Wealth	
	Demand Deposit $D^{**}(t)-D(t-1)$	Time Deposit $T^{**}(t)-T(t-1)$	Securities $S^{P**}(t)-S^{P}(t-1)$	Loans $L^{**}(t)-L(t-1)$	Saving H (t)	Capital Gains $K_{t-1}(p_t-p_{t-1})$
(1′)$\Delta D(t)$	+.30	−.08	−.08	−.30	1.00	0
(2′)$\Delta T(t)$	−.10	.20	−.10	0	0	0
(3′)$\Delta S^{P}(t)$	−.15	−.10	.20	0	0	0
(4′)$\Delta L(t)$	0	0	0	.40	0	0
$\Delta V(t)$	−.05	−.02	−.02	−.10	0	1.00
Totals	0	0	0	0	1.00	1.00

<u>Source</u>: Brainard-Tobin, 1968, p. 108.

The first terms represent the adjustment coefficients and the disequilibrium conditions including "cross" and "own" departures from equilibrium. The last two terms are the change in wealth--saving and capital gains.

Empirical estimates were prepared in 1980 for savings institutions, insurance and pensions funds, commercial banking, and households. For illustrative purposes, the results for the household sector are reproduced in Table XI.6. The table has three parts: short- and long-run interest rate responses and adjustment coefficients. Three estimates are offered for the nine financial variables: "prior," "OLS," and "mixed."

The adding-up constraints are applied in these tables. The interest-rate effects sum to zero over all equations. Unlike the sample adjustment behavior in Table XI.5 above, the estimates of the adjustment coefficients sum to unity. The reason for the difference from the sample table is that the adjustment coefficients include a wealth effect. For example, in the first column (prior row) with the asset being DDC, the partial adjustment is .9 with the remainder of the increase in wealth being allocated to the next two assets TDB and TDS. For "OLS" and "mixed" estimation the partial adjustments are more complex.

The household interest rate equations contain two additional variables not covered by the pitfalls matrix. These are the price expectations variable ($\frac{P^e}{P}$) and a transactions variable ($\frac{\sqrt{Y}}{W^e}$). The coefficients are constrained to sum to zero. Unexpected capital gains ($\frac{W - W^e - CGEQ - CG_{NON}}{W^e}$) are an additional explanatory variable in the adjustment coefficients table. The coefficients in this case sum to one.

The explicit use of "highly subjective" prior information is another innovation. The reason for the innovation is the poor results from unconstrained OLS estimation. Fewer than half of the short-run rate responses and only half of the adjustment coefficients were significant. Many of the coefficients are of the wrong sign (Backus et al., p. 183). The use of so many interest rates invites multicollinearity and may explain

TABLE XI.6 HOUSEHOLD PORTFOLIO ADJUSTMENT

HOUSEHOLDS

Dependent Variable	Interest Rate Responses										
	I	$\ln(RTDB)$	$\ln(RTDS)$	$\ln(RSHORT)$	$\ln(RLONG)$	$\ln(REQUITY)$	$\ln(RMORT)$	$\ln(RLOAN)$	$\ln \frac{RE}{RSHORT}$	$\frac{P'}{P}$	$\frac{\sqrt{Y}}{W^*}$
A. Short-Run Estimates											
*ΔDDC/W**											
prior	none	−0.0200	−0.0200	−0.0040	0.0000	0.0000	0.0000	0.0000	0.0000	0.0000	1.6000
OLS	0.1659*	−0.0201*	0.0063	0.0043	−0.0095	−0.0003	0.0295*	−0.0053	0.0048	0.0002	5.8456*
mixed	0.2947	−0.0224	0.0117	0.0022	−0.0086	−0.0008	0.0085	−0.0028	0.0007	0.0009	1.4387
*ΔTDB/W**											
prior	none	0.1767	−0.1382	−0.0045	0.0020	−0.0900	−0.0115	0.0095	0.0150	0.0000	−0.7850
OLS	0.0142	0.0141*	0.0092	−0.0007	0.0018	0.0018*	−0.0143	0.0011	−0.0004	0.0003	−1.3460*
mixed	0.1229	0.0089	0.0364	−0.0007	−0.0086	0.0033	0.0024	−0.0026	0.0006	0.0007	−0.2757
*ΔTDS/W**											
prior	none	−0.1382	0.1767	−0.0078	0.0100	−0.1475	0.0105	−0.0105	0.0150	0.0000	−0.5000
OLS	−0.0438	0.0027	0.0087	0.0020	−0.0026	−0.0005	−0.0004	−0.0136*	0.0012	−0.0001	−0.2972
mixed	0.0894	0.0015	0.0221	−0.0007	−0.0027	0.0014	0.0061	−0.0083	0.0017	−0.0004	0.2399
*ΔSHORT/W**											
prior	none	−0.0085	−0.0085	0.0200	−0.0100	−0.0200	−0.0040	−0.0040	0.0250	0.0000	−0.1600
OLS	0.2582*	0.0019	−0.0021	0.0018	−0.0051	0.0004	0.0057	0.0109*	−0.0006	−0.0003	1.0537
mixed	0.1168	0.0012	−0.0281	0.0076	−0.0038	−0.0025	−0.0017	0.0079	0.0047	−0.0007	−0.5397
*ΔLONG/W**											
prior	none	−0.0080	−0.0080	−0.0015	0.0830	−0.0525	−0.0145	−0.0145	−0.0475	0.0000	−0.0700
OLS	0.0179	−0.0055	−0.0127	−0.0037	0.0138	−0.0001	−0.0054	0.0035	−0.0018	−0.0002	−1.2089
mixed	0.1126	0.0062	−0.0181	−0.0043	0.0171	0.0017	−0.0062	0.0030	−0.0058	−0.0002	−0.2738
*ΔEQUITY-CGEQ/W**											
prior	none	0.0000	0.0000	−0.0025	−0.0800	0.2650	−0.0220	−0.0220	0.0000	0.0000	−0.0500
OLS	0.0770*	0.0011	−0.0030	−0.0011	0.0076*	0.0002	−0.0071*	−0.0007	0.0003	0.0001	−0.3860
mixed	0.0947	0.0022	−0.0033	0.0005	0.0038	−0.0002	−0.0093	−0.0011	0.0005	0.0001	−0.1231
*ΔNONMKT-CGNON/W**											
prior	none	0.0000	0.0000	0.0000	0.0000	0.0750	−0.0100	−0.0100	0.0000	0.0000	0.0000
OLS	−0.0230	−0.0039	−0.0024	0.0014	−0.0030	−0.0007	−0.0004	−0.0007	0.0014	0.0000	−0.4794
mixed	0.0321	0.0029	−0.0017	−0.0007	−0.0047	0.0008	0.0068	−0.0018	0.0001	0.0002	−0.0867
*ΔMORT/W**											
prior	none	0.0000	0.0000	0.0000	0.0000	−0.0550	0.0690	−0.0150	0.0000	0.0000	0.0000
OLS	0.0471*	−0.0007	0.0038	−0.0008	0.0033	−0.0004	−0.0091*	0.0028*	0.0001	0.0001	−0.9970*
mixed	−0.0011	0.0024	−0.0039	−0.0022	0.0027	0.0000	−0.0005	0.0043	−0.0002	−0.0001	−0.1038
*ΔLOAN/W**											
prior	none	−0.0020	−0.0020	0.0003	−0.0050	0.0250	−0.0175	0.0665	−0.0075	0.0000	−0.0350
OLS	0.4865*	0.0104*	−0.0078	−0.0033	−0.0063	−0.0005	0.0015	0.0019	−0.0050*	−0.0001	−2.1848*
mixed	0.1380	−0.0030	−0.0152	−0.0017	0.0047	−0.0036	−0.0062	0.0013	−0.0022	−0.0004	−0.2758

Dependent Variable	Adjustment Coefficients								
	$\frac{\varphi DDC}{W^*}$	$\frac{\varphi TDB}{W^*}$	$\frac{\varphi TDS}{W^*}$	$\frac{\varphi SHORT}{W^*}$	$\frac{\varphi LONG}{W^*}$	$\frac{\varphi EQUITY}{W^*}$	$\frac{\varphi NONMKT}{W^*}$	$\frac{\varphi MORT}{W^*}$	$\frac{\varphi LOAM}{W^*}$	$\frac{W - W^* - CGEQ - CGNON}{W^*}$
*ΔDDC/W**										
prior	0.9000	0.1000	0.1000	0.1000	0.1000	0.1000	0.1000	0.1000	0.1000	0.2500
OLS	1.1300*	0.0465	−0.0362	0.2831*	0.2440*	0.1909*	0.2342*	−0.1022	0.4735*	0.1962*
mixed	0.9201	0.2329	0.3299	0.2308	0.2191	0.2860	0.1856	0.2856	0.2427	0.2888
*ΔTDB/W**										
prior	0.0500	0.8000	0.1000	0.0500	0.1000	0.0500	0.0500	0.0000	0.1000	0.1200
OLS	−0.1580*	0.1060	0.0767	0.0122	−0.0274	0.0383	−0.0848	−0.0110	−0.0264	0.0276
mixed	0.0316	0.3246	0.2379	0.1133	0.1485	0.1887	0.0922	0.1577	0.1335	0.1870
*ΔTDS/W**										
prior	0.0500	0.1000	0.8000	0.0500	0.1000	0.0000	0.1000	0.1000	0.0000	0.1700
OLS	−0.1670*	−0.1074*	0.0174	−0.1133*	−0.1908*	−0.0532	0.0129	−0.0111	−0.0013	−0.0473
mixed	0.0235	0.1120	0.1726	0.1005	0.1296	0.1191	0.1380	0.1593	0.1065	0.1232
*ΔSHORT/W**										
prior	0.0000	0.0000	0.0000	0.7000	0.1000	0.1000	0.0000	0.1000	0.1000	0.0800
OLS	0.1861*	0.3349*	0.0497	0.4995*	0.3906*	0.2658*	0.3733*	0.1935	0.2195*	0.2828*
mixed	0.0079	0.0593	0.0409	0.3982	0.1249	0.0891	0.1175	0.1539	0.1122	0.0865
*ΔLONG/W**										
prior	0.0000	0.0000	0.0000	0.0500	0.5000	0.1000	0.0000	0.0000	0.0000	0.0300
OLS	−0.1248	−0.0077	0.0090	−0.0718	0.1184	−0.0018	−0.0053	0.0813	−0.0687	−0.0095
mixed	0.0040	0.0572	0.0403	0.0800	0.2404	0.1106	0.0738	0.0307	0.0199	0.0955
*ΔEQUITY-CGEQ/W**										
prior	0.0000	0.0000	0.0000	0.0000	0.0000	0.5000	0.1000	0.0000	0.0000	0.1500
OLS	−0.0157	0.1820*	0.0411	0.0493	0.0860*	0.0720*	0.0752*	0.0636*	0.0963*	0.0666*
mixed	0.0028	0.0403	0.0297	0.0058	0.0039	0.0747	0.1201	0.0320	0.0162	0.0711
*ΔNONMKT-CGNON/W**										
prior	0.0000	0.0000	0.0000	0.0000	0.0000	0.0000	0.5000	0.0000	0.0000	0.0500
OLS	−0.0040	−0.0913*	−0.0476	−0.0930*	−0.0986*	−0.0364	−0.0540	−0.0205	−0.0978*	−0.0362
mixed	0.0018	0.0389	0.0310	−0.0011	0.0053	0.0377	0.0385	0.0423	0.0288	0.0422
*ΔMORT/W**										
prior	0.0000	0.0000	0.0000	0.0000	0.0000	0.0000	0.0000	0.5000	0.1000	0.0500
OLS	0.0303	−0.0115	0.3385*	0.0039	0.0268	0.0499*	−0.0571*	0.2801*	−0.1485*	0.0413*
mixed	0.0077	0.0623	0.0560	−0.0196	0.0151	0.0048	−0.0055	0.0233	0.0695	0.0052
*ΔLOAN/W**										
prior	0.0000	0.0000	0.0000	0.0500	0.1000	0.1500	0.1500	0.2000	0.6000	0.1000
OLS	0.1231	0.5986*	0.5514*	0.4302*	0.4509*	0.4745*	0.5056*	0.5261*	0.5534*	0.4785*
mixed	0.0005	0.0725	0.0617	0.0921	0.1132	0.0893	0.2398	0.1150	0.2708	0.0975

(continued)

(Table XI.6 continued)

Dependent Variable	1	ln(RTDB)	ln(RTDS)	ln(RSHORT)	ln(RLONG)	ln(REQUITY)	ln(RMORT)	ln(RLOAN)	ln $\frac{RE}{RSHORT}$	$\frac{P^*}{P}$	$\frac{\sqrt{Y}}{W^e}$
B. Long-Run Estimates											
DDC/W^e											
prior	none	−0.0250	−0.0250	−0.0050	0.0000	0.0000	0.0000	0.0000	0.0000	0.0000	2.00
OLS	−1.0630	−0.0312	1.0983	0.0729	1.9618	0.1108	−1.6634	−0.9775	0.4169	0.0088	98.32
TDB/W^e											
prior	none	0.2500	−0.2000	−0.0050	−0.0100	−0.1000	0.0000	0.0000	0.0250	0.0000	−1.00
OLS	−3.3552	0.0080	3.4397	0.2100	6.1785	0.3550	−5.2952	−3.0534	1.2850	0.0273	293.40
TDS/W^e											
prior	none	−0.2000	0.2500	−0.0100	−0.0100	−0.1500	0.0000	0.0000	0.0250	0.0000	−0.60
OLS	−4.7424	0.0555	4.7771	0.2824	8.2979	0.4912	−7.0642	−4.1929	1.7137	0.0345	399.27
SHORT/W^e											
prior	none	−0.0100	−0.0100	0.0300	−0.0200	−0.0500	−0.0100	−0.0100.	0.0500	0.0000	−0.20
OLS	2.8961	0.0330	−3.0621	−0.1795	−5.5802	−0.3186	4.7331	2.7907	−1.1490	−0.0232	−258.03
LONG/W^e											
prior	none	−0.0150	−0.0150	−0.0050	0.2000	−0.2000	−0.0200	−0.0200	−0.1000	0.0000	−0.10
OLS	−0.9319	−0.0133	0.8919	0.0338	1.7010	0.1005	−1.3866	−0.7982	0.3237	0.0060	78.67
(EQUITY-CGEQ)/W^e											
prior	none	0.0000	0.0000	−0.0050	−0.1600	0.5000	−0.0400	−0.0400	0.0000	0.0000	−0.10
OLS	3.4009	0.0398	−2.4356	−0.1381	−4.4074	−0.2436	3.6738	2.1716	−0.9005	−0.0175	−224.27
(NONMKT-CGNON)/W^e											
prior	none	0.0000	0.0000	0.0000	0.0000	0.1500	−0.0200	−0.0200	0.0000	0.0000	0.00
OLS	−6.8426	−0.0098	7.1121	0.4450	12.5590	0.7276	−10.6665	−6.3405	2.6126	0.0505	604.65
MORT/W^e											
prior	none	0.0000	0.0000	0.0000	0.0000	−0.1000	0.1500	−0.0600	0.0000	0.0000	0.00
OLS	6.5981	−0.0770	−6.6427	−0.4014	−11.5652	−0.6890	9.8517	5.8362	−2.3961	−0.0481	−556.43
LOAN/W^e											
prior	none	0.0000	0.0000	0.0000	0.0000	−0.0500	−0.0600	0.1500	0.0000	0.0000	0.00
OLS	5.0402	−0.0054	−5.1787	−0.3251	−9.1457	−0.5340	7.8178	4.5640	−1.9064	−0.0381	−435.60

Notes: $\Delta X = X - X_{-1}$, $\Psi X = X^* - X_{-1}$ (the actual regressor is X_{-1}). Sample period is 1954.I to 1973.III (99 observations).

*t-statistic is greater than 2.0 in absolute value.

Source: Backus et al., 1980, pp. 284-86.

Where DDC = demand deposits and currency
TDB = time deposits in commercial banks
TDS = time deposits at savings institutions
SHORT = shorts
LONG = longs
EQUITY-CGEQ= equity less capital gains
NONMKT-CGNON= nonmarketables less capital gains
MORT = mortgages
LOAN = loans
We = expected wealth
P = price level
Pe = expected prices
RE = expected short-term rate
Y = personal income

unacceptable interest rate results. The long-run priors are of higher value than the short-run coefficients and assume that most pairs of assets are gross substitutes. This means that asset demands depend positively on own rates and negatively on other rates. The assumed elasticities are low, usually in the range of .1 to .3 percent. In the adjustment matrix, the priors for the diagonal elements (own adjustment coefficients) have values between 0 and 1 with liquid assets adjusting more quickly than illiquid ones.

The use of prior information results in mixed estimates for the adjustment coefficients that are superior to the unconstrained OLS estimates. The test of "improvement," however, seems to be whether the mixed estimation moved the adjustment coefficients in the direction of the priors. On the other hand, mixed estimates of the interest rate coefficients were not better than the OLS estimates.

Simulations. The unsatisfactory quality of the empirical estimates results in a kind of imaginary simulation based on the prior means. The simulation is confined to the financial block of equations. The idea is to test for consistency of the whole system: while each individual sector may behave sensibly, the system as whole may not. Simulations revealed problems with the volatility of capital flows. They induce large fluctuation in rates and asset demands. The assumption that banks fully accommodate loans, forces unrealistic reallocations of bank portfolios. "Slow" partial adjustment of quantities also results in large fluctuations in interest rates.

A variety of disturbances are simulated with similar results for open market operations, reserve requirements, mortgage support operations as reported in Hendershott. One difference from other models, however, is the assumption of imperfect substitutability between interest-paying financial assets and equities ("capital"). Variations in rates in government securities as a result of monetary policy operations exceed variations in the required rate on capital (the yield on equities).

An Integrated Model. In the basic Brainard-Tobin model, saving is exogenous. In the household model now to be considered, the consumption, saving, and asset decisions are made simultaneously (Backus and Purvis, 1980). Asset flow demands are no longer conditional upon an exogenously given change in wealth. Total wealth at the end of the period is as much a result as it is a constraint on asset demands (Purvis, 1978, pp. 403, 407).

The integrated model consists of two equations (Purvis, 1978):

$$c = \sum_i b_i X_i + \sum_s e_s y_s(-1)$$

$$\Delta y_r = \sum_i \alpha_{ri} X_i - \sum_s \gamma_{rs} y_s(-1) \quad \text{for } r = 1, \ldots, n$$

Where X_i = exogenous explanatory variables (X_o = income)

c = consumption

y_r, y_s = individual assets; (-1) refers to initial values

The n + 1 equations solve simultaneously for the n assets and consumption.[19]

Consumption is a function of assorted variables (X) and the combined effect of individual asset holdings at the beginning of the period. Changes in assets are determined by the total impact effect of a change in the ith explanatory variable on the desired flow demand less initial asset holdings.

Two differences from the Brainard-Tobin wealth model are the simultaneous determination of saving and portfolios, and secondly, the significance attached to individual assets in influencing consumption. Differences in the rates of return on individual assets affect the optimal time path for each asset and therefore also affect consumption (saving) (Purvis, 1978, p. 403).

The authors (1980) find the results of applying the integrated pitfalls approach encouraging. Their "lattice of models" is reproduced in Figure XI.1.

FIGURE XI.1 LATTICE OF MODELS: THE INTEGRATED MODEL AND SOME SPECIAL CASES

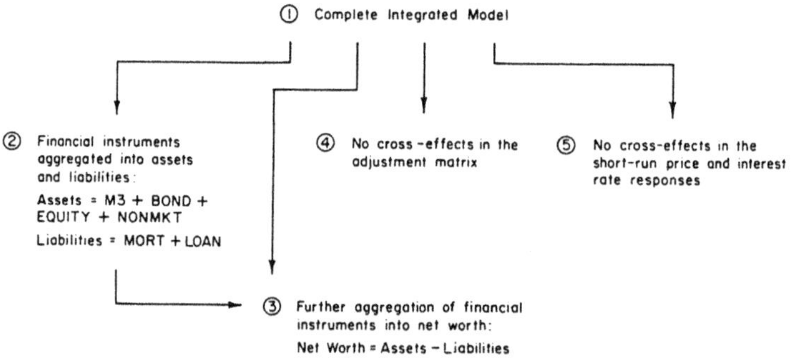

Note: Arrows indicate nesting of models; e.g., ③ is nested in ② and ①.

Beginning with the completed integrated model, the alternative models arise when the indicated parameter restrictions are imposed on the integrated model. The restricted models are each treated as a null hypothesis. As shown in Table XI.7, the null hypothesis is uniformly rejected in favor of the alternative (integrated model) hypothesis.

TABLE XI.7

RESULTS OF TESTS OF ALTERNATIVE MODELS

Equation	Null Hypothesis*			
	2	3	4	5
CON	12.15	9.97		
CDEXP	12.53	10.05	12.80	4.03
HEXP	3.35	3.56	4.41	1.04
M3			1.90	2.30
BOND			2.37	4.85
EQUITY			4.62	5.01
NONMKT			4.42	10.51**
MORT			7.34	5.24
LOAN			16.01	1.42
Critical value (5%)	F(4,70 = 2.51	F(5,70) = 2.35	F(7,70) = 2.15	F(6,70) = 2.23

*Numbers refer to figure 1. The alternative hypothesis is always the complete integrated model (model 1). The null hypotheses are model 2: financial instruments aggregated into assets and liabilities; model 3: financial instruments further aggregated into net worth; model 4: no cross-effects in the adjustment matrix; and model 5: no cross-effects in the short-run price and interest rate responses.

**There is no own rate for this equation so all seven price and interest rate coefficients have been set to zero. Degrees of freedom are (7,70).

Source: Backus and Purvis, p. 408.

Where:

CON = consumption outlays on nondurables and = services

CDEXP = expenditures on consumer durables

HEXP = expenditures on residential structures

M3 = currency, demand deposits, time deposits, and savings accounts

BOND = U.S. securities except savings bonds, state and local government obligations, corporate and foreign bonds, and open market paper

EQUITY = corporate equity and investment company shares

NONMKT = "nonmarketable" assets: life insurance reserves, pension fund reserves, savings bonds, and various miscellaneous assets

MORT = mortgage liability

LOAN = liabilities except mortgages (mostly consumer credit)

A Disequilibrium Financial Model. A disequilibrium feature is introduced into pitfall models in a study of savings and loan associations (Smith and Brainard, 1982).[20] A disequilibrium model is developed and the results compared with an earlier equilibrium model (Smith and Brainard, 1976; Smith, 1980). The authors conclude that there are apparently little or no disequilibrium effects on S&L's: their notional asset demand equations apply.[21] Households on the other hand, are rationed at times. This means that the mortgage market is either in equilibrium or there is an excess demand for credit (excess supply of securities). Institutions get what they want while borrowers are sometimes frustrated. A Theil-Goldberger mixed estimation procedure was used to combine the time series data with a priori assumptions about the model's parameters (Smith and Brainard, p. 1288).

While three additional assets are considered besides mortgages (currency and demand deposits, short-term marketable securities, and long-term bonds), only the possibility of disequilibrium in the mortgage market is considered. Other asset markets are affected by spillovers from the mortgage market as a result of disequilibrium. If S&L's cannot make all the mortgage loans they wish, they will invest in cash and bonds. These effects turned out to be small.

The key to understanding the rationing coefficients are equations (I) and (II) of their model:

$$\text{(I)}\quad A_i^h = E_i^h + {}_{ii}^{h}\, SE_i = N_i^h + \sum_{j \leq k} \alpha_{ij}^h\, SE_j$$

Where

A = actual transactions

E = effective demands

SE = excess effective demands

N = notional demands

α = the fraction of excess effective demand absorbed by the hth agent in the ith market with spillover from the jth market ($j \leq k$), while k = the number of rationed markets

$$\text{(II)}\quad \Delta\left(\frac{1}{r_M}\right) = SE$$

Where

r_M = the mortgage rate

λ = the speed of rate adjustment

These two equations imply

$$A_i = \ldots + \frac{\alpha}{\lambda}\,\Delta\,(1/r_M)$$

The rationing coefficients are $\frac{\alpha}{\lambda}$. A low value could be due to a small α (S&L's do not have to absorb market disequilibria--they get what they want), or to a large λ --rapid rate adjustments keep the disequilibria small. The a priori values assumed for α (the "prior means") are .4 when there is an excess demand for mortgage notes (SE $>$ 0), .2 when the mortgage market was near equilibrium and only .04 of an excess supply (SE $<$ 0). To the extent that S&L's satisfy this excess supply they will have to make more loans than they want to. The low prior mean on α(.04) indicates a belief that S&L's will not make many of these emergency loans.

FIGURE XI.2

EXCESS SUPPLY AND DEMAND IN THE MORTGAGE MARKET

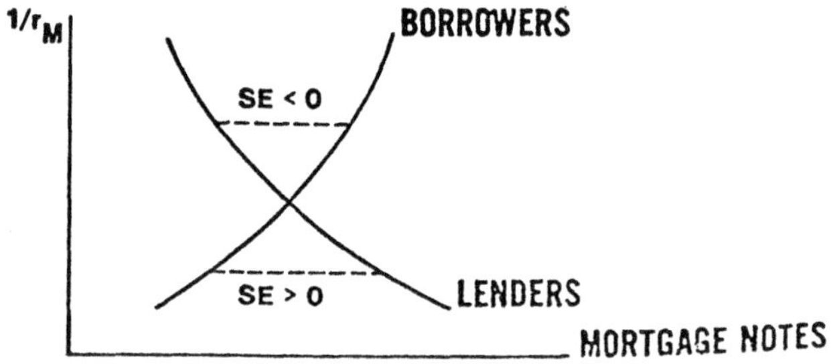

Source: Smith and Brainard, 1982, p. 1288.

The authors assume that the speed of adjustment (λ) is greater with an excess supply of mortgages (SE $>$ 0). In terms of Figure XI.2, when r_M is above the market clearing level, an excess supply of $1 billion will move the mortgage rate toward the equilibrium level by 5 basis points. Below the equilibrium level, it would take an excess demand of $4 billions to lower the mortgage rate by 5 basis points and move toward equilibrium (p. 1288). The combined effect of α and λ is to make the priors for the rationing coefficient negligible for SE $<$ 0 ($|20|$) and make it substantial for SE $>$ 0 ($|800|$). This is in keeping with the mixed estimation results that S&L's are likely to be on their notional demand curve when yields are below equilibrium levels and off their curve when yields are above equilibrium levels. The results confirm the "minimum quantity" assumptions of disequilibrium analysis. Above the equilbrium point, savings and loans are on their notional demand curve. Below it, however, borrowers are on their notional supply (of mortgages) curve and S&L's are rationed. While this would seem to be the most important finding of the study the authors curiously emphasize S&L's being on their notional demand curve for mortgages consistent with earlier equilibrium studies.

AN INTERIM APPRAISAL

In four empirical chapters we have moved from less complex to more complex flow-of-funds models. This is a retrospective pause. It is impossible to estimate left-hand variables as dual-decision variables, that is, to find a single time series that will measure a specific use of funds and the corresponding source of funds. Empirical work must link sources and uses by means of identities, by regressing one flow against another and/or by substituting choice-theoretical variables for the right-hand flow variable. Identities (Chapter VIII) have been seen to have a considerable usefulness for identifying the dynamic and passive sectors in the economy, for formulating hypotheses about sector deficits and their financing, and for forecasting real-financial flows. As illustrated by the London Business School Forecasting Centre, the underlying constraints can be integrated with econometric analysis.

Flow-flow modeling makes the jump from identities alone into equation-fitting. Its strength as well as its weakness is a system of fixed coefficients linking uses of funds to sources of funds or uses to uses and sources to sources. In the Stone input-output models, investment and saving are the disturbance variables generating the multiplier matrix. Our own (circular flow) preference assigns this role to financial flows. That fixed coefficients cannot be relied on to generate stable financial flows is a clear lesson from flow-flow models. But the stability of the linkages between real uses and real and financial sources seems well established with supporting evidence from many other sources.

The rationale of the stock market model is to begin with flow-flow relationships and then move on to a second round of equations. The first round equations identify substitutionary flow relations on the demand side and complementaries on the supply of securities side of the market. These substitute and complementary flows are then analyzed further by introducing a broad spectrum of stock, flow, and price variables. The two-tier approach to financial market analysis parallels the approach suggested earlier in Chapter V to sector expenditures and exemplified later in Chapter XIV.

Of the three portfolio balance models, pride of place belongs to the Hendershott model. In a book-length treatment, it does what it sets out to do. Adding-up constraints are neatly satisfied in the sector tables. Flow variables are both flow- and price-constrained. Simulations for the most part make economic sense. It is the only study taking a chance with ex ante forecasting. At best it breaks even with the competition--the bank reserves model. I would see the exogeneity of GNP expenditures as the major weakness. Most satisfying is the discovered importance of flow-flow linkages even where they might be least suspected, as in the case of the bank sector.

The Bosworth-Duesenberry study is disappointing in its ad hockery. Maximizing the R^2 seems to take over and the study fails to deliver on its conceptual promises. It has two redeeming features, however. First, it is eloquent on the weaknesses of conventional money market models. Second, it emphasizes the importance of the demand for bank credit in bank portfolio behavior (as does Hendershott). This fits in with the theoretical framework of the first six chapters.

The most sophisticated approach to model-building is taken in the Backus et al. study. But possibly because of this, it is the most significant failure. Too many interest rates produce impossible multicollinearities. Resort must be had to subjective "priors" both in the estimation and simulation exercises. No linkage is provided to real economic activity, despite the title of the study.

Flow-Flow vs. Choice-Theoretical Relations. Both flow and choice-theoretical variables make an appearance in portfolio balance models. Their respective explanatory value can only be evaluated by fitting separate sets of equations.[22] This has been done for the household sector (Cohen and Kenkel, 1986). Rival hypotheses were applied to household uses of funds, quarterly, 1952-1983 covering four nonfinancial expenditures categories and twenty financial asset categories. Flow variables (sources of funds, dissaving) track better than choice-theoretical variables (prices, interest rates, stock values). Price and interest rate variables are highly trended and as a result have less explanatory power than the flow variables. The problem of multicollinearity for choice-theoretical variables shows up in a comparison of correlation matrices. These results confirm the difficulties with the Backus et al. model.

In limited ex post forecasting, however, based on root mean square errors, the flow-flow models had less of a marked superiority. They forecast better for fourteen variables, with the choice-theoretical relations proving superior for ten variables.

In a more complete model of household behavior (and the same generalization applies to other sectors) there is no conflict between the two methodologies. A two-tier strategy would endogenize the right-hand flow variables in choice-theoretical terms.

Notes

1. A troublesome bit of terminology in the literature is the double use of "sector" to refer on the one hand to decision making units, and on the other hand to a form of activity or function. For example, the Bosworth-Duesenberry study refers to the financial sector when it means financial or credit market activity and to the real sector when it means spending activity and prices, wages and employment. We restrict "sector" to its decision-making context.
2. While not stated empirically, it applies <u>mutatis mutandis</u> to the liability equation.
3. While central bank action is independent of business loan demand in the BD model, the two can be linked via the government securities market. The central bank will respond to the pressure placed on the government securities market when banks sell off securities by supporting the market. In this way more reserves are supplied to the banks (Cohen, 1975).

   The endogeneity of central bank policy in response to the demand for bank credit is a central tenet of post-Keynesian econometric models. See Eichner, 1979; Forman, Groves, and Eichner, 1985. Unlike the BD model, however, the post-Keynesian models play down the importance of restrictive actions. See also below, Chapter XIII.
4. As a result the experiments with the model tell more about the model than the real world (see comments of Goldfeld, 1974, p. 359).
5. Detailed tables for each simulation are given in terms of the variables of the national income accounts, individual sectors, interest rates, and issues of credit market instruments.
6. Goldfeld is puzzled by the fluctuations seen in the CD rate and the unexplained fluctuations in the bank loan rate. They suggest that "something funny is going on in the dynamics of the adjustment" (1974, p. 359).
7. An extensive Canadian study has modeled itself after the Hendershott model (Brox and Maclean, 1987, forthcoming). The results confirm the strong influence of expenditures on financial flows. Similar flow- flow relationships were found in the Bain, Day, Wearing study of nonfinancial companies in the United Kingdom (1975).
8. The scale variable HOUS allows for the greater amount of mortgage finance as home values go up with inflation. The MOR equation, however, underestimated the dollar volume of mortgages when it was used for forecast purposes. Instead of HOUS, which measures current residential purchases and thus reflects new homes only, the stock of housing would have been a better scale variable (Hendershott, pp. 94-95).
9. Ibid., p. 84. The concentration of the weights for commercial paper in the first three quarters explains why the adjustment is largely completed in three quarters.

10. Evidently, the CG_e subtracted from financial asset change ΔFA, refers only to capital gains on current asset purchases and not on past asset purchases. Otherwise, past capital gains could not be embodied in financial assets.
11. The derivation of internal funds for nonfinancial corporate business is given in the detailed flow-of-funds accounts. For the first quarter 1985, the figures are as follows:

1	Profits before tax	$ 41.3 bns.
2	- Profit tax accruals	16.3
3	- Domestic net dividends	20.0
4	= Domestic undist. profits	5.2
5	+ Capital consumption adj.	16.9
6	+ Depreciation charges NIA	59.6
7	+ Earnings rec. from abroad	2.1
8	= U.S. internal funds, book	83.8
9	+ Fgn. earnings ret. abroad	2.7
10	+ Inv. valuation adjustment	-.4
11	= Total internal funds + IVA	86.1

SOURCE: Federal Reserve, Flow of Funds Accounts, December 1985, p. 10.

12. To all intents and purposes, however, statistical estimation according to a flow-constrained approach would result in the same formulation. That is, MB--a financing of financial asset purchases by money creation--would be estimated by B = B(M, etc.). Alternatively to escape any "moneys advanced" connotation bank lending could be made a function of effective reserves (potential demand deposits). On this procedure, see Chapter XIV below.
13. These results are similar to those of Hester and Pierce, 1975, Chapter 6.
14. The Bosworth-Duesenberry model unites business borrowing decisions with investment functions by means of identities for sector deficits. Investment generates sector deficits and borrowing via various financial instruments are then made a function of the deficit. This approach is of dubious validity because the deficit is the sum of borrowing less the acquisition of financial assets.
15. In his final summing-up chapter (19), Hendershott is less sanguine about these results and calls them implausible (p. 299). The failure of the interest rate on longs to increase is blamed on the model's deficiencies in estimating substitution between long- and short-term securities. High on the author's agenda for future flow-of-funds modeling is improving this capability. Paradoxically, he concedes that term-structure relations might have to replace market-clearing equations.
16. Hendershott's analysis of crowding out in a flow-of-funds setting has been extended in two subsequent articles (Zahn, 1978; Dalamagas, 1982). While Zahn queries Hendershott's "crowding-in" results, they are supported in the later article.

17. Subsequent comments on the model (Ladenson, 1971, 1973; Clinton, 1973; G. Smith, 1975) fail to modify the validity of the original model as an estimation technique. The assumed exogeneity of saving and wealth can be challenged, however. See "An Integrated Model" below.
18. Disequilibrium in the equities market is not shown because it is the residual asset. Adjustments in the ΔV row satisfy the column adding-up constraints. It is not possible then to have an independent disequilibrium column for equities.
19. Because of the budget constraint creating linear dependency among the n+1 equations--$X_o = c + \Sigma_r \Delta y_r$--one of the equations could be solved for residually.
20. Positive evidence for disequilibrium in the Norwegian Treasury bill and government bond market has previously been cited (see Chapter IX above).
21. My understanding of this article has been helped by a letter from one of the authors (G. Smith, September 29, 1983).
22. The dialectics of flow-flow vs. choice-theoretical relations were illustrated early on in the history of flow-of-funds analysis. When Duesenberry tested such relationships (1962), he was rebuked by Tobin (1962). Using the analogy of the substitutability of margarine for butter, Tobin told Duesenberry that one should not use the quantity of butter consumption to "explain" margarine consumption. Rather, one should relate both consumption quantities to the relative prices of the two commodities. The reasoning is that the flow-flow relationship may be unstable. For example, capital expenditures may be positively related to bond sales when interest rates are falling but have a negative relation with bond sales when income is increasing. (At that time both real uses and bond purchases are increasing.) The sign of the bond flow variable is therefore unpredictable.

    On the other hand, in a later study of demand for financial assets, Silber (1970) defended the flow-flow relationships when a value-theoretical explanation was inadequate. In such circumstances, the flows of other financial assets should be inserted into the sector asset demand equations. Similarly, a case can be made for regressing financial uses of funds against financial sources of funds.

    The controversy is ultimately an empirical one: whether flow-flow relations display more stability and are more predictable than choice-theoretical relations.

CHAPTER XII
DISEQUILIBRIUM MODELS

The models of this chapter have ther greatest interest in the role of the bank credit market in promoting disequilibrium in both financial and nonfinancial markets. Besides a series of credit market models, the Fair model and fixprice models are considered. The Fair model has a unique way of measuring constraints in a flow-of-funds setting. The fixprice section surveys the scanty evidence on the quasi-equilibrium models of Chapter III. We begin with the latter two models.

THE FAIR MODEL

Ray C. Fair sees his accounting for all flows of funds in the system and satisfying the related constraints as one of the distinguishing features of his model (Fair, 1976, p. xviii; 1984, pp. 39, 97, 104-05).[1] While all flows are accounted for, this is done on a very high level of aggregation. Thus twenty-four kinds of securities in the Federal Reserve flow-of-funds accounts are aggregated into five categories: demand deposits and currency, bank reserves, borrowing at Federal Reserve Banks, gold and foreign exchange, and an all-embracing "all other." Moreover, rather than behavioral equations, financial assets are solved for residually by means of the accounting identities. As the author admits, it is beyond the scope of his study to consider the detailed portfolio behavior of his original five sectors (households, firms, financial, foreign, government, including the monetary authorities). A sixth sector--state and local government--was added in 1984. This means neglect of the assorted adding-up constraints of the pitfalls model (1976, p. 21).

The paucity of asset categories is not the end of netness in the Fair model. Saving for all sectors sums to zero which means that saving has been defined as net financial investment (1976, p. 28). Borrowing equations are missing except for bank borrowing from the Fed.

The outstanding feature of Fair's empirical model is his recognition of the estimation problems posed by the constrained behavior of economic agents and his attempts to deal with these problems. Unconstrained decision variables are equilibrium values--the sector is on his supply or demand curve. Fair points out that such variables can only be observed if there are no binding constraints. To identify constrained decision value some proxy variable must be found for the constraint.

The challenge is to find a variable Z_t such that

XII.1 $$\frac{CS_t}{CSUN_t} = Z_t^{\gamma_1}, \quad \gamma_1 > 0$$

Where CS_t = the actual values (say, household expenditures

$CSUN_t$ = the unconstrained value

If households are not constrained then the ratio has a value of one. If households are constrained, the ratio will be less than one. With $CSUN_t$ having its own functional relation based on equilibrium values, an equation in observed values can then be estimated:

XII.2 $$CS_t = Z_t^{\gamma_1} f(.....)$$

For the household sector, Fair deals with two possible constraints--an hours constraint and a loan constraint. The hours constraint measures departures from labor market tightness. When the labor market is tight households are not constrained (the ratio is one). A value of less than one reveals an absence of tightness and constraint (1976, p. 94).

Fair's measure of labor market tightness is the detrended ratio of total hours paid for in the economy to the total population 16 and over (represented in his model by J_t^*). A variable Z_t now has to be constructed that is a function of J_t^* and shows the desired shape (Figure XII.1).

Point A is an unlikely high value for labor market tightness. From B to A it is assumed that the household sector is not constrained. The positively sloping curve depicting constraint is approximated by the following density function:

XII.3 $$Z_t = e^{-\alpha (J_t^* - A)^2}$$

FIGURE XII.1 DESIRED SHAPE OF ZJ_t AS A FUNCTION OF J*

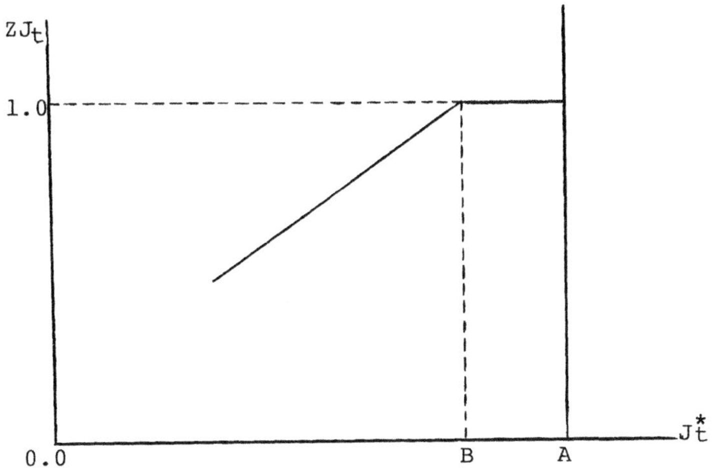

Source: Fair, 1976, p. 95.

The loan constraint is handled in parallel fashion, with the objective to find a proxy for financial market conditions when conditions are loose and households are not constrained and for conditions when they are constrained. The detrended Treasury bill rate is chosen for this purpose. As before, a Z variable has to be constructed that is a function of the bill rate showing the desired properties. Figure XII. 2 shows the desired shape of Z as a function of $RBILL_t^*$. With RBILL being solved by the model of eighty-three independent equations, the loan constraint is endogenous (1976, p. 35).

FIGURE XII.2 DESIRED SHAPE OF ZR_t AS A FUNCTION OF $RBILL_t^*$

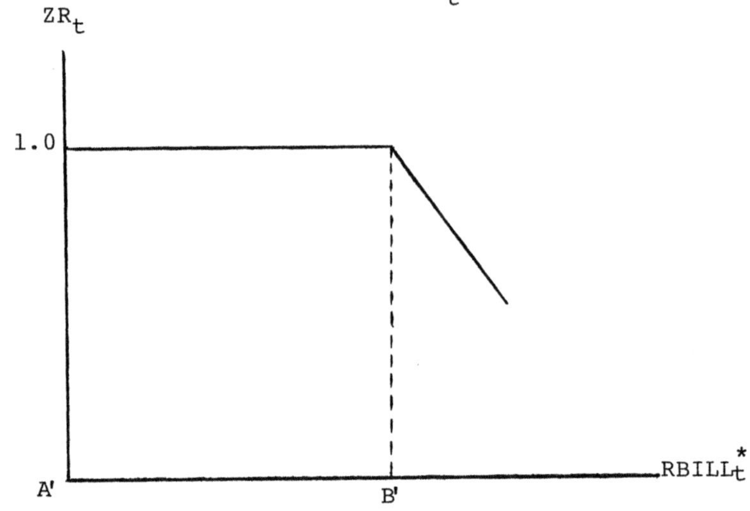

Source: Fair, 1976, p. 96.

An approximation to the curve is given by the following density function:

XII.4 $$Z_t = e^{-\alpha_2 (RBILL_t^* - A')^2}$$

The hours constraint is now represented by ZJ_t to distinguish it from the loan constraint ZR_t. Once arguments are given for $CSUN_t$ an equation can be estimated for CS_t. Thus given,

XII.5 $$CSUN_1 = e^{\beta_0} Q_t^{\beta_1} e^{\varepsilon_t},$$

where Q_t is the one explanatory variable and t is an error term, and the following interactive effect of the two constraints

XII.6 $$\frac{CS_t}{CSUN_t} = ZJ_t^{\gamma_1} ZR_t^{\gamma_2} \quad \gamma_1 > 0, \ \gamma_2 > 0,$$

then by substitution, the expression in logs for CS_t is:

XII.7 $$\log CS_t = \beta_0 + \beta_1 \log Q_t - \gamma_1 \alpha_1 (J_t^* - A)^2 - \gamma_2 \alpha_2 (RBILL_t^* - A')^2 + \Sigma_t.$$

Given values for A and A', this last equation can be directly estimated (Fair, 1976, p. 97).

The coefficient for the hours constraint is positive in the consumption equations and work effort equations in which it appears (pp. 46-48). The negative effect of the hours constraint depends on negative values for the constraint variable $(J_t^* - A)$. When slack increases in the labor market and the hours constraint becomes more binding this value becomes more negative. With a positive coefficient the constraining effect on consumption and labor force participation increases. On the other hand, when the Treasury bill rate rises the loan constraint of $(RBILL_t^* - A')$ becomes more binding. We would expect then a negative coefficient but it is positive in the housing equation, the only equation in which it appears.[2] It is of interest that when the hours constraint is applicable consumption expenditures are "flow-constrained" by wage income. On the other hand, when this constraint is not binding, then only the wage rate is relevant as an explanatory variable (p. 103).

The treatment of constraints in the 1976 model can be compared with Fair's earlier treatment of financial disequilibrium in the housing market (Fair, 1971, Fair and Jaffee, 1972). In the earlier approach supply and demand equations for housing starts were estimated. A key assumption is that the observed quantity is equal to the minimum of the quantity demanded and supplied. The quantity demanded is estimated from the household sector, the quantity of housing starts supplied from the financial sector. In disequilibrium, either the household sector is constrained (supply is less than demand at prevailing interest rates) or the financial sector is constrained (demand is less than supply). When in the current study, the loan constraint is binding, it corresponds to the household sector being rationed in the previous approach (p. 104).

In the business sector, the same (1976) loan constraint was tried. The firm is also constrained in the amount of labor it can hire as compared with the amount is wishes to hire at the wage rate it set. Similar constraint measures were constructed as in the household sector. In Fair's theoretical model a binding loan constraint has a positive effect on the price set by the firm and thus a negative effect on its production, investment, and employment. This was not verified, however, in the empirical model. Its only effect was in the dividend equation (equation 17, p. 52), where a more binding loan constraint resulted in less dividends being paid. The labor constraint was measured by one minus the unemployment rate. The results are in accord with the theory--a tighter labor market (a decline in the unemployment rate) results in higher prices (equation 9, p. 49). A major departure in the 1984 model was the abandonment of the loan constraint (1984, p. 461). Simplification of the econometric model and the failure to find much evidence for the loan constraint in his empirical work are the reasons given.

FIXPRICE MODELS

Tests of the four regimes discussed in Chapter III appear to be confined to Howard (1976), Kornai (1985), and unpublished papers reviewed by Laffont (1985). What is of interest is that they find repressed inflation to be true for both centralized and western European economies. Howard finds verification of the Barro-Grossman disequilibrium model with excess demand for output spilling over to the labor market resulting in curtailment of production in the Soviet Union. Kornai, in extensive writing, (cited in his 1985 comments on Laffont) reports similar results for the shortage (nonprice) economies of eastern Europe. The studies for western Europe reported by Laffont have the key difference that excess demand in the product market spills over to imports rather than the labor market. When demand is constrained, imports complete demand (Laffont, pp. 342-43).

CREDIT MODELS

Availability Models

Five credit models fall into two categories. The first three focus on the availability of credit. The last two are business cycle models. In the first three models credit market constraints limit expenditures. The result is disequilibrium in the product market with expenditures ex post being less than planned expenditures.

Post-Keynesian Models. Econometric estimation is based on the post-Keynesian short-period model developed by Eichner (1979b) using both the U.S. and U.K. flow-of-funds accounts. This model has five blocks, solved recursively. Block I explains the rate of growth of discretionary expenditures. Block II predicts the aggregate growth rate of economic output. In block III the "cash flow feedback effect" is determined. This is the difference between discretionary expenditures (capital expenditure items) and discretionary funds (money income less nondiscretionary spending). Discretionary expenditures are seen as the most volatile component of total spending and thus the fundamental source of cyclical movements in the economy (Eichner, 1979b, p. 41). Because "discretionary expenditure" and "discretionary funds" are wider terms, their ex ante equality should replace the conventional savings equals investment equilibrium statement (Arestis, Driver, and Rooney, 1985-86, p. 165). The cash flow feeds back into block II modifying the effects on aggregate output of the multiplier-accelerator process. The deflators used in block I to derive real expenditures and compensation rates used in block III are explained in block IV. Finally in block V liquidity effects are determined. Here the demand for bank credit is traced to imbalances between discretionary expenditures and discretionary funds. This imbalance is compared with the growth of the money base as determined by the central bank. The difference between the two reflects the degree of liquidity pressure and is called the "liquidity" effect. (The liquidity effect is discussed in detail in a 1983 working paper--by Forman, Groves, and Eichner.)

The following equation for U.S. corporate plant and equipment expenditures illustrates the estimation technique and the choice of explanatory variables (Forman and Eichner, 1981, p. 132). As evidenced in the definition of the quantity variables, the model is intended to explain cyclical movements in aggregate output, employment, and prices.

$$\overset{*}{A}_1 = \underset{(0.04)}{-0.0001} + \underset{(8.0)}{1.9}\,(\overset{*}{G}_m) + \underset{(4.0)}{1.86}\,(1/4 \sum_{t=-3}^{0} \overset{*}{G}_m)_{-1} +$$

XII.8

$$\underset{(2.3)}{0.13}(C\bar{a}p) - \underset{(2.1)}{0.001}\,(\dot{E}_1-\dot{F}_1) - \underset{(2.5)}{0.24}\,(1/4 \sum_{t=-3}^{0} \hat{L})_{-5}$$

$R^2 = 0.97$

D-W = 1.89

(t statistics are shown in parentheses)

Where

$\overset{*}{A}1$ = the quarterly deviation of the observed growth rate of expenditures from the secular growth trend (1952:2-1978:4) of 4.5%.

$\overset{*}{G}m$ = the increase in aggregate output above its secular growth trend of 3.5%

$C\bar{a}p$ = the rate of capacity utilization--manufacturing relative to mean value of index (83)

$\dot{E}1-\dot{F}1$ = the net cash deficit of the corporate sector

$\hat{L}$ = the degree of liquidity pressure: the deviation from trend of the ratio of short-term credit to short-term liabilities (deposits) within the commercial banking sector

The interpretation of the "G" terms is that a one-percentage increase in aggregate output above its secular growth trend will in the same quarterly time period cause corporate plant and equipment expenditures in real terms to increase by 1.9 percentage points above their secular growth trend (of 4.5 percent). Persistence in the growth of aggregate output above trend boosts expenditures another 1.8% (per each one-percentage increase). A one-percentage increase in capacity utilization above mean value raises expenditures by .13 percent.

The last two variables introduce financial constraints. A greater dependence on external finance (E_1-F_1) results in a slight decline in expenditures. The other side of external finance--its availability--has a more substantial negative effect. A one-percentage point increase in the ratio of short-term credit (loans) to short-term liabilities (deposits) (measured as deviation from trend) if maintained over four quarters and with a lag of five quarters, leads to an expenditure decline of approximately one quarter of a percentage point below the secular growth trend.

It is noteworthy that no long-term interest rate was found to be significant once the liquidity variable was included. The long-term interest was an explanatory variable in the original formulation (1979b). The authors conclude that it is primarily through the availability of short-term finance that monetary factors affect the corporate sector (Forman and Eichner, p. 123).

These econometric results are confirmed in a 1985 U.K. study covering the 1965:1-1980:4 period (Arestis, Driver, and Rooney).

Cohen-Kenkel Credit Model. Disequilibrium in the product market in the Cohen-James L. Kenkel model (1980) is consistent with financial markets clearing. Disequilibrium arises when expenditures ex post are constrained by the flow of external finance and as a result differ from planned expenditures, an argument in the demand for credit equation.

<u>The Model</u>. The model consists of nine behavioral equations, one equilibrium condition, and three identities for a total of thirteen equations. The demand for credit (equation 9) is explained by changes in personal saving (PS), gross business saving (GBS), real GNP (RGNP), the GNP price deflator (PGNP), all lagged a quarter (as indicated by the "1" subscript), and the corporate bond rate (RCB). The hypothesis was that lagged changes in the saving rate would have a negative effect on current-quarter borrowing. While GBS had a highly significant coefficient with the expected sign, the effect of personal saving was positive. One interpretation is that a buildup of financial and physical assets by the household sector increases its sense of solvency leading to more borrowing.

The remaining variables had the expected signs. The lagged RGNP variable is a proxy for planned expenditures possibly based on a variety of factors such as expectations. The price level had the expected effect on the dollar amount of borrowing. The interest rate had the expected negative effect on borrowing.

The hypothesis underlying the supply of credit to the private nonfinancial sector (equation 10a) was that it would be positively related to gross saving (the sum of personal and gross business saving), changes in the monetary base, and the basic interest rate. The results confirm the hypothesis. For purposes of estimating the complete model, the equation was normalized on the interest rate, RCB (equation 10b). Equations 11, 12, and 13 feed into the first equation by providing estimates for PS and GBS, and personal income (PI). Equation 14 provides the linkage between external finance and real output. This equation, coupled with the previous five "feeder" equations, explains the demand side of the product market. While a current price variable is not present in these equations, its effect shows up in the real total credit (RTC) variable and the exogenous government borrowing variable (RTG). Higher price levels for given nominal values of total credit and government borrowing reduce their value. In this way, the demand for output is

TABLE XII.1

THE COHEN-KENKEL CREDIT MODEL

XII.9 $TC_d = -35.3485 + 0.323295\ \Delta PS_1 - 1.19051\ \Delta GBS_1 +$
(−9.04655)* (2.55876) (−8.95687)
$0.154428\ RGNP_1 + 0.403918\ PGNP_1 - 2.62448\ RCB$
(4.60162) (4.33647) (−2.18013)

1952/III 1976/II $R^2 = 0.8254$ DW = 1.4064

XII.10a $TC_s = -8.20625 + 0.170268\ GS + 1.46582\ MB + 3.69691\ RCB$
(−3.48350) (1.61260) (3.02354) (4.80782)

1952/I 1976/II $R^2 = 0.6799$ DW = 1.7336

XII.10b $RCB = 2.28813 + 0.0533882\ TC + 0.0834496\ GS - 0.0587529\ MB$
(12.2671) (4.80782) (8.73030) (−0.967516)

1952/I 1976/II $R^2 = 0.7967$ DW = 0.9871

XII.11 $PS = -0.549776 + 0.0966602\ PI - 0.00528237\ NHFA_2$
(−0.60889) (7.59173) (−2.33345)

1952/III 1976/II $R^2 = 0.7178$ DW = 2.1102

XII.12 $GBS = -4.4002 + 0.030876\ NBFA_1 + 0.102517\ BSLS$
(−1.6387) (1.66655) (4.67056)

1952/II 1976/II $R^2 = 0.8558$ DW = 1.7192

XII.13 $PI = -162.092 + 0.369476\ RGNP + 2.87707\ PGNP$
(−72.2279) (15.8746) (44.9033)

1952/I 1976/II $R^2 = 0.9955$ DW = 1.1203

XII.14 $RGNP = 114.9 + 1.2\ RTC + 1.7\ RTC_1 + 1.9\ RTC_4 + 1.45\ RTG +$
(26.8) (3.7) (8.6) (6.29) (4.7)
$.9\ RTG_1 + 1.07\ RTG_2$
(3.0) (3.5)

1953/I 1976/II $R^2 = 0.9065$ DW = 0.3777

XII.15a $PGNP = 26.2803 - 0.006955\ RGNP + 19.0284\ WAGES +$
(39.0021) (−1.02206) (30.9074)
$0.005902\ PWM$
(1.05369)

1952/I 1969/IV $R^2 = 0.9957$ DW = 0.3358

*t statistics are shown in parentheses.

TABLE XII.1 continued

XII.15b PGNP $= 31.133 - 0.045503$ RGNP $+ 20.4976$ WAGES $+$
(8.13427)(−3.93952) (14.7223)
0.034012 PWM
(4.30767)

1970/I 1975/III $R^2 = 0.9968$ DW $= 1.6878$

XII.15c PGNP $= 23.0583 - 0.039313$ RGNP $+ 22.4388$ WAGES $+$
(55.2361) (−6.64220) (47.8995)
0.024518 PWM
(8.19424)

1952/I 1975/III $R^2 = 0.9984$ DW $= 0.9083$

XII.16 WAGES $= -1.41118 + 0.055195\ PGNP_4 - 0.0045557$ IGAP $-$
(−68.6216) (195.729) (−4.9508)
$0.0043925\ IGAP_1$
(−4.84416)

1953/I 1975/III $R^2 = 0.9981$ DW $= 0.5989$

XII.17 ULU $= 3.87461 + 0.151826$ IGAP $+ 0.152679\ IGAP_1$
(48.8563) (11.1913) (10.9492)

1952/II 1975/III $R^2 = 0.7807$ DW $= 1.1019$

Equilibrium condition:

XII.22 $TC_d = TC_s$

Identities:

XII.23 GS = PS + GBS
XII.24 IGAP = [(POUT − RGNP)/POUT] X 100
XII.25 RTC = TC/PGNP

TABLE XII.1 continued

Variables: definition and sources

TC	Total credit	(ONFST − SLG).
ONFST	Funds raised (excl. USG)	Board of Governors of the Federal Reserve System, Division of Research and Statistics, "Total Funds Raised by Private Nonfinancial Sectors," *Flow of Funds Table Codes* (1976), p. 22, line 6 (294102005). All flow of funds references are to this code book. Data thus identified were secured from Federal Reserve data tapes.
PS	Personal saving	F/F Gross Saving and Investment Account, p. 20, line 2 (156007105).
GBS	Gross business saving	F/F Sector Statements of Saving and Investment, p. 42, line 2 (146000105).
GNP	Gross national product	F/F National Income and Product Accounts, p. 16, line 1 (86901005).
RCB	Corporate bond rate	Federal Reserve Board, *Data Directory, Quarterly Econometric Model*, January 1975 (X91).
PGNP	Price deflator (1972 = 100) (seasonally adjusted)	F/F National Income and Product Accounts, p. 16, line 16 (71000003).
RGNP	Real gross national product	(GNP/PGNP).
GS	Gross saving	(PS + GBS).
MB	Change in monetary base	(MBR + COB).
MBR	Change in member bank reserves	F/F Subsector Statements for Component Groups in Commercial Banking, p. 49, line 19 (723030005).
COB	Change currency outside banks	F/F Sector Statements of Saving and Investment, p. 47, line 20 (713125001).
NHFA	Net household financial assets	(THFA − THFL) (end of quarter values).
THFA	Total household financial assets	F/F Sector Statements of Financial Assets and Liabilities, p. 541, line 1 (154090005).
THFL	Total household financial liabilities	F/F Sector Statements of Financial Assets and Liabilities, p. 541, line 26 (154190005).

TABLE XII.1 continued

PI	Personal income	F/F Personal Income and Outlay Account, p. 17, line 13 (156010005).
NBFA	Net business financial assets	(TBFA – TBFL).
TBFA	Total business financial assets	F/F Sector Statements of Financial Assets and Liabilities, p. 542, line 1 (144090005).
TBFL	Total business financial liabilities	F/F Sector Statements of Financial Assets and Liabilities, p. 542, line 7 (144190005).
BSLS	Manufacturing and trade sales	Dept. of Commerce, *Business Statistics*, 1971, p. 23; *Survey of Current Business.*
RTC	Real total credit	(TC/PGNP).
RTG	Real government borrowing	(SLG/PGNP) + (USG/PGNP).
USG	U.S. government borrowing	F/F Credit Market Funds Raised by Nonfinancial Sectors, p. 22, line 3 (314102005).
SLG	State and local government borrowing	F/F Credit Market Funds Raised by Nonfinancial Sectors, p. 22, line 26 (204102005).
WAGES	Average hourly wages in manufacturing	Dept. of Commerce, *Business Statistics*, 1971, p. 82; *Survey of Current Business.*
PWM	Price of imported raw materials	*Quarterly Econometric Model* (E92).
ULU	Rate of unemployment (seasonally adjusted)	*Quarterly Econometric Model* (X150).
IGAP	Income gap	[(POUT – RGNP)/POUT] × 100.
POUT	Potential real GNP	Data provided by Data Resources, Inc., based on Council of Economic Advisers series. For the rationale underlying the series' construction, see Peter K. Clark, "Potential GNP in the U.S., 1948-1980" (Washington, D.C.: Council of Economic Advisers, May 1977).

indirectly affected by prices in the expected way.[3] The significance of the lagged terms for both RTC (total private-sector borrowing) and RTG (total government borrowing) is consistent with sectors' raising funds in advance of actual expenditures, with interim investment in short-term assets.

The supply side of the analysis begins with equation 15a. Equation 16 feeds into equation 15a. Equation 15a states that prices are set on the basis of expected output (assumed equal to actual output), wage levels, and import prices. The period was broken into two with the resultant three equations. The expected greater impact of import prices (PWM) after 1970 is confirmed; what is surprising is the strength of the equation for the period as a whole (equation 15c) as compared with the subperiods. The "Harrod dichotomy" is supported by the negative relation between RGNP and PGNG.[4] When the period is taken as a whole, a billion-dollar increase in RGNP would cause a .03 point decrease in the price index. Wages are the most influential variable, with a dollar increase in average wages in manufacturing causing a 20 point increase in the index. This is not an unduly large effect when it is realized that a dollar increase represents a 30 percent increase in the average wage rate of $2.75 (for the period as a whole).

Wages are well explained in the following equation (equation 16); prices lagged four quarters have the expected positive effect, and the percentage gap between potential and actual output (IGAP) in both the current and previous quarters has a negative effect. This does not imply that wages lack an exogenous component such as market power, but rather that lagged relations seem to capture these effects. While in equation 17 wages lag prices by a year, in the markup equation (equation 16), prices react to wages in the same period.

Policy questions are generally stated in terms of tradeoffs between inflation and unemployment rather than between inflation and output. Using unemployment instead of output allows for changes in labor productivity. An additional equation of the model (equation 17) introduces the rate of unemployment by explaining it in terms of the "income gap." A 1 percent increase in the IGAP causes a substantial .15 of 1 percent increase in the unemployment rate in both current and subsequent quarters.

Simulations of the Model. Both nondynamic and dynamic simulations based on the model were attempted for the fourth quarter of 1963 through the second quarter of 1976. The model suggests that monetary and fiscal policy can exert real output effects rather than leading to purely inflationary effects. The results contrast with the theory of rational expectations which questions the effectiveness of government efforts to alter the course of the economy through fiscal or monetary intervention.

The Liquidity Constraint in Expenditure Models. The main point of our Chapter V was that wealth, debt, and permanent income deserve a place in intermediate equations explaining dissaving or borrowing. The latter then ought to make an appearance in correctly specified expenditure equations. The literature on the liquidity constraint is a move in this direction (Tobin-Dolde, 1971; Tobin, 1980, pp. 57-58; Hayashi, 1985; Kades, 1985c, pp. 30-32). The permanent income hypothesis assumes that the household maximizes its lifetime utility function subject only to the lifetime budget constraint (Hayashi, p. 186). The implication is that current and future borrowing constraints are irrelevant (p. 193).[5] Investigators have challenged this assumption by sampling or simulating the behavior of high-saving households or households with ample liquid assets. The conclusion of the Tobin-Dolde and Hayashi studies is that households without access to financial markets are indeed liquidity-constrained. They consume less during the earlier working years than they would prefer to consume (Hayashi, p. 202). Diagrammatically, there is a corner solution for such consumers. That is, in two-period space, and assuming higher borrowing than lending rates, tangency of the consumer indifference curve occurs at the coordinates of this year and next year's income (see Kades,

1985c, pp. 31-32).

While the two previous credit models focused on the effects of the availability of credit, the present approach focuses on its nonavailability. The models complement each other. The availability approach has the advantage of simplicity and provides a continuum of measurable effects from the flow of credit.

Business Cycle Models

The Sinai Model. Beginning in 1974, the already mammoth DRI model (300 equations in 1971) was expanded with the introduction of Federal Reserve flow-of-funds data. The resultant financial model is the handiwork of Allen Sinai.[6] Table XII.2 summarizes the variables and equations that were originally included in the model. Sixty-one of the 201 equations explain sector sources and uses behavior. Another 62 equations capture the information provided by flow-of-funds sector and transaction identities.

The financial-real linkages in the Sinai model rely heavily on a flow-of-funds framework. Each transactor-sector has in mind long-run values ("targets") for financial assets, physical assets, and financial liabilities. Rates of return and costs for each balance sheet item help to determine the long-run targets. Adjustment takes place through acquisition of assets (uses of funds) and financing activity (sources of funds). The result of interaction of sources and uses activities is a new balance sheet position.

The point of departure in the DRI portfolio balance model from the pitfalls models of Brainard-Tobin is the emphasis on financial risk generated by changing balance sheet compositions.[7] The generalized equation is

TABLE XII.2 FINANCIAL SYSTEM OF THE DRI MODEL

	Behavioral	Identities	Total
I. Financial Sector	44	17	61
A. Monetary and reserve aggregates	8	13	21
B. Interest Rates	24	1	25
1. short-term	15	-	15
2. intermediate-term	1	-	1
3. long-term	8	1	9
C. Loans and investments of commercial banks	6	1	7
D. Stock market	6	2	8
II. Flow of Funds	61	62	123
A. Households	20	16	36
B. Nonfinancial corporations	24	34	58
C. Mortgage activity	17	12	29
1. commercial banks	1	1	2
2. savings and loan associations	3	2	5
3. mutual savings banks	4	2	6
4. life insurance companies	6	2	8
5. mortgage rates, aggregate concepts and miscellaneous	3	5	8
III. Miscellaneous: Inflation Expectations, Installment Credit at all Financial Institutions	11	6	17
New Issues of U.S. Government Debt, New Issues of State and Local Government Debt	116	85	201
Total			

Source: Sinai 1977 Preliminary Draft, p. 171.

$$\frac{\bar{A}}{NW_{-1}} = F_1E\left(\frac{\bar{X}}{NW_{-1}}\right) + (1 - F_1)\left(\frac{\bar{A}_{-1}}{NW_{-1}}\right) + F_2\left(\frac{\bar{Z}}{NW_{-1}}\right)$$

where $\bar{A}$ is a column vector of the current, actual assets and liabilities

$\bar{X}$ is a column vector of explanatory (noncontrollable) variables such as expected own and alternative rates of return, rental prices, costs and output

E is a matrix of long-run response coefficients

F_1 is a matrix of adjustment coefficients

F_2 is a matrix of reaction coefficients

$\bar{Z}$ is a column vector of variables which affect the speed of adjustment

NW is net worth

"$\bar{Z}$" includes the cash flow of corporations or other variables that reflect illiquidity, potential bankruptcy, and the variance of expected returns (Sinai, 1977, p. 267). According to the author, Tobin failed to integrate the balance sheet and its potential instability into his model of investment spending. The credit crunches of the 1970s highlight the importance of financial factors in the business cycle. Instead, Tobin has stressed the effects on business capital expenditures of divergences between market values and reproduction costs (Tobin's q) (Sinai, 1977, pp. 176, 179).

Unlike the previous portfolio balance models, the adding-up constraints are not part of the estimation procedure. The behavior of the flow of funds in full model simulation was regarded as more important than the "niceties" of the theory (p. 268).

A "linear" description of linkages in the Sinai-DRI model

is given in Table XII.3. It begins with monetary policy and ends up with final spending ("real final demands"). An initial change in high-powered money affects interest rates and stock prices. These in turn affect the cost of capital (in row IV). Sector portfolios in V and VI respond to interest rates and money flows. While real final demands are treated sequentially in VI, they can be considered as decisions made at the same time that financial decisions are made in V. The effect of balance sheet adjustments on financial risk (section V) is a unique feature of the DRI model.

Eckstein and Sinai (1986) have documented the flow-of-funds cycle for the postwar period. Systematic changes in the liquidity and balance sheet positions of households, businesses, and depository institutions are depicted graphically in precrunch/crunch, reliquification and accumulation phases. The econometrics are limited to some simulation results. The flow-of-funds cycle has operated as both an impulse and propagation mechanism. The impulse comes "mostly" from changes in non-borrowed reserves and the resulting fluctuations of interest rates (Eckstein and Sinai, pp. 79-80). Propagation is via the channels outlined in Table XII.3.

The description of the Eckstein-Sinai simulation procedures (1986, appendix 1.1) reveals the complexity of the model and attendant problems. Offsetting "add" factors were needed in five hundred behavioral equations to remove the errors of a dynamic historical simulation. This complexity explains why until now the model has only been described in schematic form. It also explains why the Sinai financial version no longer is used by DRI in forecasting exercises.[8] The necessary add factors became huge so quickly and changes in the model were so difficult to make that the financial version was replaced by simpler forecasting tools.[9]

The Wolfson "Crisis" Model. Wolfson has sketched a business cycle model of financial crises--"a sudden, intense demand for money"--which focuses on the bank credit market

TABLE XII.3

MONETARY POLICY AND SPENDING: MAJOR CHANNELS IN THE DRI MODEL

I. Monetary policy
- A. High-powered money
- B. Federal funds rate

II. Interest rates
- A. Money market
  1. Federal funds
  2. Treasury bills
  3. Commercial paper
  4. Eurodollars
  5. Large CDs
- B. Deposits
  1. Commercial banks
  2. Savings & loan assocs.
  3. Mutual savings banks
  4. Credit unions
- C. Loans
  1. Prime business
  2. Auto installment
  3. Mortgage
- D. Long-term
  1. Corporate bond
  2. U.S. government
  3. Municipal

III. Stock market
- A. Stock market
  1. S&P 500 common stock index
  2. Dividend yield on S&P 500

IV. Rental prices
- A. Avg. cost of financial capital
  1. Weighted avg. cost of short- and long-term financing after tax
  2. Expected return on stock: dividend yield plus growth in earhings per share
  3. Capital structure: proportion of debt and equity
- B. Rental price of capital
  1. Supply prices of capital goods
  2. Avg. cost of financial capital; after tax
  3. Tax parameters
     - a. Investment tax credit
     - b. Tax savings for depreciation expense rate
     - c. Profits tax rate
     - d. Tax allowable lifetimes for depreciation
- C. Rental price of autos
  1. Supply price of automobiles
  2. Auto installment rate
  3. Price of gasoline

V. Sectoral portfolio behavior: balance sheet and flow-of-funds adjustments in response to changing yield differentials, "new money" flows, and existing portfolio positions.
- A. Households (new money-disposable income)
  1. "Financial risk":
     - a. Debt service burden with components interest rates, outstanding debt, disposable income
     - b. Loan repayment burden relative to disposable income
  2. Financial wealth
     - a. Market value-equity
     - b. Market value-bonds
     - c. Money and deposits
- B. Commercial banks (new money-deposit inflows and repayments)
  1. Mortgages outstanding
- C. Savings & loan assocs. (new money-deposit inflows and loan repayments)
  1. New mortgage commitments
  2. Mortgages outstanding
- D. Mutual savings banks (new money-deposit inflows and loan repayments)
  1. New mortgage commitments
  2. Mortgages outstanding
- E. Life insurance cost (New money-reserves less policy loans and loan repayments)
  1. New mortgage commitments
  2. Mortgages outstanding
- F. Corporation (new money-cash flow)
  1. "Financial risk" debt service burden with components interest rates, outstanding debt, cash flow
- G. State and local govts. (new money-tax receipts)
  1. "Financial risk" debt service burden with components interest rates, outstanding debt

VI. Real final demands
- A. Consumption
  1. Durables
     - a. Real hh. financial wealth
     - b. Hh. debt service burden
     - c. Loan repayment burden
     - d. Rental price of auto
  2. Nondurables
     - a. Real hh. financial wealth
     - b. Loan repayment burden
  3. Services
     - a. Real hh. financial wealth
     - b. Loan repayment burden
- B. Housing and residential construction
  1. Demand
     - a. Mortgage rate
     - b. Mortgage debt service
     - c. Treasury bill rate
  2. Supply
     - a. Mortgage rate
     - b. New mortgage commitments
     - c. Outstanding mortgages
- C. Investment
  1. Business fixed
     - a. Rental price of capital
     - b. Debt service burden
  2. Inventories
     - a. Debt service burden
- D. Government spending--state and local; public construction
  1. Outstanding state Local government bonds
  2. Municipal bond rate

Source: Sinai, 1977, pp. 186-87.

(1986b, chapter 10). Wolfson summarizes his model in nine points (1986b, p. 131):

1. Because of increased reliance on debt during the expansion phase of the business cycle, the corporations' financial condition increasingly deteriorated.

2. As profits declined, the corporations experienced increasing difficulty in meeting debt payment requirements and other fixed commitments such as those due to involuntary investment.

3. Corporations borrowed to try to obtain the funds they needed to meet debt payment requirements and involuntary investment commitments; they relied primarily upon bank loans, and, for large corporations, also on commercial paper borrowing.

4. The banks suffered losses on their business loans, which adversely affected their own financial condition, and were restricted by tight monetary policy; they tightened their lending policies, but at the same time attempted to meet the necessitous loan demands from their long-standing customers.

5. They did so by decreasing the growth rate of investments in relation to loans and by decreasing the growth rate of nonbusiness loans in relation to business loans, by restricting the business loans they extended to new customers (as opposed to established customers), and by relying on purchased funds, particularly large negotiable certificates of deposit.

6. A surprise event--either the sudden imposition of an institutional constraint or an unexpected bankruptcy (or the threat of one)--disrupted these financing patterns.

7. The disruption of financing patterns initiated a financial crisis--a sudden, intense demand for money.

8. The urgent demand for money came either from corporations or banks whose sources of funds were disrupted, or from investors who feared the loss of their funds.

9. The immediate crisis was resolved by lender-of-last resort operations of the central bank, the Federal Reserve Board.

Wolfson finds that the model stands the test of the data

very well (Chapter 11). Five financial crises are identified in the 1961-1982 period which fit in with the previous scenario. This validation relies on a noneconometric analysis of time series data most of which are flow-of-funds numbers.

<u>The New Financial Environment</u>. Wolfson admits that his theory of financial crises is not all-encompassing. The theory does not attempt to explain financial crises after 1982 (e.g., the bankruptcy of Continental-Illinois). His chapter 13 is devoted to the changes taking place in the 1980s that have made the economy more vulnerable to financial crises.[10] Past scenarios may not hold. The recent rapid growth in debt has raised fears of financial instability in new circles and may lead to new theories of financial instability (see Volcker, 1986; B. M. Friedman, 1986; Carlson, 1986; Cohen, 1986c; Federal Reserve Bank of Kansas City, 1986). Policy-wise, the new financial environment has upset the stability of money-income and credit-income linkages (see Chapter XIII below).

DEPARTURES FROM EQUILIBRIUM

The anatomy of equilibrium provides a reference point for this study of disequilibrium models. In equilibrium dual-decision situations (restricted here for illustrative purposes to two markets only), the left-hand variables represent matching flows responsive to the same market clearing interest rates and prices. Assume that we are dealing with the bond (B) and product markets (P). The matching flows are BP and PB--the planned supply of bonds to finance a similar planned demand for output, and a planned supply of output to finance the same amount of bonds. When one market clears, so does the second.[11]

Constrained disequilibrium models separate out the dual-decision variables and in various techniques relate one variable to the other. Perhaps Fair's search for proxies for constrained variables is the most subtle.[11] Next in complexity are liquidity constraint analyses.

Empirical implementation of fixprice models carefully

specify constraints for consumers and producers in the Keynesian unemployment case and for consumers in the repressed inflation case (which turns out to be the important case empirically) (Laffont, 1985, pp. 332-36).

In contrast, stand the post-Keynesian and Cohen-Kenkel credit models. They establish direct linkages between market flows (or proxies for such flows). In both of these models the supply of output is determined by expenditures ex post. The Cohen-Kenkel model attempts to identify planned expenditures in the demand for credit equation. The inevitable difference between the solution for expenditures and the value of planned expenditures measures disequilibrium. A further difference in the two models is the retention of market clearing in credit markets in Cohen-Kenkel.

The Cohen-Kenkel credit model deals with aggregate expenditures which rules out the use of an aggregate income (output) variable as a right-hand variable. In contrast, in sector expenditure models income can make an appearance. The rationale for external finance in expenditure equations is thereby clarified. In the same way that individual sectors can be regarded as "income takers," so they can be regarded as "finance takers." A major contention of this study is that finance in expenditure functions deserves a parallel treatment to the income variable.

The flow constraints in the Sinai model are not as explicit as in the previous models. It is nonetheless a disequilibrium model because balance sheets are always out of kilter, signifying stock disequilibrium even though markets may clear. The matrices of adjustment and reaction coefficients and the Z column vector, including among other disturbances a cash flow variable, make for chronic disequilibrium.

In a simpler approach founded on flow-of-funds time series data, Wolfson effectively demonstrates that upper turning point of the business cycle and financial crises have their roots in fluctuations in cash flows and in bank lending. In Wolfson's scenario, interest rates play a less important role than in Sinai in precipitating "credit crunches" or financial crises.

Notes

1. The underlying theoretical model was published earlier (Fair, 1974).
2. Fair (mistakenly, it would seem), says a positive coefficient is expected for the loan constraint (p. 101).
3. A conventional demand curve would relate quantity demanded (in real terms) to the price level, income, and other explanatory variables. The demand for output in the present model is a function of external finance (private and public borrowing). Since it lacks a price variable, it is not a demand function in a strict sense. The credit variables, however, can be written as nominal values deflated by the price level. In this sense, an inverse relation exists between price changes and the demand for output.
4. The "Harrod dichotomy" refers to the differential effects of output on prices when average costs are falling and rising, respectively (Harrod, 1970).
5. As initially stated in Tobin and Dolde (1971, p. 103), this is equated with perfect capital markets and equality of borrowing and lending rates. Why costs of financial intermediation should be assumed to be zero in perfect markets is not clear to me.
6. The discussion in this section relies on O. Eckstein (1983, esp. chapters 1 and 4), and a 1977 preliminary draft by Eckstein and Sinai which incorporated both the 1983 material and a detailed discussion of the financial model. The latter material is to be published at some future date as a companion volume under Sinai's authorship (Eckstein, 1983, p. 77). Since the 1983 volume, Eckstein has died and Sinai has moved to Shearson-Lehman. For earlier discussions of the DRI model, see Fromm and Sinai (1974); Eckstein, Green, and Sinai (1974).
7. For the underpinnings of DRI financial modeling in portfolio choice theory, see Eckstein, 1983, pp. 81-82.
8. This information is based on a 1986 conversation with DRI economists.
9. In fairness to Sinai, the early flow-of-funds detail in the DRI model evidently "paid off" with its forecasts of short-term interest rates being the best of four forecasts --DRI, Wharton, chase, and GE (General Electric) (McNees, 1979, p. 48).
10. The five broad trends in this new environment--innovation, competition, deregulation, securitization, and the growth of trading--are discussed in detail in Frydl (1986) and the Group of Ten Countries Study (1986).
11. This is in accord with Walras's law although with more than two markets a more complex submarket analysis is required.
12. The Smith-Brainard rationing coefficients (Chapter 11) are of similar sophistication but their analysis only identifies rationing in a single market, excluding intermarket constraints.

CHAPTER XIII
"DIRECT LINKAGE" POLICY MODELS

In the theoretical chapters, it was argued that flow-of-funds theory pointed to credit as the preferred intermediate policy target. This chapter studies the evidence. We begin with single equation models linking external finance and rival targets to the GNP. We next move from aggregate relations to components of GNP expenditures.

GENERAL CONTROLS: CREDIT VS. MONEY

The Pros and Cons. The attraction of credit as the policy target in controlling GNP is the constancy of income in relation to the credit aggregates in comparison with the income velocity of M1. This constancy suggests the possibility that GNP can be accurately controlled if sufficiently close control over credit is maintained. Chart 1 portrays the stability of the income velocity of credit variables in relation to M1 through 1982.

Bank credit is the narrowest measure, being limited to commercial bank loans and investments. The debt proxy includes financial claims held by nonfinancial domestic sectors (Kaufman, 1978). The largest total is nonfinancial domestic credit which takes the liability side of domestic nonfinancial sectors including the public sector. All magnitudes are measured in stock terms.

As Table XIII.1 shows, the differences in the coefficients of variation for the various ratios virtually disappear when the velocities are adjusted for their trends and respective means. This might be the key comparison. If the policymaker can predict the trend, the size and variability of the fluctuations around the trend are what matter (Fackler and Silver, p. 4).

The stability of income velocity as a test for predictability lacks the quantitative rigor of regression analysis. Moreover, such analysis oversimplifies by omitting other variables such as lagged values of the aggregates. A

FIGURE XIII.1 INCOME VELOCITIES OF M-1 AND VARIOUS CREDIT AGGREGATES

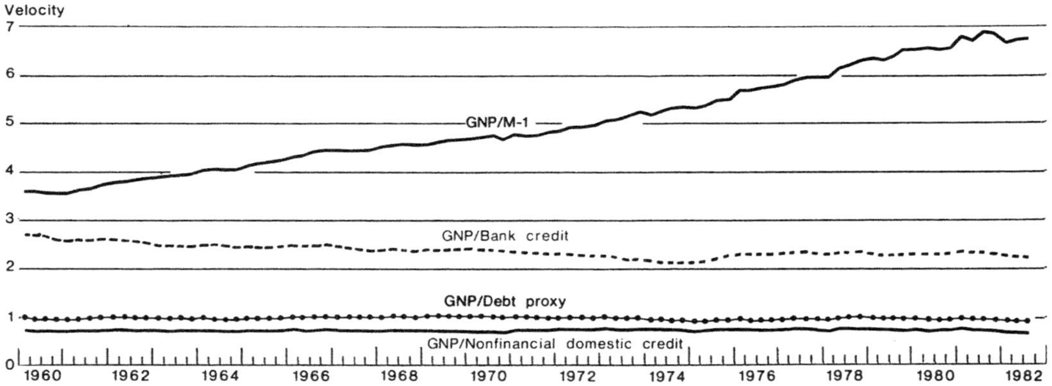

Sources: Board of Governors of the Federal Reserve System; United States Department of Commerce, Bureau of Economic Analysis.

<u>Source</u>: Fackler and Silver, 1983, p. 5

TABLE XIII.1

COEFFICIENTS OF VARIATION OF VELOCITIES:
MONEY AND CREDIT AGGREGATES*
1960-I THROUGH 1982-I

Velocities	Raw data	Detrended data
M-1	0.205	1.20
Bank credit	0.058	1.32
Debt proxy	0.015	1.17
Nonfinancial credit	0.013	.22

*The coefficient of variation is defined as the standard deviation divided by the mean.

Source: Fackler and Silver, p. 4.

considerable number of studies, (most notably those by Benjamin Friedman), have subjected the monetary and credit aggregates to regression analysis (Friedman, 1981, 1982a, b, 1983, 1984, Davis, 1979, 1982; Earley et al., 1976; Aburachis, 1973; Cohen, 1968b). We focus on the results reported by Friedman in his 1982a study. Friedman takes as his point of departure the U.S. economy's reliance on credit. What he finds remarkable is the overall stability of the credit-GNP ratio (he uses the broadest credit category as defined above), despite the sharp diverse movements in the components (1982a, chart 2, p. 236).[1]

Friedman makes use of vector autogression techniques in his support of the credit target (for the period 1959-80). The method is so named because it investigates the relation between a set of current variables (i.e., a vector), and prior values of that set of variables (i.e., an autoregression [Fackler and Silver, p. 5]). His autogressive system (1982a, pp. 233-41) demonstrates that credit plays a more significant role in the variation of either real income or prices than does money. Nor is there support for a money-income-credit hypothesis.

Friedman finally tests for controllability (the link between policy instruments and the intermediate target (1982a,

p. 242). The growth rates of four financial aggregates are related to two policy instruments--unborrowed reserves and the federal funds rate. Additional variables are past values of nominal income growth, the Federal Reserve discount rate and in some equations, the lagged dependent variable. The results again favor the credit target with smaller standard errors and higher $\bar{R}^2$'s.

Friedman's work with vector autogressive methods has inspired careful study of his conclusions (Porter and Offenbacher, 1983; McMillin and Fackler, 1984; Fackler, 1985). As Friedman points out in his rebuttal to Porter and Offenbacher (Friedman, 1983b), he is in basic agreement with their finding that VAR methods are not capable of distinguishing the proper monetary target (p. 33). This is in keeping with an earlier stated position (1982a). A two-target money and credit framework are proposed for the Fed. The key advantage is that information would now be provided from both sides of the public's balance sheet--money on the asset side and debt (credit) on the liability side (Friedman, 1982a, pp. 242-44). Friedman retreats further from a credit-only stance by suggesting three alternatives: abandoning the intermediate target approach to monetary policy; targeting both money and credit; and "better still," adding interest rates as a third target (1983a, pp. 186-89).

The strongest influence on nominal GNP found by Porter and Offenbacher in a three-variable system (1954.2-1982.4) is the commercial paper rate regardless of the ordering of the variables. One of the weaknesses of VAR is its sensitivity to the ordering of the variables. The importance of a given variable in terms of its explanatory power depends critically on the arbitrary ordering that is chosen (Porter and Offenbacher, p. 20).

Their discussion does not consider the signs of the coefficients of the lagged interest variables. This is relevant because a positive relationship suggests that it is the demand side of credit markets which is affecting the interest rate rather than the exercise of monetary policy. The influence of the interest rate on nominal GNP in VAR analysis is then irrelevant to the choice of targets. Friedman's defense of credit policy because it provides credit market information supplementary to the interest rate is not as incisive as it could be (1982b, p. 32).

The same criticism can be offered of Fackler's VAR analysis (1985). In his multivariate model (1962.1-1980.III) interest rates provide the primary link between the financial and real sectors. Neither money nor credit directly affects real output. Credit has an indirect effect when the commercial paper rate is included. In a second model with the corporate bond rate replacing the short-term rate, it loses this indirect role (Fackler, 1985, pp. 39-40). No attention again is paid to the sign of the interest coefficients or for that matter to the signs of any of the coefficients. One has to conclude that VAR analysis is not the answer.

Credit targeting has been challenged on the grounds of timeliness in the availability of data. Friedman's response is that the Federal Reserve maintains on an unpublished basis a monthly credit data file and that potentially 95 percent of the total net credit aggregate could be available monthly. The policy maker does not have to depend on quarterly data (1982a, pp. 240-41). Even so, the credit figures are likely to be less quickly available and less reliable than the money numbers (Davis, 1982, p. 258).

"Controllability" has been challenged because of the absence of reserve requirements against total financial credit. This makes for an unstable reserve multiplier (Davis, 1979, p. 22; Davis, 1982).[2] The relative weight to be given controllability and predictability is an important issue in choosing the target. The instability of the M1-GNP link because of velocity is a persuasive argument for targeting debt (credit). Debt's deviations from its guideline best reveals concurrent changes in GNP thereby prompting the correct reaction by monetary policy. Even though debt cannot be controlled closely, it does respond to changes in the supply of reserves (Kopcke, 1983).[3]

Considerable support is given the predictability argument by the recent superior performance of the credit variable as a leading indicator of recessions (Palash and Radecki, 1985). Nonfinancial sector debt has excelled in the 1980s as a predictor of recessions (1980 and 1981) (Palash and Radecki, pp. 41-42). At the same time the monetary aggregates failed badly. It is also of interest that the commercial paper rate (which performed so well in VAR analysis) has the weakest indicator record of any financial variable 1953-1981.

A counterfactual question, and a critical one, is how would the use of a credit aggregate have modified policymaking in the past? Fackler and Silver have identified differences in policy signals between M1 and credit 1970:1 to 1982:3 (Fackler and Silver, 1983, table 2, p. 8). The specific criterion was a discrepancy between the four-quarter growth rates of M1 and the credit aggregates of more than two standard deviations.[4] The term "looser" is entered in the table when consideration of a joint target would have resulted in a more expansionary policy than one based only on M1. In terms of the observed behavior of credit, this means money growth greatly exceeded credit growth. "Tighter" signifies a reverse situation when credit growth exceeded money growth by more than two standard deviations. Focusing on nonfinancial domestic credit--the widest of three credit concepts considered--in three periods policy would have been altered by a two-target framework. It would have been tighter in 1973:3-4, and 1980:2 and looser in 1980.4-1981.2. When the underlying economics of these periods are studied in detail, however, the policies followed become more credible (according to Fackler and Silver). Central bankers must perform a delicate balancing act! For example, a tighter policy might not have been appropriate in 1973 because accelerating inflation was caused by rising food and oil prices and the rate of real economic growth was declining (Fackler and Silver, p. 8). In two of the three periods in which more than one credit measure would have led to the same modification of policy, the possibility existed of going in the wrong direction. The Fackler-Silver test for targeting credit may be question-begging since it assumes that the degree of tightness or ease of monetary policy was right to begin with! The endogeneity in part of Fed policy-making makes such labeling suspect. Accommodation alternating with control may underlie the postwar data leading to problems of interpretation.

Resort to Theory. The collinearity of money and credit and the endogeneity of central banking policy bedevil the debate on targeting. Moreover, the sharp growth in debt in relation to GNP since 1982 (Carlson, 1986; Volcker, 1986; B. M. Friedman, 1986), at the same time that the money-income relationship has weakened (Siegel, 1986; Gavin, 1986; Taylor, 1986; Kopcke, 1986) casts doubt on both approaches. The unsatisfactory state of the empirical debate hastens a return to our earlier policy framework. Working out recent empirical developments in this framework might be helpful in determining the relative merits of money versus credit targeting. Our strategy is to search for likely substitutionary relationships.[5]

Comparing Substitution Possibilities. As discussed in Chapter VI (see Figure VI.1), with credit targeting and an increase in planned investment spending at the initiative of deficit units, income will be stabilized because of opposite movements in the BB and IS curves. The money stock, M1, given total M2 (the mirror-image of bank credit), is at the discretion of holders of money balances. The higher return on savings deposits and the stabilization of total transactions should discourage increases in M1 holdings.

The above analysis assumes that bank credit is being targeted. The possibility of substitution between bank and nonbank credit has to be considered. Substitution means that the flow supply of credit increases so that the BB curve fails to shift upward given an increase in investment demand. Credit targeting will be unsuccessful. Lower interest rates on savings deposits and more transactions requirements will result in accommodating increases in M1.

When M1 is targeted the supply of credit expands as financial institutions take advantage of differential reserve requirements and engage in "liability management" to finance an increased volume of credit. The result is a lesser movement upward in the BB curve and a greater expansion in money income.

The relevant empirical question in comparing credit versus M1 targeting is the respective degree of substitutability between commercial bank credit and nonbank credit, and between M_1 and other bank liabilities. Under credit targeting, will the assumed upward shift in the BB function fail to take place because of credit substitution? Blinder and Stiglitz offer anecdotal evidence against this possibility (pp. 300-01). Stronger evidence is the historical record of crunches and financial crises (Eckstein and Sinai, 1986; Sinai, 1975, 1976, 1977; Wolfson, 1984, 1985, 1986a, 1986b). Financial innovation may delay their onset (Wojnilower, 1980), but once they occur substitutability is limited.

A simple regression test of substitutability made nonbank credit a function of commercial bank credit. At the same time, other liabilities of commercial banks were made a function of their checkable deposits. The hypothesis being tested is that nonbank credit exhibits a complementary relation (positive coefficient) with bank credit and that other bank liabilities have a negative (substitute) relation with checkable deposits. The results as given in the first four equations of Table XIII.2 offer general support. A change in the flow of bank credit is associated with a strong positive change in nonbank credit (equation 1). A significant negative relationship exists between checkable deposits and nonmonetary liabilities (corporate equity issues, credit market debt, profit taxes payable, miscellaneous liabilities) (equation 3). The remaining relations for checkable deposits are not significant although the sign in the combined equation 4 is the expected negative one (other monetary liabilities in equation 2 include other deposit liabilities, federal funds, and security RP's).

TABLE XIII.2 BANK CREDIT VS. CHECKABLE DEPOSITS: TESTING FOR SUBSTITUTABILITY

Dependent Variables	C	BC	CD	FR	DEF	$\bar{R}^2$	SEE	DW
1. NBC	6333.85 (1.81571)	2.123 (12.8957)				.573	28393.1	1.48
2. OML	10722.3 (10.8404)		.0054 (.0719)			0.0081	10774.5	.5342
3. OBL	2975.39 (6.9527)		-0.6789 (-2.107)			.0272	4656.91	1.3395
4. OL	13708.7 (10.8416)		-.06253 (-0.651)			-.00464	13759.8	.4937
5. $\frac{NBC}{BC}$	3.4993 (6.29144)			.08 (.5706)	.4672 (1.91651)	.0688	1.7008	.6140
6. $\frac{OML}{CD}$	2.3262 (16.1832)			-.0087 (-.2401)	.2977 (-4.7264)	.4821	.4395	1.2421
7. $\frac{OBL}{CD}$	.1495 (2.2895)			-.04985) (-3.02771)	-.1931 (-.6747)	.6628	.1996	.8850
8. $\frac{OL}{CD}$	2.47397 (12.8625)			-.05929 (-1.2222)	-.4913 (-5.8284)	.5584	.5881	1.1798
9. DISS	5712.06 (3.5102)	.7471 (8.8787)				.3657	14954.6	1.1417
10. DISS	15236.5 (9.28099)		.1690 (1.3087)			.00525	18727.5	.3300
11. $\frac{DISS}{BC}$	1.4258 (6.21103)			.01362 (.2353)	.07403 (.7358)	0.0	.702	1.1008
12. $\frac{DISS}{CD}$	-7.9189 (-0.3555)			9.2785 (1.6517)	-7.4882 (-.7671)	.05203	68.1076	2.1420

Sources: Except for FR and DEF, Federal Reserve flow-of-funds accounts. FR and DEF were provided by Shearson Lehman Brothers, New York, 1987.

Where NBC = net credit market borrowing by domestic nonfinancial sectors other than credit market funds advanced by commercial banking

OML = change in monetary liabilities of commercial banks other than checkable deposits

OBL = change in other bank liabilities

OL = OML + OBL

BC = credit market funds advanced by commercial banking (bank credit)

CD = change in checkable deposits

FR = free to total reserves ratio

DEF = cyclically adjusted federal deficit to GNP ratio

DISS= financial dissaving: the sums in every period of negative changes in financial assets, household and corporate nonfinancial business sectors, with signs reversed.

Note: Equations 1-4 are based on quarterly seasonally unadjusted data (1952.1 to 1982.2). Equations 5-8 are based on annual data, 1959-1985. The left-hand quarterly values are summed to provide annual values similar to the two right-hand variables FR and DEF. Equations 9 and 10 are based on quarterly values 1952-1985. Equations 11 and 12 sum up the left-hand values to provide annual values similar to the two right-hand variables FR and DEF.

A more refined analysis converts the left-hand variables in the above equations into ratios and makes these ratios a function of monetary and fiscal policy (Table XIII.2, equations 5-8). The easy-tight money index is a weighted average of the ratio of free reserves to total reserves. For fiscal policy, the index used is based on changes in the full employment budget deficit relative to nominal GNP (Sinai, 1986, p. 4).[6]

Now the hypothesis is that a change in the free reserve ratio will not affect bank-nonbank credit substitution: the coefficient should not be significant. On the other hand, it is expected that substitution for checkable deposits will be affected. Tighter money will increase the importance of liability management as banks seek additional funds. The sign of the coefficient on the free reserve ratio should be negative. The left-hand ratio will rise at the same time that the free reserve ratio declines.

Easier fiscal policy (larger deficits) is expected to be neutral on the credit ratio although substitution might decline to the extent that the banks increasingly support the government bond market. The sign in the latter case would be positive (larger deficits [bigger negative values] being associated with lower values of the left-hand ratio). For checkable deposits the expected sign is negative. Substitution is expected to increase (a positive left-hand ratio becomes larger) as deficits (minus values) increase.

The results are favorable to these hypotheses. Beginning with the monetary policy variable, (FR) the coefficients for checkable deposits have the expected negative sign although only the coefficient in equation 7 is significant at the 5% level. The positive but nonsignificant coefficient for credit in equation 5 is not inconsistent with expectations. For fiscal policy (DEF) all the coefficients in 5 through 8 are significant or close to it (equation 5). The signs are the expected ones.

The relevance of these results for policy-making is that targeting bank credit because of its complementarity with nonbank credit will be more successful in hitting the GNP target than aiming at M1. Stated graphically, the BB function will shift up to a greater extent with credit targeting than with monetary targeting, thus counteracting the initial IS disturbance.

This discussion of substitution has assumed a stable relation between the total flow of credit and aggregate demand. Changing saving-investment patterns and the "fluff" in money-flows (as described in Chapter VI) may affect this stability. Recently attention has been drawn to fluff resulting from the "double counting" of credit (Volcker, 1986). There is a clear linkage between external finance for the corporate nonfinancial business sector and its financial lending (Cohen, 1986c). The policymaker in targeting credit has to be aware of financial arbitrage.[7]

Instead of dynamic shocks in the product market being at the behest of deficit units, a less likely situation is these shocks being at the initiative of surplus units. The analysis of Chapter VI gave the advantage to monetary targeting in these circumstances. Now, however, in a broader "real world" context we must allow for the dissaving of financial assets beyond the savings deposit liabilities of commercial banks. (Dissaving of these assets will shift the ownership of M1 balances and not affect total M1 balances as in the case of savings deposits.) The issue now posed is the substitutability of these assets for bank credit versus their substitutability for checkable deposits. Financial dissaving (including reductions in M1 balances) were run as a function of BC,CD; the ratios of DISS/BC and DISS/CD were run as a function of FR and DEF (equations 9, 10, 11, 12 in Table XIII.2). Only in equation 9 do we find a significant coefficient: dissaving is correlated with bank credit movements. The failure of the ratio to respond to monetary policy in equation 11 may also be taken as support for targeting bank credit. On the other hand, equations 10 and 12 do not suggest a substitutionary relationship between checkable deposits and dissaving which would have argued against targeting money balances.[8]

Autonomous shifts on the demand side of the money market must finally be evaluated. The evidence since 1982 is that monetary targeting has been replaced with interest rate targeting (Gilbert, 1985; McNees, 1986). Assuming that increases in M1 demand have been financed out of savings deposits, such interest rate targeting is defensible (see Chapter VI).

SELECTIVE CREDIT CONTROLS[9]

The question of substitution is central to the workability of selective controls. The likely substitution effects of selective credit controls can be simulated by a study of the comparative effects of "tight" and "easy" money policies. If the relationship between individual categories of spending and borrowing in particular financial markets is a close one and remains so under the pressure of tight money, the feasibility of selective controls as a way of controlling particular types of spending will have been demonstrated.[10] On the other hand, if several spending categories are associated with financing via a given financial market, and if borrowers can readily move between markets and are stimulated to do so by tight money, the likely advantages of selective controls over conventional monetary policy (control of the reserve base) are greatly lessened and possibly disappear.

What needs empirical estimation, then, is the impact of tight money on the mobility of borrowers among financial markets. Two aspects can be distinguished: borrowers intent on financing a certain type of expenditure may move among alternative financial markets in response to changes in interest rates and related credit terms. Second, substitution may result in different expenditure categories relying on the same financial market.

It is also necessary to estimate whether external and internal finance are substitutes in the financing of particular expenditures. These estimates are relevant to the evaluation of selective versus indirect controls, given the objective of selective control of expenditures or control of expenditures in general.

The Analytical Framework. The proposed test of substitution among financial sources relies on the effects observed when the scope of the borrowing variable is varied in multiple regression analysis. If we successively widen the scope of the borrowing variable so that it includes additional borrowing instruments, the borrowing instruments involved are considered to be substitutes if this combined variable has a greater impact than more narrowly defined variables. The impact of a variable is measured by its regression coefficient expressed in standard error units (that is, the t ratio). The improvement in the explanatory variable is taken to mean that, in response to changes in interest rates or credit terms (without any attempt being made to isolate or measure these respective changes), borrowers will shift between markets in the financing of given expenditures. Expenditures can then be considered to be financed out of a single pool of funds represented by the combined variable.[11] Four expenditure categories were studied: consumer durables and residential construction for the household sector; inventories and plant and equipment for the business sector.

The second kind of substitution, several expenditure categories being possible substitutes in the utilization of a given source of funds, was tested for by regressing aggregate capital expenditures for a sector against the single financial instruments that proved best with respect to the component categories. Coefficients in excess of unity for these instruments indicated capital expenditure substitution.

In testing for substitution between internal and external finance, I compared the t ratios for the combined internal and external finance variable (personal income or gross business saving plus net increase in financial liabilities) with the t ratios for each of these variables separately (given in a second regression equation). By having two coefficients (two ratios of t ratios), it is possible to test for the direction of substitution--whether internal finance is a substitute for external finance or vice-versa. If the coefficient exceeds one for the ratio of the combined variable to income, external finance is a substitute for income. Similarly, income may be a substitute for external finance if the coefficient for the combined variable over external finance exceeds unity.

Defining Tight and Easy Money. I have estimated these three kinds of substitution for both easy and tight money conditions. I define tight and easy money as a condition of excess demand or supply of loanable funds respectively. Although this implies that "tight money conditions" are being defined, rather than tight money policies, a switch from an excess supply situation to an excess demand situation requires passive acquiescence by the Federal Reserve even if they did not initiate it.[12] The behavior of interest rates was taken to be the appropriate indicator of market ease and tightness. Accordingly, following an earlier study by Hendershott and Murphy (1964), the quarterly data for 1952-67 were classified on the basis of quarterly changes in the Treasury bill rate and also some supplementary measures (see for details, Cohen, 1970, pp. 28-29). The number of easy money and tight money quarters totaled 23 and 41 respectively.

Empirical Results. The results of the analysis are presented in Tables XIII.3-6. The upper "easy money" strips provide the benchmark for measuring the effects of tight money.

In the left-hand column of these tables, the t ratio for the "best" individual credit instrument is given in the denominator and the corresponding t ratio for the best combined variable in the numerator. The latter always includes the financial flow shown in the denominator. Among the individual financial flows tested for was financial dissaving--the sum of proceeds from the sell-off of financial asset holdings (including reductions in money holdings). The most comprehensive variable--net increases in financial liabilities (NIFL)--was evaluated including and excluding dissaving. If the coefficient of financial substitution (the ratio of t ratios) equaled or exceeded one, substitution was said to exist among credit instruments in the finance of given categories of expenditures.[13]

Beginning with household expenditures on consumer durables in Table XIII.3, an increase in financial substitution is evident in tight money periods. Consumer credit is the leading financial instrument in both tight and easy money periods and net increase in financial liabilities becomes relatively more significant in tight money periods. Some doubt is cast by these results on the effectiveness of consumer credit controls as a means of limiting consumer durable expenditures. The financial substitution coefficient rises above one in tight money periods (the criterion for substitution), and net increase in financial liabilities encompasses all external finance except dissaving, thus suggesting a wide range of substitutability. In contrast, the dependence of residential construction on mortgage finance in both tight and easy money periods (Table XIII.4), is clear except that the relative importance of "other" mortgages increases slightly in tight money.[14] The results argue for the feasibility of controlling housing expenditures via mortgage finance.

The most substantial increase in borrower substitution in tight money periods occurs in the case of plant and equipment expenditures (Table XIII.6). Corporate bonds, the leading instrument in both easy and tight money periods now enjoys a substitute relationship with corporate stock, mortgages, bank loans, and other loans. Assuming that selective controls were applied to corporate bonds or more broadly to capital issues so that corporate stock was also included, one would have doubts about their likely effectiveness.

In contrast to the other three categories of expenditures, the decline of the financial substitution coefficient for inventories (Table XIII.5), indicates the presence of increased

TABLE XIII. 3

EFFECTS OF TIGHT MONEY ON SUBSTITUTION, CONSUMER DURABLES[a] QUARTERLY DATA, 1952-67

t ratio of combined variables ÷ *t* ratio of best individual variable[b]		*t* ratio for combined income + financial liability variable ÷ (a) *t* ratio for income variable (b) *t* ratio for financial liability variable		*t* ratio for capital expenditure equation ÷ *t* ratio for individual expenditure equation[c]	
Ratio	$\bar{R}^2$	Ratio	$\bar{R}^2$	Ratio	$\bar{R}^2$
		Easy money			
$\frac{5.0292^{**}}{5.1719^{**}} = .9724$	.9405** .9423**	(+Dis)[d] (a) $\frac{16.4885^{**}}{14.8613} = 1.1095$	.9155** .9405**	$\frac{5.1954^{**}}{5.1719} = 1.0045$	.9128** .9423**
		(+Dis) (b) $\frac{16.4885^{**}}{5.0292^{**}} = 3.2796$			
		Tight money			
$\frac{6.8092^{**}}{6.3350^{**}} = 1.0749$	.9439** .9393**	(a) $\frac{18.9924^{**}}{17.1790^{**}} = 1.1056$	.9069** .9439**	$\frac{5.0562^{**}}{6.3350^{**}} = .7981$	.9025** .9393**
		(b) $\frac{18.9924^{**}}{6.8092^{**}} = 2.7892$			

[a] Dependent variable: original data for consumer durables.
[b] Net increase in financial liabilities (NIFL) ÷ consumer credit.
[c] Consumer credit.
[d] (+Dis) indicates the combined income and external finance variable is enhanced in importance by including financial dissaving.
** indicates significance at the 1 percent level.
Sources: Board of Governors of the Federal Reserve System, Division of Research and Statistics, Flow-of-Funds and Savings Section, IBM printouts and periodical releases of quarterly unadjusted data.

(These sources are for all tables)

TABLE XIII.4
EFFECTS OF TIGHT MONEY ON SUBSTITUTION, RESIDENTIAL CONSTRUCTION[a]
QUARTERLY DATA, 1952-67

t ratio of combined variables ÷ *t* ratio of best individual variable[b]		*t* ratio for combined income + financial liability variable ÷ (a) *t* ratio for income variable (b) *t* ratio for financial liability variable		*t* ratio for capital expenditure equation ÷ *t* ratio for individual expenditure equation[c]	
Ratio	$\bar{R}^2$	Ratio	$\bar{R}^2$	Ratio	$\bar{R}^2$
		Easy money			
5.1068** / 5.1331** = .9949	.5014** .5041**	(+Dis)[d] (a) .7382 / 1.4821 = .4981	.0000 .0650	1.5625 / 5.1331** = .3043	.9224** .5041**
		(+Dis) (b) .7382 / 1.7818 = .4143			
		Tight money			
5.7836** / 5.6523** = 1.0323	.5137** .5028**	(a) 2.1560* / .7822 = 2.7563	.0898* .1433*	2.5437* / 5.6523** = .4500	.8575** .5028**
		(b) 2.1560* / 1.9647 = 1.0974			

[a] Dependent variable: original data for residential construction.
[b] Long-term liabilities ÷ (1-4 family mortgages); long-term liabilities = 1-4 family mortgages + "other" mortgages.
[c] 1-4 family mortgages.
[d] (+Dis) indicates the combined income and external finance variable is enhanced in importance by including financial dissaving.
* indicates significance at the 5 percent level.
** indicates significance at the 1 percent level.

TABLE XIII.5
EFFECTS OF TIGHT MONEY ON SUBSTITUTION,
CHANGE IN INVENTORIES[a]
QUARTERLY DATA, 1952-67

t ratio of combined variables ÷ t ratio of best individual variable[b]		t ratio for combined income + financial liability variable ÷ (a) t ratio for income variable (b) t ratio for financial liability variable		t ratio for capital expenditure equation ÷ t ratio for individual expenditure equation[c]	
Ratio	$\bar{R}^2$	Ratio	$\bar{R}^2$	Ratio	$\bar{R}^2$
		Easy money			
$\frac{3.0943^{**}}{3.1595^{**}} = .9794^{**}$	.5137** .5093**	(+Dis)[d] (a) $\frac{4.1934^{**}}{3.2068^{**}} = 1.3077$	.3988** .3143**	$\frac{4.0170^{**}}{3.1595} = 1.2714$	.9496** .5093**
		(+Dis) (b) $\frac{4.1934^{**}}{.7766} = 5.3997$			
		Tight money			
$\frac{3.1046^{**}}{6.3100^{**}} = .5880$	.4201 .5552**	(+Dis) (a) $\frac{2.7653^{*}}{2.9126^{**}} = .9494$	.1523** .1492*	$\frac{4.8129^{*}}{6.3100^{**}} = .7545$	.9051** .5552**
		(+Dis) (b) $\frac{2.7653^{*}}{1.4431} = 1.9162$			

[a] Dependent variable: original data for change in inventories.
[b] Σ significant liabilities ÷ mortgages; significant liabilities = other loans + other liabilities + dissaving + mortgages.
[c] Mortgages.
[d] (+Dis) indicates the combined income and external finance variable is enhanced in importance by including financial dissaving.
* indicates significance at the 5 percent level.
** indicates significance at the 1 percent level.

TABLE XIII.6
EFFECTS OF TIGHT MONEY ON SUBSTITUTION, PLANT AND EQUIPMENT EXPENDITURES[a]
QUARTERLY DATA, 1952-67

t ratio of combined variables ÷ *t* ratio of best individual variable		*t* ratio for combined income + financial liability variable ÷ (a) *t* ratio for income variable (b) *t* ratio for financial liability variable		*t* ratio for capital expenditure equation ÷ *t* ratio for individual expenditure equation[b]	
Ratio	$\bar{R}^2$	Ratio	$\bar{R}^2$	Ratio	$\bar{R}^2$
		Easy money			
2.4267**[c]** / 4.0674** = .5966	.9245** .9449**	(+Dis)[d] (a) 13.2811** / 11.4262** = 1.1623	.8752** .9059**	1.5625 / 4.0674** = .3841	.9224** .9449**
		(+Dis) (b) 13.2811** / .4202 = 31.6066			
		Tight money			
7.0372**[e] / 5.6447** = 1.2467	.9429** .9278**	(+Dis) (a) 14.8947** / 13.5514** = 1.0991	.8565** .9007**	2.5329* / 5.6447** = .4471	.8667** .9278**
		(+Dis) (b) 14.8947** / 3.6916** = 4.0348			

[a] Dependent variable: original data for plant and equipment expenditures.
[b] Corporate bonds.
[c] Σ long-term liabilities ÷ corporate bonds; long-term liabilities = corporate bonds + corporate stock + mortgages.
[d] (+Dis) indicates the combined income and external finance variables are enhanced in importance by including financial dissaving.
[e] Σ liabilities ÷ corporate bonds; liabilities = corporate bonds + corporate stock + mortgages + bank loans + other loans.
* indicates significance at the 5 percent level.
** indicates significance at the 1 percent level.

lender substitution in tight money. The coefficient declines as compared with easy money as a result of the sharp increase in the importance of mortgage finance. Given borrower discretion (rising interest rates due to an increased business demand for funds), the falling coefficient implies that banks, the mortgage lender to business, substituted mortgage lending to corporations for other kinds of lending in periods of tight money (lender substitution).

The absence of bank loans not elsewhere classified (commercial and industrial loans) in the "best" combined variables shown in the numerator of the ratios appears to run counter to usual assumptions about the close relation between this variable and inventories. When the same analysis is repeated on the annual data for 1946-67, however, without a tight-easy-money separation, the expected relationship does appear (see also Cohen, 1963). Bank loans show up as the dominant variable and a lack of substitution is apparent with other short-term sources of funds, the best combined variable in this case. The "long-run" relationship is then with bank loans whereas on a quarterly basis mortgage credit extended by banks is more important for inventory financing. The dependence of inventories on bank financing is in any case clearly established.

When we examine the two remaining types of substitution, the substitution between internal and external finance, and capital-expenditure substitution (the second and third columns of the tables), we are struck by the opposing effects of tight money on residential construction and purchase of inventories. Tight money increases substitution in all possible cases for residential construction (external-internal finance substitution constitutes two cases) and reduces it for inventory change in all three cases. If tight money imitates the effects of selective controls, one would anticipate that controls would generate offsetting substitution effects in the case of residential construction and reinforcing effects in the case of inventory change.

Controlling Total Spending. The discussion up to this point has been concerned with the choice of policies to curb particular expenditure categories. If this objective is replaced by one of controlling expenditures in general, the interpretation of the substitution results is substantially modified. Substitution within finance does not increase the total amount of credit extended. Capital expenditure substitution also becomes irrelevant if the desideratum is the control of expenditures in general.

The substitution between external and internal finance is still relevant, however. Substitution of internal for external finance becomes a virtue rather than a weakness of either direct or indirect controls. To the extent that saving out of current income is encouraged and capital expenditures become more dependent on such saving the aggregate demand for credit is curtailed and inflationary financing is reduced.

From a policy point of view, one should wish to see the impact of the income variable increase in tight money quarters relative to the impact of the external finance variable and the combined income-external finance variable. In this way, as the substitution measures are constructed, income would become more of a substitute for external finance, measure (b), and external finance would become less of a substitute for income, measure (a). These requirements are not met, however, as is shown by the tables. In the case of consumer durables the income variable increases slightly more relative to the combined variable and not by as much as the external finance variable. The result is a reduction in the mutual substitutability of income and external finance, with the reduction in the substitution of income for external finance being greater than the reduction in the substitutability of external finance for income. For residential construction, the changes in the t-ratios result in an increased mutual substitution. In the business sector, the t-ratios in the inventories and plant and equipment expenditures equations change in such a way as to reduce mutual substitutability in a more marked way than was true of consumer durables. The ideal substitution results are thus not achieved by tight money.

Notes

1. B. M. Friedman may have been responsible for the Fed announcing in February, 1983, that henceforth it would watch a broad credit total. The flow-of-funds accounts have since featured as the opening table in their quarterly releases growth rates of various credit aggregates. Friedman's work may have made the growth rates in the debt aggregates the best known feature of the flow-of-funds accounts.
2. Shadow reserve requirements might be one way of implementing a credit target (Arak, 1982). Reserve availability could be tied to credit growth by adjusting nonborrowed reserves when credit deviates from its target level.
3. The argument is supported by a series of velocity equations for various financial aggregates.
4. The mean and standard deviation for a given quarter are calculated from five-year data prior to the quarter.
5. That the empirical debate should make contact with theory has been urged by Cover (1986). He criticizes B. M. Friedman's empirical support of credit targeting as being inconsistent with the credit theory of Blinder and Stiglitz (1983). Our framework is more comprehensive than Blinder-Stiglitz' and our empirical approach is more oblique than that of Friedman. We attempt to identify changes in substitution relations and evaluate them for targeting purposes.
6. Problems of simultaneous equation bias in measuring tight-easy money policy or tight-easy fiscal policy are well known (see McNees, 1986; Sinai, 1986, n.3, p. 31). Nevertheless, we assume that swings in free reserves stem from changes in Federal Reserve policy rather than from changes in the demand for credit. The use of a full-employment budget deficit concept should take care of Treasury discretion.
7. A substantial dose of skepticism must be reserved for any selected target such as credit. It has been argued that the very selection of a particular monetary aggregate will render it useless for ultimate control purposes ("Goodhart's law"). The evidence on substitutability, however, makes bank credit less vulnerable than checkable deposits on this score.

   Our underlying assumption is that the causal linkage is between credit and expenditures and control of checkable deposits works via its effects on the flow of credit. The direct control of bank credit, it is being argued, will succeed better than indirect control via checkable deposits.
8. On the importance of dissaving, see also the discussion below under selective controls, including footnote 13.
9. Much of this section is based on Cohen, 1970. See also Chapter VI above.
10. The linkages between detailed spending categories and

borrowing without regard to tight and easy money periods has been studied in Cohen, 1961, 1968a; Cohen and Kenkel, 1986.

11. The following relationships were tested:

(a) $E_{ik} = a_{11} + b_{11}Y_i + b_{12}B_m$.

(b) $E_{ik} = a_{21} + b_{21}Y_i + b_{22}B_j$.

(c) $E_{ik} = a_{31} + b_{31}Y_i + b_{22} (B_m + B_j)$.

If the t ratio for the coefficient of the combined variable, b_{32} in (c), exceeds the t ratios for both significant component variables (represented by b_{12} and b_{22} in (a) and (b)), we say that each has been improved by being treated as part of a single financial variable. The substitution is then two-directional. Whatever financial market variable is considered first, adding the second market increases the explanatory value of the first financial variable. It is possible, of course, that substitution is one-directional, that is, that substitution exists when we begin with less significant financial market variables. In later testing, I have tested only for two-way substitution.

An alternative test for substitution would be to run the various individual flow variables in one multiple regression equation. That is,

(d) $E_{ik} = a_{41} + b_{41}Y_i + b_{42}B_m + b_{43}Bj$.

Such a test would consider all significant flows as substitutes. This approach was rejected, however, since a series of financial flow variables could be significant without demonstrating that spender-borrowers substituted among these markets. The significance of several financial variables could show that different borrowers depended on different financial markets for expenditures. Moreover, as running such regression equations indicated, one encounters serious problems of intercorrelation.

12. A step in the direction of removing the ambiguity of tight-easy-money terminology is to distinguish between financial restraint and monetary restraint. Financial restraint is what I mean by tight money, since the money stock may be growing rapidly simultaneously, suggesting monetary ease. See Horwich and Hendershott (1969), pp. 34-35.

13. The use of "dissaving" as one of our financial variables provides some measure of the effects of tight money on shifts out of money and money substitutes. The results show more appearances of dissaving in easy money periods than in tight money periods (see consumer durables,

residential construction, second column cf Tables XIII.3 and XIII.4. These results, however, are not conclusive about the total expenditure effects of financial dissaving in tight money periods. First, the tables record only the expenditure effects of dissaving by the spending sectors and do not measure the effects of dissaving by the sectors lending to them. Second, the dissaving of spending sectors may finance the purchase of financial instruments (not recorded in the tables). Such purchases directly or indirectly (via the financial sector) may lead to additional expenditures. Nonetheless, the results support earlier statements (under general controls) about limited dissaving of surplus sectors under credit control.

14. The residential construction category of expenditures makes no distinction between multiple unit construction and one-to-four-family dwellings so that it is not surprising the "other" mortgages are a substitute for one-to-four-family mortgages.

CHAPTER XIV
THE STRENGTH AND LIMITATIONS OF FLOW-OF-FUNDS ANALYSIS

A FLOW-CONSTRAINED FRAMEWORK

The flow-of-funds framework begins with the budget constraint. Assuming transactor (sector) activity in all markets we have from Chapter I:

$$P_i+B_i+L_i+M_i = {}_iP+{}_iB+{}_iL+{}_iM \quad (I.1)$$

Summing over all transactors (all sectors) in all markets, Walras's Law is satisfied.

$$\sum_{i=1}^{h}(P_i - {}_iP) + \sum_{i=1}^{h}(B_i - {}_iB) + \sum_{i=1}^{h}(L_i - {}_iL) + \sum_{i=1}^{h}(M_i - {}_iM)=0$$

As suggested in the first chapter, the Walrasian system is a dual-decision model when there are two markets. Supply in one market finances demand in a second. Excess supply in one market corresponds to excess demand in a second. Beyond two markets, however, the Walrasian system does not identify intermarket flows.

The flow-constrained framework is designed to identify such intermarket flows and to exploit the theoretical and empirical implications. Thus:

$$\sum_{i=1}^{h} ({}_iXY_i - {}_iYX_i) = 0$$

Where X and Y represent markets in their alternative roles as sources and uses of funds.

The joint plans of decision-makers constitute a single dependent variable on the demand side of one market and the supply side of a second. As described in Chapter I, each dependent variable is a function of a series of explanatory variables.

A Generalized Framework. A flow-constrained framework provides a wide basis for theorizing. Both equilibrium and disequilibrium theories can be expressed in such a framework. Equilibrium growth theory featuring surplus-deficit analysis (the work of Gurley-Shaw) requires a dual-decision framework encompassing all markets.

The Information Content of the Flow of Funds

Contemporary economic theory has become coterminous with the economics of knowledge and information (Hirshleifer and Riley, 1979; Machlup, 1984; Cohen, 1986a; McKenna, 1986). How do we describe the present study in terms of this larger theoretical context? Our study highlights the informational content of the transaction. Realized flows have an informational value in explaining other flows. The economics of uncertainty (the raison d'etre for economics of information) is concerned with the probabilities of future events (transactions) in determining transactors' current decisions. The uncertainty calculus based on incomplete information belongs on the right-hand side of our dual-decision equations (Chapter 1).

CONTRIBUTING TO THEORY

Interest Rate Theory. A Walrasian system of equations which drops either the money market or the bond market in solving for the interest rate is saying that the one financial market is the mirror-image of the other. But the bond market is interrelated with the other chief markets and only a consistent dual-decision statement of markets can capture this interdependence.

When loanable funds analysis breaks down the bond market into two component markets--the money market and the product market (saving-investment)--it has to run the gauntlet between inconsistent rates or forced intersections at the same interest rate. Reformulation of the bond market in dual-decision terms again resolves the problem.

Disequilibrium Analysis. Flow-of-funds theory embraces disequilibrium analysis in a "natural" way because of the flow-constrained nature of such analysis. A flow-constrained presentation, however, has to go beyond the income-constrained process as described in the literature.

Flow vs. Stock Analysis. Flow-of-funds theory is "flow-flow" theory as opposed to "stock-flow" theory. On "stock" variables in expenditure functions rests the burden of measuring their flow effects. But this assumes a one-to-one relation between the size of the stock variable and the magnitude of its flow-effect. I have suggested that the real balance effect confuses the real balance variable with the real balance effect. Similar statements can be made about wealth and liability variables. The implication for empirical estimation is clear. The splitting of the dual-decision left-hand variable and the transfer of one component to the right-hand side requires that it be treated as a flow variable. In turn, the flow variable is to be explained in a second equation in terms of stock and choice-theoretical variables. A two-tier approach to expenditure equations is the innovation. The missing equations in macro-monetary theory are seen to be second-stage equations explaining dissaving and borrowing.

The Key Role of Bank Credit. Flow-of-funds theory shifts the emphasis from the money market to the bank credit market. The purchase of IOUs by the banking system financed by money creation (MB) corresponds to sector borrowing for expenditure purposes (BP). By focusing on the bank credit market, flow-of-funds theory shows a sympathy with the post-Keynesian paradigm.

Introducing the bank flow-of-funds statement into IS-LM analysis enhances the usefulness of this dominant approach. A major contribution is to clarify saving-investment concepts. No longer are bond purchases identified with saving and bond sales with investment. The complexities of interaction among an equilibrium bank credit function, conventional LM1, IS, and a total deposit liabilities function (LM2) can be fully explored.

Flow-of-funds theory acknowledges the importance of money. Money is the ultimate means of payment. But the theory has to combat a "social accounting" approach to the means of payment. While such an approach seems inherent in the accounting framework, it misinterprets the role of money-creating banks. Demand (checkable) deposits are to be seen as a credit entry or product of the banks rather than a source of funds for the banking system. Banks are not simply conduits for private sector saving, perhaps the most frequent interpretation of money and banking in the flow-of-funds framework.

The money supply process is best appreciated in a dual-decision general equilibrium framework. Bank lending has its second side in the money market. Now the money market is specified with its "own" interest rate--the implicit/explicit return on checkable deposits. With an increase in the supply of checkable deposits (the other side of banks acquiring IOUs), the concept of "disequilibrium money" becomes central to the analysis of the adjustment process. Holders of money balances are "forced off" their demand curve until an expansion in income and shifts into bank nonmonetary liabilities restores monetary equilibrium.

<u>Policy Implications</u>. The theoretical analysis points to the policymakers' targeting credit instead of the monetary aggregates (Chapters II, VI). What is lost in controllability is compensated for by greater predictability. Predictability is improved because less substitutability for a bank credit target than for an M1 target makes for a more dependable relation with total spending (Chapter XIII).

The variance of income under credit and M1 targeting provides a test of relative predictability. Given a disturbance in IS, targeting the flow of credit was shown to have a smaller destabilizing effect than targeting monetary growth. On the other hand, targeting M1 or, better still, interest rates, may be preferable when money demand shifts but the IS function does not. Because the evidence on targeting is so conflicting, one has to fall back on theoretical considerations.

The question of substitutability is also crucial to the effectiveness of selective controls. A technique based on widening the breadth of the sources of funds variable confirmed "policy linkages" between controls on mortgage finance and residential expenditures.

THE PRACTICE

The Data Base. The flow-of-funds accounts are now regularly published in a number of countries. When summarized in matrix form they are seen to be capital accounts since current account nonfinancial data is no longer covered. While offering financial information widely used on a piecemeal basis, the usefulness of the accounts is still limited by data inadequacies and delays in publication. The size of the sector discrepancies casts doubt on the reliability of the data. The inevitability of discrepancy suggests that it be treated as one more variable and incorporated in forecasting exercises.

Despite data limitations, the flow-of-funds accounts have fulfilled their original purpose of describing the interrelation of transactions in financial instruments and transactions in goods and services. Historical study of the raw data (or the data slightly massaged) reveals the contours of a flow-of-funds cycle.

Flow-Constrained vs. Choice-Theoretical Models. The rationale of the flow of funds is to solve for product market expenditures by solving for the elemental flows which add up to such expenditures (see Chapter V). It is an impossible task, however, to solve the market matrix for the necessary elemental flows. Statistical time series are not available for two-ended flows in the individual submarkets which can then be related to a series of explanatory variables. The strategy has been to identify second-market flows by regression analysis. Essentially this means relating expenditures to internal and external finance variables.

The direction of causation in such an approach has been challenged (Bain, 1973, p. 1075; Kaminow and O'Brien, 1975, p. 16). Several defenses can be offered for making expenditures a function of credit. The obvious one is that it fits the case of credit rationing--when moneys advanced impose a limit on spending. But in the more general case of market clearing, it can be defended on the macro-level on the basis of the inequality of planned and actual expenditures--the existence of perpetual disequilibrium in product markets. The approach puts external finance on the same footing as income in expenditure functions. Planned expenditures condition the supply of inputs in input markets and the demand for credit in financial markets, but expenditures ex post are explained by the quantity solution in input and financial markets.

Flow-flow relations can be considered as first-stage relations with flows being explained in turn by choice-theoretical (price) variables along with stock and additional flow variables. It is in the sense of the first stage that we say there are no income, substitution, or wealth effects--only flow-of-funds effects. Choice-theoretical relations as second-stage equations, complement flow relations. The two-stage estimation approach was exemplified in the stock market model (Chapter X). Flows as independent variables were constrained in the first stage so as to be consistent with the financing of purchases and the disposal of the proceeds from new security issues. The approach has the potential of being applied to sector spending in the product market.

What deserves attention is the relative performance of flow-flow relations when put in head-on competition with choice-theoretical relations (briefly mentioned in Chapter XI). The surprises (in limited comparisons to date) are that there is little to choose between the two approaches in explaining household nonfinancial expenditures; flow-constraints outperform choice-theoretical relations in explaining financial uses of this sector, and finally, the choice-theoretical relations do not win out when financial asset equations are disaggregated.

Both types of equations deteriorate with financial disaggregation. Disaggregation does not increase the comparative explanatory power of interest rates as might have been expected. A major difficulty with choice-theoretical relations (as demonstrated in the Yale portfolio balance models) is collinearity in interest rates. The same deterioration in financial equations showed up in the detailed sector-by-sector study of Canadian-U.S. financial flows (Chapter VIII).

Equilibrium vs. Disequilibrium. The regressing of expenditures on external finance--the trademark of our empirical work on the flow of funds--implies a disequilibrium situation in the product market. Planned expenditures are not alone in explaining the demand for credit, nor is the demand for credit the only side of the market. For this reason, we would expect that the expenditures of nonfinancial sectors depart from planned expenditures.

Whether market disequilibrium goes beyond the demand side of the product market depends on our definition of equilibrium. Empirical demonstrations of nonclearing markets are rare. The Fair model (Chapter XII) provides signals as to when work hours and loan constraints affect observed behavior in the product and labor markets but without any assessment of their quantitative importance. Smith-Brainard (Chapter XI) find no support for disequilibrium in the mortgage market (although their results are subject to other interpretations).

In a command economy, rationing behavior can be safely assumed. Thus Howard's well-known study of repressed inflation contains few surprises. Less obvious are the cases of repressed inflation in western Europe reported in fixprice models (Chapter XII).

If disequilibrium goes beyond notional and effective

concepts to embrace cyclical behavior in the flow of funds, then the accounts confirm its existence. As best pictured in the Minsky-Sinai models, balance sheets are perpetually out of kilter and the adjustment process is a never ending one.

SUMMING UP

Two major surveys of the flow of funds a decade and a half ago were pessimistic about the progress that had been made in the previous thirty years (Cohen, 1972; Bain, 1973). Our present evaluation is similarly pessimistic about the empirical fruits of the accounts. On the other hand, one can be more sanguine about the theoretical progress. I have tried to suggest a theory of the flow of funds, one that integrates the real and financial on a consistent flow basis. Perhaps it will encourage further econometric estimation. But it should also discourage reliance on econometric models for forecasting purposes. Equations based on the flow-of-funds accounts have special infirmities because of the fragility of such equations. Outside of the estimation period, the tracking performance is unsatisfactory. The fragility of financial equations has many explanations--financial innovation, the speed with which financial markets can adjust to changes in rates. Most importantly, market perceptions and expectations can change rapidly. Econometric models have so far not been successful in capturing the process whereby expectations are formed. Expectations remain the Achilles heel of financial forecasting. At this juncture, forecasting efforts might be better served by a more modest approach--one that combines the discipline of the flow of funds with "judgment" and selective estimation. The use of "priors"--an admission that financial equations are fragile--makes most sense in an iterative procedure organized around the flow-of-funds matrix. The projection techniques of Chapter VIII may have a substantial payoff.

REFERENCES

Aburachis, A. T. "Monetary Policy, High Employment and External Finance." Ph.D. dissertation, University of Pittsburgh, 1973.

Alford, R.F.G. Flow of Funds. (Aldershot, England, 1986).

Anderson, W. H. L. Corporate Finance and Fixed Investment. Division of Research, Graduate School of Business Administration, Harvard University, 1964.

Arak, Marcelle. "Control of a Credit Aggregate." Federal Reserve Bank of New York, Quarterly Review (Winter 1982-83), 10-15.

Arestis, P., C. Driver, and J. Rooney. "The Real Segment of a U.K. Post Keynesian Model." Journal of Post Keynesian Economics 8 (Winter 1985-86), 163-81.

Atkinson, Sue N. "Financial Flows in Recent Business Cycles." Journal of Finance 20 (March 1965), 14-35.

Attfield, C. L. F., D. Demery, and N. W. Duck. Rational Expectations in Macroeconomics. Oxford, England, 1985.

Azariadis, Costas. "Implicit Contracts and Underemployment Equilibria." Journal of Political Economy 83 (December 1975), 1183-1202.

Backus, David, William C. Brainard, Gary Smith, and James Tobin. "A Model of U.S. Financial and Nonfinancial Economic Behavior." Journal of Money, Credit and Banking 12 (May 1980, special issue, "Financial Market Behavior, Capital Formation, and Economic Performance"), 159ff.

Backus, David and Douglas Purvis. "An Integrated Model of Household Flow-of-Funds Allocations." Journal of Money, Credit and Banking XII (May 1980, special issue, "Financial Market Behavior, Capital Formation, and Economic Performance)," 400-21.

Bain, A. D. "Surveys in Applied Economics: Flow of Funds Analysis." Economic Journal 83 (December 1973), 1055-93.

Bain, A. D., C. L. Day, and A. L. Wearing. Company Financing in the United Kingdom: A Flow of Funds Model. London, 1975.

Balbach, Anatol B. "How Controllable is Money Growth?" Federal Reserve Bank of St. Louis, Review, 63 (April 1981), 3-12.

Bank of England. "Personal Saving and Financial Investment: 1951-65." Quarterly Bulletin (September 1966).

______. "Company Finance, 1952-65." Quarterly Bulletin (March 1967).

______. "The U.K. Banking Sector, 1952-67." Quarterly Bulletin (June 1969).

______. "The Personal Sector, 1966-1975." Quarterly Bulletin (March 1977).

______. "Financial Forecasts in the United Kingdom." Quarterly Bulletin (June 1977).

______. "United Kingdom Flow of Funds Accounts: 1963-1976." (1978).

Bank of Japan. Flow of Funds Accounts in Japan 1970-1977. (September 1978).

______. The Japanese Financial System (1978).

________. "Flow of Funds of the Japanese Economy in 1984." Special paper no. 125. Tokyo, August 1985.

Bankers Trust Company. Credit and Capital Markets. New York, 1984.

Barro, Robert J. and Herschel I. Grossman. "A General Disequilibrium Model of Income and Employment." American Economic Review 61 (March 1971), 82-93.

______. Money, Employment and Inflation. Cambridge, England, 1976.

Barten, A. P. "The System of Consumer Demand Functions Approach: A Review." Econometrica 45 (January 1977), 23-51.

Batchelor, Roy A. "Comments on Bruce Brittain's Paper: On Monetary Targets." In Monetary Targets, ed. Brian Griffiths and Geoffrey E. Wood. New York, 1981, pp. 81-85.

Begg, David K. H. The Rational Expectations Revolution in Macroeconomics. Baltimore, Md., 1982.

Benassy, Jean-Pascal. "Neo-Keynesian Disequilibrium Theory in a Monetary Economy." Review of Economic Studies 43 (February 1976), 69-81.

______. "On Quantity Signals and the Foundation of Effective Demand Theory." Scandinavian Journal of Economics 79, no. 2 (1977), 147-68.

Bennett, Robert L. and Barbara R. Bergmann. A Microsimulated Transactions Model of the United States Economy. (Baltimore, 1986).

Berkman, Neil G. "Abandoning Monetary Aggregates." In Controlling Monetary Aggregates III, Federal Reserve Bank of Boston, Conference Series No. 23. Boston, Mass., 1980, pp. 76-100.

Bernanke, Ben S. "Nonmonetary Effects of the Financial Collapse in the Propagation of the Great Depression." American Economic Review 73 (June 1983), 257-76.

Berry, John M. "Big Merger Borrowing Does Not Pull Capital from Productive Use." Financier 7 (April 1984), 6-9.

Bharat, Trehan. "The Information Content of Credit Aggregates." FRB San Francisco, Economic Review (Spring 1985) 28-39.

Blinder, Alan S. and Joseph E. Stiglitz. "Money, Credit Constraints and Economic Activity." American Economic Review, Proceedings 73 (May 1983), 297-302.

Bosworth, Barry and James S. Duesenberry. "A Flow of Funds Model and Its Implications." In Issues in Federal Debt Management, Federal Reserve Bank of Boston, Conference Series No. 10. Boston, 1973, pp. 39-149.

Brainard, William C. and James Tobin. "Pitfalls in Financial Model-Building. American Economic Review 58 (May 1968), 99-122.

Branson, William. "Causes of Appreciation and Volatility of the Dollar." Working paper no. 2777, National Bureau of Economic Research (December 1985).

Brox, James A. and Wendy A. Maclean. A Model of the Canadian Financial Flow Matrix. Ottawa, Canada, forthcoming.

Brunner, Karl. "A Schema for the Supply Theory of Money." International Economic Review 2 (January 1961), 79-109.

________. "The Role of Money and Monetary Policy." Federal Reserve Bank of St. Louis, Review (July 1968), 8-14.

________. "Federal Reserve Policy and Monetary Analysis." Targets and Indicators of Monetary Policy. San Francisco, 1969, pp. 268-71.

Buiter, Willem H. "The Theory of Optimum Deficits and Debt." In The Economics of Large Government Deficits, Federal Reserve Bank of Boston, Conference Series No. 27. Melvin Village, N.H., 1983, pp. 46-69.

Burger, Albert E. The Money Supply Process. Belmont, Calif., 1971.

Büttler, Hans-Jürg, Gertrud Frei, and Bernard Schips. Estimation of Disequilibrium Models (Heidelberg, 1986), Chapter 5.

Cacy, J. A. "Monetary Policy in 1981 and 1982." Federal Reserve Bank of Kansas City, Economic Review (December 1981), 3ff.

Cargill, Thomas F. "Japanese Monetary Policy, Flow of Funds and Domestic Liberalization," Federal Reserve Bank of San Francisco, Economic Review (Summer 1986), 21-32.

Carlson, John B. "Debt Growth and the Financial System," Federal Reserve Bank of Cleveland, Economic Commentary, October 15, 1986.

Carter, Michael and Rodney Maddock. Rational Expectations. Atlantic Highlands, N.J., 1984.

Clinton, K. "Pitfalls in Financial Model Building: Comment." American Economic Review 63 (December 1973), 1003-04.

Clower, Robert. "The Keynesian Counterrevolution: A Theoretical Appraisal." In The Theory of Interest Rates, ed. F. H. Hahn and F. B. R. Brechling. New York, 1965, pp. 118-125.

Coddington, Allan. "Keynesian Economics: Search for First Principles." Journal of Economic Literature 14 (December 1976), 1258-1273.

________. Keynesian Economics: The Search for First Principles. London, 1983.

Cohen, Jacob. "A Money Flows Approach to Consumer Behavior." Southern Economic Journal 27 (January 1957), 245-55.

________. "The Treatment of the Means of Payment in Social Accounting." Journal of Finance 12 (December 1957), 423-37.

________. "Sector Investment and the Availability of Finance." Southern Economic Journal 27 (January 1961), 200-29.

________. "What Do Bank Loans Really Finance?" In Banking and Monetary Studies, ed. Deane Carson. Homewood, Ill., 1963, chap. 21.

________. "L'incidenza della borsa sul flusso dei fondi" (The impact of the stock market on the flow of funds). Rivista Internazionale di Science Economiche e Commerciali (September 1965), 882-900.

________. "Integrating the Real and Financial via the

Linkage of Financial Flow." Journal of Finance 23 (March 1968a), 1-26.

______. "Statement in Compendium on Monetary Policy Guidelines and Federal Reserve Structure pursuant to H. R. 11, Subcommittee on Domestic Finance of the Committee on Banking and Currency, House of Representatives, 90th Cong., 2d Session (Washington, D.C,, December 1968b), pp. 115-19.

______. "Direct Versus Indirect Controls as Instruments of Monetary Policy." Quarterly Review of Economics and Business 10 (Fall 1970), 25-34.

______. "Copeland's Money Flows After Twenty-Five Years: A Survey." Journal of Economic Literature 10 (March 1972), 1-25.

______. "Tieing Loose Ends in Monetary Theory in a Moneyflows Framework." Rivista Internazionale di Science Economiche e Commercialia 21 (March 1974), 246-76.

______. "Borrower Discretion, the Government Securities Market and Monetary Policy." Journal of Economics and Business 27 (Spring 1975), 233-43; errata, 28 (Fall 1975), 78.

______. "A Financial Research Program for Hong Kong." Academia Economic Papers, 4 (March 1976), 165-84.

______. "Beyond IS-LM." Malayan Economic Review 27 (April 1982a).

______. "A Creditist Approach to Monetary Theory." Nebraska Journal of Economics and Business 21 (Spring 1982b), 1-25.

______. "The Saving-Leakage Effect of Financial Intermediation." Journal of Post Keynesian Economics 5 (Fall 1982c), 153-56.

______. "The Money Supply Process: How Much Progress Since C. A. Phillips' Bank Credit?" Kredit und Kapital 17 (March 1984a).

______. "International Implications of U.S. Macroeconomic Policy." Singapore Economic Review 29 (October 1984b), 11-26.

______. "Fritz Machlup's Swan Song," Economics of Education Review 5, no. 3 (1986a), 319-23.

______. Money and Finance: A Flow-of-Funds Approach. Ames, Iowa, 1986b.

______. "The Efficiency of the Financial System: Micro-Macro Paradox," paper presented at the Southern Economic Association meetings, New Orleans, November 1986c.

Cohen, Jacob and Morton Grodzins. "How Much Economic Sharing in American Federalism?" American Political Science Review 57 (March 1963). Reprinted in Daniel J. Elazar, Cooperation and Conflict: Readings in American Federalism (Itasca, Ill., 1969), 206-32.

Cohen, Jacob and Steven Husted. "An Integrated Accounting Matrix for Canada and the United States." American Economic Review Proceedings 75 (May 1985a), 211-16.

______. "Modeling Canadian-U.S. Linkages in a Flow-of-Funds Framework." Unpublished, 1985b.

______. "A Comparison of the Effects of Canadian and U.S. Policy Shocks on Canadian Flow-of-Funds Variables," forthcoming, Journal of International Economic Integration.

Cohen, Jacob and James L. Kenkel. "A Credit Model Featuring External Finance and Scale Economies." Journal of Post Keynesian Economics 2 (Winter 1979-80), 255-56.

______. "The Information Content of the Flow of Funds: The Household Sector." in Transactions of the Second Financial Congress. Chicago, Illinois, 1986, pp. 264-389.

Cohen Jacob and W. L. L'Esperance. ."An Econometric Model of the Flow of Funds in the Stock Market." Paper presented at the Econometric Society meeting, New York, December 1965.

Cohen, Jacob and Richard C. Miller. "A Flow-of-Funds Model of the Stock Market." Journal of Economics and Business 25 (Winter 1973), 71-82.

Cohen, Jacob and William A. Schmalzl. "Simulating the Economy with a Flow-of-Funds Model Organized Around the Government Securities Market." Proceedings of the Fifth Annual Modeling and Simulation Conference, Part I, University of Pittsburgh, April 1974, pp. 275-80.

Congdon, Tim. "A New Approach to the Balance of Payments." Lloyds Bank Review 146 (October 1982), 1-14.

Copeland, Morris A. A Study of Moneyflows in the United States. New York, 1952.

Correa, Hector. Integrated Economic Accounting: Theory and Application to National, Real, and Financial Economic Planning (Lexington, Mass., 1977).

Cover, James Peery. "A Note on the Empirical Evidence for the Role of Credit in Macroeconomic Policy and Analysis." Southern Economic Journal 52 (April 1986), 1145-50.

Cox, Donald. "The March 14 Credit Controls, Consumer Credit and Spending: Progress Report." Research paper no. 8010, Federal Reserve Bank of New York (November 1980).

Dalamagas, Basil A. "A Flow of Funds Analysis of Crowding Out: Some International Evidence," Southern Economic Journal 53 (April, 1987), 997-1010.

Davis, Richard G. "Broad Credit Measures as Targets for Monetary Policy." Federal Reserve Bank of New York Quarterly Review 4 (Summer 1979), 13-22.

______. "Discussion." In Monetary Policy in the 1980s, Federal Reserve Bank of Kansas City, 1982, pp. 257-65.

de Leeuw, Frank. "Measuring Private Saving," mimeo, U.S. Department of Commerce, Washington, D. C., 1984, pp. 1-31.

Denison, Edward F. "Comment" [on Morris Mendelson, "The Optimum of Grossness in Flow-of-Funds Accounts,") in The Flow-of-Funds Approach to Social Accounting. Princeton, N.J., 1962, pp. 425-29.

Dernburg, Thomas F. and Duncan M. McDougall. Macroeconomics. 4th ed., 1972, pp. 241-42.

Diamond, Peter A. "Aggregate Demand Management in Search Equilibrium." Journal of Political Economy 90 (October 1982), 881-94.

Dimitrijevic, Dimitri. "The Use of Flow-of-Funds Accounts in Monetary Planning in Yugoslavia." Review of Income and Wealth 15 (March, 1969), 101-15.

______. "Monetary Planning in a Changing Economy: The Case of Yugoslavia." In Econometric Research in European Central Banks, ed. F. Masera et al. (Rome, 1975), pp. 495-505.

Dornbusch, Rudiger. Open Economy Macroeconomics. (New York, 1980).

Dornbusch, Rudiger and Stanley Fischer. Macroeconomics. 2nd ed. New York, 1981.

Dorrance, Graeme S. National Monetary and Financial Analysis. New York, 1978.

Drazen, Allen. "Recent Developments in Macroeconomic Disequilibrium Theory." Econometrica 48 (March 1980), 283-306.

Dudler, H. and J. C. Chouraqui. Flow of Funds Analysis in a Short-Term Context. Banque de France, Seminaire des Banques Centrales et des Institutions Internationales. Paris, April 1977.

Duesenberry, James S. "A Process Approach to Flow-of-Funds Analysis." The Flow-of-Funds Approach to Social Accounting. (New York, 1962), pp. 173-89.

Duesenberry, James and Barry Bosworth. "Policy Implications of a Flow-of-Funds Model." Journal of Finance 29 (May 1974), 331-47.

Earley. James S. et al. Money, Credit and Expenditure: A Sources and Uses of Funds Approach. New York University Bulletin, 1976(3).

Eckstein, Otto. The DRI Model of the U.S. Economy. (New York, 1983).

Eckstein, Otto, E. Green, and Allen Sinai. "The Data Resources Model: Use, Structure, and Analysis of the U.S. Economy." International Economic Review 15 (October 1974), 575-615.

Eckstein, Otto and Allen Sinai. "The Mechanisms of the Business Cycle in the Postwar Era." NBER Conference on Business Cycles. San Juan, Puerto Rico, March 1984.

______. "The Mechanisms of the Business Cycle in the Postwar Era," in Robert J. Gordon, ed., The American Business Cycle: Continuity and Change, National Bureau of Economic Research Studies in Business Cycles, Vol. 25 (Chicago, Ill., 1986), pp. 39-120.

Edgar, Michael S. "Dynamic Character of the Flow of Funds Model of the Stock Market." Journal of Economics and Business 29 (Spring/Summer 1977), 230-34.

Eichner, Alfred S., ed. A Guide to Post-Keynesian Economics. White Plains, N.Y., 1979.

______. "A Post-Keynesian Short-Period Model." Journal of Post Keynesian Economics 1 (Summer 1979), 36-63.

______. Towards a New Economics: Essays in Post-Keynesian and Institutionalist Economics. Armonk, N.Y., 1985.

Eichner, Alfred S. and J. A. Kregel. "An Essay on

Post-Keynesian Theory: A New Paradigm in Economics." Journal of Economic Literature 13 (December 1975), 1293-1314.
Eltis, Walter. "The Failure of the Keynesian Conventional Wisdom." Lloyds Bank Review 122 (October 1976), 1-18.
Enthoven, Alain C. Mathematical Appendix, to Gurley and Shaw, 1960.
Evans, M. K. Macroeconomic Activity. New York, 1969.
Fackler, James S. "An Empirical Analysis of the Markets for Goods, Money, and Credit." Journal of Money, Credit and Banking 17 (February 1985), 28-42.
Fackler, James S. and Andrew Silver. Money and Credit: Exploring Alternatives. Federal Reserve Bank of New York Quarterly Review (Winter 1982/83), 1-9.
Fair, Ray C. A Short-Run Forecasting Model of the United States Economy. Lexington, Mass., 1971.
__________. A Model of Macroeconomic Activity, Vol. I: The Theoretical Model. Cambridge, Mass., 1974.
__________. A Model of Macroeconomic Activity, Vol. II: The Empirical Model. Cambridge, Mass., 1976.
__________. Specification, Estimation and Analysis of Macroeconometric Models. (Cambridge, Mass., 1984).
Fair, Ray C. and Dwight M. Jaffee. "Methods of Estimation for Markets in Disequilibrium." Econometrica 40 (May 1972), 497-514.
Fand, David I. "The Debt-Expenditure Hypothesis and Residential Construction." Southern Economic Journal 26 (July 1959), 21-32.
Federal Reserve. Flow of Funds in the United States 1939-1953. Washington, D.C., 1955.
______. "A Quarterly Presentation of Flow of Funds, Saving, and Investment." Federal Reserve Bulletin 45 (August 1959), 1049-53.
__________. Flow of Funds/Saving Estimates Supplementary Distribution No. 1, Washington, D.C., November 1959.
______. Flow of Funds/Saving Estimates Supplement No. 2. Washington, D.C., May 1960.
______. "Flow of Funds Seasonally Adjusted." Federal Reserve Bulletin 48 (November 1962), 1393-1407.
______. Introduction to Flow of Funds. Washington, D.C., June 1980.
__________. Balance Sheets for the U.S. Economy 1945-81. Washington, D.C., October 1983.
______. Flow of Funds Accounts, Third Quarter 1985. (Washington, D.C., 1985).
__________. Balance Sheets for the U.S. Economy, 1945-84. Washington, D.C., October 1985.
Federal Reserve Bank of Kansas City. Debt, Financial Stability and Public Policy. (Jackson Hole, Wyoming, 1986).
Fischer, Stanley. "Long-Term Contracts, Rational Expectations and Optimal Money-Supply Rate." Journal of Political Economy 85 (February 1977), 191-206.
Fisher, Franklin. Disequilibrium Foundations of Equilibrium Economics. Cambridge, England, 1984.

Fleming, Miles. "The Timing of Payments and the Demand for Money." Economica 31 (May 1964), 132-57.

Forman, Leonard, Miles Groves, and Alfred S. Eichner. "Modeling the Monetary-Financial Sector." Working paper no. 14, Center for Economic and Anthropogenic Research (CEAR) (August 1983).

________. "The Cyclical Dynamics of the American Economy: Preliminary Results from a Post-Keynesian Econometric Model." Revised version (July 1985) of a paper presented at the Conference on the Cyclical Behavior and Long-Term Structural Movements of the Contemporary Economies: An Analysis of Their Financial Structure and of the Structures of Production and Distribution, Ottawa University, October 3-6, 1984.

Forman, Leonard and Alfred S. Eichner. "A Post Keynesian Short-Period Model: Some Preliminary Econometric Results." Journal of Post Keynesian Economics 4 (Fall 1981), 116-35.

Friedman, Benjamin M. "The Relative Stability of Money and Credit 'Velocities' in the United States: Evidence and Some Speculations." Working paper no. 645, NBER (March 1981).

________. "The Roles of Money and Credit in Macroeconomic Analysis." In Macroeconomics, Prices and Quantities: Essays in Memory of Arthur M. Okun, ed. James Tobin. Washington, D. C., 1983a, pp. 161-89.

________. "Using a Credit Aggregate Target to Implement Monetary Policy in the Financial Environment of the Future." Federal Reserve Bank of Kansas City, Monetary Policy Issues in the 1980s, 1982a, pp. 223-48.

______. "Debt and Economic Activity in the United States." In The Changing Roles of Debt and Equity in Financing U.S. Capital Formation, ed. Benjamin Friedman. (Chicago, Ill., 1982b), pp. 91-110.

______. "Money, Credit, and Federal Reserve Policy: Reply to Porter and Offenbacher." Federal Reserve Bank of Richmond, Economic Review 69 (November/December 1983b), 30-35.

______. "Money, Credit, and Interest Rates in the Business Cycle." Working paper no. 1482, NBER (October 1984).

______. "Increasing Indebtedness and Financial Stability in the United States," NBER Working Paper #2072 (Cambridge, Mass., 1986), reprinteed in Federal Reserve Bank of Kansas City, Debt, Financial Stability, and Public Policy (Jackson Hole, Wyoming, 1986), pp. 27-54.

Friedman, Milton. A Theory of the Consumption Function. Princeton, N.J., 1957.

Fromm, G. and Allen Sinai. "A Policy Simulation Model of Deposits, Mortgage Flows and Housing." Paper presented at the Econometric Society meeting, San Francisco, December 1974.

Fry, Maxwell J. An Application of the Stone Model to Financial Planning in Turkey (mimeo). Nathanya, Israel: Eleventh General Conference of the International Association for

Research in Income and Wealth (1969).

Frydl, Edward J. "The Challenge of Financial Change," in Federal Reserve Bank of New York, Seventy-First Annual Report for 1985 (New York, 1986), pp. 3-27.

Gaines, Tilford C. "Financial Innovation and the Efficiency of Federal Reserve Policy." In Monetary Process and Policy, ed. George Horwich. Homewood, Ill., 1963, chap. 22.

Gale, Douglas. Money: In Equilibrium. Cambridge, England, 1982

______. Money: In Disequilibrium. Cambridge, England, 1983.

Garcia, Gillian. "The Right Rabbit: Which Intermediate Target Should the Fed Pursue?" Federal Reserve Bank of Chicago, Economic Perspectives (May/June 1984), 15-31.

Gavin, William T. "Monetarism and the M1 Target," Federal Reserve Bank of Cleveland, Economic Commentary (October 1, 1986).

Georgiadis, H. G. Balance of Payments Equilibrium. Pittsburgh, Pa., 1964.

Gilbert, R. Alton. "Operating Procedures for Conducting Monetary Policy," Federal Reserve Bank of St. Louis, Review, 67 (February 1985), 13-21.

Gilbert, R. Alton and Mack Ott. "Why the Big Rise in Business Loans at Banks Last Year?" Federal Reserve Bank of St. Louis, Review 67 (March 1985), 5-13.

Goldfeld, Stephen M. "Discussion." Journal of Finance 29 (May 1974), 358-60.

Goldsmith, Raymond W. Financial Intermediaries in the American Economy. Princeton, N.J., 1958.

______. The Flow of Capital Funds in the Postwar Economy. New York, 1965.

______. Financial Structure and Development. New Haven, Conn., 1969.

______. Comparative National Balance Sheets: A Study of Twenty Countries, 1968-1978 (Chicago, 1985).

______. The National Balance Sheet of the United States, 1953-1980 (Chicago, 1982).

Goodfriend, Marvin. "A Model of Money Stock Determination with Loan Demand and a Banking System Balance Sheet Constraint," Federal Reserve Bank of Richmond, Economic Review 68 (January/February 1982), 3-16.

Gordon, Robert J. Macroeconomics. 2nd ed. Boston, 1981a.

______."Output Fluctuations and Gradual Price Adjustment." Journal of Economic Literature 19 (June 1981b), 493-530.

Gramley, Lyle E. and Samuel B. Chase, Jr. "Time Deposits in Monetary Analysis." Federal Reserve Bulletin (October 1965). Reprinted in Targets and Indicators of Monetary Policy, ed. Karl Brunner. San Francisco, 1969, pp. 219-49.

Grandmont, Jean-Michel. "Temporary Equilibrium Theory." In The Handbook of Mathematical Economics, Vol. 2, ed. Kenneth J. Arrow and M. Intriligator. Amsterdam, 1982, pp. 879-922.

Great Britain, H. M. Treasury and Central Statistical Office. "Financial Wealth of the Non-Bank Private Sector." Economic Trends 333 (July 1981), pp. 105-18.

Grossman, H. E. "Money, Interest and Prices in Market Disequilibrium." Journal of Political Economy 79 (September/October 1971) 943-61.

Group of Ten Countries. Recent Innovations in International Banking (Bank for International Settlements, Basel, Switzerland, April 1986).

Guentner, Kenneth J. "The Impact of Monetary Policy on the Government Securities Market: An Econometric Analysis." Ph.D. dissertation, University of Pittsburgh, 1977.

Gurley, John G. and Edward S. Shaw. "Financial Aspects of Economic Development." American Economic Review 45 (September 1955), 515-38.

______. "Financial Intermediaries and the Saving-Investment Process." Journal of Finance 11 (May 1956), 257-76.

______. "The Growth of Debt and Money in the United States, 1800-1950." Review of Economics and Statistics 39 (August 1957), 250-62.

______. Money in a Theory of Finance. Washington, D.C., 1960.

Hafer, R. W., Scott E. Hein, and Clemens J. M. Kool. "Forecasting the Money Multiplier: Implications for Money Stock Control and Economic Activity." Federal Reserve Bank of St. Louis Review 65 (October 1983), 22-33.

Hahn, Frank. Equilibrium and Macroeconomics. Cambridge, Mass., 1984.

Harcourt, G. C. "G. L. Shackle." Journal of Post Keynesian Economics 4 (Fall 1981), 136-44.

Harrod, Roy. "Keynes' Views on Money." Journal of Political Economy 78 (July/August 1970), 623-25.

Harris, Laurence. Monetary Theory. New York, 1981.

Hayashi, F. "The Effect of Liquidity Constraints on Consumption: A Cross-Sectional Analysis." Quarterly Journal of Economics 100 (February 1985), 183-206.

Hendershott, Patric H. Understanding Capital Markets, Vol. I: A Flow-of-Funds Financial Model. Lexington, Mass., 1977a).

__________. "The Likely Impact of Increases in Deposit Rate Ceilings on Thrift Earnings and Housing Construction" American Real Estate and Urban Economics Association Journal 7 (1977b), 177-89.

______. "Deregulation and the Capital Markets: The Impact of Deposit Rate Ceilings and Restrictions Against Variable Rate Mortgages." In Deregulation of the Banking and Securities Industries, ed. Lawrence G. Goldberg and Lawrence J. White. Lexington, Mass., 1979, pp. 71-99.

______. "Analysis of the Impact of Capital-Specific Policies or Legislation." Journal of Money, Credit and Banking 12 (May 1980), 377-99.

Hendershott, Patric H. and Chang-tseh Hsieh. "Inflation and the Growth in Home Mortgage Debt, 1964-78." Journal of Financial Research 3 (Fall 1980), 189-202.

Hendershott, Patric H. and James L. Murphy. "The Monetary Cycle and the Business Cycle: The Flow-of-Funds Re-Examined," National Banking Review, 1 (June 1964), 531-50.

Hendershott, Patric H. and James P. Winder. "Commercial Bank Asset Portfolio Behavior in the United States." Journal of Banking and Finance 3 (1979), 113-31.
Hester, Donald D. and James L. Pierce. Bank Management and Portfolio Behavior. New Haven, Conn., 1975.
Hewitt, M. E. "Financial Forecasts in the United Kingdom." Bank of England, Quarterly Bulletin (June 1977), 188-96.
Hicks, John. The Crisis in Keynesian Economics. (New York, 1974).
______. "IS-LM: An Explanation." Journal of Post Keynesian Economics 3 (Winter 1980-81), 139-54.
Hirshleifer, J. and John G. Riley. "The Analytics of Uncertainty and Information: An Expository Survey," Journal of Economic Literature, XVII (December 1979), 1375-1421.
Hoffman, Stuart. Component Ratio Estimation of the Money Multiplier, Research Paper No. 4 (Federal Reserve Bank of Atlanta, June 1979).
Hood, William C. Financing of Economic Activity in Canada. Ottawa, 1958.
Horwich, George and Patric H. Hendershott. "The Appropriate Indicators of Monetary Policy," Savings and Residential Financing 1969 Conference Proceedings (Chicago, United States Saving and Loan League, 1969), 32-52.
Hosek, William R. and Frank Zahn. Monetary Theory Policy and Financial Markets. New York, 1977.
Hotson, John H. et al. Stagflation and the Bastard Keynesians. Waterloo, Ontario, 1976.
Howard, D. H. "The Disequilibrium Model in a Controlled Economy: An Empirical Test of the Barro-Grossman Model." American Economic Review 66 (December 1976), 871-77.
Howitt, Peter. "Transaction Costs in the Theory of Unemployment." American Economic Review 75 (March 1985), 88-100.
Johannes, James M. and Robert H. Rasche. "Predicting the Money Multiplier," Journal of Monetary Economics 5 (July 1979), 301-25
______. "Can the Reserves Approach to Monetary Control Really Work?" Journal of Money, Credit and Banking 13 (August 1981), 298-313.
Johnson, Christopher. Anatomy of U.K. Finance, 1970-75. London, 1977.
Jonson, Peter D. "Money, Prices and Output: An Integrative Essay." Kredit und Kapital 9, no. 4 (1976), 499-518.
Jorgenson, Dale W., "Econometric Studies of Investment Behavior: A Survey." Journal of Economic Literature IX (December 1971), 1111-47.
Judd, John P. and Brian Motley. "Innovation and Monetary Policy I." Federal Reserve Bank of San Francisco, Weekly Letter (September 11, 1981).
Judd, John P. and John L. Scadding. "Liability Management, Bank Loans and Deposit 'Market' Disequilibrium," Federal Reserve Bank of San Francisco, Economic Review (Summer, 1981), 21-43.

Kades, Eric A. "New Classical and New Keynesian Models of Business Cycles." Federal Reserve Bank of Cleveland, Economic Review 4 (1985), 20-35.

______. "Fixprice Models for Dynamic Studies." Working paper no. 8504, Federal Reserve Bank of Cleveland, (August 1985a).

______. "Dynamics of Fixprice Models." Working paper no. 8505, Federal Reserve Bank of Cleveland, (September 1985b).

Kaminow, Ira and James M. O'Brien. "Issues in Selective Credit Policies: An Evaluative Essay." In Studies in Selective Credit Policy, ed. Ira Kaminow and James M. O'Brien. Federal Reserve Bank of Philadelphia, 1975, pp. 1-34.

Kaufman, Henry. "Economic Outlook for Fiscal Years 1978 and 1979." Testimony before the House of Representatives Committee on the Budget, February 6, 1978.

Kendrick, John W. Economic Accounts and Their Uses. New York, 1972.

Kohn, Meir. "In Defense of the Finance Constraint," Economic Inquiry 19 (April 1981), 177-195.

Kopcke, Richard W. "Current Accounting Practices and Proposals for Reform." New England Economic Review (September/October 1976), 3ff.

______. "How Erratic Is Money Growth?" Federal Reserve Bank of Boston, New England Economic Review (May/June, 1986), 3-20.

Kornai, Janos. "Comment" [on Jean-Jacques Laffont, "Fix-Price Models: A Survey of Recent Empirical Work"]. In Frontiers of Economics, Kenneth J. Arrow and Seppo Honkapohja. Oxford, England, 1985, pp. 328-67.

Krugman, Paul R. "International Aspects of U.S. Monetary and Fiscal Policy." In The Economics of Large Government Deficits, Federal Reserve Bank of Boston. (Boston, Mass., 1983), pp. 112-33.

Ladenson, Mark L. "Pitfalls in Financial Model Building: Some Extensions." American Economic Review 61 (March 1971), 179-86.

______."Pitfalls in Financial Model Building: Comment." American Economic Review 63 (December 1973), 1005-08.

Laffont, Jean-Jacques. "Fix-Price Models: A Survey of Recent Empirical Work." In Frontiers of Economics, Kenneth J. Arrow and Seppo Honkapohja. Oxford, England, 1985, pp. 328-67.

Laidler, David W. "The Definition of Money." Journal of Money, Credit and Banking 1 (August 1969), 508-25.

Lavoie, Marc. "Systemic Financial Fragility: A Simplified View," Journal of Post Keynesian Economics, IX (Winter, 1986-87), 258-66.

Lawrence, Robert Z. and Robert E. Litan. "Living with the Trade Deficit: Adjustment Strategies to Preserve Free Trade." The Brookings Review 4 (Fall 1985), 3-13.

Leijonhufvud, Axel. On Keynesian Economics and the Economics of Keynes: A Study in Monetary Theory. New York, 1968.

Lindbeck, Assar. "Some Fiscal and Monetary Policy Experiments in Sweden." Federal Reserve Bank of Boston, Credit Allocation Techniques and Monetary Policy, Conference Series No. 11, pp. 209-10.

London Business School. Financial Outlook. Vol. 1, No. 1. London, December, 1983.

________. The London Business School Quarterly Econometric Model of the United Kingdom Economy (London, 1985).

Lucas, R. E. "An Equilibrium Model of the Business Cycle," Journal of Political Economy 83 (December 1975), 1113-44.

Machlup, Fritz. Knowledge: Its Creation, Distribution, and Economic Significance. Vol. III of The Economics of Information and Human Capital (Princeton, 1984).

Machlup, Fritz. The Stock Market, Credit and Capital Formation. London, 1940.

Malinvaud, Edmond. The Theory of Unemployment Reconsidered. New York, 1977.

Martin, Preston. Statement to Congress, May 3, 1985. Federal Reserve Bulletin (July 1985), 514-17.

McKenna, C. J. The Economics of Uncertainty. (New York, 1986).

McMillin, W. Douglas and Thomas R. Beard. "The Short Run Impact of Fiscal Policy on the Money Supply." Southern Economic Journal 47 (July 1980), 122-135.

McMillin, W. Douglas and James S. Fackler. "Monetary vs. Credit Aggregates: An Evaluation of Monetary Policy Targets." Southern Economic Journal 50 (January 1984), 711-23.

McNees, Stephen K. "The Forecasting Record for the 1970s." Federal Reserve Bank of Boston, New England Economic Review (September/October 1979), 33-53.

______. "Modeling the Fed: A Forward-Looking Monetary Policy Reaction Function," New England Economic Review, (November/December 1986), 3-8.

Meltzer, Allan. "Discussion." Journal of Finance 29 (May 1974), 360-63.

Mendelson, Morris. "The Optimum of Grossness in Flow-of-Funds Accounts." In The Flow-of-Funds Approach to Social Accounting, National Bureau of Economic Research, Conference of Research in Income and Wealth. (Princeton, N.J., 1962), pp. 411-25.

Minsky, Hyman P. John Maynard Keynes. New York, 1975.

________. "A Theory of Systematic Fragility." In Financial Crises: Institutions and Markets in a Fragile Environment, ed. Edward I. Altman and Arnold W. Sametz. New York, 1977, chap. 6.

______. Can "It" Happen Again? Essays on Instability and Finance. (Armonk, N.Y., 1982a).

______. "The Financial-Instability Hypothesis: Capitalist Processes and the Behavior of the Economy," in Financial Crisis: Theory, History and Policy. Ed. C. P. Kindleberger and J. P. Laffargue. New York, 1982b.

____________. "The Financial Instability Hypothesis: A Restatement," in Philip Arestis and Thanos Skouras, eds., Post Keynesian Economic Theory (Armonk, N.Y., 1985), pp. 24-55.

______. Stabilizing an Unstable Economy (New Haven, Conn.,

1986).
Mishkin, Frederick. "Household Liabilities and the Generalized Stock-Adjustment Model." Review of Economics and Statistics 38 (November 1976), 481-85.
______. "What Depressed the Consumer? The Household Balance Sheet and the 1973-75 Recession." Brookings Papers on Economic Activity 1 (1977), 123ff.
Modigliani, Franco. "Monetary Policy and Consumption." Consumer Spending and Monetary Policy: The Linkages. Federal Reserve Bank of Boston, Conference Series No. 5 (June 1971), 9-84.
Modigliani, Franco and Lucas D. Papademos. "The Structure of Financial Markets and the Monetary Mechanism," in Federal Reserve Bank of Boston, Controlling Monetary Aggregates, III, Conference Series No. 23 (October 1980), pp. 111-55.
Moore, Basil J. "Unpacking the Post Keynesian Black Box: Bank Lending and the Money Supply." Journal of Post Keynesian Economics 5 (Summer 1983), 537-56.
______. "Unpacking the Post Keynesian Black Box: Wages, Bank Lending and the Money Supply." Thames Papers on Political Economy, 1984a.
______. "Contemporaneous Reserve Accounting: Can Reserves Be Quantity-Constrained?" Journal of Post Keynesian Economics 7 (Fall 1984b), 103-13.
Mooslechner, Peter and Ewald Nowotny. Gesamtwirtschaftliche Finanzierung und Öffentliche Verschuldung (Macroeconomic financing and public indebtedness). (Linz, Austria, 1980).
Moulton, Harold G. The Formation of Capital. (Washington, D.C., 1935).
Muellbauer, John and Richard Portes. "Macroeconomics When Markets Do Not Clear." In Macroeconomic Theory and Policy, ed. William H. Branson, 2d ed. New York, 1979, chap. 16. (Originally published in Economic Journal 88 (December 1978), 788-821.
Nagatani, Keizo. Macroeconomic Dynamics. Cambridge, England, 1981.
OECD, Committee on Financial Markets. Report of the Special Session of the Group of Financial Statisticians on the Uses of Flow of Funds Tables. (October 24, 1978).
______. Financial Statistics, Methodological Supplement. 1981, p. 170.
______. Financial Accounts. Part 1, 1982, pp. 18-19.
Okun, Arthur M. "An Efficient Strategy to Combat Inflation." The Brookings Bulletin 15 (Spring 1979), 1-5.
______. Prices and Quantities. Washington, D.C., 1981.
Olson, Mancur. "A Microeconomic and Evolutionary Approach to Macroeconomics." Paper presented at the International Economic Association meetings, Kiel, Germany, June 1984.
Orcutt, Guy H., Martin Greenberger, John Korbel, and Alice Rivlin. Microanalysis of Socioeconomic System: A Simulation Study. (New York, 1961).
Palash, Carl J. and Lawrence J. Radecki. "Using Monetary and Financial Variables to Predict Cyclical Downturns."

Federal Reserve Bank of New York Quarterly Review 10 (Summer 1985), 36-45.

Patinkin, Don. Money, Interest and Prices. 2d ed. New York, 1965.

________. "Money and Wealth: A Review Article," Journal of Economic Literature VII (December 1969), 1140-60.

Pesek, Boris P. "Monetary Theory in the Post-Robertson 'Alice in Wonderland' Era." Journal of Economic Literature 14 (September 1976), 856-84.

Pesek, Boris P. and Thomas R. Saving. Money, Wealth and Economic Theory. New York, 1967.

______. The Foundations of Money and Banking. New York, 1968.

Pettigrew, C. W. "National and Sector Balance Sheets for the United Kingdom." CSO, Economic Trends 325 (November 1980).

Phillips, C. A. Bank Credit. New York, 1924.

Poole, William. "Optimal Choice of Monetary Policy Instruments in a Single Stochastic Macro Model." Quarterly Journal of Economics 84 (May 1970), 197-216.

Porter, Richard D. and Edward K. Offenbacher. "Empirical Comparisons of Credit and Monetary Aggregates Using Vector Autoregressive Methods." Federal Reserve Bank of Richmond, Economic Review 69 (November/December 1983), 16-29.

Purvis, Douglas D. "Dynamic Models of Portfolio Behavior: More on Pitfalls in Financial Model Building." American Economic Review 68 (June 1978), 403-16.

Quandt, R. "Econometric Disequilibrium Models." Econometric Reviews 1 (1982), 1-63.

Quarterly Bulletin of the National Bank of Yugoslavia, No. 3, 1986.

Rasche, Robert H. "A Review of Empirical Studies of the Money Supply Mechanism." Federal Reserve Bank of St. Louis, Review (July 1972), pp. 11-19. Reprinted in Current Issues in Monetary Theory and Policy. 2d ed. Thomas M. Havrilesky and John T. Boorman. Arlington Heights, Inc., 1980, pp. 296-314.

Reserve Bank of Australia. Submission to the Committee of Inquiry Into the Australian Financial System. Occasional Paper No. 7 (December 1979), esp. section 1, "Finance."

__________. Statistical Bulletin. Financial Flow Accounts Supplement 1953/54-1979/80. June 1981.

______. Financial Flows. Bulletin Supplement (March 1982).

Review of Income and Wealth. "Special Issue on the Review of the United Nations System of National Accounts," Income and Wealth Series 32 (June 1986), 109-216.

Roe, Alan R. "The Case for Flow of Funds and National Balance Sheet Accounts." Economic Journal 83 (June 1973), 401-20.

Ronk, Sally. "Sources and Uses of Funds Analysis." In Financial Institutions and Markets. 2d ed. Ed. Murray E. Polakoff, Thomas A. Durkin et al. Boston, 1981, pp. 545-70.

Ruggles, Richard and Nancy D. Ruggles. "Integrated Economic Accounts: Reply." Survey of Current Business (November

1982), 198-214.

______. "Integrated Economic Accounts for the United States, 1947-80." Survey of Current Business (May 1982), pp. 1-75.

Rymes, T. K. "Inflation, Nonoptimal Monetary Arrangements and the Banking Imputation in the National Accounts," Review of Income and Wealth, 31 (March 1985), 85-96.

Shackle, G. L. S. Decision, Order and Time in Human Affairs. Cambridge, England, 1961.

______. Expectation, Enterprise and Profit. London, 1970.

______. "The Romantic Mountain and the Classic Lake: Alan Coddington's Keynesian Economics. Journal of Post Keynesian Economics 6 (Winter 1983-84), 241-51.

Sheffrin, Steven M. Rational Expectations. Cambridge, England, 1983.

Sheppard, D. and C. Barrett. "Financial Credit Multipliers and the Availability of Funds." Economica 32 (May 1965), 198-214.

Shuford, Harry C. "The Outlook for Financial Markets in 1985: A Flow of Funds Approach." In Understanding Capital Markets, Vol. II: The Financial Environment and the Flow of Funds in the Next Decade, ed. Arnold W. Sametz and Paul Wachtel. Lexington, Mass., 1977, pp. 267-305.

Siegel, Diane F. "The Relationship of Money and Income: The Breakdowns in the 70s and 80s," Federal Reserve Bank of Chicago, Economic Perspectives (July/August, 1986), pp. 3-15.

Silber, William L. Portfolio Behavior of Financial Institutions. (New York, 1970), pp. 16-17.

Simpson, Thomas D. et al. "Recent Revisions in the Money Stock: Benchmark, Seasonal Adjustment and Calculation of Shift-Adjusted M1-B." Federal Reserve Bulletin (July 1981), 539-44.

Sinai, Allen. "The Integration of 'Financial Instability' in Large-Scale Macroeconomic Models: Theory, Practice, Problems." Paper presented at Midwest Economics Association meeting, Chicago, April 1975.

______. "Real-Financial Interaction in the Corporate Sector: Some Theory, History and Evidence." Paper presented at the North American Economic Society Association annual meeting, Atlantic City, September 1976.

______. "Crunch Impacts and the Aftermath." DRI Review (June 1980), 1ff.

______. "Policy Mix and the Economy," Economic Studies Series (Shearson Lehman Brothers, February 1986, No. 19).

____________. The Financial System of the U.S. Economy. Forthcoming.

Sinai, Allen and Andrew F. Brimmer. "The Effects of Tax Policy on Capital Formation, Corporate Liquidity and the Availability of Investable Funds: A Simulation Study." Journal of Finance 31 (May 1976), 287-308.

Smith, Gary. "Pitfalls in Financial Model Building: A Clarification." American Economic Review 65 (September 1975), 510-16.

______. "Further Evidence of the Value of A Priori Information." Journal of Finance 35 (March 1980), 181-89.

______. Money and Banking. (Reading, Mass., 1982).

Smith, Gary and William Brainard. "The Value of A Priori Information in Estimating a Financial Model." Journal of Finance 31 (December 1976), 1299-1322.

______. "A Disequilibrium Model of Savings and Loan Associations." Journal of Finance 37 (December 1982), 1277-93.

Smith, Paul F. Economics of Financial Institutions and Markets. Homewood, Ill., 1971.

______. Money and Financial Intermediation Englewood Cliffs, N.J., 1978.

Spindt, Paul A. "Money Is What Money Does: A Revealed Production Approach to Monetary Aggregation." Federal Reserve Special Studies Paper No. 177. Washington, D.C., 1983.

Stafford, L. W. R. The Modern Economy. London, 1976.

Statistics Canada. Financial Flow Accounts Quarterly. (Ottawa, Canada).

______. Financial Flow Accounts (Catalogue 13-002).

______. Financial Flow Accounts (Catalogue 13-563).

______. The National Balance Sheet Accounts, 1961-1985 (Ottawa, Canada, 1986), catalogue 13-214.

Stiglitz, Joseph E. "Equilibrium in Product Markets with Imperfect Information." American Economic Review,Proceedings 69 (May 1979), 339-45.

Stone, Richard. "Simple Transaction Models, Information and Computing." Review of Economic Studies 19 (February 1952), 67-84.

______. A Program for Growth (3): Input-Output Relationships, 1954-1966 (Cambridge, Mass., 1963).

______. "The Social Accounts from the Consumer Point of View." Review of Income and Wealth 1 (March 1966), 17-28.

______. Mathematical Models of the Economy and Other Essays. (London, 1970).

Stone, Richard and Alan Roe. A Programme for Growth No. 11: The Financial Interdependence of the Economy 1957-66. London, 1971.

Taylor, Herb. "What Has Happened to M1?" Federal Reserve Bank of Philadelphia, Business Review (September/October, 1986), pp. 1-14.

Taylor, John B. "Aggregate Dynamics and Staggered Contracts," Journal of Political Economy, 88 (February 1980), 1-23.

______. "Rational Expectations Models in Macroeconomics." In Frontiers of Economics, Kenneth J. Arrow and Seppo Honkapohja. Oxford, England, 1985, pp. 391-425.

Taylor, Lance and Stephen A. O'Connell. "A Minsky Crisis," Quarterly Journal of Economics C (Supplement 1985), 871-85.

Taylor, S. P. "Uses of Flow-of-Funds Accounts in the Federal Reserve System." Journal of Finance 18 (May 1963),

249-58.

_________. "Revision Experience in Flow of Funds Accounts." Washington, D.C., December 12, 1973, processed.

______. "A Financial Background for Project Independence." Washington, D.C., August 12, 1974, processed.

Thore, Sten. "Credit Networks." Economica, 36 (February 1969), 42-55.

______. "Programming a Credit Network Under Uncertainty." Journal of Money, Credit and Banking 2 (May 1970), 219-46.

Thore, Sten and Finn Kydland. "Dynamic Flow-of-Funds Networks." In Applications of Management Science in Banking and Finance, ed. Samuel Eilon and Terence R. Fowkes. (Epping, England, 1972), pp. 259-76.

Thore, Sten and Erling Vardal. "A Programming Model for National Credit Budgeting in Norway." Economie Appliquee 27 (1974), 423-56.

Tice, Helen Stone. "Report on a Conference on the Proposals for Revision of the United Nations System of National Accounts." Review of Income and Wealth 1 (March 1967), 36-102.

Tinbergen, J. and D. B. J. Schouten. "National Income Accounts as a Means of Currency Analysis." Int. Econ. Papers 5 (1955), 179-93.

Tobin, James. "Comment." In "A Process Approach to Flow-of-Funds Analysis," in The Flow-of-Funds Approach to Social Accounting, ed. James S. Duesenberry. (New York, 1962), pp. 190-93.

_________. "Commercial Banks as Creators of 'Money.'" In Banking and Monetary Studies, ed. Deane Carson. Homewood, Ill., 1963, chap. 11.

_________. "A General Equilibrium Approach to Monetary Theory." Journal of Money, Credit and Banking 1 (February 1969), 15-89.

______. "Money and Finance in the Macroeconomic Process." Journal of Money, Credit and Banking 14 (May 1984), 171-204.

Tobin, James and Walter C. Dolde. "Wealth, Liquidity, and Consumption." Consumer Spending and Monetary Policy, Federal Reserve Bank of Boston, Conference Series No. 5, June 1971, pp. 99-147.

Townsend, Robert M. "Optimal Multiperiod Contracts and the Gain from Enduring Relationships Under Private Information," Journal of Political Economy 90 (December 1982), 1166-86.

Tsiang, S. C. "Keynes 'Finance' Demand for Liquidity: Robertson's Loanable Funds Theory and Friedman's Monetarism." Quarterly Journal of Economics 94 (May 1980), 467-91.

Tucker, Donald P. "Credit Rationing, Interest Rate Lags, and Monetary Policy Speed." Quarterly Journal of Economics 32 (February 1968), 54-84.

United Nations. A System of National Accounts. New York, 1968.

United Nations Economic and Social Council. "Review of the Implementation of the Revised System of National

Accounts." (E/CN.3 507, May 12, 1978).

________. "Review and Development of the System of National Accounts (SNA) Report of the Secretary General." (E/CN.3/121938/5; July 21, 1982).

U.S. Department of Commerce, Bureau of the Census. Implicit Price Deflators, United States Income and Output. Washington, D.C., 1958.

________. Enterprise Statistics, Part 3, "Link of Census Establishment and IRS Corporation Data." 1958, 1963, and 1967.

Vickers, Douglas. The Theory of the Firm: Production, Capital and Finance. New York, 1968.

Volcker, Paul A. "The Rapid Growth of Debt in the United States," Federal Reserve Bank of Kansas City, Economic Review (May 1986), 3-12.

Wachtel, Paul. "Econometric Models of the Financial Sector." In Financial Institutions and Markets. 2d ed. Ed. Murray E. Polakoff, Thomas A. Durkin et al. Boston, 1981, chap. 26.

________. "Financial Prerequisites for Economic Growth." In Financial Institutions and Markets. 2d ed. Ed. Murray E. Polakoff and Thomas A. Durkin et al. Boston, 1981, pp. 587-88.

Webb, Roy H. "Vector Autoregressions as a Tool for Forecast Evaluation." Federal Reserve Bank of Richmond Economic Review 70 (January/February 1984), 3-11.

Weintraub, Sydney. An Approach to the Theory of Income Distribution (Philadelphia, 1958).

________. A General Theory of the Price Level, Income Distribution, and Economic Growth (Philadelphia, Pa., 1959).

________. Capitalism's Inflation and Unemployment Crisis (Reading, Mass., 1978).

Weise, P. and Kraft, M. "Minsky's View of Fragility: A Game Theoretic Interpretation," Journal of Post Keynesian Economics, III (Summer, 1981), 519-27.

Weiss, Laurence. "Comment" [on John B. Taylor, "Rational Expectations Models in Macroeconomics"]. In Frontiers of Economics, Kenneth J. Arrow and Seppo Honkapohja. Oxford, England, 1985, pp. 437-44.

White, William H. "The Case for and Against 'Disequilibrium' Money." IMF Staff Papers 28 (September 1981), 534-72.

Wichers, C. Robert. "Complex Transactions." Southern Economic Journal 46 (October 1979), 359-88.

Wojnilower, Albert M. "The Central Role of Credit Crunches in Recent Financial History." Brookings Papers on Economic Activity 2 (1980), pp. 277-326.

________. "Private Credit Demand Supply and Crunches: How Different Are the 1980s," American Economic Review, 75 (May, 1985), pp. 351-56.

Wolfson, Martin Henry. "Financial Crises: Theory and Evidence in the Postwar U.S. Economy." (Ph.D. dissertation, American University, 1984).

______. "Financial Crises in the Postwar Economy." Paper presented at the Allied Social Science Association meetings, New York, December 28, 1985.

______. "Some Empirical Issues in the Analysis of Financial Crises." Paper presented at the conference on Economic Dynamics and Financial Instability, New School for Social Research, New York, April 15, 1986a.

______. Financial Crises: Understanding the Postwar U.S. Experience (Armonk, N.Y., 1986b).

Wood, John H. "A Model of Federal Reserve Behavior." In Monetary Process and Policy: A Symposium, ed. George Horwich. Homewood, Ill., 1967, pp. 135-66.

Zahn, Frank. "A Flow of Funds Analysis of Crowding Out," Southern Economic Journal 4 (July, 1978), 136-153.

Zarnowitz, Victor. "Recent Work on Business Cycles in Historical Perspective," Journal of Economic Literature, XXIII (June, 1985), pp. 523-580.

NAME INDEX

Aburachis, A. T., 278
Alford, R.F.G., 146, 161n9, 162n19, 176
Anderson, W. H. Locke, 208n6
Arak, Marcelle, 299n2
Arestis, P., 257
Atkinson, Sue, 70
Attfield, C. L., 41
Azariadis, Costas, 73
Backus, David, 39, 232, 235, 239
Bain, A. D., 170, 184, 195n2, 209, 248n7, 307
Balbach, Anatol B., 106n8
Bank of England, 146
Bank of Japan, 179n1
Bankers Trust, 168
Barrett, C., 22
Barro, Robert, 72
Barten, A. P., 29n10
Batchelor, Roy, 119n1
Beard, Thomas, 110
Begg, David K. H., 41
Benassy, Jean-Pascal, 72
Bennett, Robert, 161n13
Bergmann, Barbara, 161n13
Berkman, Neil, 92n14
Bernanke, Ben, 77n18
Berry, John M., 208n2
Bharat, Trehan, 57n24
Blinder, Alan, 283, 299n5
Bosworth, Barry, 210, 215, 216
Brainard, William, 23, 39, 165, 242, 243
Branson, William, 165
Brimmer, Andrew, 70
Brox, James A., 29n10, 248n7
Brunner, Karl, 83
Buiter, William, 101n2
Burger, Albert, 83, 106
Büttler, Hans-Jurg, 91n9
Cargill, Thomas F., 146
Carlson, John, 273, 282
Carter, Michael, 41
Chase, Samuel, 79, 80
Chouraqui, J. C., 156
Clinton, K., 249n16
Clower, Robert, 4, 71, 101n6
Coddington, Alan, 77n16
Cohen, Jacob, 15, 25, 41, 49, 72, 77n14, 81, 83, 90n1, 90n3, 21n5, 91n7, 110, 119n4, 129, 138, 160n8, 162, 165, 168, 176, 178, 179n5, 187, 188, 191, 195n6, 199, 205, 208n1, 247, 248n3, 259, 273, 278, 287, 290, 296, 299n9, 300n10, 309
Commission of the European Communities, 160n3
Congdon, Tim, 179n2
Copeland, Morris, 79, 109
Correa, Hector, 184
Cover, James Peery, 299n5
Dalamagas, Basil A., 249n16
Davis, Richard G., 110, 278, 280
Day, C. L., 248n7
De Leeuw, Frank, 138

Dernburg, Thomas F. 55n5
Dimitrijevic, Dimitri, 155
Dolde, Robert, 119n8, 266, 275n5
Dornbusch, Rudiger, 55n5, 165
Dorrance, Graeme S., 160n1
Drazen, Allen, 73
Driver, C., 257
Dudler, H., 156
Duesenberry, James, 210, 215, 216
Earley, James, 278
Eckstein, Otto, 70, 270, 275n6, 283
Edgar, Michael, 108n7
Eichner, Alfred, 77n15, 248n3, 257, 258, 259
Eltis, Walter, 164
Enthoven, Alain, 55n1
Evans, M. K., 204
Fackler, James, 276, 279, 280, 281
Fair, Ray, 251, 255, 275n1
Fand, David, 188
Federal Reserve, 129, 138, 139, 161n8, 168
Federal Reserve Bank of Kansas City, 273
Fischer, Stanley, 55n5, 73
Fisher, Franklin, 41, 72
Forman, Leonard, 77n15, 248n3, 258, 259
Frei, Gertrud, 91n9
Friedman, Benjamin M., 99, 278, 273, 279, 282
Fromm, G., 275n6
Fry, Maxwell, 195n3
Frydl, Edward, 275n10
Gaines, Tilford, 79
Gale, Douglas, 41, 56n15, 72
Gavin, William, 282
Georgiadis, H. G., 193
Gilbert, R. Alton, 109, 288
Goldfeld, Stephen, 217
Goldsmith, Raymond W., 70, 110, 179n6
Goodfriend, Marvin, 85
Gordon, Robert, 55n5, 77n14
Gramley, Lyle, 79, 80
Grandmont, Jean-Michel, 72
Great Britain, HM Treasury and CSO, 149
Green, E., 275n6
Grodzins, Morton, 179n5
Grossman, Herschel, 72
Group of Ten Countries, 275n10
Groves, Miles, 77n15, 248n3, 258
Guentner, Kenneth, 210, 212, 213
Gurley, J. G., 35, 55n1, 79, 82, 188
Hafer, R. W., 106
Hahn, Frank, 41
Harcourt, G. C., 74
Harris, Laurence, 11, 82, 101n1
Harrod, Roy, 275n4
Hayashi, F., 102, 266
Hein, Scott, 106
Hendershott, Patric, 14, 15, 138, 161n11, 210, 212,

217, 300n12, 221, 225, 232, 290, 300n12
Hewitt, M. E., 170, 208n6
Hicks, John, 75n2
Hillabold, A. B., 160n8
Hoffman, Stuart, 106
Hood, William C., 161n14
Horwich, George, 300
Hosek, William, 42, 57n17
Hotson, John, 55n5
Howard, D. H., 256
Howitt, Peter, 73
Husted, Steven, 138, 162n16, 176, 178, 255
Jaffee, Dwight, 255
Johannes, James M., 106
Johnson, Christopher, 163
Jonson, Peter, 92n11
Judd, John, 85, 87
Kades, Eric, 72, 75n2, 266
Kaminow, Ira, 307
Kendrick, John W., 161n8
Kenkel, James L., 77n14, 188, 247, 259, 288, 399n10
Kohn, Meir, 41
Kool, Clemens, 106
Kopcke, Richard, 92n14, 280, 282
Kornai, Janos, 76n9, 256
Kraft, M., 77n17
Kregel, J. A., 77n15
Krugman, Paul, 165
Kydland, Finn, 19
L'Esperance, W. L., 199
Ladenson, M. L., 149n16
Laffont, Jean-Jacques, 72, 73, 256, 274
Laidler, David, 92n16
Lavoie, Marc, 77n17
Lawrence, Robert, 165
Leijonhufvud, Axel, 71, 72, 74
Litan, Robert, 165
London Business School, 78n21, 173, 176
Lucas, R. E., 41, 73
Maclean, Wendy, 29n10, 248n7
Maddock, Rodney, 41
Malinvaud, Edmond, 72
McDougall, Duncan, 55n5
McMillin, Douglas, 110, 279
McNees, Stephen, 288, 299n6
Meltzer, Allan, 216
Miller, Norman, 205, 208n1
Minsky, Hyman, 70, 110, 119n3
Mishkin, Frederick, 99, 102n7
Modigliani, Franco, 42, 43, 45, 57n17, 85
Moore, Basil, 90n3, 110
Mooschlechner, Peter, 162n22
Muellbauer, John, 72
Murphy, James L., 290
Nagatani, Keizo, 56n10, 69, 75n3
Nowotny, Ewald, 162n22
O'Brien, James, 307
O'Connell, Stephen, 77n17
OECD, Committee on Financial Markets, 155
OECD, 156
Offenbacher, Edward, 279
Okun, Arthur, 69, 77n14

Olson, Mancur, 73
Ott, Mack, 109
Palash, Carl, 281
Papademos, Lucas, 42, 43, 45, 57n17, 85
Patinkin, Don, 40, 71, 82, 96
Pesek, Boris, 81, 87, 90n2, 91n5
Pettigrew, C. W., 149
Phillips, C. A., 83
Porter, Richard, 279
Portes, Richard, 72
Purvis, Douglas, 239, 240
Quandt, R., 72
Quarterly Bulletin, Bank of England, 150
Radecki, Lawrence, 281
Rasche, Robert, 83, 106
Review of Income and Wealth, 161n12
Roe, Alan, 182, 184
Ronk, Sally, 168
Rooney, J., 257
Ruggles, Nancy, 139, 160n2
Ruggles, Richard, 130, 160n2
Rymes, T. K., 91n5
Saving, Thomas, 81, 87
Scadding, John, 85, 87
Schips, Bernard, 91n9
Schmalzl, William, 110
Schouten, D.B.J., 179n3
Shackle, G.L.S., 74
Shaw, E. S., 35, 55n1, 79, 82, 188
Sheffrin, Steve, 41
Sheppard, D., 22
Shuford, Harry, 168
Siegel, Diane, 282
Silbert, William, 212, 250n22
Silver, Andrew, 176, 281
Simpson, Thomas, 88
Sinai, Allen, 70, 86, 110, 242, 243, 249n16, 250n21, 269, 270, 275n6, 283, 286, 299n6
Smith, Gary, 23, 25, 162n18, 232, 242, 249n16, 250n21
Statistical Bulletin Supplements, Australia, 144
Statistics Canada, 140
Stiglitz, Joseph, 73, 283, 299n5
Stone, Richard, 29n12, 181, 182, 184
Taylor, Lance, 73, 77n17
Taylor, John, 73, 140, 282
Taylor, Stephen, 160n8, 176, 180n11
Thore, Sten, 19, 23, 184
Tobin, James, 23, 39, 79, 56n10, 119n8, 232, 250n22, 266, 275n5
Townsend, R. M., 73
Tsiang, S. C., 40
United Nations Economic and Social Council, 160n4
Vardal, Erling, 184
Vickers, Douglas, 36
Volcker, Paul, 273, 282, 287
Wachtel, Paul, 14, 168, 170
Wearing, A. L., 248n7
Weintraub, Sydney, 69

Weise, P., 77_n_17
Weiss, Laurence, 73
Winder, James, 232
Wojnilower, Albert, 70, 283
Wolfson, Martin, 70, 77_n_18, 272, 283
Zahn, Frank, 42, 57_n_17, 249_n_16

SUBJECT INDEX

Adding-up constraints, 210, 218-19, 235
Allocational models, 13-16
Australian flow-of-fund accounts, 144-46
Balance sheet constraints, 210, 218-19
Balance sheet variables in expenditure equations, 99-100
Balanced growth, 30-35
Bank accommodation of borrowers, 215
Bank and nonbank credit, substitution possibilities, 282-88
Bank credit, key role of, 304-05; as monetary target, 103-21
Bank loan and money market model, 84-86
Bank of England forecasting, 170-73
Bank portfolio decisions, 215
Bank sector, in national income accounts, 95n5; interest rates vs. flow-flow linkages, 227-28
Bankers Trust forecasting, 168-69
Barro-Grossman disequilibrium model, 256
Base money, as target, 109
Bond market, 10; submarkets, 11-12
Bond submarket of the product market, 105
Bosworth-Duesenberry model, 210-17
Brainard-Tobin pitfalls model, 231-42
Bulls, bears, and sheep, 165-67
Business cycle, 69-71; models of, 267-73
Cambridge financial interdependence model, 182-84
Canadian and U.S. financial accounts, comparison of, 143-44
Canadian flow-of-funds accounts, 140-44
Cash flow problem, 86
Cash-funds accounting, 81-82
Cash-or-equivalent accounting, 79-81
Circular flow models, 185-94; in an open economy, 193-94
Classical unemployment, 67
Cohen-Kenkel credit model, 259-66
Consumer credit, 99
Controllability of vs. predictability in monetary policy, 103-09, 278-81, 305
Credit availability models, 257-67
Credit crunch, 71

Credit market equilibrium, 42-50
Credit models, 257-74
Credit multiplier, 106-07
Credit rationing, 68, 105
Credit targeting, 106-07; vector autoregression (VAR) results, 278-80
Credit vs. money, pros and cons, 276-88
Credits and debits vs. sources and uses of funds, 81-82
Crowding-in, crowding-out, 229-31
Debit and credit entries, "purchasing power" interpretation, 162n20
Deficit-surplus sectors, 42-50, 100, 163-66
Degree of netness, 93-102
Demand deposits, as product, 81-82; exogeneity of, 227
Demand for money, 42-49, 80-81, 105, 113-18
Direct linkage policy models, 276-301
Disequilibrium, 58-78, 304, 308-09; in submarkets, 12
Disequilibrium models, 242-45, 251-75
Disequilibrium money, 86-87, 304-05; as buffer stocks, 87; in Switzerland, 91n9
Dissaving in two-equation models, 94-96, 101n3
Dual-decision process, 1-13; importance of, 302-05
End-of-period vs. beginning of period stocks, 93-94, 99-100
Equation stacking, 15
Equilibrium, 30-57
Expenditure functions, real balances in, 98; external finance in, 274, 307
External finance, control of, 108-09
Fair disequilibrium model, 251-56
Federal Reserve flow-of-funds accounts, 129-39
Federal Reserve forecasting, 176-77
Finance motive, 39-40
Financial dissaving, 10-11, 185-93, 288-89
Financial flow accounts, Canada, 140-44
Financial forecasting, two-country integrated matrix, 177-78
Financial input-output models, 181-84
Financial instability, 69-71; as post-Keynesian short-period theory, 77
Financial market analysis, two-tier approach, 246
Financial market identities, 166-76
Financial model-building, 39
Financial multipliers, 188-93
Financial substitution, 222-

25, 239, 305-06; theory of, 111-17; tight-easy-money test of, 289-91
Financial fragility, 17, 70, 77
Fixprice equilibrium, 58
Fixprice models, 256
Flow-constrained model, number of equations, 11; compared with value-theoretical approach, 119n3, 247, 306-07; importance of, 302-09
Flow-flow models, 181-95; criticism of, 250n22
Flow of funds, and interest rate theory, 303; cycle, 69-71; constraints, 5-16; idealized set of accounts, 121-23; information content, 303; microsimulation models, 161n3; optimal degree of grossness in, 100-01; prognosis, 309; simple model-building, 163-80; statistical discrepancy, 133-39
Flow-of-funds accounts, Australia, 144-46; Japan, 146-47; United Kingdom, 146-50; Yugoslavia, 150-55; other countries, 155-59
Flow-of-funds analysis, an evaluation of, 245-47, 250n22, 302-09
Flow of funds constraints, 5-16
Flow of funds cycle, 69-71
Flow-of-funds data limitations, 306
Flow-of-funds effects as generalized effects, 100, 307
Flow-of-funds identities, 129-33
Flow-of-funds theory, policy implications of, 103-21
Flow vs. income constrained adjustment process, 71-72
Flow vs. stock equilibrium, equivalence of, 101n1
Flows vs. stocks, 304
Fluff in money flows, 109-10
Fringe of unsatisfied borrowers, 68
Fundamentalist Keynes, 74
Germany, financial accounts for, 156-58
Goodhart's law, 299n7
Group of financial statisticians, view on financial accounts, 155
Growth rates in debt, data for, 299n1
Hendershott model, 217-32; IS-LM framework, 231; weakness of, 228-29
Hydraulic Keynes, 72
Income averaging, 99
Income multiplier, 86
Income variance, 305-06
Input market, 10
Inside vs. outside money, 82
Integrated economic accounts, U.S., 139-40

Integrated pitfalls model, 239-42
Interest rate ceilings, 113
Interest rate targeting, 103, 117
Interest rates vs. flows, bank sector, 227-28
Interest rates, substitution effect on household portfolios, 97-98
Interest symmetry constraints, 14, 210, 217
Internal funds, business sector, derivation of, 249n11
IS-LM analysis, 38-41; extension of, 42-50
Issues-income ratio, 30-35
Iterative process, 176
Japanese flow-of-funds accounts, 146-47
Keynesian mode, 59-64
Kirchoff conservation conditions, 22
Leakages, into money balances, 86
Liability management, 91n11, 283
Linkages in monetary policy, 103-21; reverse causality, 110
Liquidity constraints, 102n7
Liquidity-constrained models, 266-67
Liquidity crises, 86
Liquidity cycle, 69-71
London Business School forecasting, 173-76; rational expectations assumption, 179-80n10
M1 and other bank liabilities, substitution possibilities, 282-88
Market analysis from the "outside," 196-209
Market equilibrium, balanced growth, 30-35
Market identities, 6
Market matrix, 5-7; own submarkets, 9; submarkets, 6-12; equations, 7-12; disequlibrium in submarkets, 12; demand and supply functions, 8-11; unit sum identities, 6; equilibrium conditions, 9-11
Means of payment, social accounting view of, 79-80, 88-89
Micro vs. macro views of the banking system, 83
Minimizing income variance, 113-18
Missing equations, in macromonetary theory, 95, 98
Monetary dissaving, real balances as proxy for, 95-96; effect of interest rates on, 96-98
Monetary policy, 103-21; minimizing income variance, 113-18

Monetary targeting, 103-21
Money and credit, collinearity of, 282
Money as target, 103-21
Money, definition of, 87-88; importance of, 305
Money market, 9-10; in stationary state, 10; planned dissaving in, 10
Money market models, criticism of, 215
Money multiplier, 105-06
Money, social accounting approach, 305
Money supply process, general equilibrium framework, 84-87; in models of reserve and money markets, 83-84; New View of, 80-81, 83; post-Keynesian view, 90n3
Neoclassical synthesis, 38-41
Notional and effective values, 58-68
NOW accounts, 88
Octuple entry accounting, 4
OECD financial accounts, 155-59
Open market transactions, in transmission process, 105
"Other countries'" financial accounts, 155-59
Payments as a Markov chain, 23-26
Payments matrix, 16-19
Payments network, 19-23; high-powered money, 21; limitations of, 23
Permanent income, 99
Pitfall models, 230-40
Portfolio balance models, 176, 210-50; ranking of, 246-47
Post-Keynesian credit availability models, 257-59
Predictability in monetary policy, 109-110, 280-81
Product market, 6-7
Programming models, 184-85
Public sector borrowing requirement, 170
Public sector deficits, and the current account, 163-64
Quadruple-entry accounting, 3-4
Quantity adjustment with clearing markets, 69
Quantity constraints, in utility maximization models, 72-73
Quasi-disequilibrium, 58-68
Rational expectations, 41; 179-80n10; disequilibrium in, 73-74
Real balance effect, 82; as dissaving, 94-98
Repressed inflation, 65-67
Saving flow, asymmetry in, 107-08
Saving leakage effect, 107-08
Say's law, correctness of, 91n8

Sector constraints, 13-16
Sector equilibrium, 36-37, 51-54
Sector identities, 13-16
Sector surplus-deficit rotation, 179n6
Selective credit controls, theory of, 111-13; empirical results, 288-97; and total spending, 297-98
Shortage economy, 76
Simple model building, transaction and sector identities, 163-80
Simultaneous equation bias, problem of, 299n6
Sinai business cycle model, 267-70
Slippage effects in monetary policy, 105-07
Spillover effects, 67, 76n10, 86, 243
Stickiness of wages and prices, explanation of, 72-73
Stock adjustment models, 96
Stock adjustment vs. flow-of-funds models, 101n5
Stock market absorption of funds thesis, 196; 208n2
Stock market model, dynamic vs. impact multipliers, 208n9
Stock market model, 196-209; two-stage strategy, 199-200; reduced form, 205
Stock vs. flows, 93-102
Successive approximations method of forecasting, 176
Targeting credit, criticism of, 191n1
Targeting credit vs. money, 103-21
Transaction, emphasis on, 1; the basic building blocks, 3-26; payments side, 16-26.
Transaction accounts, 88; as numeraire, 106-07
Transaction matrix, 3-4
Transactor-sectors, 7
Transmission process, monetary policy, 105
Two-country integrated matrix, 177-78
Two-endedness in flows, 1-13
Two-stage approach to market modeling, 196-209
Two-tier approach in expenditure equations, 304
Unbalanced growth, 35
Underconsumption model, 67-68
United Kingdom, flow-of-funds accounts, 146-50; zero sum matrix, 149-50
Unit-sum identities, 13-16
UN system of National Accounts, 123-39
Vector autoregression (VAR), problems with, 279-80
Walras' law, 40, 302
Walrasian system, 12-13, 302-303
Wealth and debt effects, 98-

100
Wealth vs. liquidity constraints, 119n8
Wolfson crises model, 270-73
Yugoslav flow-of-funds accounts, 150-55
Zero-sum constraints, 13
Zero-sum matrix, 149-50

FINANCIAL AND MONETARY POLICY STUDIES

1. Multinational Enterprises – Financial and Monetary Aspects.
   Editors: J.S.G. Wilson and C.F. Scheffer, with 16 contributors.
   1974. ISBN 90-286-0124-4
   (SUERF Colloquium Nottingham University, England, April 1973)
2. Floating Exchange Rates – The Lessons of Recent Experience.
   Editors: H. Fournier and J.E. Wadsworth, with 14 contributors.
   1976. ISBN 90-286-0565-7
   (SUERF Colloquium Venice, October 1974)
3. The Development of Financial Institutions in Europe, 1956–76.
   Editors: J.E. Wadsworth, J.S.G. Wilson and F. Fournier, with 26 contributors.
   1977. ISBN 90-286-0337-9
   (SUERF Colloquium Brussels, April 1976)
4. New Approaches in Monetary Policy.
   Editors: J.E. Wadsworth and F. Léonard de Juvigny, with 29 contributors.
   1979. ISBN 90-286-0848-6
   (SUERF Colloquium Wiesbaden, September 1977)
5. Europe and the Dollar in the World-wide Disequilibrium.
   Editor: J.R. Sargent, with 17 contributors.
   1981. ISBN 90-286-0700-5
   (SUERF Colloquium Basel, Switzerland, May 1979)
6. Bank Management in a Changing Domestic and International Environment: The Challenges of the Eighties.
   Editors: Donald E. Fair and F. Léonard de Juvigny, with 25 contributors.
   1982. ISBN 90-247-2606-9
   (SUERF Colloquium Helsingør, Denmark, October 1980)
7. International Lending in a Fragile World Economy.
   Editors: Donald E. Fair in co-operation with Raymond Bertrand, with 25 contributors.
   1983. ISBN 90-247-2809-6
   (SUERF Colloquium Vienna, April 1982)
8. Currency Competition and Monetary Union.
   Editor: Pascal Salin.
   1984. ISBN 90-247-2817-7
9. Government Policies and the Working of Financial Systems in Industrialized Countries.
   Editors: Donald E. Fair in co-operation with F. Léonard de Juvigny, with 24 contributors.
   1984. ISBN 90-247-3076-7
10. Jelle Zijlstra, A Central Banker's View.
    Editors: C. Goedhart, G.A. Kessler, J. Kymmell and F. de Roos.
    1985. ISBN 90-247-3184-4
11. Monetary Conditions for Economic Recovery.
    Editors: C. van Ewijk and J.J. Klant.
    1985. ISBN 90-247-3219-0
12. Shifting Frontiers in Financial Markets.
    Editor: D.E. Fair.
    1985. ISBN 90-247-
13. Central Bankers, Bureaucratic Incentives, and Monetary Policy.
    Editors: E.F. Toma and M. Toma.
    1986. ISBN 90-247-3366-9
14. International Monetary and Financial Integration – The European Dimension.
    Editors: D.E. Fair and C. de Boissieu.
    1987. ISBN 90-247-3563-7
15. The Flow of Funds in Theory and Practice.
    Jacob Cohen.
    1987. ISBN 90-247-3601-3